BRITISH 'SPY FEVER' IN THE FIRST WORLD WAR

BRITISH 'SPY FEVER' IN THE FIRST WORLD WAR

Fearing the Enemy Within

Harry Richards

BLOOMSBURY ACADEMIC
LONDON • NEW YORK • OXFORD • NEW DELHI • SYDNEY

BLOOMSBURY ACADEMIC
Bloomsbury Publishing Plc, 50 Bedford Square, London, WC1B 3DP, UK
Bloomsbury Publishing Inc, 1359 Broadway, New York, NY 10018, USA
Bloomsbury Publishing Ireland, 29 Earlsfort Terrace, Dublin 2, D02 AY28, Ireland

BLOOMSBURY, BLOOMSBURY ACADEMIC and the Diana logo are trademarks of
Bloomsbury Publishing Plc

First published in Great Britain 2025

ISBN: HB: 978-1-3505-2343-2
ePDF: 978-1-3505-2345-6
eBook: 978-1-3505-2346-3

Typeset by Newgen KnowledgeWorks Pvt. Ltd., Chennai, India

For product safety related questions contact productsafety@bloomsbury.com.

To find out more about our authors and books visit www.bloomsbury.com
and sign up for our newsletters.

CONTENTS

FIGURES

TABLES

PREFACE

Following the declaration of war in 1914, German spies were sighted across Britain as a potent form of 'spy fever' gripped the nation. It was widely believed that a clandestine network of spies and saboteurs, mostly comprised of naturalized aliens domiciled in Britain, had successfully infiltrated all elements of society. When war came, these nefarious agents would carry out acts intended to disrupt or incapacitate Britain's war effort from within and gather vital intelligence designed to support attacks from without. Although that danger never fully materialized, parts of British society remained convinced that German agents remained at large. Contemporaries labelled this atmosphere of fear and anxiety a 'spy fever', but such a term has distorted historical interpretations of popular reactions. This book questions the extent to which British society was truly terrified of German spies and explores the political, social and cultural impacts of secret warfare during the early stages of the First World War.

This book contends that our understanding of spy fever needs revising. Whereas previous studies have argued that spy fever was characterized by extreme terror and hysteria, this book shows that it encompassed a wider variety of emotions and experiences. Each chapter examines different emotional experiences related to the spy peril: alarm, terror, excitement, anxiety, hope, anger and enjoyment. British society was certainly obsessed with the imagery of German espionage, but this did not constitute a severe physical or psychological condition. This fascination with secret warfare and covert activities is what we might term 'spy fever'.

ACKNOWLEDGEMENTS

This book has been many years in the making, and I could not have started it, let alone finished it, without the help of many wonderful people.

First, I would like to extend my heartfelt thanks to the History Department at the University of Northampton. I am particularly grateful to Cathy Smith, Matthew Seligmann, Drew Gray and Matthew McCormack for their inspirational teaching. It is no exaggeration to say that they provided a truly formative experience for me as an undergraduate between 2009 and 2012. The completion of this book marks the end of a fifteen-year ambition that they set in motion.

I was also incredibly fortunate to complete my PhD in such a friendly and supportive environment at Keele, and so I am heavily indebted to the history staff and fellow PhD students whom I shared that time with. Philip Morgan was instrumental in providing reassurance and guidance; Rachel Bright and Siobhan Talbot were thankfully always on hand to provide friendly assistance; while Kate Cushing and Alannah Tomkins made an inexperienced graduate teaching assistant feel like part of the department. My doctoral supervisor, Professor Anthony Kauders, deserves much credit for helping me produce a passable thesis, while my examiners, Professors Adrian Gregory and Aristotle Kallis, provided constructive feedback that has hopefully turned it into a more complete and compelling book. Thanks also to Julia Coole, Glenn Price, Gemma Scott, James Williamson and Julia Lawton for helping me navigate the challenges of teaching for the first time, for commenting on ideas and pieces of work, for making academia seem accessible to an imposter like me and for generally making my PhD experience a truly memorable one.

Several people have helped me adapt my thesis into this monograph which warrants recognition here. My colleagues, Clare Stevens and Dafydd Townley, have very kindly read parts of the book and provided useful feedback and encouragement through the process of getting it published, while Rob Spalton has been a constant source of advice and support along the way. I need to thank Nick Hiley for commenting on an earlier draft and for allowing me to use images from his personal collection and to Jock Bruce for helping me uncover some of the personal stories of the soldiers included in this narrative. My biggest thanks are to Jim Beach because without him I would have never had the chance to start this project. Along the way Jim has pointed me to sources and avenues of inquiry, read and discussed ideas with me and guided me through personal and academic challenges. I am forever in his debt. Any mistakes that remain, however, are of course entirely my own.

I would also like to thank family members who have helped in various ways. In particular, I would like to express thanks to my late grandparents, Peggy and

Brian, who allowed me to stay with them during various research trips to Scotland. Although they sadly did not live to see this project come to fruition, Nan always expressed an interest in my work and without them this would have surely been a book about English spy fever. My aunt and uncle, Sue and John Cushnie, also helped in this regard by hosting and driving me around the Highlands to different archives there. At the other end of the country, my great aunt Anne and her late husband Alan, with the help of my great uncle Barry and his partner Vivian, supported research across the south of England.

My parents, Heather and Paul, deserve a tremendous amount of gratitude for being a constant source of encouragement and support throughout my life. When I decided to go university after being in full-time employment they made it possible. I cannot thank them enough for doing so, for it has irrevocably changed my life. Hopefully this book will suffice in repaying them. My parents, along with my sister Amy and her husband Cory, have provided much-needed distractions throughout the writing of this book and deserve credit for making sure I reached the end.

My greatest thanks are reserved for my wife, Yvonne. Without her unwavering love and encouragement this book would not have been possible. Her patience in rereading countless drafts and hearing me go on about spies and emotions for so long has been nothing short of extraordinary. So to my best friend, this book is dedicated to you with all my love.

ABBREVIATIONS

AGL	Anti-German League
BEF	British Expeditionary Force
BEU	British Empire Union
BL	British Library
CCAC	Churchill College Archives Centre, Cambridge
CEF	Canadian Expeditionary Force
CID	Committee of Imperial Defence
IB	War Office Intelligence Branch
IWM	Imperial War Museum, London
LHMA	Liddell Hart Military Archives, King's College London
MI5	Security Service
MI6	Secret Intelligence Service
MO5	Military Operations, Department No. 5 (Secret Service)
MO5(g)	Military Operations, Department No. 5, Section g (Counter-Espionage)
NMM	National Maritime Museum, Greenwich
NSL	National Service League
TNA	The National Archives, Kew

INTRODUCTION

During the First World War, British society ostensibly fell victim to a 'spy fever' in which widespread panic and suspicion arose from the belief that an army of German spies and saboteurs had infiltrated Britain and was poised to facilitate a sudden and crippling attack. As such, it became imperative for individuals to exercise vigilance against any potential adversary, however tenuous or abstract the threat, to protect against invasion and annihilation. Denouncing strangers and suspecting aliens of treachery became commonplace in this atmosphere of fear and anxiety, as 'spy fever' seemingly gripped the nation.[1]

From the beginning spy fever was likened to a disease that spread rapidly causing intense emotions and illogical behaviours among those it infected. These effects, according to one leading liberal pamphlet, were comparable to a psychological breakdown:

> The spy-mania is the subtlest and most contagious of epidemics. Its bacillus arises by spontaneous generation out of fear. It finds its nidus among the suspicions latent in every brain. It feeds on the universal love of mysteries, and on the general antipathy towards every stranger. It propagates itself in the close atmosphere of inactive apprehension, and sweeps through cities like bubonic plague or financial panic on the Stock Exchange. Some minds are so prone to the disease that they gibber of spies even in times of profound tranquillity. To suppose oneself haunted by spies is a symptom of approaching dementia recognised in all asylums.[2]

Following the Armistice, when it became clear that the reality of foreign infiltration in Britain was quite unlike the fictional portrayals of Germany's clandestine operations, the absurdity of spy fever became ever more apparent. As such, the feelings that had been generated by the espionage peril were frequently dismissed as foolish aberrations. One of the most commonly repeated definitions of spy fever comes from a post-war memoir, entitled *Queer People*, written by Basil Thomson. Thomson, who had headed the Criminal Investigation Department and Special Branch inside the Metropolitan Police, thus making him responsible for monitoring suspicious aliens and investigating German spies during the conflict, claimed that fears of this kind led to 'hysteria' akin to a pathological condition':

> In August 1914 the malady assumed a virulent epidemic form accompanied by delusions which defied treatment. It attacked all classes indiscriminately and seemed even to find its most fruitful soil in sober, stolid, and otherwise truthful people.[3]

While Thomson was undoubtedly well versed in the rumours and allegations pertaining to covert activities, such a description undoubtedly sensationalizes his wartime activities. But similar impressions of popular responses to the enemy within were not uncommon. Having enlisted two days after his twenty-third birthday on 8 August 1914, Ernest Lycette spent the majority of the war in uniform. Several decades later he recalled those early days of war:

> It appeared that the people of the various nations, led by their leaders as they watched the press and streets during those demented days, fell victim to the hysteria as helplessly as any of the nameless multitudes around them. It seemed as if reasons and humanity had ceased. Scares and hysteria of war filled the columns of the press.[4]

Interpreting popular reactions through the lens of 'hysteria' was fairly commonplace in regards to the outbreak of war, but how far do these sources reveal the true nature of spy fever or accurately depict emotional experiences associated with the enemy within?

The main problem here is that descriptions of spy fever, especially those produced after 1918, typically portray collective behaviour and public opinion. But these accounts have frequently been used to make inferences about individuals' experiences of spy fever and in particular about how their emotional and psychological states were impacted by fears of secret warfare. If we take Lycette's account at face value, we might assume that this popular hysteria comprised of people suffering from a heightened irrational fear, a potent delusional anxiety or some other form of distressing hyper-emotional state leading to abnormal and otherwise unexplainable behaviour. Yet descriptions of spy fever were seldom written as objective or comprehensive assessments of individuals' experiences and should not be treated as such. As many other accounts reveal, popular responses to the enemy within were often as nuanced as they were extreme. In October 1914, during what might be described as the height of spy fever, Norman Macleod, private secretary to George Lambert MP, recorded in his diary how public feeling had been 'much inflamed' by rhetoric in the press, but he appears to have been somewhat indifferent to popular outcry:

> Spy mania attack on Germans. Various stories more or less incredible of German spies since war began and agitation agst [sic] Germans commenced by *Globe*. H[ome] O[ffice] rather opposed it. Suspicions grew however. Evening news started on campaign agst [sic] German waiters and succeeded in getting many hotels to dismiss German employees – agitation grew owing to stories of what Germans had done in France, Belgium – *John Bull* and *British Weekly* joined in

demanding stricter measures – most Germans in E[astern] districts rounded up and interned – this might have been a necessary step tho' doubtless spy peril exaggerated.[5]

Whereas Lycette recalled how spy scares filled the pages of the press, Macleod more accurately highlighted the predominance of anti-German sentiment in certain right-wing publications. The prevalence of similar ideals and attitudes across society more generally is less clear, and Macleod even insinuates that conflicting views existed. Despite assuming that this opposition was ineffectual, Macleod himself seems to be critical of the spy peril and questions the validity of the stories being circulated. Macleod's experience of spy fever implies that there was a difference between individuals fervently expressing feelings and attitudes consistent with spy fever and a general acceptance of the rhetoric targeting a perceived enemy. From this interpretation, it is entirely possible that repressive measures – and the emotions that sustained them – were tolerated primarily because wartime conditions had made it the norm to do so.

This distinction between the individual and the collective is something that has dominated the study of popular reactions and experiences of the war in recent years. Over the past two decades, social and cultural historians have been focused on uncovering details that reveal how different groups of people lived through the conflict. These historians have been re-examining all aspects of the war to move away from interpretations 'weighed down with symbolism, or dominated by over-arching theories'.[6] One of the most significant studies of the British Home Front resulting from this 'cultural turn' has been Adrian Gregory's *The Last Great War*. Here Gregory draws upon local histories to highlight the plethora of individual voices and regional variations during the conflict. As a result, he finds that British people understood the war in very complex and often conflicting ways. While the British public often explicitly demonstrated their support for the war, which could also appear fairly uniform across society, individuals could still maintain their own feelings of indifference or dismay.[7] Whereas Gregory exposes the variations evident between national and regional perspectives, Janet Watson contends that the differences between men and women, rich and poor, urban and rural, professionals and volunteers, combatants and non-combatants, all created diverse experiences and feelings. Britons, according to Watson, were all fighting different wars according to their role and position within society, and so all had different interpretations of the conflict.[8] Summarizing the vastness of everyday lives with catchall terms that denote a single, dominant experience – like that of 'spy fever' – is therefore no longer tenable. In her analysis of popular reactions to the enemy within in France, for example, Deborah Bauer finds a multitude of emotions such as terror, excitement, courage, anger, hatred, joy and hope, all found expression through popular perceptions of spying.[9] In light of these findings, our understanding of 'spy fever' in Britain needs further analysis.

While the interaction between social and cultural history has done much to disentangle myth and memory from lived experiences,[10] the burgeoning study of emotions in the past – commonly regarded as an 'emotional turn' – has illustrated the complexity of emotional experiences.[11] Catriona Pennell's study of 'war enthusiasm', for example, demonstrates the limitations of monolithic labels because they cannot possibly account for the 'multiplicity of emotions' experienced by a society at war. While British society consented to the war, this was not akin to unconditional or unequivocal support and was more stoic than euphoric. Although some people certainly displayed enthusiasm in response to the crisis of August 1914, this was far from ubiquitous. For the majority of people Britain's entry into the conflict was met with 'shock, tension, anxiety, dread, and defiance', rather than just jubilation. By examining how British society went to war in 1914 Pennell shows that there cannot be a single experience among a population of 40 million people.[12] In a similar vein, the idea that the Armistice resulted in simple emotional responses has also been debunked. Whereas historians have typically viewed the end of the war as a period of relief and joy, or resentment and despair, depending on the nationality of the subject, Ute Frevert has demonstrated that the emotional landscape in 1918 was not neatly divided between victorious and defeated nations. It is entirely possible that people welcoming loved ones home were not much concerned about the political circumstances in which soldiers were demobilized, whereas bereaved families may have cared little about whether their loss had been for a victorious cause or not. In showing the discrepancies between individual feelings and collective sentiment, Frevert highlights the differences that may have existed between emotions privately felt and openly displayed.[13] As such, descriptions of collective attitudes and sentiments like that given by Basil Thomson do not necessarily accurately convey the feelings and experiences that may have been fashioned by images of an enemy within.

However, that is not to say that such sources are not useful in gaining a better understanding of spy fever. Given that newspapers played an essential role in constructing and propagating the danger, they are helpful in identifying the cultural resources – the language, phrases, customs and behaviours – used to describe and understand the phenomenon. These inevitably shed light on the emotional standards and cultural norms used to interpret the enemy within and form experiences of spy fever. Through a careful reading of newspaper articles, personal correspondences and official records, this book uncovers the diverse ways people felt about German secret agents and in doing so assesses the political, social and cultural impacts of the enemy within. The fact that warring societies developed extreme emotions in response to the outbreak of the First World War was almost inevitable. The mobilization of millions of people in the pursuit of international power and prestige required political ambitions to be felt as well as thought. But these feelings could be interpreted in various ways.[14] If fear and anxiety were indeed the principal emotions felt in response to the German spy peril, who felt afraid or anxious? How did these emotions manifest? What attitudes or behaviours did they provoke? Although there was undoubtedly a widespread obsession with German spies, the degree to which this fascination actually became hysterical is difficult to verify; but if it did, it surely differed significantly across society as a whole. The diverse emotional reactions to the enemy within, and thus popular experiences of spy fever, form the subject of this book.

The German spy system

Despite exaggerated depictions of the German spy system in Britain, the reality was quite different. The origins of German intelligence in Great Britain can be found in the 1890s as the Imperial Navy's growing size necessitated a reorganized naval structure, which led to the Admiralstab being formed. This new organization immediately set upon the creation of a naval intelligence department, intended to mirror the General Staff's own intelligence bureau, Sektion IIIb.[15] Despite an initial lack of funds, by 1900 the Admiralstab had created its own *Nachrichten-Abteilung* (intelligence department), colloquially know as 'N'. Because the Royal Navy was Germany's main rival at sea – British ships were stationed in all theatres the German navy would ever be deployed to – it was N, and not Sektion IIIb, that was principally tasked with gathering intelligence on Britain.[16]

N's early attempts to establish an intelligence apparatus in Britain proved less than successful. Their initial plan was to recruit agents, typically Germans domiciled in Britain's naval ports, who could then send coded telegrams to the German naval attaché in London regarding the movements of British ships. This organization never became fully operational because of the difficulty in recruiting people willing to spy on their host country, while successive naval attachés, who reported to the Naval Office and not to the Admiralstab, were reluctant to become involved in espionage. Such work not only comprised their status at the embassy, but to most German officers spying was considered deceitful and abhorrent. Yet had this system ever become fully operational, it would have never worked in wartime because of the centrality of the naval attaché who would be expelled in the event of war with Germany.[17]

Following Britain's support for France during the Agadir Crisis in 1911, though, Germany abandoned its *Weltpolitik* and instead concentrated its foreign policy on Europe. This meant that the Imperial Navy's strategic focus was firmly fixed on the Royal Navy, and this obligated N to expand its intelligence efforts in Britain. Rather than use naval attachés to recruit and control agents, N placed Gustav Steinhauer (self-styled as 'the Kaiser's Master Spy') in control of this network.[18] Until 1911, Steinhauer had personally communicated with agents by mail or in person. Because this arrangement made it difficult to manage large numbers of informants, Steinhauer established a series of *Mittelsmänner*, or intermediaries, that could forward correspondence to and from agents. This also ensured that frequent letters from Germany did not arouse the suspicions of provincial postmasters. However, Steinhauer continued to face difficulties in recruiting agents. There were roughly 56,000 Germans living in Britain in 1911, but many of those were political émigrés who had left Imperial Germany, in part to avoid compulsory military service. Although a few agreed to act as intermediaries, the majority of German ex-patriots were either averse to engage in illicit activities or had successfully assimilated into British society. The German operatives that were employed were typically seeking excitement and adventure, or were ex-convicts looking for a lucrative career, which hardly formed the basis of a competent and reliable intelligence system. Most were discovered soon after the start of their spying career.[19]

Although British counter-intelligence was also very much in its infancy, it was more than capable of dealing with this clumsy, and not very covert, attempt at intelligence gathering. In 1907, Lieutenant-Colonel James Edmonds became head of MO5, the 'Special Section' of the War Office's Military Operations Directorate, and began a dedicated investigation into Germany's covert activities. But Edmonds sought to prove his wild theories, rather than determine an accurate assessment of the threat. Although he was able to uncover N's early attempts at intelligence gathering in Britain, Edmonds was preoccupied with stories of Germany's military agents in France who were thought to be more focused on sabotage than espionage and so remained intent on finding a similar threat in Britain. Rather than look for patterns in German naval intelligence, MO5 instead systematically catalogued reports of German spies from members of the public alarmed by stories they had read in the newspapers. Because these allegations confirmed his preconceptions, Edmonds presented them as evidence that a huge network of spies existed, and that an army of mobile saboteurs was hidden in Britain intent on destroying 'bridges, tunnels, aqueducts, etc.'. Both, he believed, were intent on aiding a German invasion of Britain.[20]

Despite Edmonds's erroneous assessments of Germany's secret service, by 1909 he had convinced the 'Foreign Espionage' subcommittee of the Committee of Imperial Defence (CID) that he had uncovered an extensive system of foreign espionage. As a result of Edmonds's 'investigations', the CID approved the creation of a Secret Service Bureau to handle the matter. By 1910, the Bureau was split into two sections: a 'Foreign Section' (espionage) under Commander Mansfield Cumming and a 'Home Section' (counter-espionage) led by Captain Vernon Kell, Edmonds's former right-hand man. Both were nominally attached to MO5, and Kell's branch was entitled MO(t).[21] These two sections provided the forerunners to the Security Service (MI5) and the Secret Intelligence Service (MI6).

By the outbreak of the First World War, MO(t) had unearthed most of N's peacetime operatives in Britain. In August 1911, Kell's unit had captured a letter from a certain 'F. Reimers' living in Potsdam trying to recruit a naturalized German. Upon receipt of the letter, Kell quickly realized its significance and began intercepting more of his correspondence. 'Reimers' was soon identified as none other than Steinhauer himself, and his letters revealed three of his intermediaries based in London: Karl Ernst, Otto Kruger and August Klunder. By the end of September 1911, interceptions had provided the names of several agents as well: Heinrich Schutte in Weymouth, Johann Engel in Falmouth and Walter Rimann in Hull. Rather than detain these spies, Kell placed them on an arrest list to be rounded up in wartime. Fortuitously for Kell, these 'Reimers' intercepts continued to produce new names. Frederick Apel was discovered working as an agent in Barrow in April 1913, and two months later Marie Kronauer was found to have taken over her late husband's work as an intermediary in London. Testament to the effectiveness of Kell's interceptions was the speed with which it uncovered new suspects. In February 1914 Adolf Schneider was recruited as a forwarding agent but was immediately detected by MO(t), and from the very moment Albert Celso Rodriguez arrived in Portsmouth as a spy he was placed on Kell's arrest list.[22]

A few German operatives were apprehended before the outbreak of war, and these arrests not only illustrate the difficulty Steinhauer had in recruiting agents living in Britain but also the clumsiness of those whom he dispatched to Britain. The first of these, Max Schultz, was a notorious fraudster who had been released from a German prison in early 1911 but soon found work as a spy. N sent him to Plymouth in June of that year, where he rented a houseboat, threw extravagant parties and fired guns off the side of his boat for amusement. Schultz's attempts at espionage were as inconspicuous as his extravagant lifestyle. Both of Schultz's attempts to recruit agents ended in complete failure. In each case he had the prospective agents sign agreements and then mail them personally to individuals known to MO(t). But instead of posting the letters, both recruits went straight to the police, informed them of Schultz's intrigues and handed them written proof of his crimes. Schultz was tried in November and sentenced to twenty-one months' imprisonment. Heinrich Grosse was another such example. A currency counterfeiter by background, Grosse was released from prison in 1911 and quickly recruited by N. He was sent to Portsmouth to gather intelligence and posed as a language teacher. Grosse spent more time bedding his students than intelligence gathering, and his spying career was as clumsy as it was short-lived. In his second attempt to enlist an informant, he openly claimed to work for a German company and asked a naval pensioner explicit questions about sensitive matters. The potential recruit was immediately sceptical and went straight to the dockyard police, who in turn shared his suspicions with Kell. Grosse's movements were then followed and he was arrested in May 1912, seven months after his arrival in Portsmouth. In any case, Steinhauer had long stopped paying Grosse on account of the worthless intelligence that he was providing.[23]

Following the declaration of the Precautionary Period that proceeded Britain's entry into the First World War, Kell gave orders to apprehend the suspects on his arrest list, which by then had risen to twenty-two, of which only fifteenth were thought to be in Britain. The police arrested eleven of these spies. To embellish the wartime success of his unit (renamed MO5(g) in August 1914), Kell augmented this list with individuals arrested on the initiative of local constabularies and presented it as a great spy round up – an intelligence coup that continues to serve as a founding myth for MI5.[24] In reality this was not a coherent spy ring, most of these individuals only ever acted in this capacity for a short period, and the intelligence they provided afforded no real advantage to the Admiralstab. They posed almost no security threat to Britain, and N was not in any way disrupted by their seizure.[25] That was because by July 1914 N had already abandoned its peacetime organization and had activated its wartime intelligence system comprised of 'tension travellers'. Despite having little experience with espionage, a handful of these spies reconnoitred British seaports completely undetected by the British authorities during July and August 1914.[26]

Germany's wartime intelligence gathering continued in this way. Agents were sent to Britain, usually for four to eight weeks, and were tasked with visiting seaports and report on the locations of naval vessels to establish whether or not the Royal Navy was preparing for battle. These operatives travelled disguised as salesmen and camouflaged their telegrams sent to neutral countries as commercial instructions. Despite their simplicity, these codes usually passed the censor. As Germany began targeting commercial shipping with submarines, these agents also provided the arrival and departure details of merchant vessels. Owing to a lack of focus, however, the intelligence that this system provided was typically wide-ranging and occasionally flawed. Multiple agents reported first-hand sightings of Russian troops either landing in Scotland or making their way south, for example. By May 1915 N had largely abandoned this method and instead focused on collecting information in neutral ports regarding the movements of British merchant vessels, which proved a far easier method. German naval agents did continue to operate in Britain throughout the war, but these operations had become more infrequent and less significant by the summer of 1915. During the entirety of the First World War the Admiralstab sent around 120 of these agents to Britain.[27]

Germany's sabotage operations targeting Britain were even more haphazard and ineffectual. There were two German organizations for sabotage operations during the First World War: Sektion P within German military intelligence formed in November 1914 and NIV, which was not properly set up by the navy until the spring of 1916, but the Admiralstab had been instructing agents to organize explosions on ships destined for enemy countries from as early as 1914. Germany's primitive attempts at sabotage were nothing like what Edmonds had feared. Although German sabotage operations in North America are well known,[28] as are their extensive subversive campaigns across the British and French Empires designed to provoke insurrections across North Africa, India, Persia and Ireland,[29] the First World War witnessed few successful sabotage operations.[30]

The first would-be saboteur in Britain, Horst von der Goltz (real name Franz Wachendorf), arrived in England on 4 November 1914 with a forged US passport. Initially, von der Goltz had been commissioned to blow up a canal along the US-Canadian border by Captain Franz von Paper, the German military attaché in Washington, but the mission was aborted at the last minute. So von der Goltz was instead dispatched to Britain, under the alias Bridgeman Taylor, where it was hoped his services would be put to better use. However, von der Goltz was arrested only ten days after his arrival for failing to register as an alien, and the German stamps in his passport aroused the suspicions of the arresting officers. He was sentenced to six months' imprisonment and scheduled for deportation after his release. In an attempt to reduce his sentence, Goltz contacted Captain Reginald Hall, the Director of Naval Intelligence, and offered information in exchange for an early release, but it was instead decided that Goltz be interned until the end of the war. This proved a wise decision. During von Papen's return to Germany after his expulsion from the United States, he foolishly allowed the British to seize a treasure trove of secret documents in his possession. These documents revealed that Bridgeman Taylor was in fact working for Germany's secret service and had been sent to England to offer his services as a double agent. Given von der Goltz's previous activities, it would be safe to assume that he was there to conduct some sort of seditious activity.[31]

German naval intelligence also tried to use disgruntled Irishmen in America for sabotage work against British factories, but this amounted to very little as all the planned missions were aborted due to a lack of coordination and funds. Germany's most successful sabotage operations were therefore conducted from neutral countries where they managed to destroy several cargoes bound for Britain. German saboteurs operating in Norway were particularly effective. The Norwegian authorities convicted several agents there after monitoring their correspondence and finding boxes of explosives all with labels on them containing the address of the German legation. It was not until early 1918 that Norway was finally clear of saboteurs, but this was not before they had detonated several devices on ships bound for Britain.[32] The most alarming plot against Britain, though, was devised in September 1916 when a physician in the German army proposed to drop liquid cultures of plague bacilli from Zeppelins, with the aim of instigating an epidemic. The plan was passed to General Erich Ludendorff, second only to Paul von Hindenburg in the German army, who inquired about its practicability. Fortunately for Britain, when the Kaiser heard of the scheme he categorically forbade the use of biological warfare against British civilians.[33] This did not stop livestock supporting the Allied cause being targeted with anthrax, however.[34] But overall, German sabotage against Britain was not especially prolific. Despite multiple claims that explosions in British factories were caused by duplicitous Germans, not a single case of German sabotage took place in Britain.[35]

Because the reality of Germany's covert activities in Britain was completely unlike the army of trained saboteurs and clandestine operatives believed to have overwhelmed the nation, popular fears seem somewhat unfounded. This distinction – between what was real and what was imagined – has dominated accounts of spy fever, and as a result, historians have struggled to understand the feelings and behaviours that it comprised. Emotional reactions to the spy menace are typically written off as irrational delusions based on overactive imaginations. In Christopher Andrew's seminal study documenting the rise of the British intelligence community, he claims that the outbreak of war in 1914 'provoked an unprecedented wave of spy mania'. Despite the capture of twenty-one 'real German spies' shortly after the outbreak of war, Andrew notes how 'many thousands of imaginary agents remained at liberty plotting imaginary acts of sabotage and communicating with the enemy'. 'Even more remarkable than the scale of [William] Le Queux's own fabrications and delusions,' according to Andrew, 'was the readiness with which others believed them.'[36] In Panikos Panayi's pioneering work on the growth of Germanophobia during the war, he similarly juxtaposes the reality of German espionage in Britain to accentuate the outlandishness of the 'hysteria', while James Hampshire is eager to point out that it 'was based on fallacy and fantasy'.[37] Spy fever, according to this portrayal, was little more than irrational emotionality resulting from an inability to distinguish fact from fiction.[38]

While popular paranoia may have appeared disproportionate to the veracity of the threat, this does not invalidate the emotions that spy fever represented. In a highly influential article examining the influence of false news in wartime, Marc Bloch found that shared misperceptions are born out of 'imprecise individual observations or imperfect eyewitness accounts' and arise from what he referred to as 'group psychology'. During periods of crises, such as the outbreak of war, Bloch maintained that the collective psyche suffers from a degree of anxiety and expectation. This, combined with a lack of up-to-date and well-informed news caused either by censorship or the absence of informed correspondents, leads to an overreliance on even the most far-fetched of reports. Consequently, the transmission of false news flourishes because people find a medium with which to express 'all their prejudices, hatreds, fears, all their strong emotions'. And so for Bloch, the emotions and group psychology that led to rumours of German espionage were not irrational or inexplicable, regardless of how unreasonable the symptoms may appear in retrospect.[39] For this reason, the emotions and experiences generated by the spy peril in Britain during the First World War are worthy of a serious and dedicated analysis.

A global pandemic

Bloch's observation seems particularly apt since Britain was not unique in its fear of foreign espionage and subversion during the First World War.[40] In fact, comparable feelings emerged in practically every belligerent state during the period. The idea that spy phobias were somehow irrational responses to war, therefore, seems to ignore the enduring utility of fear in motivating political discussion[41] as well as the unifying effects that creating an enemy within can bring.[42]

During the First World War, this was especially pertinent. As societies prepared for a contest that was widely expected to be far-reaching and cataclysmic, the need for an enemy 'other' to mobilize society proved crucial. Daniela Caglioti's study of enemy aliens across Europe shows that as the First World War redefined 'military necessity' the security of the state took precedence over individual rights and civil liberties. Despite the continual distinctions between soldier and civilian in international law, as the conflict became all-encompassing, national sovereignty became predominant. Subjects of hostile nations, whether combatant or non-combatant, became enemies in every respect. Yet during this conflict, and unlike in previous wars, international law mattered, at least in principle. States now required a means and rationale with which to legitimize acts of violence and curtail the freedom and liberties of minority groups. Propagating stories of espionage, sabotage, insubordination and resistance became essential in mobilizing public opinion against the enemy alien. The figure of the spy, a versatile character capable of carrying out a multitude of threats, played a central role in increasing and sustaining the rise in political oppression and social animosity that broke out across warring states.[43]

Perhaps unsurprisingly, dominion nations echoed many of Britain's concerns, and the spy featured prominently in much of the nationalistic rhetoric throughout the empire.[44] Jingoes in Canada attempted to recast Canadians of Teutonic origin as savage and devious and 'ready to do criminal work for their masters'. As the public ostensibly grew increasingly anxious about an invasion from across the Atlantic, reports of German sabotage precipitated various measures aimed at combatting spies. Following several minor incidents, all of which received front-page newspaper coverage, the relentless pursuit of suspected spies in Canada was likened to a 'witch hunt'.[45] German immigrants in South Africa were similarly depicted as 'mean-spirited spies'.[46] While Australia saw a prominent anti-alien campaign portraying Germans as an astute race predisposed to spying, which hastened discriminatory measures there.[47] Although depictions of German spies were far less conspicuous in New Zealand, the nationalist press attempted to portray the remaining aliens as a network of clandestine agents. As a result, those who challenged a renewed sense of 'Britishness' became suspected of foreign collusion as anti-German sentiment swept the nation through a wave of attacks and riots against enemy aliens.[48]

Although it is far harder to distil a single Home Front experience in India given the geographic, ethnic and religious diversities, there is evidence of a very limited spy fever. The war certainly created a series of grievances, insecurities and anxieties for Indian society, but these were focused more on the future status of Indians within the empire as well as the system of governance that might follow India's participation in the conflict. Indian nationalism could vary from being anti-British and in favour of home rule to passionately supporting Britain's cause. Unlike the dominions, there was little room for anti-German sentiment to emerge as elsewhere. That being said, India retained a strong oral culture and this ensured that rumours spread rapidly, especially when they provided glimpses into the war. Following the appearance of the SMS *Emden* in the Indian Ocean, for instance, people began to speculate that the German navy were gearing up for an attack, and paranoia about a potential invasion of the subcontinent grew. Sightings of German soldiers were reported throughout the country as a result, and spies were rumoured to be active in Lahore. Moreover, as anxieties grew in relation to Indian participation in the conflict, which intensified following the Ottoman Empire's declaration of *jihad* and Germany's attempts to foment Islamic revolt across the British and French Empires, popular fiction encapsulated these concerns by depicting spies infiltrating Indian villages intent on stirring up an insurrection. Thus, although espionage seems to have appeared far less frequently in Indian discourse and popular culture, there were nevertheless occasional references to the spy peril in the expression of certain fears.[49]

Spy phobias were certainly more noticeable beyond the British Empire. In France, fears of secret infiltration seemingly engulfed the country within weeks of the war breaking out. Because war was declared at the height of the summer tourist season, strange faces could be found everywhere. Being out of place and speaking in an alien accent was more than enough to arouse locals' suspicions. Germans who happened to be travelling or residing in France in 1914 found themselves liable to attack in the street, and sporadic bouts of violence led to several fatalities. As trench warfare set in and France became the central theatre of war, paranoia became rampant. Women working close to the front line were often considered out of place and were thus commonly suspected of being spies. Because legislation and security measures discriminated against outsiders, denouncing strangers became a civic duty designed to strengthen national cohesion and eliminate internal threats. Like in many warring nations nervousness among French soldiers tasked with preventing foreign intrusion flourished and several civilians were shot as a result. Although France was a relatively homogenous nation compared to countries like Russia or Austria-Hungary, spy scares were not simply a way of re-establishing national identities but also a way of exonerating military defeat. According to popular thinking at the time, French soldiers had not been defeated on the battlefield but betrayed by a nefarious enemy within. Cultivating stories of illicit activities provided a convenient explanation for France's military failures.[50]

Given the ongoing ethnic tensions in Russia, Russian society experienced intense fears of an enemy within. Germans and Jews were the primary target of the resulting hostility. As Russia suffered a swift military defeat at the Battle of Tannenberg in August 1914, rumours quickly claimed that Jewish saboteurs had poisoned wells, supplied provisions to the invading army, harboured enemy soldiers and reported Russian troop movements to German HQ. Because much of the fighting took place in close proximity to Jewish communities, they provided a convenient scapegoat to explain Russian setbacks. But as Russian society became more fractured and more desperate owing to subsequent defeats, soldiers and civilians began blaming spies for every strange occurrence and military setback. Accusations of suspected German agents became so widespread that soldiers began rounding up hostages as a punishment for locals thought to be spying. But even away from the front line the espionage peril captivated newspaper readers across the country, at the same time as a sanctioned effort to root out enemy spies took place throughout the Russian Empire. Roughly 50,000 German, Austrian and Ottoman citizens were interned as potential spies during the first few months of war, and by February 1915, the military began deporting all enemy subjects. Tens of thousands of Germans, including Russian subjects of German descent, were deported under the auspices that they were likely recruits for German intelligence.[51]

Even before joining the war on the side of the Entente, spying had become a predominant issue in both Italy and America. In Italy, where immigrants comprised less than 1 per cent of the population, concerns about spying prompted the government to target enemy aliens, with legislation combatting the espionage threat passed under the guise of military defence and economic security. Notwithstanding the lack of immigrants in Italy, nationalists enflamed tensions and exaggerated the enemy within to incite suspicion and fear. This rhetoric equated foreigners with spies and saboteurs and gave rise to the belief that aliens were part of an elaborate network of German treachery.[52] Before America's entry into the war, perceptions of Germany varied and were somewhat ambiguous given that many Americans were of German descent. Yet wartime anxiety, anti-radicalism, xenophobia and anti-German hostility were all galvanized by nationalist propaganda emphasizing the importance of 'Americanism', which created a volatile and repressive atmosphere. Immigrants soon found themselves targeted, and German-Americans received the bulk of this aggression. Fundamental to this was the belief 'that every German soldier was a violent beast; that spies and saboteurs lurked behind every bush ... and that Russian Bolsheviks were merely German agents'. From the spring of 1915 American newspapers began reporting that Germans had been engaged in espionage, sabotage and propaganda campaigns within the United States for months previously. The US military, and especially their counter-intelligence organizations, were convinced of the omnipotence of German secret service and routinely rounded up innocent suspects based on whether they looked or sounded German. Even President Wilson suspected that 'the country is honeycombed with German intrigue and infested with German spies'. This erroneous belief was founded on mythic stories of German intelligence during the Franco-Prussian War but became incredibly hard to dispute after Franz von Rintelen, the Naval Intelligence Officer conducting Germany's sabotage campaign in the United States, was apprehended in London in 1915. Rintelen's 'plans' were leaked to the press that revealed Germany's intentions to set fire to munitions factories, incite strikes among American workers and plant bombs on Allied cargo ships, which fuelled anti-German sentiment even further. This manifested most noticeably in the creation of the American Protection League, a group of 250,000 'quasi-vigilantes', which sought to incite further aggression against immigrants and even offered their services to the Justice Bureau as self-styled spy catchers.[53]

Perhaps with the exception of Russia, panic and suspicion were far more potent and pervasive among the Central Powers. As one of the most ethnically diverse nations, the Austro-Hungarian Empire experienced a particularly acute paranoia and 'spies' were swiftly rounded up following the outbreak of war. In the western corner of the monarchy, Habsburg Italians were denounced as traitors and were thought to be carrying out treacherous activities. In the northern region of Galicia, all civilians became suspected Russian agents. While in the east, in Hungary, the Romanian minority could 'hardly move for gendarmes and police spies ... all rumours flourished ... everyman spied on his neighbour, no matter how placid and peace-loving'. Because Vienna imposed strict censorship from the outset, and the military swiftly imposed a dictatorial system of governance, rumours and denunciations became commonplace as society attempted to fashion their own system of legality and fairness. Newspapers, of all political affiliations, alleged that a network of spies controlled from Belgrade had infiltrated Habsburg society. Local authorities were inundated with reports of deceitful individuals, and the police began arresting anyone deemed suspicious. Reporting people for spying essentially became a way for citizens to enforce newly instigated wartime legislation that regulated everything from food provisions to public behaviour. Violence, including hostage taking, arson, harassment and even summary executions, was not uncommon as society attempted to rid itself of spies.[54]

Arguably the most severe reaction to the spy threat occurred in Germany where long-held fears of encirclement had amplified collective concerns and convinced society that they were victims of international aggression. The dearth of war news during the early weeks only exacerbated this sentiment further. Every aspect of the war became the subject of wild rumours; stories alleged that enemy agents were poisoning the water supply, attacking railway and telegraph lines, guiding aircraft with flash lights and directing an invading force with carrier pigeons. Government notices publicizing the presence of Russian spies only inflamed society's sense of terror. On 2 August 1914 the public was requested to assist the authorities in the detection of foreign agents and civilians began arming themselves and administering their own forms of social justice. The following day an official report claimed that Russian agents had overrun Germany, and that sixty-four 'spies' were discovered in Berlin alone. But German paranoia took on a particularly sinister character as angry mobs began lynching potential suspects. Despite many of the rumours being implausible, stories of foreign infiltration were readily believed because society was so desperate for news about the war. Contemporaries even began referring to this as 'war psychosis' or 'mass hypnosis', which had serious consequences for Germans and aliens alike. In a single German state at any one time, over a hundred people were likely to be detained on suspicion of spying, while at least twenty-eight German civilians were killed by anxious sentries fearful of spies.[55]

Although the Ottoman Empire had a long history of allowing Christians and immigrants to live and prosper within the caliphate, the nineteenth century had seen a reversal in religious and ethnic tolerance. As such, Ottoman nationalism increasingly identified with the Turks and Arabs and less so with other Muslim (like the Kurds) and non-Muslim groups.[56] Because Turkish nationalism increasingly sought to alienate Christian communities, most notably the Armenians, and because of conflict with European powers over the Balkans and Caucasus regions, perceptions of both the internal and external enemy were already firmly fixed in the Ottoman mind. Although anti-Christian pogroms had been a feature of Ottoman rule throughout the nineteenth century, as Ottoman power in the region waned, anti-Christian chauvinism was further exacerbated by a *jihad* declared in November 1914 targeting Christians and enemy aliens.[57] But much like other belligerent states, the Young Turk Committee of Union and Progress (CUP) leaders had to create a 'war narrative' through which Ottoman society could make sense of the war, the enemy and their own role in it.[58] Although religion was central in the formation of popular patriotism during the earlier Balkan Wars, images of foreign spies interfering in Ottoman affairs were also employed to mobilize public support during the campaigns of 1912–13.[59] And so when the Ottomans were once again involved in a European War, measures against spies or the harbouring of foreign agents were part of a wider effort by the CUP to crack down on public morality, which became synonymous with the idea of national security. Minorities living in close proximity to coastal areas along the Aegean and Black Seas, for instance, found themselves relocated to Central Anatolia and their movements restricted as a result.[60]

Regardless of the reality of German secret agents, the perceived threats of espionage and sabotage provoked fear and anxiety in societies across the globe and provided governments everywhere with a recognizable danger that served to justify enhanced security measures. Such attitudes and behaviours were perfectly rational or, at the very least, conventional responses to the First World War. Experiences of the enemy within in Britain are therefore worthy cf further study to uncover why spy fever resonated with society as well as how the resulting emotions shaped public opinion and popular reactions to the war. Owing to the growing scholarship in how emotions can be used as a tool for uncovering historical experience and change, this book is able to delve into the characteristics of popular spy phobias in Britain and reconsider what this means for our understanding of spy fever during the First World War.

Writing a history of fear and anxiety

So how can historians first identify and then analyse emotions in the past? We cannot, after all, ask historical actors how they felt about particular objects or occurrences or why they thought or behaved the way they did. In a highly influential article published in *American Historical Review*, Peter and Carol Stearns make an important distinction between emotion and emotionology. The Stearns contend that whereas the former represents a complex set of interactions that are mediated through neural and hormonal functions, the latter refers to the norms, rules and discourses that govern how and when to display or supress feelings in a particular cultural context, which are easier for historians to identify. By ignoring the differences between emotion and emotionology historians have typically described emotional standards evident in discourse, rather than individual feelings that existed within the body, without necessarily acknowledging the difference.[61] The application of emotional concepts such as fear and anxiety to otherwise unexplainable human actions is therefore misguided and anachronistic without first recognizing how far historical feelings can be identified and interpreted. In other words, this book is not attempting to state categorically that historical actors were experiencing a certain type of emotion and instead argues that, based on the cultural norms linked with spy fever, different emotional experiences were possible.

The question then becomes, how can we identify emotional standards? Where, if anywhere, are the customs regarding emotional experience communicated and therefore discernible? William Reddy's theory of 'emotives' puts forward a solution to this conundrum by stressing the importance of language, which he maintains is intrinsic to understanding one's own feelings. According to Reddy, it is only through expression, and the process of translating feelings into words, that we can identify and manage our own emotions.[62] Because the terms we give to these feelings – happiness, anxiety, guilt, hope and so on – all have specific meanings and connotations, we can only understand the sensation and its implications by labelling it with such a term. Reddy refers to these terms as 'emotives'. Thus, while historians may not be able to interview their subjects and make specific inquiries as to their emotional states, they can identify efforts to assess and describe feelings, which have no physical existence beyond the individual, through the use of language and performance. In doing so, historians can observe the process through which emotions are managed, shaped and, to some extent, experienced by the individual.[63] Although Reddy's theory of emotives has helped bridge the gap between emotionology and emotion, he does not go so far as to provide a methodology for examining emotion beyond words. Thus, in line with current approaches in the history of emotion, this book merely examines the expression of emotional experiences relating to spy fever during the First World War. It does not, and cannot, make substantive claims about the exact nature of individuals' emotional states or specific feelings.

This necessitates a consideration of how emotion words can be used. Although an individual might claim to be afraid, we cannot know whether they felt that internally or if they merely imitated the feeling to achieve a desired result. Furthermore, when historical actors claim to have witnessed an individual in a state of fear, we cannot know for certain that the subject was truly afraid because the observer interpreted the situation and the emotional response according to their own values and experiences. Whereas one individual might feel fear, that same circumstance might induce anger, shame, excitement or guilt in others, and so we cannot know whether or not the observer was accurate in their assessment. Historians also inevitably apply their own interpretations of specific emotions onto the past, which can lead to feelings occurring in the past being misidentified or misunderstood. This book is not therefore intended as a history of emotion that demonstrates what fear or anxiety – or any other emotion – meant to individuals in 1914. When individuals are referred to as being fearful or anxious, based on evidence displaying certain customs or understandings, I am merely suggesting that they are displaying symptoms of fear or anxiety according to my own interpretations of those words. This does not necessarily mean that those individuals felt those specific feelings.[64]

This means that an understanding of what fear and anxiety are has to be established in order to differentiate between the two. This is complicated by the fact that there is no universally accepted definition of 'emotion', let alone 'fear' or 'anxiety'. In simplistic terms, emotions are felt experiences that have been labelled with terms like 'love' or 'hate'. Paul Ekman considered some of these – anger, disgust, fear, happiness, sadness and surprise – to be basic, universal emotions that exist within the human body.[65] Yet historians have quite clearly demonstrated that emotions have been in a constant state of flux since at least the eighteenth century, if not before.[66] In other words, the emotion terms that Ekman thought to be universal have had different meanings to different people at different times. As a result, historians rarely view emotions as a universal phenomenon, choosing instead to focus on the cultural influences that shape emotional experience. Martha Nussbaum, for example, characterizes emotions as an 'appraisal or value judgement' that is used to understand things outside of our control.[67] Barbara Rosenwein adds that those judgements are based on shared cultural standards that exist in any given society. While she concedes that there is a biological and universal human aptitude for feeling things now referred to as 'emotions', what these emotions are, what they are called, how they are felt and how they are expressed are all shaped by social customs or what Rosenwein refers to as 'emotional communities'.[68] William Reddy portrays emotions as 'overlearned cognitive habits' that are designed to facilitate or reinforce political ideals. One's interpretation of emotion, according to Reddy, is overtly shaped by an 'emotional regime' that governs the expression, and therefore experience, of emotion.[69] Recognizing the social and political origins of emotional expression is therefore essential.

Because of the centrality of fear and anxiety to the conventional understanding of spy fever we also need to distinguish between 'fear' and 'anxiety', which adds a further level of complexity.[70] Joanna Bourke proposes that fear and anxiety can be separated according to their stimulus. The word 'fear', she maintains, relates to an immediate and objective threat, whereas 'anxiety' typically refers to an anticipated or subjective threat.[71] Yet the question, 'what is fear', has perplexed psychologists and historians alike, and this has spawned a broader philosophical debate about what emotions really are. Arguably 'fear' is nothing more than the situation in which the feeling occurs, because individuals interpret emotion based on the circumstantial features that arise in any given situation. Certain threats might incite anger, rather than fear, simply because of the environment in which they are encountered. As a result, Bourke contends that historians should exercise caution when applying either fear or anxiety to individuals in the past. During the alarm caused by the spy peril, for instance, it is difficult to say with any certainty whether individuals felt afraid or anxious. Although they may have believed the threat to be real and imminent, they were reacting to abstract claims of covert activity that reflected various uncertainties caused by the outbreak of war. Moreover, what may have been fear for one individual could have been anxiety in another. What might be deemed an immediate and objective threat to one group could be considered an anticipated and subjective danger to another.[72] Because of the innate difficulty in distinguishing between fear and anxiety, this book often uses 'spy phobia' as a catchall term that encompasses both.[73]

However, fear and anxiety also elicit different responses, according to Bourke. Fear, for example, produces a physiological response: the heart rate quickens, blood pressure soars and breathing intensifies to enable the fight-or-flight instinct. Anxiety, on the other hand, correlates to an enduring state of panic because the threat is intangible or only loosely defined, making it harder to perceive or identify.[74] This distinction between fear and anxiety provides a useful framework to examine emotional responses to the spy peril as historians routinely ascribe both fear and anxiety to outbreaks of spy fever. On the one hand, such fears allegedly created a feverish response, which has overt physiological connotations affecting the body, while the resulting panic purportedly spread uncontrollably like a contagion and kept people in an abiding state of mania. Consequently, Parts II and III of this book focus on experiences resembling 'fear' and 'anxiety', respectively. This does not mean that I am only considering 'fear' or 'anxiety' exclusively; I merely use the distinction between immediate and abstract threats as a framework to examine the characteristics of spy fever in Britain. Whereas Part II examines incidents in which the spy appeared as a direct and objective danger to determine how people experienced these circumstances, Part III looks at the construction of the threat in public discourse to identify the emotional standards that shaped responses to the anticipated threat. In so doing, these two sections argue that popular phobias were not feverish or contagious; that individual fears were far less significant than collective anxieties, at least according to Bourke's distinction between fear and anxiety; and, most importantly, that 'spy fever' comprised more emotional experiences than simply fear or anxiety.

The existence of multiple emotional responses, sometimes in conflict with each other, has often made writing emotional histories difficult. Michael Roper argues that it is because historians often lack the methods and concepts to 'accommodate the contrary character of emotions'.[75] This has certainly limited the historical depiction of spy fever, as historians invariably identify only a single emotional experience, that of extreme fear. To try and uncover the range of emotional standards in 1914, this study takes a closer look at how the spy peril appeared in the press and compares this with how feelings were conveyed and interpreted in private correspondence. Whereas previous studies invariably focus on national right-wing publications, this book has carefully examined the presence of spy-related narratives in forty-four newspapers from across the British Isles.[76] From these, over 9,000 articles containing references to spying have been collected. Each article has been categorized according to its content, as outlined in Appendix 1. Categorizing articles in this way helps to assess the scope and characteristics of the spy peril more broadly and place spy phobias into their proper context. Such a large sample has furnished various insights into society's interest in spying. Most importantly, it illustrates that spies appeared in print in different ways and for different reasons. This book proposes that the images and expressions used to construct the spy peril acted as a set of emotional standards with which people could make sense of and formulate their own emotional responses to the enemy within. By showing the range of conflicting emotional norms within this narrative, this study suggests that there were multiple feelings generated by the notion of an enemy within. Whereas previous studies have taken a narrow view of spy fever, arguing that it was characterized by extreme terror and widespread hysteria, this book argues that 'spy fever' should encompass a wider variety of emotions and experiences. British society was certainly *obsessed* with images of German secret agents, but this did not necessarily constitute either a physical or psychological condition. The collective fascination is what we might term a spy fever.

This book is divided into three parts that each reconsider one of the three main claims made by historians about British spy fever during the First World War. Part I looks at the emergence of spy phobias to realign the historiography with the history of emotions. Because feelings are culturally determined, spy phobias could not have occurred spontaneously, and so the two chapters in this part show how espionage came to represent a specific threat, both to individuals and to society as a whole. Part II challenges the notion that spy phobias were typically symptomatic of hysteria or mania. Such psychological trauma was almost entirely absent from personal experiences or encounters with the spy peril and so such claims cannot be substantiated. Despite the frequency with which 'spy mania' has been used to describe the espionage peril, the related phobias seldom appear as a particularly acute or enduring fear among individuals facing the danger. Part III looks at how society was presented with the threat to contest the assumption that spy phobias became contagious and an almost ubiquitous response. By re-examining the different ways in which espionage appeared in various discourses it becomes evident that historians have mistaken the prominence of the spy peril as an indicator of the prevalence of spy phobias more generally and have therefore assumed that a particular emotional state comprised of fear and anxiety became an especially pervasive and manic response to the outbreak of war.

The three parts of this book have each been inspired by different conceptual approaches found in the history of emotion. Part I uses William Reddy's idea of 'emotional regimes', in which he connects emotional practice and custom with political ideology, to situate spy fever within the broader context of fears and anxieties regarding national and imperial decline.[77] These two chapters posit that national security discourse, and the political agitation designed to augment security measures and restrictions, gave rise to popular fears that in 1914 metastasized around the threat of German spies. Part II then examines the prevailing 'emotional styles', an idea created by Carol and Peter Stearns to refer to the trends shaping rules and methods for expressing and performing certain feelings, which influenced how popular spy phobias were interpreted and communicated.[78] Its two chapters uncover two contrasting ways in which individuals explained their own experiences or observations of spy phobias. Because Part III is concerned with the impact of spy fever on the collective psyche, it examines the various ways in which spies featured in political discourses and popular culture. It is influenced by Barbara Rosenwein's concept of 'emotional communities', which proposes that individuals can adjust their emotional judgements and interpretations according to their immediate contexts and therefore experience different and even conflicting emotions as they interact with different communities.[79] As such, its three chapters show that 'spy fever' embodied different feelings for different people at different times.

Although the spy peril certainly generated much fear and anxiety, the different chapters of this book illustrate that a range of emotions could be felt in response to the threat, and that all of these reactions should be thought of as different facets of the 'spy fever' that accompanied Britain's entry into the First World War.[80] Part II will demonstrate that the experience of fear could induce excitement as well as terror, while Part III shows that wartime anxieties could induce anger and hatred, or hope or joy, depending on circumstances in which the danger was encountered. For this reason, our current understanding of spy fever is too reductive and insufficient in describing popular reactions to the enemy within. 'Spy fever' should be reimagined as an atmosphere in which people developed an intense fascination with the German spy menace, which took many forms and provoked various emotional responses, and not as an uncontrollable mania affecting bodily functions or causing psychological impairment.

Part I

ORIGINS OF SPY FEVER, 1900–14

During the Edwardian era discourses that had once centred on imperial defence became instead increasingly fixated on issues relating to national security. As society began to perceive colonial, technological and economic adversaries as a direct challenge to the dominance of Britain and her empire, the threat of invasion coupled with the expected dangers of a foreign spy network dominated this narrative. The publication of George Chesney's *Battle of Dorking* in 1871 did much to shape the course of invasion and then espionage literature and is often credited with provoking an enduring fascination with covert activities.[1] Although the 'dastardly French', occasionally in alliance with Russia, was the primary antagonist in this genre, Germany soon emerged as the greatest colonial and industrial rival and supplanted the old enemy as the more pressing concern.[2] Yet this international rivalry and competition seldom provoked hostility against German immigrants living in Britain. Although there were undoubtedly sporadic outbursts of anti-German sentiment during this period, admiration for Britain's future foe persisted in many respects,[3] and German communities were generally left alone.[4]

Nevertheless, during the First World War British society witnessed a notable expansion of anti-alienism linked closely to fears of an enemy within.[5] In particular, a potent form of xenophobia aimed at Germans residing in Britain cultivated animosity towards anything that could be figuratively associated with Germany.[6] Importantly, though, society's aversion towards outsiders has been viewed as an organic reaction that was exploited, rather than driven, by cultural and political interferences.[7] Panikos Panayi, for example, attributes the rise in anti-German sentiment to a visceral outburst of 'spy fever' among the general population.[8] While Catriona Pennell declares that a 'fundamental characteristic' of this spy fever is that it 'emerged spontaneously at the grass roots'. Pennell maintains that large sections of society became convinced of the omnipotence of the German spy system and emphasizes the level of self-vigilance that resulted from the extreme paranoia evident across society. According to Pennell, neither the police nor the government inspired or coerced this reaction, though she concedes that their actions undoubtedly legitimized such behaviour.[9]

Pennell uses a letter written in November 1914 to illustrate the level of self-imposed vigilance. The message was addressed to the Lord-Lieutenant of Devon, Hugh Fortescue, who received numerous letters about spies in the area. The letter in question aimed suspicion at a family in Exmouth after they had vacated their rented property. According to the landlord, a hole had been dug in the garden and a saucepan had been used for reasons 'other than domestic purposes'. It was further suggested that the family had been concealing incriminating documents in a collection of stuffed birds.[10] While the author was clearly displaying suspicions symptomatic of a spy fever, the existence of coercion is more apparent than Pennell accounts for. Four days after the outbreak of war the Lord-Lieutenant had addressed the people of Devon in a speech reported in the *Exeter and Plymouth Gazette*:

> There were, continued his lordship, unquestionably a certain number of German spies in the country, and among them were secret agents who would do anything they could to delay and hinder our mobilisation by blowing up bridges, breaking down communications, and so forth … If certain bridges and communications were destroyed it would cause a great deal of delay in connection with movements of troops which would take place in the next few days.

This speech, like many others across Britain, emphasized the prevalence of the German spy network and outlined the specific threats that it posed to the British war effort. It not only defined the physical response but also the emotional reaction that befitted wartime conditions. Within this emotional framework, maintaining self-vigilance and suspicion became essential to the war effort. The extreme measures that Fortescue advocated further illustrated the significance of the threat:

> He, therefore, asked anybody, of any class and any age, who lived within reach of places he would mention to specially look after property day and night, take a shot gun with him, and a dog who disliked strangers, it would be no harm, and take any steps up to shooting to keep at a distance people who would destroy these vulnerable points.[11]

Given the nature of his public address, it is unsurprising that the Lord-Lieutenant received correspondence disclosing various local anxieties related to German espionage.[12] In his speech Devonshire society was being called upon, not to volunteer their services abroad but to fight an enemy that had successfully infiltrated British society.[13]

Panayi uses the diary of a young girl, Winifred Tower, living on the Isle of Wight in 1914 to highlight the spontaneity of spy phobias. Although Tower referred to speculation regarding various German conspiracies supposedly transpiring on the Isle of Wight in August 1914, Panayi ignores the wider context in which these concerns originated. Tower herself noted in her diary that there were warnings about spies on the island and how people should be on the lookout for people 'hanging about near the fortifications and also against giving any information to strangers which might be of use to the enemy'.[14] Admittedly this was the day after she had recorded the details of the alleged plots, but the fact that counter-espionage activities on the Isle of Wight had such a high profile, even before the declaration of war, makes it problematic to assume that her feelings developed in isolation to this.[15] For people to 'fear' German spies they needed an understanding of when, where and how secret agents posed a threat to either themselves or the nation.[16] As we shall see in the two subsequent chapters, society was made aware of the dangers of espionage and sabotage in pre-war political rhetoric and popular culture, but then as war was declared, local authorities turned what was a fictional adversary into a real and imminent peril.

William Reddy's theory of 'emotional regimes' that connects emotional standards to political ideals is helpful in understanding how spy phobias emerged. Between 1880 and 1914, frequent warnings of impending invasions and anti-alien rhetoric were arguably designed to stimulate and sustain certain feelings to benefit a certain political agenda. This emotional regime conveyed social customs, constructed a framework to interpret feelings and promoted modes of emotional expression. It was a chauvinistic regime that prioritized emotions like fear and anger to boost support for measures designed to increase national efficiency and security. Spy phobias were very much a part of this. For fear and anxiety to manifest as they did in 1914, and for them to focus specifically on German spies, cultural and social standards had to exist in which these emotions could be applied to the situation emerging in August 1914. By envisaging spy phobias as a particular facet of a wider emotional regime, we can begin to identify the political and cultural interactions that made fears of secret agents possible in 1914.

The following two chapters are thus concerned with the emotional contexts in which spy fever occurred. Chapter 1 examines how similar concerns pervaded Victorian and Edwardian discourses linked to invasion scares and xenophobia, which illustrates the tradition of promoting public uproar and trepidation as acceptable emotional responses to international disputes and internal vulnerabilities. These narratives, although not deliberately intended to stimulate spy phobias, were essential for society to understand the scale and type of threat that an enemy within posed. Without recurrent invasion scares and a growing anti-immigrant sentiment, the belief that aliens were covertly organizing the subjugation of Britain on behalf of a foreign power lacked credibility. Having identified the mechanisms through which comparable fears permeated society, the second chapter moves on to analyse the proliferation of spy phobias following the outbreak of war. Examining the characteristics of spy fever in August 1914 shows that popular suspicions were tied to official concerns and local security measures designed to ensure the continued safety of Britain. How individuals experienced these fears will be the focus of Part II.

Chapter 1

AN ERA OF ANXIETY

On his way to volunteer in August 1914 Professor Gardner recorded a 'strange spectacle' while walking along a busy London street. He found what he perceived to be an anxious crowd gathered around a hole opening up in the road. Gardiner claimed that these people were becoming hysterical at the sight of the tarmac splitting and attributed this reaction to fears that German forces had arrived in London. Fortunately for Gardner, and the safety of the capital, it turned out to be nothing more than a burst water pipe.[1] Whether this 'hysteria' was real or not, the idea that this response or observation occurred spontaneously is inconsistent with how historians treat emotions in the past. For anybody to associate cracks in the pavement with a German invasion – the idea that enemies could tunnel all the way to London is pretty far-fetched – there needed to be some sort of pre-existing understanding of what the danger consisted of and how it threatened society, as well as an emotional framework that aided the interpretation and expression of the resultant feelings.[2]

It is well established that feelings of nervousness had been mounting in Britain ever since the Enlightenment. Just as ancient Greece had developed medicine to alleviate the sickness caused by sedentary urban lifestyles, Britons also came to believe that modernity was to blame for increasing levels of psychological ailment witnessed during the nineteenth century.[3] Industrialization and global commerce, in particular, were considered responsible for mounting levels of inertia and mental illness.[4] By the beginning of the twentieth century this condition was referred to as 'neurasthenia', which quite literally meant 'disease of civilisation'. Although neurasthenia was not exclusive to Britain, psychologists there observed a notable rise in reported cases as concerns about Britain's anticipated decline began to flourish towards the end of the nineteenth century.[5] Imperial insecurities compounded this sense of national weakness. For many Britons, the overextension and grandeur of the Roman Empire prior to its demise served as a stark reminder of the dangers associated with overindulging in imperial expansion.[6] This sense of fragility was compounded by widespread concerns that the lower classes were becoming increasingly degenerate.[7] And so despite Britain's imperial and industrial ascendancy during the latter half of the nineteenth century, British society repeatedly displayed signs of anxiety, especially in relation to national security and imperial defence, but these feelings were neither automatic nor inevitable.

This chapter challenges the characterization of First World War spy phobias as a spontaneous reaction by situating them within the wider context of fear and anxiety that preceded the First World War. It first examines the invasion 'hysteria' that plagued Victorian and Edwardian discourses to highlight the role that the press played in cultivating popular anxieties. While historians of emotion posit that emotional awareness is determined by an individual's understanding of conventional practice, thereby rendering a pre-existing cultural framework essential to the interpretation of feeling, the historiography of invasion scares suggests that alarmist rhetoric provided the necessary resources to understand and express feelings of unease. Following this, the analysis turns to the development of anti-alienism in Britain. While prejudice and discrimination undoubtedly reached unprecedented heights during the course of the First World War, the expansion of Germanophobia in 1914 amounted to an evolution, not a revolution, of xenophobic discourses. The resurgence of spy fever in August 1914 should be viewed as an expression of pre-existing fears and anxieties, not as a radical or spontaneous outburst of emotion, and this has important implications for how we assess the origins and scale of spy phobias.

The final section contends that images of the Franco-Prussian War gave rise to a plethora of spy novels that fashioned varied and ambiguous stereotypes of German espionage. Yet these images of German secret warfare also saturated social and political discourses and, in doing so, familiarized society with a set of ideas relating to the characteristics and functions of Germany's Secret Service. Moreover, given the long history of spy fever – the term first appeared in the British press in 1870 – society was already familiar with the emotional standards connected to an assumed spy peril. Thus, the invention of 'spy fever' and the prevalence of espionage in popular culture and political rhetoric ensured that the reading public were acquainted with the alleged duplicitousness of Germany. As such, both the source of danger and appropriate responses to it had been established prior to 1914. Observing the mechanisms through which fear and anxiety pervaded British society, the pattern of xenophobia more generally and the construction of the spy as a particular object of danger, this chapter begins to question the value of viewing spy phobias as spontaneous and instead highlights the importance of political discourse and cultural devices in shaping emotional expression that characterized the outbreak of war. Both had been established well before August 1914.

Invasion and public emotions

Since the Romans first landed in Britain successive generations of Britons experienced or encountered anxieties about invasion.[8] Between the Battle of Waterloo and the assassination of Archduke Franz Ferdinand British society was gripped by periodic invasion scares.[9] Although the 'dastardly French', occasionally in alliance with Russia, was the initial adversary in this expected invasion scenario, Germany soon emerged as the greatest colonial and industrial rival and supplanted the old enemy as the more ominous foe. Society's increasing fixation with espionage following the turn of the century took place within this atmosphere of nervousness. One concerned journalist remarked in August 1914 that the 'detection of spies all over Great Britain ... disclose the intention to invade us when the opportunity for such a blow arises ... the blow would fall upon us like a bolt from the blue, at a moment when Britain was isolated, friendless and unprepared'.[10]

Invasion 'scares' have too often been viewed through the lens of 'hysteria' and 'panic', and not unjustifiably so, since these were often the terms used by contemporaries. Such a narrative purports that 'scaremongers' frightened the British public into adopting a more extreme form of militarism, or navalism, depending on the scare, and this coerced the government into enacting certain policies and strategies.[11] More recent historians, however, rightly view the use of 'panic' to describe collective behaviour as a social construct, one that is invariably applied to denounce the attitudes or intentions of those involved. They also stress that invasion 'scares' were entirely distinct from 'public opinion', which needs to be coherent and organized and unlike the sporadic nature of popular outbursts of emotion.[12] Yet the way in which emotive language was used to foster certain responses implies that such incidents drew upon a wider emotional regime linked to radical conservatism. This regime overtly prioritized fear of foreign intrusion and frustration at government inertia to challenge the dominant liberal ideals of the day in support of radical policies.[13] Spy scares, it is argued here, were part of that same emotional regime, and so by highlighting the mechanisms that instigated Edwardian invasion 'panics', it becomes problematic to assume the spontaneity of First World War spy 'scares'.

Neither the French nor the Germans ever seriously contemplated launching a full-scale invasion across the Channel or North Sea, but the prospect of foreign armies landing in England nevertheless dominated strategic thinking in Britain. By the 1880s invasion fears had worsened as international stability was undermined by belligerence and confrontation among the major powers. It was feared that decades of isolationism had reduced Britain's diplomatic influence on the continent and prompted collusion among her rivals.[14] In response, politicians felt compelled to take a much greater interest in how Britain's finite military and naval resources were allocated, and this inevitably meant that they had a greater influence over strategy. This politicization of military and naval affairs ensured that the most pressing issues of the day, which frequently involved home defence and the threat of invasion, dominated strategic thinking at both the War Office and Admiralty during the final stages of the nineteenth century.[15] Because Britain continued to face ongoing international uncertainty beyond the fin-de-siècle,[16] strategy was based on the assumption that Britain could enter a war with France, Russia, Germany or a coalition of all three.[17] Such a scenario would obviously pose an existential threat to Britain's global hegemony, and so the Committee of Imperial Defence (CID) was established in 1902 to increase political oversight on matters of strategic importance. Thereafter, the defence of the British Isles was almost continuously discussed and reassessed among military and naval planners.

Shortly after the turn of the century, though, the expected enemy in various invasion scenarios was firmly fixed on the German menace. Germany's long-held military prowess, supplemented by a new and powerful navy, caused considerable concern in both the Admiralty and War Office.[18] In 1898, the first of Germany's Naval Laws approved the construction of nineteen battleships and over forty cruisers. Given that Germany possessed few overseas colonies it was reckoned that this modern and capable fleet would be permanently stationed in the North Sea, only ten hours off Britain's east coast.[19] The Admiralty's fears were seemingly confirmed by the British naval attaché in Germany, Commander Arthur Ewart, who reported that Germany's expanding navy was purposely designed to challenge the supremacy of the Royal Navy.[20] Figures at the War Office were similarly preoccupied with the growing German peril. Lieutenant Colonel William Robertson, head of the Foreign Intelligence Section, strongly believed that the German General Staff had developed detailed invasion plans and, owing to Germany's combined military and naval strength, were in a position to execute them. He regularly shared such assessments with the CID.[21] And so despite some in the War Office advocating for a more offensive continental strategy that would augment the strike capability of the regular army, the CID's attention between 1911 and 1914 was predominantly focused on the Royal Navy, blockade and home defence, rather than the deployment of the BEF overseas.[22] Evan as German troops marched through Belgium and Northern France in 1914, concerns about a possible attack from across the North Sea never fully abated.[23]

As military and naval strategists almost continually re-evaluated the implications of national and imperial defence, nowhere was the fear of invasion more explicit than in the pages of the national press. Fleet Street's obsession with future wars prompted A. J. A. Morris to argue that 'before the war the nation's wits had been stolen, its nerves enfeebled, [and] a "national neurasthenia" induced' by politicians, generals and journalists consumed by the German menace.[24] Despite the CID repeatedly discounting the possibility of a full-scale invasion, as opposed to a more limited raid, their forensic scrutiny reflected the temperature of public opinion. Amateur strategists abounded in this climate, and they relentlessly foretold of Germany's illicit designs. To them it appeared inevitable that Germany would come as a 'bolt from the blue' – a swift amphibious assault designed, not necessarily to conquer but to paralyse Britain and render her subservient to Germany's will. But Morris specifically attributed this form of neurasthenia to the 'patriotic press', especially papers such as the *Mail* and *Express*, which broadcast lies and half-truths to bolster British militarism and foster an unreasonable hatred of Germany for financial and political gain.[25]

Besides Morris's seminal work, which focused on the expansion of militaristic vigour more broadly, Howard Moon's thesis attributed a series of invasion panics to doom mongering in the press. The first panic Moon addresses occurred in 1888, as deteriorating tensions between France and Germany threatened further European conflict. Because it was considered unlikely that Britain would be able to remain neutral in such a contest, the proficiency of the nation's defences came under considerable scrutiny. Lieutenant General Sir Edward Bruce Hamley led the charge against the government's alleged negligence. Hamley, a widely admired army veteran, Conservative MP and prolific writer, had been pressing for home defence reforms for several years and used this opportunity to promote his plans for fortifying London against attack from the Thames.[26] His efforts were bolstered by remarks published in the *Daily Telegraph* by Viscount Garnet Wolseley, the adjutant general of the army, second only to the Duke of Cambridge in the War Office and the pre-eminent military hero of his day.[27] Although the prime minister, Robert Cecil, launched a scathing attack against Wolseley and his 'panic producing speeches', propaganda was supposedly 'frightening the country into the idea that it is to suffer all kinds of attacks'.[28] Wolseley responded in kind and used his maiden speech in the House of Lords to appeal to the nation as he considered it unlikely that any government would ever implement 'military precautions at home or abroad until an outraged public opinion forces their hand'.[29]

Public agitation then rose sharply again at the turn of the century in response to Britain's involvement in the Transvaal. The infamous 'Black Week' of December 1899, in which three separate British forces were defeated by Boer farmers, led to a serious collapse in British confidence. Soon after, almost the entire regular army and most of the effective Auxiliary forces were deployed to southern Africa, and it quickly became apparent that Britain could do little to thwart any attacks at home if they were to occur. With the army 6,000 miles from Britain the Fleet provided the only safeguard against invasion. But an increasingly hostile Europe also gave rise to doubts relating to the navy's ability to guarantee Britain's security. The prime minister, Lord Salisbury, proved incapable of managing the crisis in British confidence. To some he appeared, at best, inconsistent on matters of defence and, at worst, completely indifferent, which inevitably aroused the ire of various political commentators. The most prominent and persistent of them was the liberal journalist William T. Stead. Stead was not known for his equivocation, and he fervently predicted that a coalition of French, Russian, German *and* American forces would soon invade southern England:

> To gradually drain away from Great Britain all her trained fighting men, to carry them off to a distance of 6,000 miles, to so entangle them in the toils of a War from which no extrication is possible for six months and probably twelve, that would obviously be a master stroke of Satanic policy ... the next move in the diabolical game would be to arrange a series of combats, each more artfully designed than its predecessor, to convince our enemies that we were lacking in every element of military power except the bulldog valour of the individual soldier.[30]

In a private letter to Major General Sir John Charles Ardagh, head of the Intelligence Department at the War Office, Stead not only reiterated his belief that Britain was soon to be attacked but also, rather menacingly, avowed that 'the public will before long be thoroughly scared'.[31] Alongside Stead was John Strachey of the *Spectator*, Leo Maxse of the *National Review* and James Knowles of the *Nineteenth Century*, and together they presented a powerful body of opinion.[32] When the government announced the Army Estimates in February 1900 it specifically attributed the War Office's concerns to 'scaremongers' in the press.[33]

The government continued to debate the issue of invasion in 1907 and 1908 and then again between 1913 and 1914. Germany's expanding naval construction elicited fearful responses in the press, but pressure groups committed to their own ideas of home defence sought to exacerbate popular resentment and trepidation. The most important of these was the National Service League (NSL). Established during the Boer War to promote universal military service for home defence, the NSL found a powerful ally in Lord Roberts. Roberts had retired from the CID in 1905 to publicly vent his frustration at the lack of army reform, views which were strongly criticized in official circles.[34] As head of the NSL Roberts made repeated and vociferous appeals for conscription on the grounds that overseas attack had become almost unavoidable and that the capacity of the navy to resist such an endeavour remained uncertain. Whereas Roberts supplied the military expertise, the Northcliffe press provided the exposure. Given the size of his press empire, Alfred Harnsworth, later Viscount Northcliffe, became the most revered scaremonger within the Tory Party and its associated press, and after a failed attempt to get elected into Parliament, Northcliffe purposefully embarked on a campaign to shape policy through crude and jingoistic journalism.[35] It was in the pages of the *Daily Mail* that Roberts and William Le Queux published a serialized form of *The Invasion of 1910*, which fictionalized a German attack that brought unrivalled terror to towns and cities across Britain.

Late Victorian and Edwardian invasion scares are seldom considered as spontaneous outbursts of social anxiety. Although the historiography of invasion scares has often inferred the extent of panic across society, it has nevertheless highlighted the political and cultural influences that inevitably provoked or shaped certain fears. If any panic did exist, it is easily attributable to outspoken individuals, sensationalist journalism or radical organizations. Explicit attempts to inculcate certain anxieties originated from the perception that wider society remained ignorant of certain threats and therefore required a more 'informed' understanding. Given that invasion scares were highly politicized displays of public emotion, they should be thought of as part of an emotional regime that corresponded to a marginalized, albeit vocal, political ideology. While certain liberals and socialists exhibited similar invasion anxieties to right-wing alarmists,[36] and although the Conservative Party were by no means united on issues of home defence or the invasion threat, historians generally agree that such panics were 'all but exclusively products of Conservative political interest'.[37] Whether this form of scaremongering induced a widespread state of fear seems unlikely, but this type of rhetoric undoubtedly conveyed emotional standards and models of expression that could be used to interpret and describe feelings encountered during periods of national vulnerability or crisis.

Germanophobia in Britain

The idea that spy fever was spontaneous derives from Arthur Marwick's seminal work highlighting the transformations brought about by the First World War.

According to Marwick's thesis these changes had a momentous and lasting effect on nearly all aspects of social and political life,[38] and so the degree of racial hatred espoused during the conflict far surpassed anything that had transpired previously.[39] Owing to the emphasis placed on the dramatic and catalytic effect of total war, wartime Germanophobia has often been seen as a radical departure from Britain's ostensibly liberal political culture.[40] In his highly influential study of wartime Germanophobia, for instance, Panikos Panayi professes that the manifestation of anti-German antagonism had little precedent in Edwardian history:

> The hostility of the war years had only a few roots specifically in this sort of economic-inspired animosity … Although the pre-War peaks did provide a foundation for the hostility during the years of armed conflict, we should not see hatred of Germans within Britain as a steadily growing plant which bore fruit in 1914. Instead, we should compare it with a smouldering fire which occasionally came alight prior to the war, but, with the outbreak of hostilities, exploded.[41]

Although this 'explosion' has now been subjected to revisionist interpretations elsewhere,[42] viewing spy phobias as an instinctive reaction to the outbreak of war neatly aligns with Marwick's earlier proposition that the war had a dramatic impact on society. Moreover, the suddenness of such antagonism also insinuates that these attitudes were generated by an organic reaction among the general public, hence why spy fever – linked closely with anti-German sentiment more broadly – is often presumed to have blossomed in similar fashion.[43]

However, the emphasis on a rapid and spontaneous transformation of ideals is inconsistent with broader studies of British anti-alienism. Colin Holmes's magisterial volumes on the history of immigration question the notion that Britain routinely displayed lenience and openness towards refugees and immigrants. Holmes identifies a number of images and stereotypes that were used to convey prejudicial beliefs relating to immigrants before the appearance of the spy in xenophobic rhetoric.[44] Although hostility was by no means consistent across Britain, a multitude of migrants and ethnicities encountered discrimination. The long-standing Protestant antipathy towards Catholicism, for example, ensured that Irish immigrants were repeatedly derided as racially inferior to the Anglo-Saxon.[45] Furthermore, tensions generated around the 1905 Aliens Act were predominantly directed against the arrival of Jews from Russian Poland, whose numbers had been steadily rising since the 1880s. Resentment towards Russian Jews originated from the economic competition they provided in the labour market and was exacerbated by the widely held belief that unlike other immigrant groups, Jews refused to assimilate.[46] Romani people also received a torrent of abuse despite their relatively small presence in Britain. While the Traveller community arrived legally and were self-sustaining, they found themselves legislated against by government, rounded up or forcibly removed by local police and discriminated against by society for their nomadic lifestyle.[47] African and Asian communities faced much animosity thanks to the rise of Social Darwinism and skewed concepts of race as well as their foreign religious beliefs.[48] Concerns that Lithuanian, Italian and Chinese workers were saturating the market with cheap labour also ensured that these groups faced intermittent abuse.[49] In sum, Holmes posits that during the period between 1871 and 1914 there was little evidence of the 'much-vaunted tradition of tolerance in Britain, let alone acceptance', and conversely argues that Britain was a fundamentally intolerant nation.[50]

David Caesarani attributes this expansion of anti-alienism during the Victorian period to the growing importance attached to national and racial identity. He argues that Social Darwinism and the eugenics movement closely entwined national characteristics with ethnicity.[51] Although the British public had displayed relatively relaxed attitudes towards immigrants up until 1880, the alien population at that point remained relatively small and was dwarfed by the volume of economic migrants relocating from within Britain. But the early 1880s reversed positive opinions as an influx of Eastern European immigrants coincided with economic decline. Aliens then became a focal point for aggression, as theories of evolution and natural selection amplified the division between alien and native. Caesarani suggests that between 1906 and 1914 anti-alienism 'developed a momentum, dynamic, and logic of its own' that was fuelled by the Home Office and prominent anti-alienists. As a consequence, he maintains:

> The roots of wartime and post-war anti-alienism are to be found in the construction of the alien in British political culture and society in the late Victorian and Edwardian eras. Policies and practices post-1914 were merely an extension of those which were tried and trusted or which had previously been mooted and experimented with.[52]

Viewing wartime Germanophobia as an aberration is therefore inconsistent with the historiography of racial and ethnic discrimination in Britain. The emergence of a spy fever in 1914 should instead be viewed as an expansion of anti-German sentiment that had been developing in Britain in years prior to 1914.

Besides the growing propensity to exhibit xenophobic tendencies towards a host of undesirable minorities, Britain was involved in an escalating diplomatic, economic, naval and imperial rivalry with Germany throughout the decades preceding 1914.[53] During the first half of the nineteenth century this conflict appeared unlikely. A common religion and closely linked royal dynasties had safeguarded good relations between the two countries, while cooperation at Waterloo seemingly confirmed Britain and Germany as natural allies. While Germany appeared to British audiences as a leading figure in literature, music, philosophy, theology and economics, Britain provided an example with which Germany could model her own growing industrialization.[54] Mutual respect and admiration thus characterized Anglo-German cultural, intellectual and political relations. It was not until Germany's unification in the 1860s and the war of 1870 that relations between the two nations began to deteriorate.[55] For some Britons a strong nation state at the heart of Europe promised to provide a bulwark against French and Russian aspirations, while others feared that a militarized neo-feudal

Germany threatened to overthrow the balance of power on the continent. The latter resonated widely thanks to Bismarck's ruthlessness and diplomatic acumen. Nevertheless, on the whole, Britain remained fairly ambivalent at the prospect of a unified Germany. The most pressing concern was that Prussia might in the future also seek to augment her military and political mastery with maritime power, which would upset the naval balance of power and pose a direct challenge to Britain's supremacy at sea.[56]

Although Prussian aggression towards Austria and France, not to mention the treatment of civilians during the Franco-Prussian War, offended British sensibilities, popular animosity could be mitigated by the continued distinction between what was perceived as inherently 'Prussian', compared to that which was considered 'German'. While Prussia was overtly militaristic and unscrupulous, thereby making it a target of political antipathy, Germany remained cultured and liberal in the minds of many Britons.[57] To get around this ambiguity Paul Kennedy identified two schools of thought: the ethical 'idealists' and the practical 'realists'. Kennedy suggested that idealists sought the continuance of peace and closer ties with Germany, whereas the realists either genuinely believed in the German peril or used the threat to advance a political agenda.[58] However, Jan Rüger contends that these categories are insufficient in explaining British opinions of Germany. Rüger warns against making a simple distinction between two opposing viewpoints because in reality there was an assortment of contradictory attitudes and opinions that varied according to personal and political circumstances.[59] Moreover, while certain Germanophobes had the most realistic outlook on Germany, some Germanophiles could be the most vociferous critics of Germany.[60] Thus, rather than a straightforward progression from affinity to antagonism, British perceptions of Germany were far more ambivalent.[61] As such, it would be a mistake to simply connect a hesitant political antagonism with popular discrimination aimed at German immigrants in Britain.

Although Kennedy fails to account for certain ambiguities, there was nevertheless an ideological split between ethical and practical considerations in British politics. Disagreements concerning relations with Germany were merely a single aspect of a larger ideological divide. Idealists and realists were often focused on more pressing matters during the 1870s, and despite growing concerns regarding Germany's intentions, Britain and Germany were actually in agreement in regards to European affairs for most of the decade.[62] But by the mid-1880s Britain's position as the leading imperial and industrial power was beginning to wane. Traditional doctrines of laissez-faire liberalism were no longer suited to the new realities Britain was faced with, and as a result, the radical right began depicting Germany as both an example to emulate and a dangerous foe, in the hope that it would increase national efficiency and stem the tide of collective degeneracy.[63] Despite the intensification of this rhetoric, published views of Germany were by no means predominantly unfriendly as many continued to recognize a shared cultural heritage.[64] Nor was Germany the only target of the radical right.[65] Rather than perceive a gradual progression of animosity, historians generally recognize constant fluctuations in public opinion.[66] And so although the

Anglo-German rivalry was often played out in popular culture, the progression of Germany into a clear and present danger was far from consistent. The appearance of invasion and espionage novels, which routinely attempted to elicit anti-German responses, typically coincided with specific episodes of political antagonism. Outside of these periods of strained Anglo-German relations, writers could adopt a much friendlier attitude towards Germany.[67]

Even Germany's militaristic, impulsive and obstinate leader, Wilhelm II, was the subject of much ambivalence in Britain. His ancestry and overt fondness for British culture was often enough to overcome any aversions towards his impulsiveness and recklessness. Even after the anger and hatred aimed at him following the Kruger Telegram[68] negative opinion quickly abated after the Kaiser's timely appearance at Queen Victoria's deathbed, which appeared to symbolize Germany's support for Britain in her hour of need.[69] Nevertheless, the idealists in Britain struggled to maintain this benevolence towards Germany indefinitely. In spite of the persistent cultural affinity between the two nations German immigrants faced sporadic forms of hostility. As with most nineteenth-century anti-alienism in Britain, though, Germanophobia was decidedly class based. Lower-class Germans, distinct from middle- and upper-class immigrants, came under attack for their perceived immorality, lack of religious adherence, alcoholism and sexual promiscuity. German workers received much condemnation for ostensibly taking British jobs, despite Germany's own soaring economic and industrial success.[70] Although these socio-economic forms of animosity were spread across minority groups, because Germany was increasingly portrayed as a threat by the radical right, the level of discrimination aimed at Germans tentatively increased. Episodic attacks against Germans in London coincided with heightened diplomatic tensions as a result, but these incidents were neither systematic nor widespread enough to suggest a consistent aversion to German immigrants.[71]

The transformation from a diplomatic rivalry to a growing social anxiety and eventual hostility was far from inevitable, especially given the continued closeness of Anglo-German cultural relations.[72] Keir Waddington contends that a rising Germanophobia was facilitated through characterizations transposed onto material objects believed to be intrinsically German. Since a greater awareness of contagious diseases had exposed the risks of foreign interference, meat became symbolic of foreign intrusion because of the potentially harmful bacteria that it carried. German sausages, for example, were commonly purported to contain 'deadly mysteries' liable to spread disease and so served as a metaphor for the encroaching danger German communities appeared to represent. In highlighting the importance of symbolism in breaking down former affiliations Waddington disputes the notion that Anglo-German friendship was easily or spontaneously displaced by a growing antagonism after 1900. Although the war fanned the flames of Germanophobia, wartime hostility, which was itself regularly aimed at Germans butchers, reflected a much longer chronology of popular anti-German sentiments. By examining the use of specific imagery to stimulate xenophobia Waddington reiterates the importance of manufactured stereotypes in the expression of discriminatory attitudes. But most importantly, he shows that embryonic forms of popular Germanophobia originated through cultural interactions carried out over a protracted period, despite a latent affinity displayed by both societies.[73]

Although British perceptions of Germany and the German people were far less belligerent during the pre-war period, wartime xenophobia was not entirely without precedent.[74] The long chronology of growing intolerance towards immigrants suggests that the manifestation of anti-German sentiment during the First World War was a culmination of animosity that had been developing during the previous half century. As a consequence, Germanophobia should be viewed as a single component within a mounting tradition of discrimination and not as a phenomenon specific to wartime conditions. Most importantly, the expansion of Germanophobia developed, in part, thanks to negative cultural constructs that helped to convey popular hostility. The appearance of the spy, which likewise portrayed individuals as emblematic of the nation from whence they came, mirrored former devices used in discriminatory rhetoric. Like the German sausage, the spy offered a simple and convenient mechanism to focus anxiety in a way that provided a sense of community and purpose during a tumultuous period. However, just as the dangers associated with diseased meat required an understanding of bacterial infection, a widespread belief that German espionage signalled a very real and immediate danger demanded a predetermined understanding of what covert activities looked like and how they threatened the nation.

Images of secret warfare

Since British society had repeatedly encountered the prospect of invasion against a backdrop of rising immigration, the emergence of a spy peril in which these two perceived threats coalesced seems almost inevitable. But popular emotions do not become fixated on images of clandestine agents and subversive activities without some degree of interference. Since political rhetoric and cultural stereotypes were evident in the propagation of fears linked with invasion and immigration, it is misguided to assume that spy fever developed spontaneously. In fact, because spy phobias were closely related to these broader anxieties, in that images of secret warfare frequently and explicitly portrayed aliens as enablers of an enemy attack or invading force, spy phobias were part of the same emotional regime linked to radical conservatism. Consequently, it is worth considering how stereotypes were formed in relation to espionage and sabotage and how those images were used in discourses prior to the First World War, as these formed the cultural and political resources that shaped emotional responses to the enemy within in 1914.

Prior to August 1914, the British public had become well versed in the apparent dangers of Germany's secret service. Images of German spies proliferated widely following Prussia's swift invasion of France in 1870, and it was during this conflict that we see the first appearance of the term 'spy fever' in Britain.[75] During the earlier Crimean War, conversely, Britain's enduring aversion to increased regulation meant that national security was generally considered subservient to conventional liberalism, and so 'spy fever' was incompatible with popular sentiment. Even *John Bull*, which would later become one of the most vociferous advocates of repression and intolerance during the First World War, captured the British distaste for spying of any sort:

> It has been the boast of this country hitherto, that the hateful system of police espionnage [*sic*] which prevails in most of the Continental States, has no existence among us ... the absence of a corrupt system of surveillance, – so alien are these things to the genius of English life that our language has not even words to express them, – is one of the primary conditions of that open freedom and honest independence, as well as the basis of that reverence for the law, which distinguish the English character. The existence of an organized [*sic*] body of spies, prying into men's affairs, is not only inconsistent with a state of legal freedom, but exercises a highly demoralizing [*sic*] influence upon society.[76]

Given the opposition to overbearing security measures and the importance of individual liberty during the eighteenth and nineteenth centuries, the British public seem to have seldom considered foreign spies as a significant threat to the nation.[77] Yet by 1871 the *Lincoln Chronicle* stressed that there was much cause for concern. There were, they claimed, 'Germans in the Royal household, Germans in the cabinet, Germans in Parliament, Germans in our army, Germans in our navy, Germans in our volunteers, German bankers, German merchants, German shopkeepers, German labourers... Spies, all of them'.[78]

The Franco-Prussian War marked a turning point in how European societies comprehended war and the challenges that it brought. As war became a contest of nations at a time when European immigration was flourishing, aliens became potentially hostile adversaries that could undermine state and society from within. As such, correspondents reporting on the fighting in France frequently told of countless spies and saboteurs aiding the invading Prussians.[79] Whereas supposedly factual representations of the Franco-Prussian War established the scale and tenacity of Germany's secret service, a deluge of novels then followed that placed spies at the centre of all Germany's intrigues and invasion plans.[80] Even in 1914 Le Queux was still using the Franco-Prussian War to substantiate contemporary fears of German espionage. In *The German Spy System from Within by Ex-Intelligence Officer*, published in October 1914 under the pseudonym Lionel James, Le Queux exclaimed that German treachery was endemic:

> The German system of military espionage can best be studied by an analysis of the working system in France from the year 1870 onwards. So far as the outside world is concerned, the military invasion of France by German began at the end of July 1870, but in reality the invasion began in the latter half of 1867, when Stieber, chief of the German secret police, began the placing of his fixed posts throughout the country. No less than 30,000 spies were place in the departments of Northern and Eastern France, and the feats of this army made possible the work accomplished by Von Moltke.[81]

Although Le Queux was essentially peddling the same lies that had circulated during the war as part of the Steiber legend,[82] by situating fictional stories of German espionage and sabotage within the real world of Prussian antagonism and treachery, authors like Le Queux established the spy as a real threat, one that would almost certainly go on to cause havoc for Britain in any future conflict.[83]

But before British audiences became immersed in the fictional world of clandestine intrigue and sabotage, it was the prospect of foreign armies landing on Britain's shores that captivated audiences. And it was here, in the pages of invasion novels, that Britons first encountered Germany as an enemy. Prompted by Prussia's swift and decisive victory in 1870, George Chesney's *The Battle of Dorking* first appeared in 1871 shortly after the Franco-Prussian armistice and introduced audiences to the idea that Germany could, if so inclined, invade southern England. *Battle of Dorking* went on to inspire an entire genre exploring contemporary diplomatic and political issues and how they intersected with home defence and imperial security.[84] Although the German menace faded shortly after the success of *The Battle of Dorking*, and subsequent invasion thrillers like Le Queux's *The Great War in England in 1897* portrayed Russia and France as the likely invaders owing to their sizable navies, as Germany's own naval construction began in earnest, the Teutonic foe once again became the likely adversary in fictional depictions of future war.

Because Prussia's alleged transgressions during the Franco-Prussian War had given rise to the understanding that it was an innately deceitful and scheming nation, it was not long before writers began including spies and intrigue into their invasion conspiracies. Widely considered as one of the founding texts of the espionage genre, and certainly one of the greatest of the Edwardian spy novels, was Erskine Childers's *The Riddle of the Sands*. Published in May 1903, it set the tone of Edwardian popular fiction and established the spy as legitimate and thrilling device that would entertain audiences for over a century.[85] Building on Chesney's invasion scenario, *Riddle of the Sands* proposed that such a plot would by facilitated by duplicitous secret agents. One of the problems set out in *Riddle of the Sands* was the difficulty in identifying and defining the spy threat. Davies and Carruthers, the men responsible for uncovering the dastardly plot, suspected the primary antagonist, Herr Dollmann, of being involved in some sort of nefarious activity after he had seemingly led Davies into an almost inescapable trap. Davies labels Dollmann a 'spy' but admits that he is unsure of what this meant and was only certain that he is 'something pretty bad'.[86] Davies's inability to unequivocally define what he means by the term 'spy' establishes espionage as a varied threat that can refer to a range of perverse occupations and not just covert intelligence gathering. Adding to this complexity, Carruthers later points out that there are no easily recognizable characteristics that can identify a spy, which further exacerbates the ambiguity and severity of the danger.[87] It later transpires that Dollmann was a former lieutenant in the Royal Navy and had been supplying his knowledge of the English coast to the Germans. The implication being that this ill-defined danger could emerge from anywhere, even from treacherous Englishmen seeking financial gain.

Davies's inability to adequately define the essence of a spy was a prevalent theme in Edwardian fiction. Whereas Childers wrote about Dollmann the spy who leaked information to covert operatives, Joseph Conrad's *Secret Agent* was an equally enigmatic figure. In an earlier life Adolf Veloc had been involved in collecting intelligence in France for an undisclosed foreign embassy but was described as an 'agent provocateur' by his handler.[88] In this capacity the secret agent was tasked with provoking insurrection as well as gathering intelligence. Unlike in *Riddle of the Sands*, the threat of espionage was not simply the leakage of information crucial to national security, but hidden saboteurs intent on causing civil unrest from within:

> The existence of secret agents should not be tolerated, as tending to augment the positive dangers of the evil against which they are used. That the spy will fabricate his information is a mere commonplace. But in the sphere of political and revolutionary action, relying partly on violence, the professional spy has every facility to fabricate the very fact themselves, and will spread the double evil of emulation in one direction, and of panic, hasty legislation, unreflecting hate on the other.[89]

Of course, this was just as perilous as information gathering, maybe even more so, for it represented a direct attack on Britain's values and way of life.[90] Thus, according to these early espionage novels spies could be engaged in a variety of exploits ranging from intelligence gatherers, political conspirators, covert saboteurs or subversives plotting unrest. The provenance of the danger was equally varied. In *Riddle of the Sands*, the antagonist was unequivocally German. But in *The Secret Agent*, the foreign embassy directing Verloc's efforts was loosely connected to both Russia and Germany, while Verloc himself, although claiming to be British, was born to a French father – once again suggesting that the spy menace could come from anywhere.

Besides the classic novels produced by the likes of Childers and Conrad, fictional secret agents flourished during the Edwardian period thanks to authors such as William Le Queux and E. Phillips Oppenheim who took full advantage of lower printing costs. Publishing spy stories at an impressive rate, these authors deliberately set out to sensationalize the German menace for financial and political gain. Le Queux, in particular, found huge success as a popular novelist and became synonymous with the spy peril in Britain.[91] It was Le Queux's explicit intention to awaken the British public to the dangers of German espionage and in so doing became an essential figure in setting out the parameters of the threat.[92] In one of his first espionage novels, *The Man from Downing Street*, Le Queux established the threat in no uncertain terms: 'England's enemies nowadays keep up a whole army of unscrupulous spies ... in every capital, almost in every one of the principal cities in the civilised world today may be found one or more agents of that wonderful organisation.'[93] Although not primarily a spy novel, Le Queux's *Invasion of 1910* went on to have a lasting impact on the genre and shaped perceptions and portrayals of the German menace throughout the period. Whereas Childers and Conrad only ever wrote about a handful of spies who seldom succeeded in their endeavours, *1910* depicted a full-scale invasion preceded by hundreds of saboteurs who had been hiding and plotting in Britain for years.[94] Shortly before the first German landing in East Anglia, for example, German agents severed cables and blew up railway lines to prevent the alarm from being raised. After Germany's initial landing, more agents then began destroying transport links and telegraph communications across Britain to further disrupt the already besieged defenders.[95]

In *Spies of the Kaiser* Le Queux returned to this theme so that he could further expose the 'vast army of German spies' – this time said to be 5,000 strong – operating in Britain. The main protagonists, Ray Raymond, John James Jacox and Vera Vallance, gradually uncover the enormity of Germany's intrigues. The conspiracy involves seemingly ordinary Germans who had been enjoying the life afforded to them in Britain as peaceful citizens. Unbeknownst to the public, though, these 'fixed agents', many of whom were employed as waiters or barbers, were trained soldiers tasked with stockpiling ammunition and explosives, monitoring aircraft and naval construction, locating transport and communication infrastructure and reconnoitring the country in motor cars to identify suitable landing points and artillery positions in readiness for the day that England is invaded.[96] Popular fiction had quite clearly established that German spies could be anywhere and everywhere, given the number of aliens residing in Britain, and that these agents posed a considerable threat to the continued safety of the nation. To anybody familiar with the work of Le Queux, individuals found to be making sketches, taking photos, driving motorcars or in possession of communications equipment could be identified as a potential spy. Although we should not assume that readers interpreted these narratives as unabridged factual exposés, the very fact that Le Queux deliberately sought to awaken his readers politically suggests that First World War spy phobias did not occur entirely spontaneously.[97]

Oppenheim's novels were, on the whole, more sophisticated and eminently more readable than Le Queux's. Whereas Le Queux greatly exaggerated the ubiquity of German spies, Oppenheim's early novels constructed a more elusive danger, albeit equally sinister in nature. Rather than legions of emissaries ready to attack Britain from within, *Mysterious Mr Sabin* (1898) portrays an unnamed secret organization controlling Europe's destiny, of which Mr Sabin was a part. Fortunately for Britain, Sabin's own plot to restore the Bourbon Monarchy by fomenting a German invasion of England was scuppered at the last minute by this mysterious organization that considered a European war inopportune, at least for the moment. As well as being an unscrupulous agent attempting to control European diplomacy, the reader also becomes acquainted with German spies who later try and assassinate Sabin after his failure to deliver crucial intelligence to the Kaiser's ambassador in London. Referred to as 'Doomschen', these spies posed as peaceful citizens who, because of prior convictions, are actually working for Germany's secret police. Although Mr and Mrs Watson appeared like innocent American citizens, they were operating under false pretences (they were neither named Watson nor married) and were obliged to fulfil any task their country asked of them in a desperate effort to commute their death sentences bestowed upon them in their native Germany.[98]

Despite the subtle threat uncovered in *Mysterious Mr Sabin*, Oppenheim's *The Great Secret* is much more reminiscent of Le Queux's *Spies of the Kaiser*. Hardross Courage, the central protagonist of the story, first discovers Germany's evil plot while staying in a famous London hotel. After risking his own life, Hardross eventually exposes an army of German saboteurs organized into societies formed of clerks, tradesmen, waiters and hairdressers who are ready for an armed uprising against Britain. After hearing of the plot, the editor of the fictional *Daily Oracle* comments, 'This is what comes of making London the asylum for all the foreign scum of the earth.'[99] Whereas writers like Kipling, Conrad and Childers introduced audiences to the figure of the spy, it was through the work of Le Queux and Oppenheim that the British public could, if so inclined, contemplate the sizable threat that German spies presented. Of course this assessment was purely fictional, but their imaginings had a lasting impact on shaping contemporaries' perceptions of the danger. The suspicions that were recorded in 1914 routinely imitated fictional stereotypes; popular narratives often associated hotel staff, café waiters and foreign hairdressers and clerks with foreign espionage, while carrier pigeons, flashing lights and suspicious motorcars were frequently given as the cause of much concern.[100]

Historians have often attached great significance to the deluge of fictional spies that saturated Edwardian literature. The appearance of spy phobias in 1914, they argue, was directly attributable to society's earlier consumption of invasion and espionage novels. David French asserts that 'a gullible British public was beginning to mistake fiction for fact,'[101] while James Hampshire claims that 'it was the blurring of the boundary of fiction and reality which made the phenomenon of spy fever so virulent'.[102] In one of the most recent analyses of Edwardian spy fiction, Danny Laurie-Fletcher argues that even 'highly educated and worldly' individuals failed to distinguish between fact and fiction. Vernon Kell himself, the head of the wartime counter-espionage bureau MO5(g), was supposedly duped by Armgaard Karl Graves's testimony simply because it mirrored the narratives and conventions used in popular spy fiction.[103] According to these historians because spy novels conflated the hidden world of espionage and intrigue with the real world of international politics and diplomacy, society almost unequivocally interpreted them as evidence of Germany's infiltration of Britain.[104]

However, this rather simple model assumes that literature invariably influences the political consciousness of the reader and that its impact is directly proportionate to its circulation.[105] In his recent thesis examining invasion literature, Harry Wood contends that historians are yet to sufficiently explore the impact of this genre and advises against assuming a direct correlation between fiction and popular fears.[106] There is no doubt that spy fiction enjoyed unprecedented levels of popularity during the Edwardian period and not just in Britain. Fictionalized interpretations of future conflict captivated audiences across Europe, but it was in Britain that readers were exposed to considerably more tales of future wars than anywhere else in Europe, and many of these stories incorporated depictions of espionage.[107]

If there were indeed a straightforward connection between the prevalence of fictional spies and the scale of popular fears, Britain would have experienced a far more potent spy fever than any other belligerent, yet that was far from being true.

But it was not just cheap fiction that told of German spies and saboteurs, as images of secret warfare also filled the pages of the national press. Here the spy was an equally enigmatic figure that engaged in an array of duplicitous acts. Spies could be foreign dignitaries colluding with an enemy, disgruntled natives selling secrets to foreign powers, covert saboteurs leading organized forces inside an enemy nation, internal subversives acting against their own government or travelling agents attempting to gather sensitive information.[108] Because secret agents were occupied in all sorts of nefarious schemes they proved incredibly effective at stimulating discussions about home defence and international relations, which made them a regular feature of popular newspapers.[109] However, the way in which spies were used as rhetorical devices certainly differed. Whereas radical journals certainly embellished the German spy threat and claimed that thousands of clandestine foes were active in Britain,[110] mainstream publications mostly focused on international intrigue and the many spies being apprehended in the great imperial capitals of Europe.[111]

Although Morris rightly identified newspapers like the *Daily Mail* as an active contributor to defence scares, it rarely gave explicit warnings about espionage in Britain and, in fact, even occasionally downplayed the threat of spies.[112] But where it was prolific was in reporting on spies and counter-spies active in Germany. This narrative purported that Germany's security forces were overzealous, and that as a consequence, the German people must be deeply irrational and prone to nervousness.[113] The arrest of Captain Bernard Trench and Lieutenant Vivian Brandon at Borkum in 1910, for example, was characterized as a 'spy mania', even though these two individuals were genuine British spies who had been sent to gather intelligence about the naval installations and coastal defences at Kiel, Brunsbüttel and Tonning. At the time of their arrest, they were conducting their second mission to Germany and were being paid by Mansfield Cumming, head of the foreign section of the fledgling Secret Service Bureau.[114] While attributing these arrests to a 'mania' was likely designed to undermine the legitimacy of Germany's actions, and was perhaps also a rejoinder to claims in the German press that Britain had itself been suffering from the most incomprehensible of spy fevers,[115] further 'attacks' of spy fever were presumed to have instigated several sensational claims of illicit activity in Germany.[116] According to reports in the *Daily Mail* outbreaks of German spy fever were sporadic but caused much sensation in the afflicted areas.[117] After the arrest of another British spy sent to Germany, Max Schultz (not to be confused with the German spy of the same name sent to Britain in 1911), German newspapers began expressing the belief that British spies had systematically infiltrated the entire country.[118] One German newspaper claimed:

There is unquestionable evidence that with the aid of English money a host of paid spies is maintained in the shipyards and other great manufacturing works in Germany, and not on the coast alone. The spies are Germans, or German-speaking foreigners, and are controlled by more highly placed British agents ... According to all appearances people in a good position and belonging to the best society in England take part in the work, their love of sport impelling them to play with danger.[119]

By conflating Germany's measured reactions to real security threats with public outcry and hyperbole in the press, the *Daily Mail* created the impression that Germany was predisposed to panic and alarm and therefore inferior to the more stoic nature of Britain. Perhaps more importantly, though, this narrative established a paradigm whereby suspicion, even when it was genuine and precise, was labelled as feverish or manic.

Based on its pre-war coverage of covert operations, it would be hard to argue that the *Daily Mail* deliberately sought to incite panic or spread fear about German spies during the period preceding the First World War. Few articles sensationalized the threat of German spies in Britain or exaggerated Britain's vulnerability to this particular menace. However, the prevalence of espionage within the pages of the *Daily Mail*, one of the most widely read newspapers in Britain at the time, undoubtedly cemented the idea that spies were a common feature of international relations in both peace and war.[120] By also portraying Germany's responses to spy threats as a form of mental illness, society became familiarized with the assumed characteristics of spy phobias. Because Germany's reaction to spies was seen as overzealous and unfounded, it was portrayed as feverish and manic to denigrate the credulity and irrationality of German society.[121] While this narrative may not have directly influenced how individuals felt about German spies, it almost certainly shaped how they viewed these fears in others. If nothing else, it gave readers the language to explain popular fears in this context. So when Britons observed similar feelings much closer to home, there was an existing linguistic framework to understand and describe them. British spy fears in 1914 were often seen as feverish, not because people made careful assessments about the mental state of those affected but because it had become commonplace to portray such emotionality as psychological disorder.

While the creation of fear and paranoia cannot be objectively attributed to the popularity of spy stories, as a creation of popular culture, they projected various customs and ideas that could shape perceptions and behaviour. Although the threat of espionage was rather broad and somewhat ambiguous, images of secret warfare, however sensational they may have been, offered interpretations of where, when and how covert activities were likely to manifest. That is not to say that society were foolishly mistaking fiction for fact, but when society experienced anxiety or fear in relation to international stability or national security, and when they were warned about the dangers of German secret agents, as they were in August 1914, these portrayals of secret warfare were the primary resource with which they could comprehend the danger in front of them. Moreover, the way in which spy phobias were commonly depicted established an emotional and linguistic framework that could help people explain and express feelings that occurred because of that same danger.[122] Thus, although spy stories did not induce popular spy phobias or panics, they did create certain conditions in which a spy fever could flourish.

***

Based on how public emotions were formed and expressed during the late Victorian and Edwardian periods, especially those associated with internal and external threats, one could argue that an emotional regime existed in which certain ideals and feelings were amplified. According to many contemporary military analysts, warfare had changed. The Franco-Prussian War, more so than any previous conflict, had demonstrated that war was a contest of nations and that the country most able to harness new technology in the pursuit of destruction would likely prevail. As a result, society had to be readied for the dangers of future conflict. This necessitated a heightened awareness of national and imperial security and in particular the potential for an invading army to land on Britain's shores. The increasing aversion to immigration was not entirely disconnected from this, since the presence of aliens symbolized an invasion of sorts while also adding an extra dimension to anticipated invasion scenarios because of the potential that they could form an enemy within. However, for security discourse to have any significant effect it needed to mobilize collective feelings through emotive language, itself reliant upon accepted customs and conventions regarding emotional expression and meaning. This emotional regime was largely tied to conservative ideals and prioritized a heightened emotional concern for international stability and national security. Whereas invasion 'scares' exaggerated external threats to expedite more stringent security measures, anti-alien rhetoric sought to mobilize society against the potential dangers of an enemy within.

These same standards made the spy peril possible, since fear and anxiety had been frequently portrayed as desirable emotional responses to ensure appropriate policies were forthcoming, and these feelings had been routinely connected to an external invasion threat as well as an internal alien menace. The emergence of the spy peril during the First World War was only possible because the lingering threat of invasion coupled with a growing xenophobia to make individual Germans living in Britain symbolic of the wider German nation. Condemning these individuals provided an outlet for various feelings generated by the war. But by exploring similar panics and situating spy phobias within the context of Victorian and Edwardian scaremongering, this chapter has highlighted the problem with understanding spy phobias as an impulsive reaction among the general population. Since emotional experiences are formed through political and cultural discourse, how society became aware of the object of danger, how they became accustomed to a particular set of feelings and how these two became connected need to be taken into consideration to understand why fears and anxieties centred on the threat of German spies in particular. While the many invasion scares in Britain demonstrate the degree of interference that was necessary to establish a specific threat and create the conditions necessary for panic, the gradual increase in Germanophobia during the same period highlights the importance of sustained mediation, especially through the use of emotive imagery, to maintain popular clamour.

The emergence of spy phobias was therefore only possible because society had access to an emotional framework that prioritized certain feelings in response to international crises and a cultural paradigm in which secret agents were a common feature of contemporary conflict. But for individuals to experience fear or anxiety, society needed to understand that the threat was imminent, and these warnings soon appeared following the outbreak of war in August 1914. Thus, although popular culture did not directly inculcate specific emotions felt by individuals witnessed during the spy peril, it did contribute to an emotional framework that helped people interpret some of the experiences generated by the outbreak of war.

Chapter 2

THE OUTBREAK OF WAR

On one sunny August afternoon James Carroll, aged twenty-seven, went for a walk close to a railway line by his home in Farnham. After coming across members of the London Territorials, responsible for guarding the railways in the area, Carroll engaged Private Wagner in conversation about the composition of local defences. The conversation was brief and Carroll soon moved on. Upon witnessing this exchange, Bugler Hardy suggested that this 'very suspicious man' be arrested. As Carroll walked away, Wagner and Hardy began shouting at him to surrender. Unbeknownst to them, however, Carroll was partially blind and deaf. Because Carroll had inadvertently ignored their challenge, on account of his disability, they directed Private Calfe to confront and arrest him:

> Hardy and Ireland came running towards me yelling at me. I saw the man. I waited till he came round the road towards my bridge. I challenged him, shouting out 'halt'. He looked up and made no reply. I challenged him again. The same thing happened, Then 5 of us challenged him. He looked up and passed under the bridge. We all crossed to the other side to meet him coming out. We challenged him once more. He began to move off at a sharp trot. He was then about 30 yards away, I thought for a few seconds what I had better do. I thought better not run down to him because he might have firearms. I fired one shot and he fell in the roadway.[1]

Later that day, at five minutes to midnight, James Carroll succumbed to his wounds and died at Aldershot military hospital. In the inquest that followed, extreme measures, even those that resulted in the deaths of innocent bystanders, were deemed vital to national security.

This chapter shows how Britain's mobilization was accompanied by an overt campaign to warn society about the dangers of enemy within at the same time as various authorities sanctioned ad hoc initiatives to combat German secret warfare, and it was in this environment that a spy fever emerged. It first looks at how society initially encountered secret enemies within the pages of the local press to examine the rhetoric and activities that gave rise to spy phobias in August 1914. While these narratives provided the problem, they simultaneously offered the solution; increased levels of suspicion and vigilance would ensure the continued security of the nation. The second section then looks more closely at the 'spy scares' that appeared in the press to try and ascertain who was most likely to feel afraid or anxious at the outset of war. From this it becomes clear that local authorities played a crucial role in the creation of spy fever. Their very overt activities designed to impede German spies gave the impression that there was a very real and imminent danger, which emboldened others to take the threat seriously. The final section then examines the interactions between government and local authorities to understand why the latter appeared so troubled by the prospect of an enemy within. The interplay between provincial and central authorities reveals much about how the spy peril became so prominent following the declaration of war and why the resulting phobias appeared so acute in August 1914.

By focusing specifically on how the spy threat was articulated and established in August 1914, this chapter shows that spy fever was not spontaneous. Like earlier invasion scares and anti-alien sentiment, emotional responses to the spy peril were stimulated by rhetoric promoting specific feelings in support of national security objectives that were publicly sanctioned and adopted by figures of authority. While newspapers conveyed the appropriate emotional customs to interpret the threats posed by German spies, local authorities simultaneously began a very overt campaign to root out German spies in their midst. Together, these actions stressed the importance of certain behaviours and feelings to wartime conditions and seemingly confirmed the existence of an elusive threat that many paranoid scaremongers had spent a decade prophesizing about.. Together these activities seemingly confirmed what many paranoid scaremongers had spent a decade prophesizing about.

Constructing the peril

The arrest of twenty-one 'known' German spies following the declaration of the Precautionary Period was one of the earliest reports to emerge after Britain declared war.[2] These arrests marked the first opportunity for society to extrapolate the magnitude of the German menace in Britain, and rumours of covert activity soon escalated.[3] Although events in London were watched with keen interest, reports of German espionage across Europe provided the most compelling evidence of hidden enemies in Britain.[4] It was repeatedly claimed during the first few days of war that 2,000 spies had already been arrested in Belgium, with at least 100 of them executed. Spies had been found wearing Belgian military uniforms, driving motorcars for nefarious purposes and armed with bombs and revolvers. Covert wireless stations had been uncovered, vital infrastructure secretly marked for destruction and thousands of German rifles discovered in cases labelled 'bacon'.[5] As arrests of German spies continued, and the depths of their treachery increasingly exposed, one journalist surmised that the Belgian public 'had been betrayed by every stranger within their gates'.[6] Immediately following the declaration of war, and before any widespread outbreak of panic could have materialized, the British public were therefore besieged by reports revealing the existence of a secret

German spy network that had infiltrated key European theatres. Such stories laid the foundation for believing that a similar menace was operating Britain.

Depictions of Germany's clandestine operatives in Belgium provided the public with a stark reminder of the risks of neglecting internal security and the direct threats they faced from an enemy within. As spies were being captured in every theatre of war, it was widely inferred that a similar menace must inevitably also exist at home.[7] Since the notoriety of the German General Staff had been well established for over a decade, it was assumed that they had already stockpiled arms and explosives inside every potential adversary and that large 'numbers of German military desperadoes have been let loose in England to work as much destruction as possible at vital points'.[8] Reports of Belgium's demise, which had been greatly assisted by this clandestine foe, provided the imperative and justification to manufacture an espionage threat in Britain. By demonstrating the existence of covert operations elsewhere, the press invented the potential for comparable problems at home.[9]

Various publications began to highlight the vulnerability of strategic points and stressed the importance of popular vigilance. The right-wing magazine, *John Bull*, characteristically reminded its readers to 'keep their ears and eyes wide open, and if they find any of the above orders being contravened, they should immediately inform the police or military authorities'.[10] Even in mainstream newspapers readers were told to inform the authorities of any suspicious aliens that come to their attention.[11] While there were occasional doubts as to the credibility of reports disclosing German clandestine activities, the prospective threat was considered too great to ignore. The *Derby Daily Telegraph* wrote:

> While there is happily good reason for believing that many of the alarms as to the alleged German spies are due to suspicion and misunderstanding, the duty upon citizens all over the United Kingdom of maintaining observation wherever there are circumstances of suspicion should not be neglected.

Notwithstanding the discomfort in discriminating against innocent Germans, dutiful citizens were reassured that:

> Scotland Yard takes rather a serious view of the possible recklessness of some of the undesirables, and that is why the authorities are placing a number under detention. If the public are reasonable in their vigilance they can render service in the protection of themselves without doing material injustice.[12]

Anxiety and suspicion were both familiar emotions promoted by the press. Consequently, as the international crisis provoked collective insecurity any resulting fears were directed towards a familiar object of danger, and people were instructed on how to react to that threat in a way that was conducive to the national effort.

On top of the hyperbole in the press, vigilance was also strongly encouraged by local figures of authority. Their personal importance within a community not only afforded a trustworthy source, but their local perspectives often compelled communities to believe that the danger was imminent. In Elginshire, for instance, the chief constable directed officers to watch all aliens in the area more diligently and gave instructions that the local community be mobilized to search for any potential suspects. Any new arrival was to be watched intently, and anybody conducting nocturnal activity was to be stopped and interrogated, by members of the public if necessary.[13] In Norfolk, civilians were strongly encouraged to participate in local defence. The chief constable directed officers to 'arrange for persons who have guns to shoot any pigeons flying seawards' to prevent illicit communications. He also ordered that constables take special steps to ensure local haystacks were protected against spies, for he was convinced enemies would try and set them ablaze. As a result, local farmers and grounds keepers were given weapons and began nightly patrols.[14]

Initiatives to thwart spies were particularly noticeable in the south-east of England. The chief constable in East Sussex had long harboured concerns that aliens posed a security threat. In 1910, he was more than willing to carry out Kell's bidding and was keen to register all foreigners in Britain so that sufficient control could be established.[15] Following the outbreak of war in 1914 he told the local Watch Committee that the dangers of undesirable aliens and their involvement in treacherous activities had imposed considerable responsibilities on the police. In response, any individual who seemed even the slightest bit suspicious was to be arrested, and officers were issued with revolvers and instructed to use them when needed. Territorial soldiers were also readied to provide additional support to combat dangerous or armed aliens.[16] While there is no suggestion that the chief constable sought to directly incite a public panic towards the threat of espionage, his personal concerns are likely to have impacted the local community. The report presented to the Watch Committee portrays a police mobilization, simultaneous to the military one, against a foreign presence within Britain that came from his own concerns rather than popular outcry. The immediate presence of police activity against foreign spies did not simply legitimize popular xenophobia; in many cases, it preceded it.

In neighbouring West Sussex, the chief constable deliberately galvanized public anxieties shortly after war was declared. By establishing a volunteer civilian guard, members of the public were called upon to assist the police in protecting the local community from spies. Their duties included:

> To undergo drill and musketry so as to become a fit and competent body to assist and support the police and thus to relieve the military …
>
> To guard bridges and other important points, i.e., water works, post offices, electric light stations, and gas works …
>
> No German or Austrian should be allowed to loiter near a bridge, culvert, or interfere in any way with telegraph poles and wires …
>
> The civil guard should report all Germans and Austrians if they know that they have in their possession any of the following articles: – FIREARMS, AMMUNITION, EXPLOSIVES; or material intended to be used for the

manufacture of explosives; any inflammable liquids any signalling apparatus; any carrier pigeons; any motor cars, motor cycles; motor-boat, yacht; or aircraft; any cipher code; any telephone installation; any camera or other photographic apparatus; any military or naval map, chart, or handbook; they should detain such persons if necessary.[17]

In a letter to the Lord Lieutenant, the chief constable conceded that several of the original duties were removed because they were technically illegal but affirmed that others, despite their illegality, were essential. He advocated their inclusion and suggested that 'every action against an enemy of our Sovereign is legal, by common law'.[18] The Surrey chief constable seemingly concurred with this sentiment. After the war he described the measures that he personally put in place:

On the first day of the war, it came to my knowledge that the Military had made no provision for guarding their line of communication, i.e. the South Eastern Railway from Aldershot to Dover, and that the whole of the Aldershot Command would be going over this line. At that time it was anticipated that the Germans living in this country would commit sabotage. Anyone with a stick of dynamite could have prevented the use of this line. To deal with this situation, I, within two days, organised a posse of civilians armed with any weapons they could get hold of, and posted them as a continuous guard on all the vulnerable points. Of course, I had no authority to do this, and there was no time to get it. There was also no time to swear in these people as Special Constables, so I had to accept the responsibility, and I wrote and told the Home Office what I had done. This arrangement was maintained for about two months.[19]

By inaugurating ad hoc civil guards to repel the combined threats of espionage and sabotage almost as soon as war was declared, chief constables bridged the gap between official concerns and popular responses. Local communities up and down Britain were essentially mobilized against the enemy within, which sanctioned feelings of suspicion and vigilance among the general public.

During the early weeks of war, the British public was frequently exposed to warnings about the dangers of German secret agents. Britain's declaration of war sent shockwaves through the nation and in the absence of reliable news 'fear, anticipation, imagination, and rumour' filled the void.[20] Local authorities inevitably shared similar apprehensions, but they possessed the most prominent voice, and so the cause of their anxiety could easily appear as the dominant, if not necessarily the most pervasive, concern across society more generally.[21] Although historians have often interpreted these fears as evidence of widespread and feverish delusions, they should refrain from presuming that these institutional perspectives represented organic attitudes and anxieties. Mostly because these concerns were by no means consistently conveyed across Britain.

In a post-war lecture Vernon Kell described local police forces as vital to his work. He claimed that such assistance required coaxing over '250 separate and independent chief constables, each of whom has to be wooed and won separately before his cooperation can be assured for any purpose in peace and war'. While Kell believed he had secured the unwavering assistance of police chiefs throughout Britain, his statement highlights the degree of agency that chief constables maintained.[22] In contrast to Kell's sanguine assessment of his own efficacy, an internal memo produced by Major General John Ewart, the Director of Military Operations, suggests that while many agreed to the War Office's demands, some chief constables remained adamant that it was not their business to carry out such activities.[23] In any case, despite Kell's best efforts, there was a clear disparity in how police constabularies responded to the peril. Despite the vigour witnessed in Elginshire, there is no evidence that the neighbouring Banffshire constabulary responded in a similar fashion. Although the chief constable complied with the War Office's demands, as was to be expected in wartime, he refrained from sharing any concerns publicly.[24] Likewise, the chief constable of Leicestershire received directives from the War Office to intern all German reservists as prisoners of war and to discover if any further culprits resided in the county. Only a few days later, he was directed that 'as much attention as possible shall be given to the guarding of bridges, power stations, waterworks ... the destructions of which by evil disposed persons would retard mobilisation or inconvenience the general community'.[25] However, he clearly regarded such duties as the responsibility of the military and instructed that ordinary policing remained paramount. Most importantly, rather than allow anxieties to escalate, he instructed superintendents to 'deal with all things at present as confidential and impress upon men to keep matters to themselves'.[26]

The Derbyshire chief constable received similar directives from the Home Office, but he appears to have been unmoved by any anxieties that he may have suffered.[27] In his correspondence with superintendents there was a notable indifference towards espionage or the presence of aliens more generally. When the problem did appear in his correspondence, the chief constable maintained that officers merely uphold their duty rather than adopt any extreme security measures. He appears to have only reacted to the spy danger following interference from another chief constable in an adjacent county.[28] Likewise in the Monmouthshire constabulary, there is almost no trace of spy fever. The chief constable at Newport seems to have given few, if any, instructions relating to foreign espionage, suspicious people or restrictions on aliens. Recorded concerns were instead focused on the potential threat of German Zeppelins, despite the relative safety of South Wales.[29] In nearby Griffithstown local issues continued to dominate police agendas.[30] Theft remained the predominant issue, but missing persons, escaped psychiatric patients, dangerous dogs, bigamy, assault and desertion all seemingly caused more concern than the prospect of German spies.[31]

Just as police responses varied, not all provincial newspapers perpetuated the anxiety focused on German espionage. Some were simply shocked that locals had been caught up in incidents occurring elsewhere.[32] The *Leicester Chronicle* reported an 'astounding' incident for it 'did not occur in Switzerland, Germany, or Belgium, but in the peaceful neighbourhood of Studley Bay'. The surprise and indignation at responses occurring in other regions suggests there was a degree of variation in how communities reacted, and that not all were familiar with the severe measures enacted in certain districts. Nevertheless, the Leicestershire man suspected of espionage found the experience to be extremely pleasing, 'for as an Englishman I was very proud of the steps the authorities had taken to ensure the safety of our little island home'.[33] Some newspapers took a more confrontational approach and explicitly denounced the threat of espionage. Readers of the *Bucks Herald* and *Bedfordshire Times* were assured that despite the arrests of spies in London, 'spy mania' had already dissipated and that adopting 'Prussian' methods of regulation should be avoided.[34] The *Northampton Mercury* went even further and condemned those responsible for such hyperbole

> Once more I remind readers against believing the loose gossip that flies round in these times ... even testimony said to be based on actual personal observation is often utterly unreliable. One of the latest yarns was that a German spy had been arrested at Teeton with enough poison in his possession to kill all the inhabitants of Northampton. I need not say there was no foundation for that report than for many other lying tales that have been in circulation.[35]

The existence of a less extreme and exaggerated response to the alleged peril provides the first indication that such fears were not ubiquitous, and that indifference and opposition to spy fever was also possible.[36]

Notwithstanding these differences, in certain areas there was a clear and deliberate attempt to expose the British public to the dangers seemingly faced in August 1914. Although the foundations for popular alarm had already been established through recurrent invasion scares, discourses that emerged in response to the outbreak of war specifically identified the 'spy' as the most pressing cause for concern. It represented an attempt to manipulate anxieties in a way that mobilized local communities against a secret enemy and encourage participation in the war effort. But the discrepancy evident across Britain insinuates that a degree of immunity from this 'national neurasthenia' existed. As such, it highlights the influence of regional perspectives in establishing popular fears. As we shall see, however, these regional concerns were themselves not impulsive or spontaneous. They were driven by national attitudes and directives issued by central government authorities. Since the existence of a rhetoric promoting spy phobias challenges the validity of understanding these emotions as a spontaneous phenomenon, it demands a reassessment of how and when spy scares occurred.

Chasing spies

Warnings in the press about secret agents also coincided with reports that 'spies' were being captured across Britain. Without any ostensible 'evidence' of German espionage, alarming narratives could be easily ignored. But what transpired during the first few weeks of war seemingly corroborated the assumption that German spies had successfully infiltrated Britain. Although historians have invariably considered these spy scares as evidence of a 'spy fever' among the general population, a closer look at how these incidents featured in the press suggests that the British public were not helplessly overcome by fear and anxiety, at least not in August 1914. Rather, it was individuals and organizations responsible for home defence that most often displayed levels of suspicion and paranoia symptomatic of spy phobias. As such, reports of spy scares in the press should not necessarily be used as an indicator of popular fears but as evidence that society was encouraged to adopt feelings of distrust and nervousness through an officially sanctioned spy hunt.

Assumptions regarding the scale of espionage phobias have been overly reliant on a speech to the House of Commons in which the Home Secretary, Reginald McKenna, claimed that the Metropolitan Police had received 9,000 reports of espionage by mid-September.[37] Such an enormous figure clearly indicates that a very anxious public were susceptible to the alarm generated by the spy peril. Yet this claim has never been corroborated by police sources, or any source for that matter, which is probably because it was little more than a retort to Joynson-Hick's criticism of the Home Office.[38] It is more likely that McKenna's 9,000 spies came not from an anxious public ready to denounce every stranger in their midst but from concerned officials ready to discriminate against innocent civilians. At the end of August there was a meeting in the Home Office in which the Chief Commissioner of the Metropolitan Police, Sir Edward Henry, warned that innumerable German and Austrian reservists marked a significant threat. Despite a lack of evidence supporting such an allegation, he claimed that these individuals were likely to commit outrages designed to create panic and disruption. In response, the Home Office proposed that the police should begin to arrest those most dangerous. It is from this meeting that McKenna's claim of 9,000 spy sightings originated. The police commissioner claimed that 4,500 German and Austrian reservists resided in London, and that there were probably no less than 2,500 scattered elsewhere across Britain.[39] Following a more detailed enquiry into the number of enemy aliens in Britain, the Home Office found that 680 had been detained in Liverpool, 220 in Hull, 140 in Cardiff, 70 in Leeds, 800 in Birmingham, and 3,000 in Manchester.[40] When you add these figures with the 4,500 arrested in London, you reach 9,410 people who had been interned under this initiative. Thus, when McKenna claimed that 9,000 'spies' had been reported to the police, he really meant that 9,000 enemy subjects had been detained under the Aliens Restriction Order after official enquiries. The figure McKenna presented to Parliament regarding the number of apprehended 'spies', therefore, is hardly illustrative of specific or popular spy phobias.

So how can we measure the extent of popular alarm in August 1914? This study proposes that analysing spy scares appearing in print offers the best way to reconstruct early responses to the enemy within. Although this approach cannot possibly account for every single instance of suspicion, reported or otherwise, it does offer the most systematic method of quantifying spy fever. Since police records rarely survive intact from this period, local newspapers provide an unrivalled opportunity to study the occasions in which British society figuratively confronted the spy menace. Based on the survey of local newspapers used here (see Table 7.3 and Appendix 3) 297 articles contained reports of spy scares during August 1914. Within these, there were 144 incidents in which 193 individuals were accused of being spies. Given the frequency of duplicated reports this represents an extensive, if not an entirely comprehensive, selection of publicized spy scares, which significantly alters our understanding of spy fever.

While there were almost certainly more than 144 instances in which individuals were suspected of being spies during August, it seems unlikely that any such cases were reported to the police, or that these suspicions were acted upon in any significant way, given that the local press did not consider them newsworthy. Despite claims that the Metropolitan Police received thousands of reports of spying within the first six weeks of war, a more systematic analysis of spy scares in the British press suggests that the number of cases being reported in England, Scotland and Wales combined was most likely in the hundreds, not thousands. Regardless of whether this survey provides an accurate measurement of suspicion in August 1914, these 144 cases nevertheless draw attention to some of the key factors behind the emergence of spy fever in August 1914, which have hitherto gone unnoticed.

Figure 2.1 shows that the overwhelming majority of spy scares occurred in a single geographic region: the British coast. The Royal Navy's dockyards in particular provided suitable locations for spy fears to flourish, while areas along the east coast, given the vulnerability to an invading German force, appear to have been especially receptive to concerns about spies. Multiple newspapers were surveyed away from these coastal areas, but besides numerous cases in London, very few cases occurred inland, presumably because the German spy peril was intimately connected to the threat of invasion. Whereas inland locations witnessed fewer spy scares, they also exhibited less interest in cases of espionage; 74 per cent of spy scares occurred in and around the sea, while coastal newspapers printed 147 articles referring to spy scares compared with only 106 from the same number of inland publications. From this, it seems likely that spy phobias were not a universal experience and that certain areas or communities were more susceptible to this type of fear. Regardless of the accuracy of McKenna's claim to Parliament, therefore, such a quip does not account for the diversities of British society and should not be used as evidence of a widespread state of anxiety.

Owing to the concentration of spy scares along the coast, it could be argued that these were driven by self-fashioned fears due to an individual's proximity to a potential invading force. Moreover, since the majority of spy scares were also an immediate knee-jerk reaction to the war (Table 2.1 illustrates that almost three quarters of the incidents occurring in August took place during the initial fortnight of the war) it is understandable that spy phobias have been seen as spontaneous. Especially since a direct correlation between scaremongering in the press and popular fears would have meant that the number of accusations and indictments would have increased as the intensity and impact of this rhetoric grew. Instead, the number of spy scares declined only two weeks into the war, and the level of suspicion and fear on display in early August 1914 never reached such heights ever again.

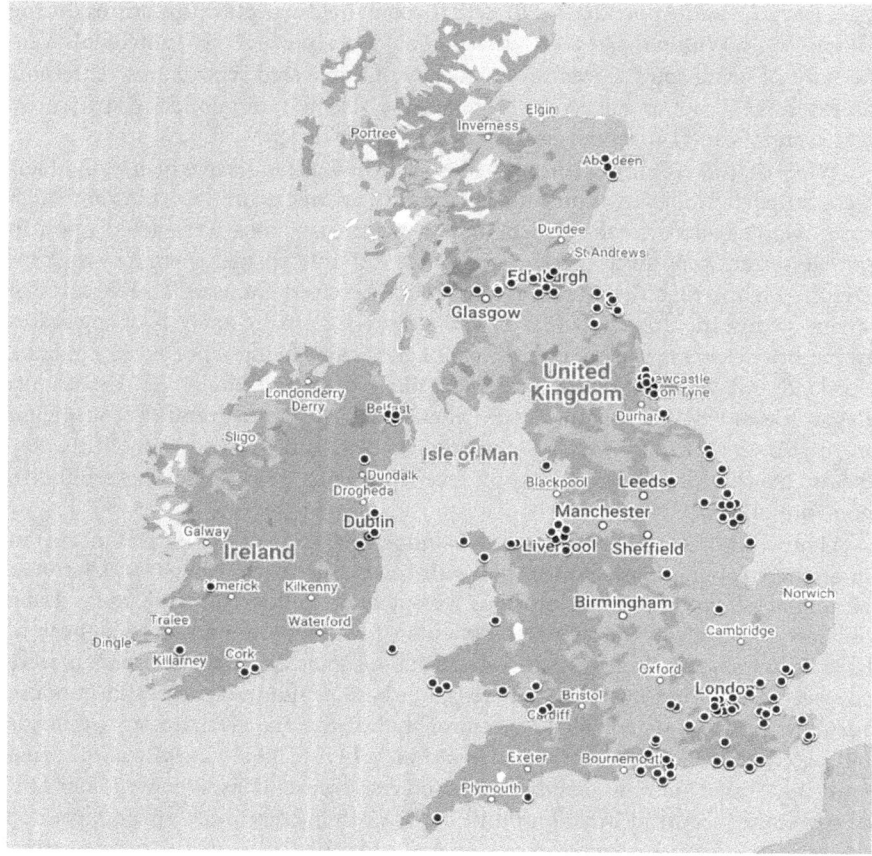

Figure 2.1 Locations of spy scares in August 1914 (see Appendix 2 for more detail).

However, as well as charting where and when spy scares were most common, it is also possible to identify the group most responsible for instigating them, and from this it becomes clear that spy scares were far from an organic social reaction. First, of the 193 suspects, 14 were apprehended because they were on a watchlist compiled by MO5(g) and had been designated for arrest prior to the outbreak of hostilities.[41] The arrests of these suspects took place after Kell had successfully intercepted their correspondence and were not the result of popular suspicions.[42] More significantly, though, of the 111 incidents in which the source of inquiry or alarm can be identified, just over 10 per cent came from concerned members of the public. During the first two weeks of the war, when spy scares were most prolific, that figure drops to less than 9 per cent. So even if all the spy scares in the survey with unknown origins were attributable to concerned civilians, they would amount to less than a third of the total number. Local authorities – territorial soldiers and police constables for the most part – were thus responsible

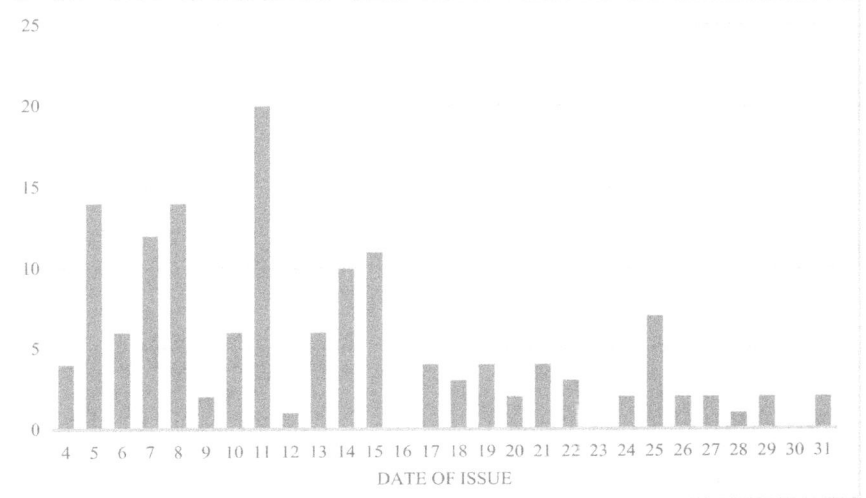

Figure 2.2 Number of spy scares appearing in print during August 1914.

for around two-thirds of all spy scares reported in the press. This means that the British public was not only inundated with warnings about the alleged threat, they were also confronted by a frantic search for a secret enemy in their midst. Despite repeated claims to contrary the phenomenon of spy hunting that became a notable feature of Britain's entry into the First World War seldom reflected an instinctive or popular reaction.

The most noticeable group displaying behaviours associated with espionage-related phobias were the Territorial soldiers scattered across Britain. Civilians in uniform, sometimes unacquainted with military practice and vulnerable to warnings about German invasions and secret agents, appeared to have conflated the home and fighting fronts during the initial mobilization period and, as a result, were responsible for the majority of recorded spy scares.[43] But how and why did these anxieties prevail?

In spite of the Haldane reforms that took place between 1906 and 1912, the effectiveness of the Territorials remained doubtful to many pre-war commentators. In the Commons Territorial MPs often criticized their own force, while the press and military analysts publicly ridiculed the state of Britain's part-time army. Weekly drills, an occasional weekend training and fifteen days' annual camp failed to convince people of the strength or value of such a force.[44] Whether they would be used for home defence, imperial security or in a European conflict remained unclear as Britain went to war.[45] As a result, their mobilization proved problematic and confusion abounded.[46] Even after being mobilized troops were kept in an abiding state of trepidation. Following an invasion warning issued by a nervous War Office staffer, troops were required to remain on appointed accommodation and were forced to sleep wearing their boots and puttees, to be

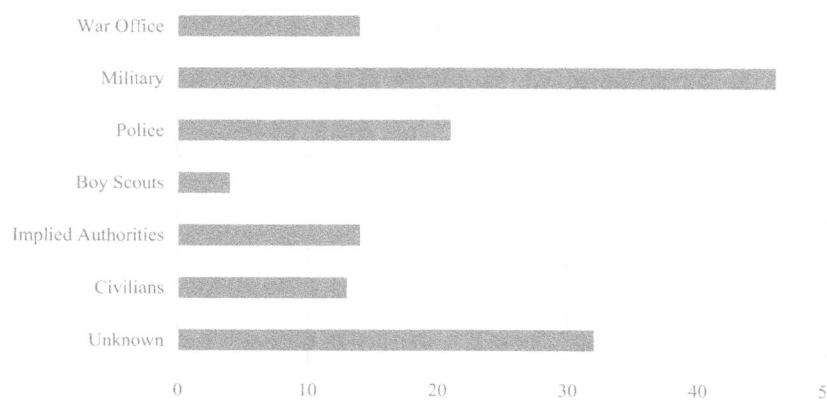

Figure 2.3 Instigators of spy scares featured in the press during August 1914.

ready at a moment's notice.[47] And yet despite this urgency, Territorial units seldom received the necessary equipment, which encumbered a battalion's readiness and morale. Territorial formations were also expecting to complete six months' further training following mobilization, but because they were dispersed across Britain protecting vulnerable points in 1914, effective coordination and company training became practically impossible.[48] Amid this confusion, the morale issues caused by inadequate equipment and the concerns owing to a dearth of training and preparation, panic could easily flourish.[49]

And it did. Nervous sentries frequently caused scenes of excitement and agitation. One local mayor labelled them the 'trigger happy Territorials' after he was fired upon by troops as he walked around his local reservoir.[50] In Edinburgh a group of Territorials thought that they had spotted a German submarine attempting to penetrate the boom defences at the Forth Bridge and so instructed the nearby forts to open fire. The suspected 'U-boat' turned out to be nothing more than a discarded whisky bottle.[51] Since they were responsible for defending against espionage and sabotage, their nervousness fixated on the spy peril. One man admiring the views near Dover found himself pounced upon by six soldiers all with fixed bayonets. He was detained and interrogated because they believed him to be a spy.[52] Another man strolling along the beach near Birkenhead found himself blindfolded and taken to a nearby fort for questioning simply for carrying binoculars along the seafront.[53] Private Smith of the Queen's (Royal West Surrey) Regiment witnessed one unfortunate incident on the Margate-Dover line in which a nervous sentry on night duty shot and killed a donkey after it had, unsurprisingly, ignored his three challenges. In defence of the donkey killer, his unit had been told to prepare for a German invasion and maintain 'special vigilance' in response.[54] Because of the need to uphold 'special vigilance', Territorial soldiers were eager to challenge and stop anybody (or anything) thought to be hiding something.[55] According to Edward Heron-Allen, the biggest danger he faced living in East Sussex was not from German spies, or even a raiding force, but 'being shot at sight by some nervous territorial'.[56]

Heron-Allen's fears were not unjustified. Upon discovering what was thought to be a German spy, Territorial soldiers at Dunfermline shot at a telegraph linesman working on the overhead cable at the local post office.[57] Motorcyclists were frequently shot at for ignoring challenges.[58] In Newcastle a man who had attracted the attention of a military patrol was shot and killed after attempting to flee.[59] Innocent bystanders were not the only casualties in this. Soldiers were themselves frequently injured in the midst of all the confusion and panic. When a detachment of troops defending the wireless station at Waltham noticed two men acting suspiciously, they raised the alarm and chased the suspects, but one soldier ended up getting bayoneted in the leg.[60] After Private Robinson thought he had discovered a spy while guarding an aircraft hangar in Surrey, he fired upon the suspect but, to his surprise, faced returning fire that hit him in the arm.[61] In a separate incident, two troops from the Scottish Rifles noticed lights coming from a nearby golf course and opened fire. They hit Private George Calder in the elbow, leading to his arm being amputated.[62] Two soldiers were even killed in the midst of this chaos. Both soldiers were inadvertently shot after alarms were raised 'that a spy was knocking about', and search parties were sent out to catch the offender. Louis Morrice was killed while on garrison duty at Bidston Hill near Birkenhead after enlisting less than a week earlier.[63] Some accounts suggest a rifle went off inadvertently, while others report that several shots were fired and Morrice was killed in the crossfire.[64] At the inquest of Private Walter Henry Smith's death, killed near Chatham waterworks, witnesses claimed he had died after sentries nervously pursued spies in their vicinity.[65]

A closer inspection of spy scares transpiring in August 1914 suggests that individuals were far more likely to imitate the frantic or excited emotions associated with spy phobias if their circumstances necessitated it. While that could involve one's proximity to a possible German landing place, spy phobias seem to have been far more pervasive among those responsible for defending against an anticipated German attack. Those at the forefront of home defence were thus most likely to embrace and perpetuate spy phobias, and so the frequency of spy scares in August 1914 does not necessarily reflect a widespread or spontaneous anxiety. The British public, therefore, were not only bombarded by warnings about the spy danger, they also witnessed enhanced security measures that reinforced and exacerbated those threat assessments. While warnings can be dismissed as abstract and immaterial, the very prominent spy hunts carried out by local authorities most likely provided a bigger indication that this threat was in fact imminent. While the social and emotional impacts of these activities are obviously impossible to measure, it would be misguided to assume that spy fever occurred spontaneously given how active the press and local authorities were in constructing the peril. This influence of these spy hunts was indeed palpable to some:

Sentries with fixed bayonets guard the great bridges, and no one ventures to penetrate the quays and the dockside. Stories which pass from mouth to mouth of shooting of sentries and captures of spies lurking about the dark places of the river, which may or may not be apocryphal, do not incite one to close investigation. One feels instinctively here that the spirit of war, terrible and death dealing, is all over.[66]

The question that remains, then, is, why did these authorities take such extreme measures against a non-existent threat?

Defending the realm

Notwithstanding certain indifferences in how provincial authorities responded to the enemy within, the only way that the spy peril could be assessed as credible and imminent by multiple authorities simultaneously was if there were some form of governmental interference. Indeed, prior to the outbreak of war, local officials had been frequently forewarned about the espionage threat and readied to neutralize the anticipated danger in the event of war. It was through this interchange that local threat assessments were shaped and concerns exacerbated. Of course panic was never the intended outcome,[67] but the vagueness in much of the directives circulated before and during resulted in an overzealous response because they allowed eagerness and paranoia to shape local responses. Examining the interactions between regional authorities and government departments highlights the state's role in cultivating local spy scares, which separates these fears and anxieties from a spontaneous spy fever among the general public.

The threat of an enemy destabilizing Britain from within became a frequent component of home defence planning in the decade leading up to the First World War. As mentioned previously the issue of invasion repeatedly resurfaced in CID debates, and espionage became a frequent component of that debate.[68] In April 1914 the Committee received the fourth inquiry in ten years looking at attacks against the British Isles from an overseas power. It reaffirmed that a potential invasion could involve either a full-scale landing designed to inflict a crippling blow at the heart of the empire or a less ambitious raid intended to distract and damage rather than subdue. The latter was considered the most plausible given the ability of a raiding party to conduct operations without first alerting the Royal Navy. It was also concluded that this form of attack was most likely following the despatch of the Expeditionary Force to the continent and before the mobilization of the Territorial Force had been completed.[69] Vulnerable points were thus most liable to attack from enemy agents immediately following any declaration of war. The need to rapidly secure a vast number of locations in the event of war meant that the activities witnessed in August 1914 were not entirely spontaneous. Since this task was considered vital to Britain's wartime security, the threat of German spies was officially ratified through an assortment of memoranda and directives emanating from the War Office in particular.

The War Office had begun to consider the implications of secret intelligence to British defence ever since the Prussians had routed French defenders in 1870. Based on his observations of the conflict Major (later Major General) Charles Booth Brackenbury strongly recommended enhanced preparations against foreign espionage:

> Surely this extraordinary development of speed in making war, demands some further preparation than used to be sufficient. Surely it demands that we should watch more carefully, and prepare ourselves more assiduously than has been the custom heretofore.[70]

Although Germany's rapid victory was indicative of their military efficacy, it also suggested that they were fully cognizant of their European foes. As such, the primary lesson to be taken from the Franco-Prussian War was that Germany maintained an extensive intelligence apparatus:

> This remarkable institution [the German Intelligence Office] was organized as a distinct permanent section of the General Staff in 1863, the year before the Danish War. All the information obtained by the other sections is handed over to it, systematically arranged and ready for use, so that it is, in peace, the one office which knows everything, and can answer all questions which Count Moltke may ask. It receives, besides, a considerable amount of secret intelligence even during peace. When we remember that service in the Army is universal in Prussian, and that a large proportion of the German merchants, clerks, and other employés [sic] working in other countries have been 'one year volunteers', we cannot but be struck by the immense faculty for gaining military information possessed by this highly organized [sic] and warlike nation.[71]

Charles's brother, General Sir Henry Brackenbury, later went on to head the Intelligence Branch (IB) at the War Office and, unlike many of his predecessors, was a firm believer in the merits of intelligence work because of his first-hand observations of the German General Staff in 1870.[72] Owing to the growing value placed upon of intelligence, Brackenbury's successors continued to stress the importance of local vigilance to deny any future adversaries the means with which to collect valuable information on Britain's defences.[73]

As head of MO5, otherwise known as the 'Special Section' within the Directorate of Military Operations (responsible for secret service work), Lieutenant Colonel James Edmonds shared many of Brackenbury's trepidations about Germany's covert plots.[74] According to Edmonds, the war of 1870 stood as evidence of France's unpreparedness and insufficient intelligence resources. With this in mind, he lectured regimental officers about the significance of widespread vigilance to contain the internal threats posed by Germany: 'Far greater vigilance, far closer watching of the enemy and far greater secrecy will be required than against foes we have been accustomed to meet.'[75] He impressed upon them the importance of personal vigilance to counter-espionage, and that 'even in peace you should look out for and report any foreigner who habitually haunts the neighbourhood of barracks, camps and fortifications'.[76] Although the full extent of his influence cannot be ascertained, his concerns regarding Germany's clandestine activities were clearly shared beyond MO5. It is entirely feasible that some of his concerns resonated with officers who would later go on to lead Territorial units. In any case, his teachings were certainly enduring. In 1918, upon joining the Intelligence Corps, George Gedye learnt about the 'Value of Intelligence' through a lecture that still focused on the role of secret service during the Franco-Prussian War.[77]

Since the War Office strongly considered espionage and attacks from ill-disposed persons as realistic threats facing Britain, its preparations for future war stressed the need for extreme vigilance at home.[78] In October 1912 the War Office circulated a memorandum outlining the methods of secret agents. It stated that the primary objectives of foreign spies would be to acquire details concerning the construction of warships, forts, aircraft, telegraphy apparatus and armaments; mobilization plans and defence schemes; and the distribution of troops and naval vessels.[79] This is hardly a surprising list of targets, and one would expect that the German General Staff and Admiralstab would be most pleased to acquire this sort of information in time of war. However, echoing the crude stereotypes found in cheap spy fiction, it reckoned that agents were particularly numerous in ports or military garrisons masquerading as hairdressers, waiters, publicans or governesses.[80] The War Book of 1914 further stressed the need to defend vulnerable points such as magazines, factories, wireless stations, the railways and lines of communications.[81] Any civilian thought to be acting suspiciously was to be arrested immediately, and sentries were directed to shoot suspected agitators if necessary.[82] It is perhaps not surprising, then, that the majority of spy scares occurred in and around these particular locations since the possibility of surprise attack and the need for Territorials to remain cautious had been repeatedly emphasized.[83]

In July 1909, a standing joint Naval and Military Committee was established to ensure the safety of vulnerable points across the British Isles.[84] Whereas initially it conceived of two types of threat to be considered by the committee: 'attacks by an enemy's organised armed forces' and 'attacks by ill-disposed persons',[85] by 1910, it was deemed most likely that attempts to commit outrages would be carried out by individuals rather than by raiding forces.[86] Against these threats the committee recommended that the naval authorities should share responsibility with the police for the protection of dockyards, while the military authorities and the police would defend vulnerable points inland. Although general terms were agreed the committee considered it unnecessary to outline specifics and advised that local police commissioners be given absolute authority.[87] Thus, while defence planners identified spies and saboteurs as a credible threat to British security, much of the responsibility for dealing with this enemy was given to untrained and ill-equipped local officials.

Veron Kell, head of British counter-intelligence, likewise directed that local police forces take active measures against this enemy within. Because Kell relied on county constabularies to monitor and arrest potential suspects, he spent much of his time visiting chief constables across Britain to ensure their cooperation.[88] Kell was more or less successful in this regard. In June of 1910, Kell visited the north-east of Scotland hoping to enlist the support of the chief constables there. Whereas Major Arthur Ferguson, His Majesty's Inspector of Constabulary in Scotland, seemed 'very anxious to assist in everyway', Major Duncan F. Gordon in Aberdeenshire 'was not enthusiastic, and said there was no cases of suspicious Germans anywhere about'.[89] In any case, Kell persisted and organized a conference among chief constables to strengthen local security measures in coastal areas.[90] The resulting memorandum set out that small bands of men armed with explosives would likely attempt to disrupt mobilization plans and early military operations. As a result, it was instructed that following the commencement of hostilities local efforts to curtail espionage should be doubled and a careful watch be kept on all undesirable aliens, friendly or otherwise.[91] Chief constables were also directed to begin enlisting men for what was to become the 'observer scheme', or the inauguration of a civil intelligence service following the outbreak of war.[92] In October 1912 a further memorandum on counter-espionage stressed that the danger of foreign communities 'cannot be too strongly insisted upon' and the need to identify whether any aliens were in a position to contribute to foreign 'Secret Service'. This included information that pointed to 'acts of espionage being committed, or about to be committed, or to preparations being made for the destruction of vital points and communications, in readiness for the time when war may break out'.[93] In sum, police forces were left in little doubt about the significance of enemy agents in any future conflict and were unequivocally instructed to thwart covert operatives.

With the declaration of the Precautionary Period on Wednesday 29 July, the government rapidly sought to mobilize the nation against a sudden 'bolt from the blue'. Local authorities were immediately given further warnings about the possibility that foreign agents could cripple the country's readiness for war.[94] To ensure the cooperation of county constabularies, the Home Office reissued a memorandum in July outlining the duties of the police in the event of war. Chief constables were implored to adopt desperate measures to strengthen their force, and if sufficient numbers were not found in the reserve, it was recommended that anyone accustomed to discipline and familiar with police work be employed to guard vulnerable points.[95] The guidance issued by the Home Office undoubtedly prompted a degree of urgency that could easily be confused with severity by its recipients. Chief constables were made aware of the importance of protecting locations liable to attack because it was anticipated that covert enemies intended to delay Britain's immediate military capabilities by sabotaging vital strategic points.[96] Local initiative here became imperative; it was recommended that 'the Chief Constable will himself take any special precautions which he may have reason to believe are immediately necessary'.[97] The Official Secrets Act (1911) had also previously stipulated that the suspicion of a chief constable was enough to secure a warrant against potential spies without the need for any incriminating evidence whatsoever.[98] Home Office circulars reiterated that particular attention was to be given to any location that may be of naval or military importance, and as war was declared, existing measures were to be strengthened as far as possible.[99] Rather than adopting a coherent national strategy against covert threats, relatively inexperienced local police officers (at least in relation to secret warfare) were left to coordinate an almost military response to an unknown and potentially hostile force.[100]

Notwithstanding the novelty of this task to police forces, the Home Office gave neither clear direction as to what constituted suspicious circumstances nor how constables should react when confronted with the threat.[101] Because the Home Secretary lacked jurisdiction over provincial forces, circulars regarding police duties were merely recommendations rather than direct commands,[102] and so precise details were not forthcoming.[103] This proved problematic because without precise instruction, the very interpretation of suspicion is inherently subjectively. Consequently, the police faced a danger that appeared imminent and perilous without the necessary experience or detailed instruction on how to locate or respond to this enemy within.[104] More significantly, though, chief constables never received a credible threat assessment from the Home Office, which left them oblivious to the scale of the threat and vulnerable to exaggerations found in the press.[105] Aside from the Home Office's attempt to publicly suppress panic, the vagueness of much of their recommendations to county constabularies stimulated unnecessary concern, which shaped local measures and generated wider anxieties among the general public.

This chapter has tried to argue that spy scares were a top-down rather than bottom-up phenomenon. Nowhere is this more evident than in how spy scares were sometimes justified in retrospect. During the inquiry into James Carroll's death, for example, the War Office was clear in their support for the Territorials' response. The defence rested on recently ratified wartime legislation.[106] While there was some initial doubt as to whether Carroll should have been arrested because the incident occurred in broad daylight, a notice issued by Lord Lucan, in command of the Territorial Brigade in question, was used to justify the shooting as it 'seems to amount to instructions'.[107] The notice, dated 6 August 1914, read:

1. All unauthorised persons are forbidden to trespass on or loiter in the neighbourhood of Railways, Railway Bridges, or Tunnel Shafts.
2. Any person found disobeying these orders will be arrested and handed over to the civil police.
3. Any persons refusing to halt when repeatedly ordered to do so by a Sentry or Patrol, or resisting Sentries or Patrols in the execution of their duty may be fired on.[108]

To substantiate their case further, the War Office suggested:

> There is no question of shooting or killing a civilian on the high road; any person of normal intelligence must know that in time of war sentries are armed with ball ammunition and that challenges must be obeyed.

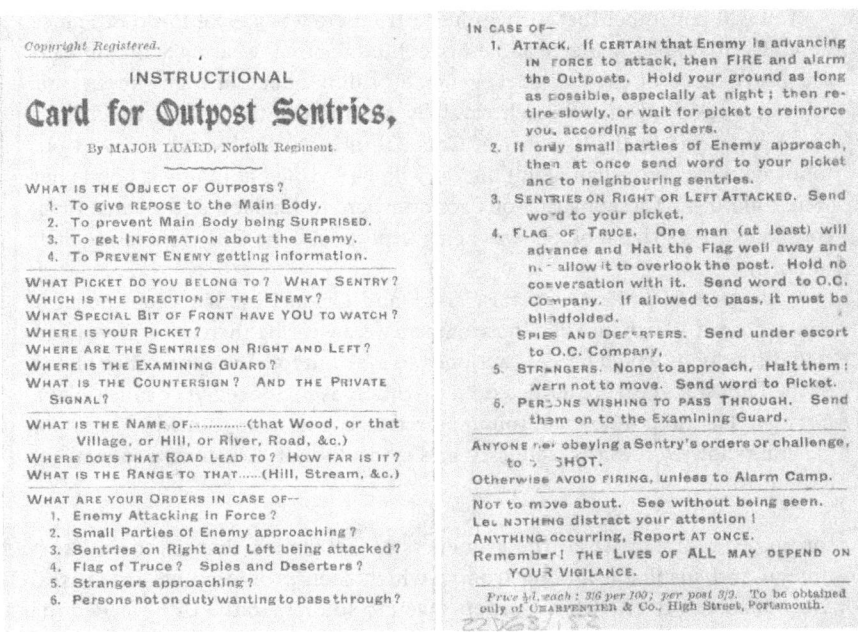

Figure 2.4 Card for outpost sentries.
Pocket-sized card explaining the duties of outpost sentries, which clearly promotes a heightened awareness and vigilant response to potential German spies among Territorial soldiers. Leicestershire Record Office, Regimental Records, 22D63/152.

Lord Lucan's notice provided sufficient validation for the behaviour that resulted in Carroll's death.[109] Indeed, Territorial officers routinely gave strict instructions that any persons ignoring a challenge should be shot.[110] The War Office also suggested that previous incidents had meant that the sentries had 'reasonable grounds for supposing that attacks might be made'.[111] The jury at the inquest deemed the soldier innocent of any wrongdoing and agreed with the War Office that the defence of the British Isles exempted violence against civilians.[112]

Following an incident in which a Canadian General Officer was suspected of espionage in Kent, Captain McInnes, an Intelligence Officer in the CEF, was tasked with investigating how such a mishap was allowed to happen. McInnes's conclusion epitomizes the link between official warnings and overzealous responses:

It has been rather a difficult matter to discover the source of the original information handed in regarding this incident as we found after starting investigations that General Carson's motor ride in this particular instance took place on our about [13 July 1915] nine months ago. However I think that we have arrived at the root of the matter or as near as possible considering the elapsed time.

You will remember that early in July 1915 there was a great to-do in France about German spies being up and down behind our lines wearing Staff uniforms especially those of the Colonies, generally riding about in high power cars. Warning was sent out to watch carefully all strange Staff Officers, especially those appearing in the uniform of Colonial units. Special word was sent out to locate three Australian Staff Officers who had visited at different points but were unknown. These instructions got over here to England at the same time, consequently a sharp look out was being kept for strange Officers wearing Staff uniform.

A dispatch rider saw General Carson and Colonel McBain stop their car and get out at Wrotham Hill. These officers were wearing the very uniform and staff distinctions which he was cautioned to look out for. The appearance of one of the Officers especially attracted his attention as he looked very much like a German. He was a little man, round fat red face, goatee or chin whisker, and a general tendency towards rotundity, and evidently not accustomed to wearing a uniform.[113]

According to McInnes it was the vagueness of instruction that led to widespread confusion and suspicion among troops, which then prompted an ardent search for German spies. Even in 1915, orders given to soldiers in the BEF warned that

any stranger, be he officer, soldier, or civilian, who makes enquiries as to the position, distribution, movement, relief, or the organization of the troops, or concerning the site and armament of batteries, must be regarded as a suspicious character, and prompt action taken ... Any officer or man who observes anything in the nature of signalling must consider it his duty to investigate the matter personally on the spot.

The same orders stated that 'anyone who permits a suspected person to escape is guilty of Neglect of Duty ... A mistake made through excess of zeal in arresting suspects can do little harm and is quite excusable; an opportunity missed through timidity in taking action is unpardonable, and may endanger the security of the Force'.[114] According to this directive, then, it was perfectly acceptable for soldiers to behave in an inordinate or intemperate way, and they may have even put themselves at risk for failing to do so.

Herein lies the link between national security and spy phobias. Individuals charged with defending areas of military significance initiated the majority of spy scares after being told that they were likely to face covert agents intent on disruption and destruction. Concerns about German spies had been cultivated during a decade of inquiries and policies that had considered and identified the threats of espionage and sabotage, which were disseminated widely upon the outbreak of war. Whether or not these official fears had any broader impact on the British public is not yet apparent, but McInnes's observation highlights the problem of assuming that spy phobias were spontaneous. Owing to the numerous attempts to encourage extreme vigilance, either deliberately or inadvertently, it is impossible to say that these efforts had *no discernible impact* and that individuals fashioned intense fears of German spies completely independently from the warnings and activities that characterized Britain's entry into the First World War.

***

Within the pages of the national and local press, customs and norms regarding appropriate responses to the outbreak of war and the enemy within were clearly on display. This rhetoric explicitly prioritized suspicion as essential to national security. Just as similar conversations about strategy and defence had done previously, this emotive narrative sought to mobilize society against a particular threat; in this instance, that threat was very clearly focused on aliens and traitors intent on weakening Britain from within. While these narratives conveyed linguistic resources and established behavioural norms that could be used to interpret feelings generated by the outbreak of war, it also stressed that these reactions were essential to the continued safety of the realm. Given that attempts to establish espionage and sabotage as imminent dangers relied upon invasion anxieties to make the spy peril a plausible threat, there was nothing particularly new in this type of apprehension. Spy phobias were thus facilitated by the manipulation of pre-existing emotional standards, rather than a spontaneous outbreak of fear and anxiety.

Analysing outbursts of spy phobia in August 1914 reveals that local officials were most often responsible for expressing these emotions in public. As a result, spy scares were more frequent in areas where there were increased security measures, which demonstrates the impact of official actions on local perspectives. Rather than evidence of widespread social anxieties, spy scares were more reflective of the nervousness felt by local authorities during August 1914. And this nervousness was not entirely spontaneous either, as those responsible for home defence explicitly directed concerns against the spy threat and sanctioned harsh and even violent preventative measures. Since the majority of spy scares occurred almost immediately following the declaration of war, the reported alarms that followed should be seen as further coercive measures, rather than evidence of spy phobias among the general population. These spy scares added a degree of legitimacy to the rhetoric promoting the espionage peril and strengthened claims for increased vigilance and suspicion. In doing so, local officials embodied the proper emotional and behavioural response to the enemy within and this provided an example for the British public to replicate.

A close analysis of spy phobias evident in August 1914 also draws attention to some of the more nuanced characteristics of these emotions. The disparity evident across different locations implies that there was a degree of agency in an individual's willingness to accept, or at least in their readiness to perpetuate, fear or anxiety. Although spy phobias were undoubtedly prominent reactions in August 1914, the fact that they most notably appeared only in certain contexts suggests that they were not the dominant reaction in how society went to war. The fact that police constables and Territorial soldiers initiated the majority of recorded spy scares suggests that spy phobias were either not widely felt or, if they were, they were not particularly severe or impactful emotional experiences, given the difficulty in finding popular suspicion in the historical record. The following chapters are thus dedicated to examining how individuals did experienced spy fever.

Part II

INDIVIDUAL FEARS, 1914–15

Because the eighteenth and nineteenth centuries witnessed various attempts to diagnose and treat mental illness, the way in which contemporaries understood the relationship between mind and body was constantly in flux. Doctors were divided as to whether these diseases originated from physical or psychological disorders, and so there was disagreement and uncertainty about what these illnesses were and how they should be treated. As a result, they were typically considered as 'functional disorders' and regarded as disturbances or changes in bodily functions not attributable to any discernible disease. This classification helped bridge the gap between mind and body and enabled doctors to offer both psychological and biological treatment without fully endorsing either as a cause.[1]

Before the First World War, mental illness was often styled as hysteria or neurasthenia. Although the former has been applied to numerous medical complaints throughout its history – epilepsy, multiple sclerosis, syphilis, to name a few – by the mid-1800s, it was commonly believed to be a disorder of the nervous system. The French clinical neurologist Jean-Martin Charcot, widely regarded as the father of neurology, considered hysteria as a dysfunction of the central nervous system, which most often took the form of a physical or emotional shock. According to this interpretation, intense feelings of 'grief ... terror, anger, distrust, and other hateful passions' were both responsible for and symptomatic of hysteria. Unlike earlier understandings, which had often attributed hysterical conditions to irregularities within the female sex organs, Charcot insisted that both women and men were susceptible to hysteria, although he conceded that the former were more likely to experience its most severe effects.[2] Whereas neurasthenic patients suffered from nervous exhaustion (i.e. somatic defects) that prohibited reasoned judgements, hysterics suffered from emotionality and suggestibility ('psychic' symptoms) that hindered coherent thought. Although doctors recognized clear similarities between neurasthenics and hysterics, the loss of will was far more prominent in the latter and hysterical patients were thought of as utterly devoid of logic and self-control.[3]

At the end of the nineteenth century, although neurasthenia (a disease of the body) and hysteria (a disease of the psyche) were thought of as separate conditions, they were both regarded as 'functional diseases' caused by a predisposing condition of 'nervous weakness'.[4] By associating psychological conditions with a physical disturbance of the nervous system, patients with emotional ailments were reassured that their pain and suffering were as real as any other illness and would not be dismissed as fraudulent ailments or consigned to the madhouse.[5] Although mania (heightened emotional state) and melancholia (lessened emotional state) were typically associated with insanity or lunacy by contemporaries, and were thus separate from hysteria, they too became thought of as symptoms of cognitive and emotional disarray. Because this period witnessed an increasing awareness of mental illness, as well as a rising number of diagnoses, it became almost impossible to be both 'weak willed' and 'normal' at the same time.[6] Consequently, the inclination to view spy phobias as a form of mania or fever coincided with how contemporaries were beginning to comprehend seemingly unexplainable afflictions.[7] Given that society was witnessing an increasing attempt to define and diagnose mental instability, it is perhaps unsurprising that many envisaged the emotionality associated with the spy peril in this particular way.

In keeping with Basil Thomson's assessment of spy fever, historians have routinely appropriated medical terminology to describe the feelings and experiences generated by the espionage peril. David French contends that the British public became 'hysterical' about the spy danger, while Catriona Pennell claims 'fever' is an appropriate term 'because it not only describes the hysteria or delirium similar to that felt by an intensification of temperature, but it also suggests a malady within the body'.[8] For Pennell, contemporaries experienced spy fever very literally because secret agents had metaphorically enfeebled Britain's immunity from foreign attack much like infection weakens the body. Yet despite the common use of 'spy fever' and 'spy mania', the origins of these terms are found in popular discourse and not medical evaluation.[9] Without psychological assessments of individuals afflicted with such fears the applicability of terms such as 'mania' or 'fever' to the experience of espionage phobias remains speculative. To establish whether these concepts were anything more than descriptions of the collective psyche, given their prominence in popular discourse rather than objective assessments of individuals' emotional dispositions, needs further analysis. By uncritically adopting terms like mania and fever, historians have transposed ideas regarding mental illness and insanity on to people who developed fears of espionage and sabotage in accordance with a broader emotional regime linked to national security.

There is, however, tangible evidence that a relatively small group of people experienced severe fears of espionage and that these feelings stimulated delusions of nefarious German spies. One woman, for example, was recorded by medical professionals as being 'unstable and emotional' because of German spies. She firmly believed that these nefarious agents were occupying the house next door and were plotting to kill her. As a result, she suffered from insomnia and later began to hear the voices of German spies in her head 'saying all sorts of nasty words which put wicked thoughts in her brain'. Notwithstanding the signs of psychological disorder present in this account, this case of spy mania did not correspond with how people generally experienced the peril. This particular individual was diagnosed with melancholia in addition to a 'mania with marked delusions and suspicions' while at Menston Asylum in 1915.[10] Despite the inference that this person was suffering from a spy mania, the fact that she was placed in an institution as a result suggests that her mental state, and the emotions that accompanied this illness, was extraordinary.

Although they might not reflect popular fears, similar cases are interesting for what they reveal about the nature and severity of delusions and suspicions that were considered symptomatic of a mania. Another patient admitted to Menston Asylum in January 1917 thought that spies had been following her and had tried to assassinate her on three separate occasions. What is more striking was that she believed they had actually succeeded, but that she had miraculously come back to life after each attack.[11] Delusions of persecution, a common theme among asylum patients, were easily linked to the spy threat. According to his wife, one newly admitted patient had been refusing to leave the house because he believed that the streets were full of spies waiting to kill him. Following initial observations doctors found that he did not sleep or eat because of his delusions, and that he regularly suffered from panic attacks and crying fits.[12] Another patient feared that a male spy had abducted the lady next door and had begun impersonating her. This subterfuge was designed to turn local residents against the patient.[13]

For others, the trauma created by the war significantly impacted their mental state and the contemporary prevalence of German spying in popular culture clearly shaped their responses to distressing experiences. After nearly being killed during the bombardment of Scarborough in December 1914, one woman became 'full of delusions that she is surround by German spies who cycle after her wherever she goes'. As well as being constantly on the lookout for Germans, she struggled with hallucinations in which she heard the sound of guns and abusive voices in her head. For what might be described today as post-traumatic stress disorder, she was diagnosed with delusional insanity and chronic mania.[14] Based on recorded descriptions of psychological illness that incorporated fears of German covert activity, any attempt to diagnose 'spy mania' in this sense would most likely require evidence of severe and sustained delusions, including vivid hallucinations, and most likely a considerable mood disorder.

Such a conclusion is supported by the findings of contemporary psychologists. At the beginning of the nineteenth century, mania was described as a disorder of judgement and reasoning commensurate with a form of madness or insanity. In Alexander Morison's *Outlines of Mental Diseases* published in 1826, he described mania as:

> marked by exuberance of ideas, expressed with rapidity, and in the utmost confusion and incoherence. The delirium extends to objects of every description – the attention is continually wandering – the efforts of volition are vague and unsteady – the affections and perverted … the irritability is great – the restlessness incessant, there being little or no sleep.[15]

Over the course of the century mania was increasingly understood as a mood disorder, with manic delusions arising from euphoria. One of the most influential psychiatric texts of the nineteenth century wrote that mania was primarily a disorder of the emotions, particularly marked by greatly exaggerated or morbidly exalted feelings, and that these intensified emotions gave rise to aberrations of intellectual capacity, restless activity and insanity.[16] Given that people experiencing spy phobias have often been portrayed as agitated, suspicious and excitable towards a very tenuous threat in a way that often defied logic or reason, it is perhaps understandable that such behaviour was associated with this type of psychological disorder.[17] Without a clinical assessment of individual cases, though, it is impossible to say with any certainty whether individuals' spy phobias outside of the asylum constituted any form of mania. However, since conceptions of mania typically referred to a protracted psychological state, personal correspondence in which spy phobias can be observed can potentially reveal the duration of such feelings, which can provide an indication of their severity.

The following two chapters uncover the 'emotional styles' through which spy phobias were expressed. In doing so, they uncover contrasting ways in which the enemy within was experienced by people supposedly encountering the threat. Chapter 3 looks at how fears were articulated to identify patterns of behaviour and distinguish them from a genuine mania. In doing so it finds that individuals expressed fear towards objects of danger initially identified by novelists, journalists, politicians and military commentators. As such, their fears were perfectly rational based on the information in the public domain. Because spy phobias were a culturally determined response to a particular scenario, individuals' fears typically reflected the situation in which they were experienced, rather than an internal hysterical state. As a result, they were typically short-lived and ineffectual, at least according to how individuals described them, and therefore distinct from a sustained psychological condition. Moreover, not only were spy phobias unlike the disorders present in the asylum, they were also far less damaging and influential than the terror created by either the threat or reality of aerial bombardment, which questions the potency and impact of spy phobias.

Chapter 4 then re-examines how popular culture shaped emotional experiences of the spy peril. Because spy phobias have typically been described as a particularly acute fear, historians have assumed that the resulting experiences primarily consisted of terror and panic, thereby associating spy phobias with psychological disturbance. Yet fear can excite and titillate, just as much as it can terrify and incapacitate. In examining the cultural portrayal of espionage, which is itself important for revealing features of emotional styles,[18] the prospect of confronting enemy agents and overcoming them with little more than one's ingenuity and courageousness was regularly portrayed as a noble and rousing endeavour. This is very different from the scaremongering of invasion-espionage literature and implies that an alternative emotional style existed with which people could interpret the danger and form different experiences of it. Consequently, the cultural depiction of spy catching as a heroic and thrilling enterprise made it possible to feel excitement rather than terror when supposedly facing the danger, and this is evident in how people described encounters with the formidable German spy. The prominence of excitement found in how people described their encounters with the 'spy' further suggests that the experience of spy fever was completely unlike the suffering caused by psychological illness.

Although attributing spy phobias to delusional insanity arose because these feelings ostensibly corresponded with how society understood psychological illness, this interpretation fails to account for how so many people, most of whom were presumably not mentally unstable, became transfixed by the spy peril. In reality espionage phobias reflected the specific historical context in which wartime fears were experienced. By uncovering this context, it is clear that individual cases of spy fever were neither feverish nor manic. Identifying contrasting emotional styles clearly highlights the limitations of characterizing such fears as a form of lunacy. The following two chapters will show that individual fears could be experienced in different ways and that even when terror became apparent, it was typically short-lived and ineffectual. When describing individuals' feelings and emotional states, therefore, historians should avoid appropriating the medical connotations of terms like mania and fever, unless there is clear evidence that they were suffering from an acute paranoia or sustained insanity.[19] Whether or not these experiences amounted to a collective mania will be considered in Part III.

Chapter 3

WARTIME SPY PHOBIAS

Fears that duplicitous foreign agents were secretly plotting against Britain from within were not exclusive to the First World War.[1] During the French Revolutionary and Napoleonic Wars, the anticipation of invasion coupled with the threat of domestic radicalism created the illusion of an enemy within. Foreshadowing the draconian measures adopted in 1914, the wars against Revolutionary France saw a range of stringent security measures justified by reports that the enemy, in conjunction with internal revolutionaries, was attempting to infiltrate and destabilize Britain with its spies and saboteurs.[2] Just as it did against Imperial Germany a century later, victory against France's Levée en masse also required national mobilization. In Britain, which maintained a radically anti-democratic stance, patriotism built on notions of loyalty and volunteerism became essential to maintain popular support.[3] Over 300,000 people joined the volunteers to defend against invasion and subversion.[4] Like the depiction of espionage in 1914 reports of French spies had little semblance with reality. One rumour claimed that Napoleon himself was disguised as a fisherman exploring British ports, while another had him canvassing the Welsh mountains.[5] Nervousness generated by the prospect of invasion was so great that it generated a story about a monkey being executed as a French spy. Legend has it that the primate was found wearing a French military uniform and was lynched by an angry mob in Hartlepool for acting as a secret agent on behalf of the republic.[6]

Similar concerns prevailed in 1940. After the fall of France, when Britain felt particularly isolated and alone, virulent conspiracy theories about a Nazi fifth column gripped British society. It was widely believed that a pro-German faction within France had facilitated the Nazi's success, just as it had done in Denmark and Norway previously. The *Daily Mail* and *Express* inflamed animosity towards those considered undesirable or outsiders, much like they had done in 1914. Aliens, Communists, Fascists, and Jehovah's Witnesses all found themselves frequently associated with a German fifth column and were used as scapegoats for Nazi triumphs throughout much of Europe. Bowing to popular clamour, the Home Office began interning enemy aliens as well as political dissidents. Although there was little truth in the fifth column rhetoric, these rumours have rarely been viewed as widespread naivety or collective madness but instead viewed by historians as an attempt to unite the British public under the banner of national security.[7]

Notwithstanding the existence of comparable fears in other wars, the paranoia witnessed during the First World War has been routinely likened to insanity. Yet despite the prevalence of 'fever' and 'mania' in describing popular reactions to the enemy within, the overt psychological and physiological connotations that accompany these concepts are problematic. The literal application of these terms has distorted our understanding about popular reactions to the enemy within. The following chapter is thus concerned with how individual experiences and feelings were articulated. It is not an attempt to psychoanalyse the individuals involved and so cannot positively determine the specific feelings encountered by the individuals mentioned, let alone ascertain whether or not the subjects were suffering from any psychological condition, such as feverish deliriums or manic outbursts. However, in identifying the style in which spy phobias were expressed and performed, based on how experiences or observations were recorded, this chapter shows a clear disparity in how these feelings were conveyed in private correspondence compared with the recorded delusions witnessed in asylum patients. Exploring how individuals documented their concerns and how they observed fear in others suggests that spy phobias were often transient and limited to certain contexts and not symptomatic of an uncontrollable contagion.

The first section of this chapter analyses correspondence that discloses individuals' encounters with potential spies to show that the resulting emotions were not particularly invasive or enduring, which questions the existence of a mania. It posits that the term 'spy fever' simply reflected the common practice of diagnosing emotionality and suggestibility, or in other words, what appeared to some as irrational behaviour, as a form of mental illness. Based on written responses to the spy peril it seems somewhat doubtful that these experiences amounted to an actual malady. The second section then continues the analysis of spy scares in the press to highlight their decline after the immediate security concerns of August 1914 had subsided. Although this reflects a general perception of the enemy within, rather than individuals' specific feelings, the declining frequency with which outbursts of fear appeared in this narrative is also perhaps indicative of how often these feelings occurred. These findings suggest that the emergence of spy fever was closely associated with the particular security issues of August 1914 and did not arise from a widespread inability to distinguish fact from fiction. The final section then examines the fears caused by Zeppelins and aerial bombardment to demonstrate the relatively limited impact that spy phobias seemingly had on individuals in comparison – at least as far as can be ascertained from the historical record. Thus, although authors like Basil Thomson found 'spy fever' a useful device to sensationalize wartime emotions and behaviours, the medical connotations of 'fever' and 'mania' have greatly distorted our understanding of popular reactions.

Deliriums that defied treatment?

Assessing emotions occurring in the past comes with an array of difficulties, not least because the written formats in which feelings are preserved are produced retrospectively, which means that the experience is only made available to the historian after some sort of appraisal. With the passage of time the interpretation of emotion can change as memory becomes distorted by hindsight. Following post-war revelations that the threat of German espionage was overstated and unjustified, it is unsurprising that many individuals sought to dissociate themselves from the collective paranoia by exaggerating the folly of such fears. Nevertheless, one of the most striking features of espionage phobias is how quickly they appear to have dissipated.[8] Although Helen Fane witnessed a 'spy' being apprehended in Leadenham for creating maps thought to be useful in the hands of an enemy, any fears that she may have developed as a result seem rather momentary and ineffectual. While the incident was deemed worthy enough for her to write about, there is no suggestion that this episode stimulated an extreme or enduring emotional reaction. She even wrote, somewhat facetiously, that 'he certainly went out very early each morning', implying that in her opinion the evidence against him was rather unconvincing which negated any enduring sense of fear. The suspected 'spy' was also released the very next day.[9]

Rather than being an uncontrollable or overwhelming outburst of suspicion, spy phobias often produced an internal struggle between individual agency and collective security. Owing to prominent warnings about the peril, people undoubtedly felt obliged to fear spies in order to maintain the continued safety of the nation, but these emotions appear to have been easily managed. In October 1914, for example, Beatrice Trefusis was undecided as to whether she had actually discovered a spy:

> We were rather suspicious about a man who sang some amusing patter songs in broken English and Yiddish over at Cowshott Camp the other night. German spies have already been caught in the new army. So I wrote a note to the chaplain, and stated our fears – [which were] probably quite unfounded.[10]

Popular suspicions were thus firmly rooted in the many rumours and stories claiming to have uncovered foreign plots. In this instance, reports that German spies had infiltrated the British army compelled Trefusis to comply with demands for vigilance, but her doubts as to the validity of her concerns suggest that her feelings were driven more by social convention and a desire to support the war effort, rather than an uncontrollable emotional state. Similarly, while Florence Schuster accepted the plausibility of a widespread system of German espionage and the necessity of countermeasures, she also disparaged that 'people in Manchester have lost their heads'. Schuster thought it outrageous that 'a tremendous amount of Germans are confined in various depots ... some of who have been a long time in England, and who are doing English work'. But her disdain towards the prevailing anti-alien discord was matched by her conviction to support the national cause. Immediately after criticizing such constraints she concluded that 'it seems ridiculous that some people ... should be so restricted, but it's got to be done'.[11] The contradiction within Schuster's account suggests that fears of German espionage could be 'performed' to resemble the prevailing custom of the time.

Through this conformity, individuals were afforded a greater reassurance that the nation remained secure and that they were a part of that effort.

This has important implications for how we understand spy fever. Although historians have occasionally distinguished between expressed feelings and 'real emotions', Barbara Rosenwein argues that 'performed emotions' are also felt. While people can certainly feign emotions, emotional experience is conditioned by an acceptance or internalization of emotional norms that dictate feeling.[12] Being compelled to fear spies, therefore, does not necessarily invalidate the reality of the feeling because individuals can only understand their true feelings through evaluation, which requires a set of cultural norms and shared values. But it does contradict the assumption that people were nominally in a perpetual state of terror, akin to a mania, especially outside of the circumstances in which fear became an appropriate response. Consequently, historians should not view spy phobias as an enduring or particularly poignant sensation but one that was mostly confined to specific situations. Frequent warnings depicted various scenarios, mostly derived from fictional exploits, as distinctively suspicious: flashing lights and strange noises near the coast, individuals loitering close to military instalments, artists sketching local scenery and motorists travelling the countryside all become justifications for increased concern.[13] As a result, when individuals confronted these situations they often aimed their resulting trepidations at innocent bystanders because they had been instructed to do so, as maintaining vigilance had become imperative to national security.[14]

Uncovering a 'secret' German was one of the most common pretexts in which suspicion could arise.[15] Anyone caught concealing a German connection or failing to disclose their foreign origins, presumably to protect themselves from discrimination, was considered treacherous and their behaviour likened to perfidious activity.[16] After Private Hill had joined the Lincolnshire Regiment, for instance, he was subsequently outed as a German named Carl Bfaff. Despite being raised in America by his mother, and only German on his father's side, he had never been naturalized in Britain. When his heritage was uncovered he was quickly labelled a spy and arrested. Claims of espionage were short-lived though, and Bfaff was promptly released.[17] However, cultural stereotypes were just as important when it came to generating suspicion. Sausage factories and certain dog breeds commonly attracted suspicion because even the most tenuous links to Germany could provoke condemnation or distrust.[18] After rumours spread that a convent near Colchester had once housed German nuns, it was widely believed that the entire institution was a centre for espionage and illicit signalling.[19]

Suspects would not necessarily need to be German for this type of suspicion to emerge; so long as there were uncertainties about their heritage, individuals with a foreign-sounding name could be suspected of treasonous behaviour. Frank Polz was working at Devonport in October 1914 when he was accused of being a German and a spy despite having served in the Royal Navy for twenty-two years and in the dockyard for fourteen. The authorities nonetheless kept him under observation and although nothing implicating him in espionage was ever found, Winston Churchill, First Lord of the Admiralty at the time, instructed the dockyard police to swiftly 'round him up'.[20] Likewise, a Polish teacher at Bentley Priory had her employment terminated as soon as war was declared on the grounds that she might be mistaken for a German. Her foreign heritage created doubts about her allegiance and provoked allegations that she was a spy.[21] Upon being forcibly relocated to the Scottish Highlands after a German U-boat had left them stranded in Britain, a group of Norwegian sailors were thought to be German spies simply because one of them could speak German. Yet rumours of their supposed transgressions dissipated as the initial excitement of their arrival in Aviemore subsided.[22] In West Horsley, Surrey, Reverend Edward Unmack, who could speak several languages, one of which was German, was reported by residents for being 'thoroughly German in his ideas and speech', for allegedly visiting Germany before the war and for supposedly giving sermons in German, which practically made him a German and a spy. The chief constable concurred and shared these concerns with Vernon Kell no less.[23]

Anybody whose identity was unknown was liable to attract suspicion. Florence Mower explained, 'If your saw somebody in the street that was a bit strange ... someone you hadn't seen near your terrace before, who just happened to be looking around, was automatically a spy'.[24] Reverend Andrew Clark noted how the residents of Little Waltham, a village on the outskirts of Chelmsford, suspected a man reconnoitring the area of being a spy. Although the suspect was indeed collecting information about the local topography it quickly emerged that he was a member of the Ordnance Survey conducting an official inquiry.[25] Strangers did not have to do anything sinister to arouse suspicion, however. While serving on the Western Front, Lieutenant Donald Weir became unduly concerned for his mother's safety after she had acquired a new friend:

> By the by, you need not tell her so, but in my opinion this friend of yours is not to be trusted a yard from you. All spies lie, the rumours are awful as the war, and I don't suppose she is any more Swiss than my old aunt so just [treat her] with a good deal of suspicion. She may make socks for British soldiers and at the same time by playing a double part. You cannot imagine what a wonderful service this German spy system is ... Anything that appears in my letters is not to be known by her.

However misguided these concerns may have been they were consistent with contemporary notions of national security. Weir's fears were explicitly linked to the possibility that he might inadvertently pass secrets to the enemy through his correspondence with his mother, which was a reasonable inference based on the warnings given to soldiers in the BEF.[26] Weir's claim that spies typically dress as old women or in British uniforms presumably derived from popular descriptions of the threat.[27]

Although fears of Germany caused by the war were often fixed on innocent Germans, spy phobias also reflected deep-rooted concerns that were not obviously linked to espionage. Flashing lights or recurring noises are not overtly dangerous, but because they had been frequently associated with an impending invasion, signalling of this kind was thought to be a considerable danger.[28] The military in particular frequently warned the public about the threat of spies messaging German naval vessels using such methods.[29] As a result people became especially concerned with preventing spies from sending secret communications from Britain.[30] While on sentry duty at Scarborough in December 1914, Reverend Monteith wrote to his wife telling her of a man found 'in great excitement'. Upon learning that mysterious lights had been seen coming from a nearby house, the sentries decided to go and investigate. When describing the incident Monteith claimed that he 'didn't really feel in the least afraid' while approaching the property, but that the 'other men got a bit jumpy'. Monteith's alleged bravery juxtaposed with the alleged nervousness of his fellow troops implies that fear had become a standard response to this type of confrontation. Having established a system of surveillance to monitor the suspicious house, Monteith claimed to be on duty throughout the remainder of the night and following day. But his involvement felt rather distasteful. 'How would you like to do that', he asked his wife, 'it seems a beastly thing to do, to spy on a man like that, but I suppose if a man spies, he must be spied on, so I lay outside and watched'. Although Monteith had some reservations, the 'evidence' of unlawful signalling placated his reservations. Upon entering the house soldiers found communications equipment, which firmly implicated the suspect in Monteith's mind.[31]

The significance of these circumstances did sometimes overcome reason and judiciousness. Shortly after enlisting as Second Lieutenant in the Liverpool Territorials, John Mallalieu observed flashing lights in nearby trees and went out to investigate. Using his friend's newly acquired range finder, Mallalieu was somewhat bemused at the distance of the signals. Puzzled at the reading the two soldiers investigated the lights more closely only to discover that they were looking at a low moon. A wooded area had obscured the celestial body, but swaying branches allowed beams of light to escape, mimicking the effects of a light signal.[32] Besides these ad hoc and amateurish investigations there were also more systematic attempts to investigate and prevent enemy communications. Police and naval officers in Devon and Cornwall began a particularly intrusive search for secret agents thought to be communicating with the enemy. Fuelled by reports of illegal lights and enemies operating in close proximity to the sea, the men of the coast watch frantically searched for spies in their respective districts, while naval officers habitually trampled on civil liberties and maintained that vague claims of signalling were the only pretext necessary for such measures.[33]

Since sketches could also be used to convey Britain's military secrets to the enemy, painting and drawing were effectively outlawed and widely condemned as unscrupulous activity.[34] Major Innes and John Grant reported a man to the police for sketching Dufftown's market square, which was hardly an area of military importance since it is 20 miles inland. Even when it was ascertained that the artist was a clergyman from Sunderland, thereby removing any suspicions regarding his identity, the police nevertheless considered it necessary to keep him under observation.[35] Grace Tollemache was arrested for sketching an old dilapidated castle, which was clearly no longer useful to any military.[36] But because sketching had been prohibited under the Defence of the Realm, onlookers felt compelled to report it as suspicious activity, not because they were delusional. George Rose was reported to the police while on holiday after locals spotted him painting the sunset but suspicions vanished after Rose verified his identity.[37] Sentries apprehended two boys in Caithness for taking photos near a local wireless station, but the police soon released them because the station was not even visible for where they had been found. The boys were simply taking photos of their school, and so any misgivings about the boys quickly dissipated.[38] There was undoubtedly an increased desire to police public spaces during the First World War, especially against strangers and outsiders, but spy scares were usually quickly and easily resolved. Culprits were often let off with nothing more than a fine.[39] The suspect caught in Dufftown, for instance, was never formerly arrested because he could prove his identity. For Rose, as soon as the minor inquiries had been completed, normality was restored and he even went for drinks with the arresting officers. Such episodes were not akin to any form of hysteria. These 'spy scares' simply reflected renegotiated ideas of national security and a desire to uphold new wartime regulations among certain individuals.

As well as seditious artists, motorcars also became indicative of surreptitious behaviour and commonly featured in official warnings.[40] Motorcars had long symbolized the growing incursion of outsiders and quickly became the source of much disdain in the British countryside. Provincial communities 'grew to hate cars for their noise, smell, danger and the unconcerned bearing of the drivers', all of which encroached upon the idyllic rural lifestyle. Even more noticeable, though, were the affluent city dwellers who had been invading the countryside with ever greater ease.[41] Some 338,000 cars were bought in Britain in 1913, which drastically increased the likelihood of encountering a stranger.[42] Unlike the railway personal forms of transport meant that strangers could disappear as suddenly as they had appeared, making cars much more suited to clandestine activity. As a result, people became especially conscious of secret agents speedily reconnoitring the British countryside using motorized transport.[43]

This was most noticeable in how local military authorities reacted to the threat of aerial bombardment. Arthur Read, a Territorial soldier in the London Irish regiment, recalled how one individual supposedly signalling from a motorcar led to detachments of Territorials sent out to guard the roads. Armed with fixed bayonets and loaded rifles, they were instructed to stop and search every oncoming vehicle and if it failed to comply they were to open fire.[44] Lieutenant William Foster, serving with the Sherwood Foresters in Essex, was similarly tasked with picketing the roads to watch out for spies in motors guiding dirigibles to their target. Although Foster found no evidence of unlawful activity he did claim that two spies were caught nearby.[45] The military's stringent response against personal vehicles presumably endorsed popular assumptions about people driving cars and that they were somehow deceitful.[46] Although this type of alarm was connected to wider concerns regarding advancing technology and the effect on social cohesion and local security, these fears were remarkably tenuous and evanescent.[47] During a Zeppelin attack on Hull, Margaret Constable and her friend were accused of spying for the enemy and a mob of people began to surround her car. Despite the crowd's initial hostility, they were placated after learning that the car belonged to Colonel Constable of the local regiment. Margaret later found out that they had been reported to the police but that the local constabulary had not taken the threat seriously.[48] A family in Kent was also suspected of conducting intelligence gathering simply for owning a car.[49] Although enquiries into the family found that their chauffeur was French, the Johnsons were proven to be English and so concerns were dropped.[50]

Many of the accusations recording contemporary concerns suggest that specific instances of fear were short-lived. Mary Anderson, enjoying retirement in the Cotswolds in 1914, recalled the thrill of encountering a potential spy but more significantly the ease with which anxieties were allayed:

> One day, talking to a friend in the road, I saw a man, looking to my mind like a typical German spy ... I told my friend I was sure the suspicious-looking individual was a spy. 'I will speak to him, and if his accent is German, ring up the police.' My friend begged me not to do so saying: 'He is a spy, I am sure, and he will shoot you as soon as you approach him.' With my heart in my feet I walked up to him and said, smiling: 'My watch has stopped, will you please tell me the time?' With an undoubted Western American accent he pulled out his watch: 'I guess my watch has gone a bit crazy in this damp country; it says half-twelve.' I thanked him, feeling very foolish ... That little episode cured me of the spy-fever.[51]

For Anderson at least, this type of fear did not necessarily arise because of an existential threat, although her friend may have felt differently, but Anderson describes it more as an exhilarating opportunity to combat a potential enemy in support of the national effort. In any case, there seems to be a range of different emotions evident in her description. Her use of the term 'spy fever' to describe her feelings is also interesting for it shows the disparity between how contemporaries used the term 'spy fever' and an actual mania. Based on her account of this 'little episode', her short-lived suspicion appears very much unlike the delusional paranoia observed in asylum patients. But because her concerns by her own admission proved foolish, she felt inclined to label them in such a way that conveyed the absurdity of her apprehension and thus drew upon the prevalence of 'spy fever' as a concept to explain her encounter.

Rather than suffer from a chronic disorder caused by the espionage peril, most individuals experiencing spy phobias seem to have suffered from a 'flush of spy fever', which is inconsistent with how contemporary psychologists understood 'mania' as a sustained psychological condition.[52] Many instances of suspicion seem to have originated with specific objects, such as cars or lights, or against certain activities like drawing or loitering. None of which are overtly threatening without some form of direction. Thus, people suspected covert activity and nefarious intentions when faced with these circumstances primarily because they were encouraged to do so and expressed heightened emotional responses because national security appeared to demand it. While this may have reflected a state of anxiety, such examples are hardly illustrative of an intense or protracted fear. Characterizing such reactions as hysteria or lunacy, therefore, seems to derive more from society's inclination to associate nervous weakness with psychological disorder. Although it is not possible to objectively analyse the mental state of the individuals mentioned earlier, there is little evidence that confirms the existence of a mania or fever. As a result, historians cannot positively associate spy phobias with a psychological disorder and so should avoid assuming that individuals suffered the effects of a mania or fever in relation to the espionage peril. Whether or not terms like 'spy fever' and 'spy mania' accurately surmise the national psyche or collective response remains to be seen, but they should not be taken literally as descriptors of individual feelings and reactions towards the enemy within.

Frequency of spy scares

As well as anecdotal evidence that suggests spy phobias were relatively short-lived for the individuals experiencing them, the way in which espionage appeared in the press also indicates that spy scares were a relatively brief phenomenon. As the previous chapter demonstrated, British society witnessed an intense level of suspicion and vigilance during the summer of 1914. However, following an official announcement confirming the capture of twenty-one spies, supposedly the entire German spy system in Britain, the Home Secretary declared that the 'public may rest assured that the great majority of Germans remaining in this country are peaceful and innocent persons from whom no danger is to be feared'.[53] Following a second statement from the Home Office, one journalist wrote that it was:

> a relief to learn from the Home Secretary that Scotland Yard has no evidence of malpractices by spies. Most of the stories that have been published in the newspapers of threatened damage to railway lines and of attacks upon sentries have been subject to reasonable explanation, and in others the cases have not been proven, and the public certainly ought to get reassurance from that fact.[54]

Of course not all newspapers concurred, but McKenna's intervention nevertheless seems to have assuaged many fears related to the spy peril.[55] Home Defence Intelligence Summaries reported that allegations of German spies had notably declined, despite the continued attention given to espionage in the press.[56] This would suggest that by October society was becoming increasingly confident in the security measures in place.[57] Notwithstanding the initial unrest McKenna was praised by some for his handling of the apparent danger:

> We have never been included among the admirers of Mr McKenna's methods at the Home Office. We have regarded him somewhat as a fish out of water, recognising that his real place is at the Treasury. But, as the Suffrage agitation proved, the detective force has lost nothing in efficiency during his tenure of office. The spy question can be left in its hands and journalists with any real

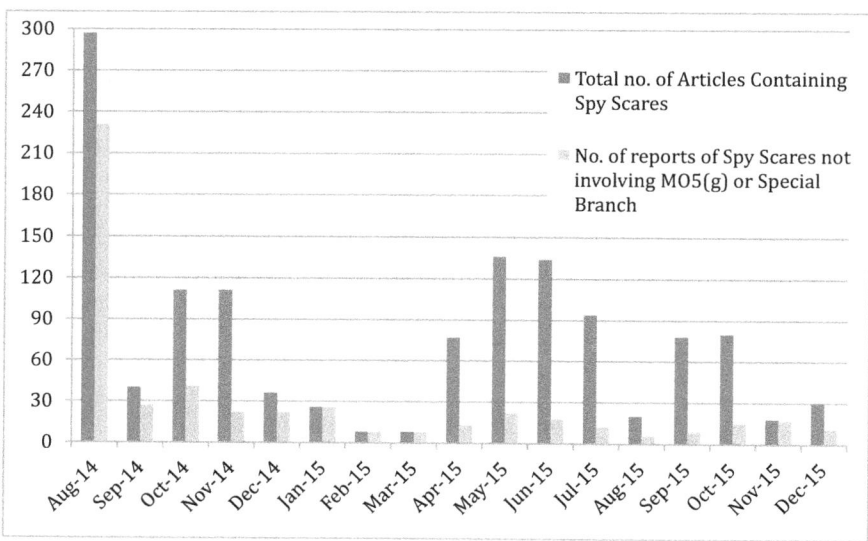

Figure 3.1 Number of spy scares reported in the press compared with the number of local spy scares, August 1914–December 1915.

information concerning suspicious actions of alien enemies will find it better to give it to Scotland Yard, rather than publish silly twaddle in the columns of newspapers. If newspaper syndicate owners have lost their poor heads, the majority of Englishmen have not.[58]

Further arrests gave the impression that the military and police forces had the situation under control.[59] Even Basil Thomson, seemingly contradicting his own description of spy fever, claimed that individuals quickly recovered from spy phobias after receiving news that the authorities were taking adequate precautions.[60] Figure 3.1 demonstrates that the number of incidents involving alleged suspects dropped significantly after the initial commotion during August 1914. This means that either very few spy scares were taking place or that public interest in them had diminished. Either way, the significance of spy phobias was in decline. Despite the inclusion of 297 articles exposing 'spies' active in Britain during August 1914, in the following month, only forty articles reported cases of espionage in Britain. This is a considerable change in how spy fever featured in the press. Although the number of suspicious incidents ostensibly rose during October and November 1914, 69 per cent of all articles that contained suspected spies related to only two suspects, Karl Gustav Ernst and Carl Hans Lody. Neither Ernst nor Lody was the victim of popular clamour, having both been investigated and arrested by MO5(g).[61] If we remove reports pertaining to official counter-espionage rather than popular fears, the number of articles depicting spy scares appearing in October and November drops to just sixty-two. Despite a superficial increase in October the impact of spy phobias during this period remained very much unlike that of August 1914.

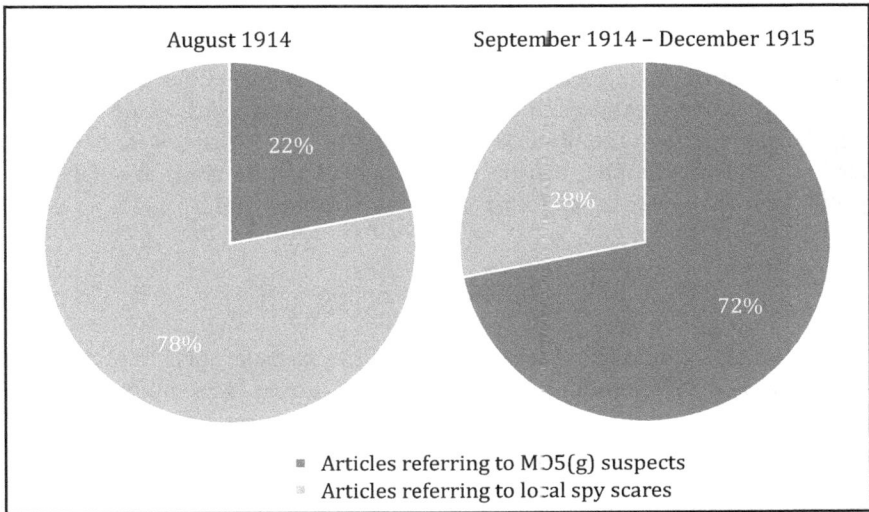

Figure 3.2 Proportion of local spy scares compared with official counter-espionage.

The decline of provincial spy scares was also a national and enduring development. Figure 3.1 also shows that in most months high-profile cases prosecuted in London, involving suspects identified and investigated by the War Office and the Metropolitan Police, received far more attention than local outbursts of suspicion. There were only seven months in which local spy scares formed the majority of the suspicious activities documented in newspapers, but these were numerically insignificant. This is because between September 1914 and December 1915 there were on average only seventeen articles per month describing arrests or investigations based on provincial suspicions, despite coming from a sample size of over 500 issues per month. As Figure 3.2 makes clear, the overwhelming majority of reports documenting the investigation, arrest or prosecution of spies only related to a handful of suspects – most notably, Carl Hans Lody, Karl Gustav Ernst, John Hahn, Karl Friedrich Müller, Anton Küpferle and Robert Rosenthal, who were either imprisoned or shot in the Tower of London because of the investigations of MO5(g) and Special Branch.[62] Although captured spies continued to generate much interest, popular suspicion seems mostly confined to the immediate period following the declaration of war.[63] August 1914 witnessed 45 per cent of all articles containing references to spy scares in print between August 1914 and December 1915. If we consider local spy scares on their own, that figure becomes 54 per cent.

Thus, while early scares most often represented officially sanctioned local counter-espionage, by September the government's response to a handful of genuine spies dominated images of the enemy within. That espionage continued to attract much interest and speculation is indisputable, but there is little evidence to suggest that society's fascination with spying resulted in intense outbursts of panic or suspicion beyond the initial mobilization period. Although the frequency of spy scares in the press does not provide an objective assessment of whether or not people felt truly afraid because of their immediate surroundings, such an analysis does suggest that this particular emotional style – a heightened sense of suspicion and apprehension – was declining in significance. If that was indeed the case, then popular fears, at least the physical manifestation of those fears, were becoming far less frequent. Claiming that these feelings were symptomatic of a persistent psychological condition, therefore, is purely speculative.

The Zeps are coming

The declining significance of spy phobias, both in terms of their impact on the individual and their prominence in national discourses, was unlike the more enduring, and more intensely felt, fears caused by the prospect and experience of aerial attack. Comparing espionage phobias with Zeppelin terrors provides a much-needed emotional context in which to analyse the severity and persistence of fear on the Home Front. As a result, it becomes clear that clandestine operatives were not the primary cause of fear in Britain, especially from December 1914 onwards.[64] The first air raids of 1915 appear to have elicited a much more extreme emotional reaction than early encounters with the spy had done. Since spy fever has been routinely likened to hysteria, whereas the more powerful and prolonged responses towards Zeppelins have not, implies that characterizing spy phobias as a form of fever or mania arose out of subsequent realizations that there was no genuine threat, rather than the actual emotional reaction itself. If terms like mania or fever genuinely reflected the degree of emotionality on display, then Zeppelin fears would have surely also been labelled as such.

In January 1915 the first two Zeppelins appeared over East Anglia and began bombing King's Lynn, Sheringham and Great Yarmouth, killing four and injuring a further sixteen in the process. In May 1915, following several aborted attempts due to poor weather, the first air raid on London killed thirty-five people. Raids over Hull and Newcastle quickly followed in June. These early raids were both a symbolic and explicit demonstration of future warfare, which fostered a growing sense of vulnerability, especially in industrial centres.[65] There were a total of fifty-one Zeppelin attacks on Britain, during which they dropped 196 tons of bombs killing 556 people.[66] Air raids went on to kill a total of 1,239 civilians in Britain and injure a further 2,886. Given the overt danger to the individual, rather than abstract threats against the nation, fears of aerial bombardment were often articulated in a very different way to spy phobias.[67]

Owing to the notoriety and prominence of espionage in 1914 people inevitably considered it a noteworthy phenomenon, but unlike the portrayal of air raids in post-war reminisces, memoirists seldom recalled their own espionage fears and typically only relayed anecdotal and vague references to the spy peril. Barbara Duguid recalled how 'there was considerable spy fever at the time', while Gilbert Bickmore noted how 'naturally there were spy scares everywhere'. Neither author chose to elaborate or disclose any personal experiences of the spy peril.[68] T. H.

Kirk similarly recounted how as a fifteen-year-old at an Officers Training Camp in August 1914, the period following the BEF's retreat from Mons became 'a time of hysteria [and] spy stories' in which innocent men were frequently shot.[69] Although these accounts convey the public's awareness of the peril, there is a lack of detail and personal connection that suggests the threat of espionage seldom created lasting impressions.

Zeppelins, on the other hand, were commonly credited with inspiring terror, and given the scale and longevity of the threat, experiences of air raids filled post-war reminisces.[70] Owing to the unmistakable and unprecedented destruction that they caused, Zeppelins were often regarded as the greatest danger facing people at home.[71] Whereas spy phobias rarely received more than a brief mention in memoirs, air raids are remembered with meticulous detail.[72] As a ten-year-old living in Norfolk Jennie McDonagh witnessed first-hand the fears that Zeppelins inspired. She recounted how her family were 'all very frightened' and could easily recall the tremble in her mother's voice during a raid.[73] Elizabeth Bracher, living alone in Surrey while her husband was serving in France, could describe her every encounter with a German Zeppelin. Although the first attack proved relatively ineffectual, the second destroyed a nearby bungalow with her friends inside. The same Zeppelin continued on to Croydon and inflicted further damage.[74] In contrast to the rather elusive spy imperilling the nation, people were able to witness first-hand the damage inflicted by air raids. This placed the individual in close proximity to the danger and created a much stronger sensation that was preserved within one's psyche.[75]

Even without the loss of loved ones or damage to personal property the devastation was often intimately felt. Hilda Davison, who lived with her parents in Sunderland, vividly recalled the state of terror that she was reduced to on account of such destruction:

> One night shortly afterwards we heard a lot of shouting in the street. I was too nervous to go outside with the others, and so I missed the sight of a Zeppelin being brought down in flames. I had several frights after this. Once I got everybody up in the middle of the night, thinking I had heard a bomb, and it turned out to be thunder. On another occasion, at about six in the morning, I heard a double crash in the house, and lay paralysed with fright. Mother got up, and discovered that a heavy picture in the front hall had fallen first on to a table.[76]

For Davison, the sense of terror was not simply confined to the situation in which the object of danger was apparent. Because of the intensity of these fears, and the very real peril that Davison felt, they had lasting effects beyond the immediate circumstance in which the threat was perceived. In describing her time training as a nurse in Sheffield, Elizabeth Cockayne could easily recall the degree of terror she felt during a raid on the nearby steel works. 'As the bombs dropped shaking the block, I stood by the centre table with my knees knocking but the next morning the patients said how brave I was. If only they knew!'[77] Evident in Cockayne's account is the way in which Zeppelins could reduce one's capacity to control bodily functions and create vivid emotional experiences.

Fear was not necessarily the only the emotion preserved in memory. Norah Bristow fondly described the excitement she felt in watching burning Zeppelins fall over London. Yet this does not mean that fear was not also present in some form. For Bristow, her delight may have resulted from the displacement of former anxieties, for example. Observing the Zeppelin's destruction removed the immediacy of the danger thereby alleviating any lingering concerns allowing her to rejoice at Zeppelin's demise.[78] J. W. Barrett remembered how his father would congregate with neighbours in their street to watch the nearby anti-aircraft guns fire upon dirigibles. According to Barrett it generated much excitement; neighbours would even bring out seats and distribute hot drinks among the crowd of spectators gathered to watch the spectacle.[79] Since this particular description referred to an attack in 1916 the onlookers had perhaps become accustomed to this type of fear, affording them the resources to manage their emotions more effectively and experience them in a different way than Davison or Cockayne had done earlier in the war. Gathering to watch Zeppelin raids seems to have become a fairly common activity, probably because passivity and ignorance can often exacerbate one's sense of fear.[80] In any case, while fears of aerial bombardment could both excite onlookers and terrorize helpless victims, they nevertheless created unforgettable experiences.[81]

Contemporaneously recorded accounts of air raids are equally revealing of the range and intensity of emotional responses generated by aerial bombardment. Even before Zeppelins had begun attacking Britain, the prospect of aerial attack was widely anticipated and a huge emotional outpouring was expected.[82] Indeed, after the first bombs had landed, numerous letters and diaries began diligently recording local casualties and the physical destruction caused by German air raids.[83] Some even went out of their way to personally examine the damage caused by air raids.[84] Although these accounts are not always explicit in how they felt in response to aerial attack, the frequency with which people recorded Zeppelin sightings and the detail that went into describing the damage suggests that the prospect of aerial attack was regularly in people's thoughts, which cannot be said for how individuals recorded their engagement with the spy danger.[85] The first time Emily Blathwayt observed a notable rise in nervousness among the British public was because of 'Germans who [threw] bombs in defenceless towns from aeroplanes'.[86] Upon hearing that a Zeppelin had bombed a nearby town for the first time, Ada McGuire expressed grave concern that she was now directly within the Zeppelin's 'line of sight'.[87] Rather than an intangible or abstract threat to collective security, aerial bombardment presented a clear and immediate threat to the individual, which seems to have incited fear far easier than German spies ever did.

While concerns for one's safety was commonly articulated in private correspondence, air raids also symbolized a noticeable change in the way war affected civilians, and so as the bombs fell people commonly articulated their concerns for loved ones' safety.[88] Captain Ashby wrote to his wife, Margery, telling her that during an air raid 'you imagine all sorts of poor folk must be blown to blazes in hundreds – the most awful great thuds – detonation that shook the whole place, with fearful flashes right on top of each other'.[89] Olive Armstrong, lecturer in history and economics at Trinity College Dublin, grew tremendously afraid for her mother's safety during a visit to London, and throughout their correspondence the location of recent raids and the likeliness of future encounters were discussed at length.[90] Although Lieutenant John Lawton found watching German aircraft 'exhilarating', as the range of Zeppelins expanded he grew increasingly anxious for his mother's safety.[91] Private Stanley emphatically sought to keep loved ones away from the danger: 'I mustn't wish you here – the London area is not a healthy place to be in … and I sincerely hope the Zepps never reach Birmingham and the Midlands', where his family lived.[92] For the same reason, Agatha Broadwood urged her cousin to take refuge from the Zeppelins and pleaded with her to leave the capital.[93]

Many people shared Nell Hague's desire to have loved ones close, not just to know that they were safe but to also provide much-needed emotional support. During her first Zeppelin raid, Hague wrote to her husband telling him of the discomfort and insecurity she felt without him:

The Zeps! are here! and from mother's bedroom window the whole town seems on fire … Last night was the second time since our arrival here that the alarm whistles have blown … however, last night (Sunday) they were blown again about 10p.m and about 11 we all went to bed. I did not feel afraid, but of course I longed to have you here, for you always bring such a sense of security to me.[94]

Although Hague did not admit to being frightened, she later described her general state as 'one of nervous tension', which explains why she sought emotional comfort to alleviate her angst. The reason for her fear was clear: 'You must just try to imagine my feelings as I laid our little one in his bed tonight and how my heart echoed his baby prayer … Oh sweetheart, I wish you were here too.'[95] Although individuals might have been reluctant to admit being afraid, the degree of concern felt for the safety of others, especially children, reveals the extent of fear many people felt and this manifested in a desire to prepare, physically and emotionally, for the next encounter.

Whereas spy phobias proved relatively inconsequential, fears of aerial bombardment were seldom benign, particularly in areas susceptible to attack from the skies.[96] Whereas one might be able to take action to deter or thwart espionage, individuals often felt helpless in the face of the indiscriminate destruction brought about by aerial bombardment, and this had a profound impact on their emotional and physical response. Jeanne Berman recorded how a Zeppelin raid over Grimsby in June 1915 caused her to 'feel faint' at the thought of it, while her teeth began to chatter uncontrollably.[97] During a night raid on Lowestoft in April 1915 residents in nearby Southwold grew particularly apprehensive upon hearing explosions. Sleep, in particular, became particularly difficult:

At 12 o'clock my maids came to my room, and said they heard gunfire and so did I. We went downstairs and after the firing ceased so we went back again [to bed]. Half an hour afterwards they again roused me. Another half hour downstairs and then to bed. Another half hour and another alarm. After this we felt that we might rest in peace, but it was not to be.[98]

As a result, many people gathered in the street to feel secure through congregation and alleviate anxieties through observation.[99] Some people felt compelled to sleep fully clothed next to emergency rations, while others even resorted to sleeping in the assumed safety of the open countryside.[100] Nell Hague described how entire communities were placed in a state of disarray as fears of Zeppelins grew:

But oh! If you could see the desolation in some parts of the town, you would never forget it. Last night the alarm was blown again ... the civic guard come found and order all lights out, cars are stopped, and practically everything is in utter darkness. Of course we made all preparations ... The most pitiable part of all was the sight of the families coming away – they were all ordered out of the congested areas into the open – parks were thrown open, and they came into the fields. It is no exaggeration to say that there were thousands of people in and around the fields and lanes at the back of mothers' – the dear little children – the cripples, the aged – oh, my dear it must be seen to be realised.[101]

The terror engendered by the prospect of aerial bombardment had a noticeable impact on people's lives. Entire towns were kept in darkness, people desperately sought out shelter and those with valuables and property signed up to government insurance scheme to protect themselves from financial ruin.[102] Unlike spy phobias, which required a specific set of circumstances to generate a sense of fear, the continuation of the war itself was the only pretence needed to sustain fears of aerial bombardment. The possibility of death and destruction at any moment and the unprecedented scale of devastation created the conditions necessary for a lasting sense of terror that dominated emotional experiences on the Home Front.

Nevertheless, as society adjusted to the new realities of warfare, many individuals learnt to manage their feelings generated by German air raids.[103] Following her first experience of aerial bombardment in Margate, in which a young child was killed nearby, Lydia Peile hoped to 'never have such a close experience of bombs again'. Unfortunately for Peile she was to be bombed again only three weeks later. This time, though, she described the affair in her diary as 'more exciting than alarming'.[104] Society's determination to outlast and overcome the destruction caused by aerial bombardment can also be seen in how Florence Shuster described her first experience of a German Zeppelin:

This was my first experience of a raid except for one Zeppelin raid in 1914 ... I was quite prepared to feel windy, but honestly did not feel in the least excited or nervous. I was most surprised that I did not have a funny feeling in my inside. I can understand it getting rather boring, having to spend half the night in a cellar which was very draughty and cold with only one small gas jet and not enough to read by.[105]

Suppressing fear in this way was not uncommon Despite living on the Sussex coast in 1914, and thus exposed to both a German naval raid and a Zeppelins attack, James Hissey felt perfectly safe as he became more accustomed to the war: 'So many exciting things are happening that nothing no longer excites us. I don't think we need worry ourselves here – we don't anyhow', he wrote to a friend regarding his current safety.[106] While this may have been an attempt to conceal his fears and express bravado in the face of danger, it is equally possible that Hissey's words marked an attempt to manage and suppress his concerns by outwardly maintaining a sense of stoicism. Yet the reality of aerial bombardment, at least during the early stages of Germany's aerial offensive, proved less destructive than originally expected, and this helped instil a degree of emotional control. In April 1915, for instance, Frank Lockwood described the damage caused by air raids in his diary: 'Zeppelin made a futile raid on the English Coast tonight. Newcastle and district was visited. Result, 2 persons slightly wounded. Fancy coming 350 miles to do such trifling damage.'[107]

As air raids became more routine and increasingly familiar the fears that often beset early observers became easier to suppress as the collective resolve, itself partly strengthened by individuals' desire for vengeance, increased.[108] Margaret Currie recounted how an entire audience remained calm during a West End production in the middle of an air raid, even as the building started to crumble around them:

Carmen Hill was singing when we heard the first disturbing sounds above us, but we tried to ignore them. The next item was a bassoon solo by Wilfred James, in the middle of which there was a crash, followed by a cracking sound, and a shower of plaster began to fall from the roof over the Promenade itself, which was packed. There was a moment of panic when people in the centre of the hall tried to disperse ... The soloist however, kept merrily on, and we soon realised it could only be shrapnel which had dislodged some plaster. The soloist got a rousing encore, and returned to play 'we shan't get home till morning' among cheers and laughter.[109]

Besides this collective spirit spurring people on, Maggie Turner felt determined to endure the ordeal of bombardment while working as a nurse at Great Ormond Street Hospital. In a letter to her mother, she wrote:

Never in my life will I forget last night ... I fell asleep in a few moments only to wake up to hear the most awful noise ... [I] felt the whole of my room shake, things falling down all over the place, screams from nurses flying down the stairs and passages, saying quickly 'Nurses the Zeppelins are here!' All lights were turned out at once from the main and we were in utter darkness ... I didn't feel a bit frightened at the time and shouted out to the Nurses as we flew downstairs not to cry out ... The gas and the sound of the bombs exploding was awful, one after the other – the noise and darkness was too terrible … Several of us slept together as we were all so shaken with fright … All the Nurses really behaved in a splendid way, only a few lost their heads.[110]

Despite reassuring her mother of her safety and emotional well-being, her account brilliantly captures the range of emotional experience. Although fear was widely felt, Turner was able to manage it and safeguard the children in her care. According to this emotional style, which prioritized calmness over panic, individuals could feel defiance, rather than terror, by supressing and overcoming their fears. In other words, while some could succumb to the situation and freeze in a moment of panic or despair, others could ignore the immediate dangers and channel their feelings elsewhere.

Besides fortitude, for people like Andrew Clark, a second lieutenant in the Royal Artillery protecting Woolwich Arsenal, air raids offered an opportunity to face the enemy directly and as such represented a thrilling opportunity. Upon spotting airships over London, described by Clark as a 'glorious view', he rushed back to the city by train to battle the invaders.[111] During the encounter, Clark claimed that there was so much excitement among the troops that one even fell out of a window after cheering too vigorously.[112] Comparable feelings of exhilaration were not confined to soldiers, however. After what proved to be a very narrow escape, Flora Evans wrote:

This is just to let you know that we were not all blown up last night by Zeppelins. It really was most thrilling as they came within 3½ miles and dropped bombs … We heard the engines at about 10:30, it sounded as if they went right over here, very high. The night nurses and some of the men swear they saw it go over. Then we all calmed down again … some of the staff have gone to see the holes today, I am going tomorrow if pos[sible].[113]

Nell Hague described to her husband how after an air raid she was 'too wide awake to go to bed', no doubt because of the adrenaline rushing through her veins, and described the encounter as a 'thrilling experience' in a letter she wrote him the following morning.[114]

Notwithstanding the severity of fear created by the prospect of aerial bombardment Susan Grayzel concludes that Zeppelin attacks induced a range of conflicting experiences and emotional reactions, including fear, defiance, pride and excitement. For some, the possibility of annihilation spawned a sense of exhilaration, while for others, acclimatization merely generated indifference in the face of adversity and derision at 'the awful fuss over these air raids'.[115] Upon learning of the Zeppelin attacks in January 1915 and the destruction that they had wrought, Alison MacIntyre questioned, 'What good can they do? Absolutely no scare created we only wish they would drop bombs on some place worth while.'[116] Despite witnessing a Zeppelin attack on London, Archibald Walker wrote about having a rather 'dull week', and that despite others in a state of 'much excitement', there had been no alarm 'except in the breast of one or two ladies occupied in plying the ancient trade. These saw fit to faint.'[117] Despite the terror that often characterized response to Zeppelin raids, there was clearly a certain emotional response that was deemed suitable, according to the norms and customs of the day. This idealized stoicism and resolve can be seen in an article appearing in *The Times* in September 1915:

> No doubt the Germans believed that with their Zeppelin war upon civilians they would cause a panic among civilians. It is part of their theory of war that civilians are generally contemptible in war. They exist but to be frightened ... It takes little to throw civilians into a panic in peace; it was natural, therefore, to expect that bomb-dropping would throw them into a panic in war ... She did expect that, and she has been disappointed. The Zeppelins appear to cause wonderfully little panic at the moment of murder, and no permanent panic afterwards. Their effect is, not a demand for peace, but a demand of the whole nation to help in the war.[118]

Because of this prevailing emotional style Grayzel contends that there was almost a complete lack of panic in Britain – at least collectively – because the principle of total war required total involvement. In this situation, survival on the Home Front demanded the entire nation to participate and remain steadfast. In the face of German militarism and aggression, civilians were to be immune to panic and remain in control of their emotions.[119]

Comparing these two types of fear raises an important question about the nature of spy fever. Namely, why were people so keen to stress that Zeppelins fears did not create widespread alarm, whereas spy phobias were often likened to panic or hysteria? Identifying the emotional standards governing these two reactions suggests that the answer lays in the conceptualization of total war and the nature of home defence. On the one hand it was essential to create a sense of control to ensure that the British public remained calm in the face of German violence and maintain their shared resolve. But at the same time there was an increasing desire among certain sections of society to oust the enemy within, ostensibly for the benefit of national security and homogeneity. These two conflicting ideals required the manipulation and control of certain types of fear. Individuals' fears of survival needed supressing for the collective good, whereas threats to the nation needed to be felt internally so that the danger could be realized and mitigated appropriately. By promoting and exaggerating individual responses to the spy peril, wartime discourse created the conditions in which the fears and insecurities linked to the enemy within appeared as a psychological condition. Examining how individuals articulated their responses to these dangers, however, suggests that the link between espionage phobias and psychological illness is unfounded, especially as they appear to have been inconsequential compared to the far more memorable fears of aerial bombardment.

***

Owing to the difficulty in assessing individuals' emotions in the past, it is helpful to examine the contexts in which particular feelings were expressed. By doing so it is possible to identify patterns of behaviour and modes of expression that shaped the interpretation and experience of individual feelings. In accordance with a wider emotional regime that prioritized fear and frustration when responding to various security threats, the spy peril focused suspicion and mistrust on certain scenarios ostensibly linked to German espionage. However, it appears that spy phobias were only expressed in certain situations, which arguably distinguishes them from a sustained and delusional paranoia and separates them from how contemporaries understood severe psychological disorders. Few, if any, individuals recorded themselves as experiencing spy phobias on multiple occasions.

Given that fears of the enemy within were seldom depicted as hysterical or manic either before or after the First World War, the specific medical context of 1914 was thus important in influencing how contemporaries rationalized and viewed comparable fears within their own time period. Without a proper psychological assessment, it is of course impossible to verify the existence or non-existence of a related disorder. Yet the frequency with which medical language has been used to describe spy phobias is particularly striking. Arguably the application of terms like 'spy fever' to individuals' fears was driven, not by the characteristics of contemporary suspicions but because of growing attempts to diagnose and treat different forms of nervous weakness. The emotionality and suggestibility of individuals displaying spy phobias made them vaguely comparable to increasingly popular understandings of mental illnesses like hysteria or neurasthenia, which gave rise to concepts such as 'spy mania'.

Presuming that these fears were irrational ignores the wider appeal of the enemy other. Especially since society had been frequently warned that there was a very real threat posed by Germany's secret service, it is problematic to assume that popular suspicions amounted to delusional paranoia. Situations mimicking the fictional exploits of German spies, involving light signals directing enemy forces, drawings that might betray Britain's defences, motorcars being used to reconnoitre the countryside or plots to destroy communications infrastructure and transportation links, not only legitimized the threat but also became common pretexts for displaying certain emotions. Being aware of these threats and maintaining vigilance, in accordance with ill-conceived ideas of national security, is not the same as hallucinations involving German spies. Because spy phobias were predominantly expressed in specific contexts, they became less likely after the initial weeks of the war as these contexts became less apparent. But because these feelings were contingent on the perceived existence of a defined danger, the suspicions stimulated by the spy peril were often momentary as reality made the absence of threat clearer. If the circumstances in which the spy was observed were found to be erroneous or misleading fears would quickly dissipate. As a result, spy phobias were not akin to a malady that 'defied treatment'. Notwithstanding the cases in which an individual may have suffered a heightened sense of fear owing to the spy threat, these feelings were driven by social conventions regarding the expression of certain feelings, which were then mitigated through appraisals of the threat.

Comparing spy phobias with Zeppelin terrors also shows a clear disparity in how these two fears were articulated, which further questions the impact of spy fever on individuals' emotional dispositions. Describing espionage fears as a feverish response insinuates that these emotions manifested physically as well as psychologically. Yet fears of Zeppelins were often conveyed with a degree of severity often lacking in how spy phobias were portrayed. The frequency with which Zeppelin raids appeared in personal correspondence produced during the war demonstrates just how potent this feeling could become.[120] Although spies posed a threat to national security, wartime conditions created physical dangers that posed a direct risk to the individual, which was, for most people, a far more pressing concern than abstract fears of an enemy within. This comparison implies that espionage phobias were less influential to individuals than society's interest in spying implied, which suggests that spy fever was more of a collective anxiety, instead of an individual malady within the body.

Given the dearth of evidence suggesting that people suffered from particularly enduring or crippling fears of espionage, characterizing individuals' reactions as a form of 'mania' is problematic. Such an assessment is premised on the idea that spy phobias were hysterical and irrational, neither of which can be substantiated by how people articulated their own fears in writing. Moreover, this conclusion can only be reached if one assumes that the hyperbole surrounding the spy peril was symptomatic of people's feelings. Failing to distinguish between the two is problematic given the disparities in how people perceive and interpret their emotions. As the following chapter will make clear, portraying spy phobias as a form of mania overlooks the popular appeal of combatting a secret and nefarious enemy and obscures the variety of emotions that could be felt when encountering this foe.

Chapter 4

PLAYING THE GREAT GAME

Before we completely discount the idea that 'spy fever' induced a psychosomatic condition, it is worth considering why people felt inclined to hunt spies. Historians who have encountered spy phobias typically claim that these emotions originated from the consumption of popular invasion and espionage literature. According to this interpretation, spy fever occurred because of a shared belief that fictional portrayals of espionage depicted a literal reality. While this offers a convenient narrative to explain a seemingly irrational response, it is obviously impossible to determine whether or not individuals genuinely accepted works of fiction as factual exposés, which makes it rather problematic to attribute spy fever to a widespread gullibility. In an attempt to decode Britain's fascination with spying, Nicholas Hiley has offered an alternative interpretation of the purpose and attraction of spy novels. Hiley contends that spy novels serve a similar purpose to an urban legend. Both merge the real world with myth and fairy tale to construct a narrative relating to recent or foreseeable events involving ostensibly 'normal' people. Believed or not, spy stories, like urban legends, 'served an underlying need to know about and to try and understand bizarre, frightening, and potentially dangerous or embarrassing events that may have happened'.[1] However, the principal function of spy novels, according to Hiley, is not to accurately depict events or intrigues taking place in the real world but to facilitate the subconscious fantasies of adolescents and insecure middle-class men.[2] Spy novels provide a way for people to access the esoteric world of international politics and diplomacy while also confirming the importance of the individual to national success. In doing so, spy novels offer a sense of excitement and opportunity to readers.[3]

The main problem in assuming that spy novels directly induced widespread fears of secret agents is that it ignores the fact that spy novels transcend different genres and incorporate a variety of themes. Not all spy stories of the period fabricated or embellished existential threats facing Britain. Thomas Hitchner's work shows a clear dissonance between the pessimism of counter-spy and invasion literature on the one hand and the relative optimism of spy and adventure novels on the other. Whereas the former advocated suspicion and paranoia, the latter promoted 'cleverness, courage, and honourable competition, best represented by the tradition of sportsmanship'.[4] Rudyard Kipling's *Kim* (1901), for instance, conveys a very different tone to the explicit jingoism of William Le Queux. Unlike Le Queux, Kipling's work contains less threat of annihilation and focuses more on the exciting adventures found in the world of intrigue and deception, colloquially referred to by Kipling as 'the Great Game that never ceases day and night'. Although the allied Russian and French agents symbolized a considerable danger – an invasion of India, the jewel in Britain's imperial crown – the narrative centred on Kim's wit, ingenuity and bravery that saw him succeed through a number of trials that coincidentally upheld the security of the empire. Whereas Le Queux relentlessly warned of national defeat and imperial demise, Kipling instead emphasized the adventure and fulfilment found in individual enterprise and agency.[5] It is unlikely that readers of *Kim* drew the same conclusions and formed the same emotional responses as readers of *Spies of the Kaiser*, and so although the connection between fictional spies and popular fears has been widely accepted, historians need a better understanding of the different ways that fictional depictions of secret warfare shaped responses to the First World War. Only then can we appreciate the nuances of spy fever.

Despite much of the historiography assuming that a widespread and delusional paranoia was manufactured by gripping tales of German invasion and intrigue, spy novels are written to excite and entertain audiences just as much, perhaps even more so, than they are to frighten or alarm. Although historians have hitherto focused on the inherent dangers of covert infiltration clearly on display in invasion literature, the sense of adventure found in encountering literary spies was just as influential in forming individual responses to the First World War. By identifying two distinct themes within the espionage genre, it becomes possible that readers could access two contrasting emotional styles that shaped perceptions of the German spy menace and their experiences derived from it. Whereas Edwardian spy novels reflected contemporary politics and uncertainty, and so drew upon social and political anxieties, the central protagonist was invariably successful, much to Britain's benefit, through heroic endeavour and exciting adventure. Envisaging and a secret enemy within, therefore, afforded individuals an emotional connection to the war effort precisely because of the way in which heroism and adventure had been represented in popular culture.

This chapter postulates an alternative explanation as to why people expressed fears of German spies. It moves away from the suggestion that British society was unable to distinguish fiction from fact and instead argues that emulating the familiar tropes of popular spy novels provided people, mostly men, a sense of purpose and adventure. While this contrasting emotional style may not be as easily observable in the hyperbole featured in the right-wing press, it can certainly be seen in how people privately recorded their experiences of hunting for spies. For these individuals, fear often stimulated a sense of exhilaration rather than terror because the threat of espionage presented a unique opportunity to display one's military bravado and gallantry. Because spy catching came to resemble actual military activity it gave meaning and value to individuals otherwise detached from the war effort, while the opportunity to engage the enemy served to excite and distract from more pressing concerns. Most importantly, spy catching served to re-establish masculine identities in line with notions of patriotism and courage and solidify the position and importance of unenlisted men to the war effort. The way in which people described their interactions with suspected spies suggests that these encounters were thrilling rather than debilitating, and that most attempts to thwart this deadly foe were generated by a desire for excitement and adventure, rather than because of uncontrollable hysteria.

Becoming the hero

Because historians have focused so much on the relationship between spy novels and popular fears, the significance of fragile masculinity to the perpetuation of spy phobias has gone somewhat unnoticed. Yet representations of patriotism, glory and honour – all of which shaped experiences of spy fever – were themselves fashioned from assumptions regarding appropriate roles for men and women.[6] The analysis of spy scares carried out in Chapter 2 highlights a hitherto neglected aspect of the peril. Of the 144 incidents examined, eighty-five originated with Territorial soldiers, boy scouts or police constables, thirteen were initiated by concerned civilians (of which at least five were men), while forty-six reports did not explicitly state who originated the claim. A conservative estimate, therefore, is that men instigated at least two-thirds of these reported spy scares. Equally significant, though, is the gender of those suspected. Of the 193 suspects, 165 of them were male and only 13 were described as female.[7] Despite a few exceptions, the threat of female spies was often overlooked or diminished during the First World War because women were often reckoned to be somehow unsuited to clandestine work.[8] In any case, the overwhelming proportion of spy scares seem to have involved men asserting their authority over other men deemed inferior or threatening.[9] Since masculine identities had long been formed around heroism and military participation, it is unsurprising that these concepts aroused wartime emotions. In order to understand why individuals became fixated on the threat of German spies, the creation of Edwardian masculinity, and in particular how this appeared in espionage literature, needs examining.

Ideas of manliness during the Edwardian period largely derived from images of imperial adventure and military endeavour. Throughout the nineteenth century the most frequent depiction of idealized masculinity had been the imperial soldier hero.[10] Since colonialism primarily served the political and social elite, continued popular support for the British empire required the cultivation of imperial identities that appealed to the lower classes. Masculine culture thus sought to romanticize the adventurer and soldier tasked with exploring and defending the frontiers of empire.[11] This characterization of the imperial soldier hero focused on his endurance, adaptability, courage and unrelenting service to his country.[12] This 'pleasure culture of war', as Michael Dawson has termed it, promoted an intense fascination and excitement among men and had a significant impact upon their future identities as well as nationalist policies. As such, heroic and romantic representations of conflict became essential to the development of popular militarism, which made the prospect of war palatable and presented individual participation as an invaluable component of international struggles.[13]

The protagonist of the spy novel closely resembled the imperial soldier hero of the nineteenth century and encapsulated the ideals and qualities that he represented. Robert Baden-Powell wrote:

> To be a really effective spy, a man has to be endowed with a strong spirit of self-sacrifice, courage, and self-control, with the power of acting a part, quick at observation and deduction, and blessed with good health and a nerve of exceptional quality.[14]

The historian David Stafford argues that fictional spy catchers were 'scrupulous, dutiful, fair, and loyal to country, family, and God. He was a man of the right social class and with the correct education carrying out his duty to his country regardless of cost or sacrifice.' He was, in short, the ideal gentleman. As an incorruptible force in the fight against internal and external threats his distinctive 'Britishness' separated him from foreign adversaries.[15] More than the imperial soldier or adventurer, though, the amateur spy catcher offered a glimpse into an otherwise secret world of international intrigue and clandestine operations.[16] Placing the familiar military hero into the unfamiliar context of international diplomacy offered stability in an ever-changing world and reassured the reader of Britain's position within it. Replicating popular Victorian heroes also alluded to the endurance of British masculine identities despite the challenges that emerged following the turn of the century. Although inexperienced, the central male protagonist always led Britain through increasingly complex global tensions and confirmed that national prosperity would continue to thrive through individual enterprise.[17]

Central to the success of espionage novels was the amateur sleuth or accidental spy who stumbled across a malevolent foreign plot. Armed with little more than his wits and ingenuity, he eventually prevailed against a wretched and more equipped foe. Le Queux stressed that spy catching was thus the ultimate challenge for it required both physical strength and intellectual reasoning in equal measure.[18] In contrast to the protagonist was the professional spy in the employ of foreign powers. In *The German Spy System from Within* (1914), Le Queux (this time writing under the pseudonym Lionel James and falsely claiming to be an ex-intelligence officer) described espionage as a 'despicable business. Your perfect spy is a man of criminal impulse, a moral pervert of sorts.'[19] Before 1914 Britain's fictional spies could justify their clandestine exploits because they remained, for the most part, amateur adventurers.[20] Although professional espionage work was often thought of as incompatible with traditional British values prior to 1914, following the outbreak of war it became increasingly acceptable for protagonists to be engaged in this work.[21] In Escott Lynn's *In Khaki for the King* (1915), Vivian, an ingenious British agent operating in Germany, repeatedly outwits enemy soldiers, manages to escape from foreign lands, warns of dastardly plots and takes up a commission in the Belgian army. However, after Vivian is given the opportunity to meet the enemy on the battlefield, the vulgarity of espionage is juxtaposed with the honour of conventional combat. Upon commissioning into the Belgian army,

Vivian remarked: 'Thank goodness! I can now throw off this disguise, and can meet these Germans as I've always longed to, in the field, face to face, and with a good sword in my hand.'[22] The professionalism, and thus depravity, of Germany's spies nicely juxtaposed with Britain's intuitive amateur investigators, whose ingenuity repeatedly thwarted Germany's military proficiency and served as an ideal for British men to aspire to.

The construction of the British spy catcher proved indispensable to individuals on the Home Front. Because 'most people viewed the war through the lens of popular culture', themes of civilian heroics and amateur espionage played an important role in shaping people's perceptions of their own purpose and value during the war.[23] An example of how popular culture formed this association can be found in *The Man Who Stayed at Home*. Inspired by their own frustrations after being denied entry into the military, the authors wrote the play with the explicit intentions to demonstrate that 'diplomacy and espionage are amusing recreations for men at home.'[24] First performed in 1914, the play celebrated the sacrifice and bravery of ordinary citizens and became one of the most successful espionage thrillers of the First World War.[25] Although the main protagonist, Christopher Brent, is a composed and fearless character, he is repeatedly berated for his apparent unwillingness to enlist. It soon transpires that he is secretly working for British intelligence and through his creativity and astuteness foils a network of spies and prevents German U-boats operating along the British coast. As a dashing figure Brent captures the interest of Molly early on, but her infatuation is met with indignation from her father who considers Brent a coward. After it becomes clear Brent was actually a hero, because of his espionage work, Molly is able to reaffirm her admiration and disparages her father's earlier derision: 'And that's the man we all sneered at because he stayed at home.'[26]

The depiction of masculinity ingrained throughout the espionage genre proved particularly useful following the onset of war. That men instigated the majority of spy scares in August 1914 insinuates that latent male insecurities were becoming more pronounced. Indeed, gender historians frequently indicate that masculine identities grew increasingly fragile during the conflict.[27] Because combat was seen as an intrinsically male endeavour, the Home Front became a distinctly feminine space and this diminished the status of men not in khaki.[28] To compensate, chauvinistic demonstrations of masculinity became synonymous with national security, ostensibly making it vital to the war effort.[29] Less than a fortnight after war was declared, *John Bull* professed the importance of virility to Britain's struggle:

> We hear the call of the bugle and the beating of the drum and the tramping of the troops ... Let every Briton, therefore, gird his armour. It is not necessary to be a soldier – but it is necessary to be a MAN. There is a mental armour and a moral armour – more enduring than steel. Gird it on.[30]

Owing to the gendering of combat, as well as the intense pressure on men to enlist, the war threatened to subordinate the importance of non-military men.[31] Through images like the 'Rape of Belgium', German aggression was specifically shown to target women and children, which amplified the necessity of male volunteerism.[32] The palpable degree of war enthusiasm in Britain and Germany left men in both countries with a deep-seated desire to take part and instilled a sense of guilt among those not able or willing to contribute.[33] For Alfred Tufnell Robinson, a retired British colonel, the compulsion to serve was so great that he ended his own life as he felt unable to 'do anything good' for his country and feared becoming nothing more than 'an additional mouth to feed'.[34] In a similar but less extreme vein, Percy Ward regularly struggled with the anxiety caused by his civilian status. During his final year at King's College London he repeatedly deliberated on whether to join the army or not and then had a 'nervous breakdown' after choosing not to enlist.[35]

For many men facing similar difficulties, taking deliberate steps against the enemy within assuaged feelings of inertia. Even Basil Thomson acknowledged that spy phobias were most acute among those 'who were doing nothing in particular' for the war effort.[36] Because of the challenges facing masculinity, Laura Ugolini argues that male civilians made considerable efforts to bridge the gap between themselves and the front line to avoid being relegated, at least figuratively, to subordinate 'non-men'.[37] Despite their civilian status, private vigilance and surveillance provided an activity for men on the Home Front to maintain an emotional connection to the war. Because of the links made between the amateur spy catcher and contemporary ideas about masculinity and military service, individuals could overlook their physical separation from the battlefront by confronting a secret enemy at home.[38] It was for this reason that one campaign ran by the Anti-German League, notable for its extreme prejudicial beliefs and propagation of the German spy menace,[39] declared, 'If you cannot join the Army, join the Anti-German League' to help protect the nation from the greatest threat it has ever faced and eradicate the German spies who were, they claimed, 'scattered all over the universe'.[40]

The spy peril was perfectly engineered to provide satisfaction and meaning to civilians not otherwise engaged in the war effort. In October 1914 the *Globe* published a letter advocating the formation of local committees to monitor espionage activities in 'every town throughout England'. These committees would, it was claimed, provide many men, specifically 'civilians and old soldiers', with an opportunity to serve their country.[41] Another letter proposed the creation of a 'Royal Corps of Spy Hunters' to destroy the German menace.[42] Thus, while the military value of spy hunting was widely proclaimed, the responsibility was often explicitly given to male civilians. In one of his allegedly factual treatises on German espionage in Britain published in 1915, William Le Queux wrote:

> Nothing is too large, or too small, for the net of German espionage; no agent can be too highly, or too lowly, placed ... Never let it be forgotten that an apparently trivial incident may be the key for which the spy is patiently seeking, and that even a seemingly baseless rumour transmitted by the humble German, as the result of eavesdropping during his employment, may set the master brain at work upon some matter of overwhelming importance.[43]

While the anti-alien tones are clear here, as is the exaggerated scale of German espionage, the burden of responsibility to prevent even the most trivial of activities is placed firmly upon the individual because even the smallest intrigues, according to Le Queux, could prove invaluable to the German war effort. Because members of the public became duty bound to investigate and root out the spy menace, emulating popular depictions of heroic and masculine endeavour became useful ways to maintain positive roles for men on the Home Front.[44]

The editor of the *Globe*, a paper known for its jingoism and radical conservatism, frequently called upon readers to report observations of German espionage so that the government could finally appreciate the scale and significance of the danger. It was instructed that letters be sent in envelopes marked 'confidential', thus giving the impression that people combatting the spy peril were somehow imperative to the nation's security.[45] The editor responded with an announcement that the information provided had been conveyed to the military authorities and had rendered 'valuable service in securing the arrest of suspicious aliens'.[46] This sense of importance was undoubtedly felt among those reacting to the alleged danger. Sir Richard Pennefather, a retired civil servant living in Essex, appeared rather pleased with himself after he claimed to have caught a spy,[47] while a newly appointed special constable became a local hero in Shepton Mallet after apprehending his first 'spy'.[48] Facing charges of drunkenness and assault after shouting abuse and attempting to stab a man along Victoria Embankment, Patrick Kerr pleaded to the magistrate that 'I thought I was doing something for my country. I thought he was a spy'.[49]

Male adolescents were particularly keen to engage with this peril because of the heroism that spy hunting afforded them.[50] For Augustus and Arthur Alexander, two brothers who had been indoctrinated into the importance of military service, the war offered an opportunity to demonstrate greatness. Throughout the war Augustus's diary documented numerous stories describing the sort of military bravado that he aspired to. Capturing a potential spy became an important part of this narrative:

> I heard that an officer at Aldershot went to a German hairdresser to have his hair cut, and began talking about the war, and the German began insulting the British. Then the Officer got suspicious and thought he would investigate, and burst a door open, and found 6 other Germans with rifles and maps of Aldershot on a table in front of them, they were all immediately arrested and shot.[51]

Augustus's fascination with stories of officers arresting duplicitous German spies reinforced his perception of the innate courage and righteousness of British servicemen.[52] Although this sentiment might be expected in children brought up on enthralling tales of military heroism, men of all ages went to extreme lengths to achieve the heroism that they believe spy catching afforded them.[53] One man was so desperate for such accolades that he fabricated a story about chasing a spy near Dover while under enemy fire. Unfortunately for the would-be hero, he was proven to be a liar and was prosecuted under the Defence of the Realm Act for spreading false information.[54]

William Freeland Waddell's *The Patriot and the Spies*, published in 1915, perfectly captures the importance of spy hunting to wartime masculinity. Written as a parody of the increasingly popular custom of spy hunting as well as xenophobia more generally, *The Patriot and the Spies* strongly indicates that these attitudes and behaviours were primarily designed to allay the guilt and shame felt by civilians unable or unwilling to engage the enemy directly. Wardell tells the story of a man named Dugald MacBitter (a rather obvious play on words) who resided in a fictional town on the west coast of Scotland called Drumlie. As a melodramatic and satirical rendition of overzealous patriots, it ridicules the stupidity and recklessness of amateur spy catchers. Through a series of increasingly absurd exploits, Dugald faces the trials and tribulations of an amateur spy catcher. His initial effort focused on capturing a foreign visitor called Gecherstein. After witnessing Gecherstein reading a newspaper, Dugald thought that it was 'a clear case o' espionage, if ever there was ane'. Unbeknown to Dugald, Gecherstein was really a local man named Geraldson who had lived in Drumlie in his youth.[55] Adamant that a 'successful capture would lead, if not to recognition by the War Office, at least to increased importance in Drumlie', Dugald continued in his quest:

> Armed with binoculars, Dugald marched with firm step to the shore, and trained them on some curious object out at sea. 'I'm richt!' he ejaculated, with great fervour. 'It's jist whit I thocht – a mine, an' nae mistak'. I could wager ma lugs on't.'[56]

However, despite courageously towing the explosive back to shore in front of a gathering crowd, he fails to secure the adoration of the town as the object turns out to be nothing more than a fallen tree and Dugald is humiliated.[57]

Owing to his frenzied and incongruous search for spies, Dugald is repeatedly disgraced and shown to be a liability. After being approached by a man named Diddle, supposedly a like-minded patriot equally incensed by the refusal to take the internal threat seriously, Dugald readily discloses the deprived state of local defences. After Dugald shows Diddle Drumlie harbour, informs him of the number and location of Territorials in the area, points him to the most suitable place for landing an invading force and confesses that a Royal Navy vessel had never visited the region, Diddle departs. Dugald is then shocked to discover a note that had fallen from Diddle's pocket. Unable to read the foreign language with which it was written, he took the message to Dr Whitlow who translated it for him:

ARMY SECRET SERVICE, BERLIN.
    HERR VON GREBERSTEIN, – Code 1193. Immediate. Ascertain particulars of coast at Drumlie, and all particulars, as usual. To save time and to obtain accurate information, get in touch with a native. You know the rest. Last enclosure serviceable. Remittance enclosed herewith. All well with the fatherland. Kaiser jubilant on account of the war. God bless him! – FUNKLESTEIN.

'Well, well,' said the doctor, half amused, 'all we can say is he has "diddled" you, Dugald, most completely.'[58] In response, the disgraced Dugald becomes determined to catch Diddle/Greberstein and sets out to reconnoitre the nearby Windymoor Territorial camp following reports of a man fitting his description staying nearby. During Dugald's investigation, however, a nervous sentry stops and searches him. In a final touch of irony, the sentry detains Dugald and finds Greberstein's note in his pocket. Dugald is then himself arrested as a German spy.[59]

Although primarily a satirical exposition, and despite Dugald's eventual success in capturing Greberstein and uncovering a network of German spies in Drumlie, *The Patriot and the Spies* reflects contemporary perceptions of masculinity and military participation. Before the war, Dugald was seldom aggressive but became insular and intolerant as the war dragged on.[60] But the impetus behind Dugald's quest to discover German spies in his remote little town was palpably clear:

A man was 'nae patriot ava' unless he could pass with ease from the pacific mood to a belligerent one.

'I'll let them see,' was his oft-repeated remark, 'that I'm at least willin' an' ready tae souse the Germans, supposing; they were as atrocious an' wily as the deil himsel'.'

Despite suffering from various disabilities preventing him from joining the colours, Dugald desperately sought to prove his worthiness and support his country:

'A patriot canna remain inactive. I'm as guid the day as the day I first met ye. Ower auld at forty! Let them spin that theory try Dugald MacBitter. I'll mak' them change their minds. If I had been at the front there wad hae been nae fall o' Namur. I hae a plan.'

'Ma plan will be usefu' at home. Ye ken, Janet [Dugald's wife], there's German spies aboot, an' ma plan is tae collar some o' them. Will that no aye be helpin' the country?'[61]

As a satirical commentary on contemporary culture, Dugald's belligerence reflects the type of remorse many men felt because of their civilian status, which fashioned a desire to combat an enemy within. Dugald's esteem for soldiering was sharply juxtaposed with feminine passivity. Whereas news of the front only stimulated Dugald's desire to eradicate the internal threat, Janet, Dugald's wife, is distressed by the thought of death: 'I dinna see hoo you men can tak' sich delight in sheddin' bluid … War's no a thing tae mak' sport o'', she pronounced.[62] Because of the close association between contemporary notions of masculinity and military participation, the importance of non-combatant males finding additional ways to reassert their masculinity became crucial.

Although historians are right to suggest popular spy fears emerged, in part, as a consequence of popular culture, individual fears did not merely result from a naïve inability to separate fact from fiction. The consumption of popular culture and its portrayal of amateur spy catchers stimulated belligerence among many non-combatants because replicating the heroics found in spy fiction offered emotional sustenance. Rather than associate spy fever simply with irrational thought, a burgeoning xenophobia or a collective gullibility, the *Daily Herald* recognized the significance of spy hunting in moderating civilian guilt. It claimed that 'every nation suffers in some degree in wartime from spy-fever' but insisted that there was a fathomable reason:

> The soldiers who are at the front work off the passions of war in action. Their hatred of the enemy, if they feel any, is blown away with the smoke of their rifles. It is the non-combatant at home who nurses his wrath, and for lack of a healthy vent for it, turns to brooding on spies and inventing conspiracies.[63]

Since counter-espionage seemingly offered an opportunity to confront the enemy, containing the internal threat legitimized the presence of male civilians on the Home Front and alleviated the guilt caused by their non-combatant status. For many people, then, spy phobias reflected an anxiety borne out of gendered identities being in a state of flux, which threatened the status of non-military men. To compensate, overly chauvinistic civilians disillusioned or ashamed of their passive existence found gratification through emulating the celebrated heroics of espionage fiction. Testimony to this practice was the ridicule that these individuals faced for their hypocrisy in avoiding actual military service:

> Eh, Jack, but we'd some sport on Sat'day night!
> You never 'eard of it? Why, where was you?
> We said we'd 'ad enough of these 'ere spies:
> Pretending to be English – English wives,
> And kiddies speakin' English, and all that:
> But reely 'Uns – 'a menace to the state' –
> 'The enemy in our midst' – that's what they are
> So out we goes, some fifty chaps or more,
> And crowds comes with us, just to see the fun.
> Ah, fun it was, and make no mistake. The brutes!
> Spy-'untin' 's better sport and safer, too
> I tell yer, Jack, you missed a proper treat.
> Next time, it's on I'll come and … What?
> What's that?
> You've been and gone and 'listed? Lord deliver us![64]

Although pointing out the irony in such chauvinism epitomizes the alienation many overzealous patriots faced in certain communities, it nonetheless demonstrates the correlation between spy phobias and war service. While espionage fiction enabled fears of spies and saboteurs because it defined the parameters and characteristics of the threat, it also shaped the way in which certain individuals perceived the unfamiliar wartime context surrounding them. Many men felt compelled to combat the enemy within, not necessarily because they unequivocally accepted the hyperbole surrounding the spy peril but because for certain individuals, a heightened sense of national loyalty demanded it.

The sport of spying

Having established a framework in which people could perceive the threat as well as contemplate their own role in combatting it, it becomes easier to appreciate how individuals may have felt when responding to the spy peril. However, attributing suspicion and paranoia to a desire for recognition and acclaim, rather than an inability to distinguish fact from fiction, does not overturn the centrality of fear in these encounters. The need to conform to prevailing masculine stereotypes and participate in spy hunts was as much driven by a need to dispel one's own fear of obscurity and inadequacy, for instance.[65] But as individuals' correspondence shows, fears of espionage were frequently likened to a sporting contest, complete with feelings of pride, joy and inclusion. The range of feelings on display within these accounts suggests that a contrasting emotional style existed besides the one identified in the previous chapter. By uncovering the rationale behind people's willingness to adopt the customs promoted in the rhetoric and warnings surrounding the spy peril, the following section can further differentiate between espionage phobias and mental disorder.

Despite the prevalence of sensational spy stories, the reality of intelligence work is often quite different and typically involves mundane office work rather than dramatic chases or armed confrontations. In any case, the latter most often influences how people perceive espionage. Winston Churchill, for instance, deliberately conflated fiction with reality while reflecting on the environment of 'spy mania' during the First World War:

> In the higher ranges of Secret Service work the actual facts in many cases were in every respect equal to the most fantastic inventions of romance or melodrama. Tangle within tangle, plot and counter-plot, ruse and treachery, cross and double-cross, true agent, false agent, double agent, gold and steel, the bomb, the dagger and the firing party were interwoven in many a texture so intricate as to be incredible and yet true.[66]

Practitioners also routinely likened the reality of espionage to fictional spy stories. In a lecture on intelligence work given to army officers, Count (Lord Edward) Gleichen, Assistant Director of Military Operations and Intelligence between 1907 and 1911, explicitly called upon his students to familiarize themselves with fictional detective novels and espionage stories to acquire the necessary skills for spying.[67] Even Vernon Kell presented intelligence gathering as a most exciting chase, and Mansfield Cumming, the first head of the Secret Intelligence Service, or MI6, described espionage as an amusing 'capital sport'.[68]

This 'Sport of Spying', as Baden-Powell referred to it, was well established before the First World War and widely shaped perceptions of espionage work.[69]

Edwardian newspapers routinely likened warfare to a sport or game like chess or hunting, and spying was no exception. While the complexity of international intrigue required a keen intellect, covert operations were seen as inherently dangerous and thus exhilarating.[70] Despite the apparent hysteria commonly associated with spy fever, sport brings opportunity, pleasure and excitement; for those emulating the amateur heroics of espionage fiction, spy catching appeared to offer similar rewards. In a letter written to his mother in August 1914, for instance, Private Joss used the spy peril to frame his enthusiasm at the prospect of going to war. Figure 4.1 shows a self-portrait Joss made of him chasing a German 'spy'. Since he drew the spy wearing a traditional Prussian Pickelhaube, Joss had very little idea of what a spy looked like, but the expression on his face as he chases the suspect illustrates the satisfaction and excitement he believed would be attained through such endeavour. Owing to his fascination with the murky world of secret agents Joss would later go on to participate in a 'German hunt' that he claimed caused a riot in Winchester.[71]

Joss was not the only soldier eager to catch a German spy. Much like Territorials in Britain, soldiers in the British Expeditionary Force (BEF) received numerous warnings about spies lurking behind the front line. Whereas orders regarding spies on the Home Front seem to have abated quite quickly after the period of

Figure 4.1 Sketch by Private Joss of himself chasing a 'German spy'.
Joss made the sketch in August 1914 while serving with the Honourable Artillery Company. C. G. W. Joss Papers, Letter dated 10 August 1914.

crisis waned, warnings of espionage on the Western Front contained a much more explicit threat and continued long after the danger dwindled at home. Almost as soon as the BEF arrived in France troops were warned that enemy spies were numerous: 'They may disguise themselves as French or Belgian Offices, soldiers, gendarmes, policemen, priests etc. the only safe rule therefore is to hold no conversation on military matters with any person until his identity is established.'[72] Troops were instructed to 'detain any suspicious character until he can be interrogated by an officer', and it was intimated that 'every inhabitant of the villages in our area should be regarded as a potential spy and treated as such.'[73] Private Leonard Smith, of the 2/4 Battalion of the Queen's (Royal West Surrey) Regiment, was instructed that 'spies are everywhere and the greatest caution is necessary to prevent them from obtaining information which might easily cause the loss of many English lives.'[74] If that was not enough to incite paranoia, sentries were given a license to enact extreme responses to potential spies; one order reminded troops that 'it is better to cause inconvenience to an number of innocent persons than let one spy escape.'[75] In reality, British commanders vastly overstated the significance and scale of German espionage along the British front. After the declaration of war, Sektion IIIb, responsible for German army intelligence, struggled to dispatch new agents to France or contact existing agents in the field,[76] but this did not stop soldiers believing that an army of secret agents had penetrated their lines and were surreptitiously spying for the enemy.[77]

There are many reasons why men in the BEF expressed fears of German espionage. Chris Kempshall argues that spy phobias reflected a 'circumstantial paranoia' driven by the soldiers' cultural isolation while serving at the front as well as the ongoing uncertainty about the prosecution of the war.[78] For this reason, spy catching proved thrilling as a distraction from the monotony and insecurity of trench life.[79] Private Reginald Watts, who served behind the front line, claimed that a spy tried to sneak into his building to accentuate the degree of excitement and significance to an otherwise mundane job.[80] Even being apprehended as a spy could bring excitement that provided an escape from the boredom often encountered at the front.[81] But for soldiers in the line of fire, the spy peril also seems to have helped them make sense of what was going on around them as well as offer a distraction from the precariousness of their situation. While working in the 4th Division's Ammunition Column around the town of Ermenonville in September 1914, Private Percival Cobb wrote in his diary how he had had a 'very memorable day indeed which no-one will ever forget. All men except drivers were called up with rifles and ammunition. Paraded and told off in sections to scout out in village for spies.'[82] His unit's war diary, however, records a rather different encounter:

Marched for Baron. Passed Néry where the cavalry (2nd Dragoons) and 'L' RHA were bivouacked, and heard firing shortly after. Arrived Baron. All available gunners turned out with rifles to act as infantry to repel and expected attack. Left 1st section at Baron and marched remainder of column to Montagny. About 300 Uhlans and 4 guns debouched from the woods ¾ mile north of Montagny and went towards Ermenonville. All gunners turned out and took up position north of camp. A few shots fired at German scouts and one prisoner captured by a staff officer (Lt K) in motor car.

Given that 300 Uhlans stood between him and the frontline infantry battalions at Baron, Cobb was facing a threat much greater than a few spies. By confusing such a perilous situation with an extraordinary, but relatively benign, exploit mirroring popular fiction, Cobb may have downplayed the tangible danger to avoid facing the reality of the conflict. Comprehending the true horror of modern war was perhaps too much for some to grapple with, and so comprehending it through familiar stereotypes lessened their struggle.[83]

The fact that Cobb chose to describe his early encounter with the enemy by linking it with German espionage also suggests that spies were considered as the ultimate adversary, and that facing them was a demonstration of one's courage and strength. As well as providing distraction, from both the tediousness and volatility of warfare in 1914, the spy peril also provided a means of finding excitement and adventure in frontline service. Brigadier-General John Charteris, Haig's Chief of Intelligence at GHQ from 1915, placed a high value on spy hunting because it provided a sense of exhilaration like no other:

> The prevailing ailment is spy-fever. Everyone sees a spy in every un-uniformed human being, and a spy-signal in every inanimate feature of the landscape. So long as we are fighting on French soil, there is not much chance of successful German spying. But when we get to Germany it will be different, and suspicion is a healthy atmosphere to encourage against that time, so when the spy tales come to me, as most of them do, however ridiculous they are, I do not pour too much cold water on them – indeed, yesterday we had a pleasant interlude in our monotony. Some German spies were reported to be hiding in some caves in a wood near our head-quarters, so we organized a hunt and drove the woods. It proved a blank, of course, but it was quite amusing and greatly encouraged our amateur Sherlock Holmeses.[84]

Rather than characterizing such behaviour as hysterical delusions, Charteris's belief that spy scares amounted to a form of sport aligned with much of the fictional portrayals of espionage appearing during this period.[85] Thus, while spy phobias have often been interpreted through the pessimism and xenophobia of invasion literature, the excitement and sense of sportsmanship evident in romanticized depictions of the 'great game' had an equally profound impact on how people experienced spy fever.

Nowhere was this more evident that among soldiers in the BEF. For them, spying was not an abstract danger threatening the nation but something each and every soldier had to contend with.[86] Soldiers became duty-bound to actively hunt for spies, and when they wrote about these experiences, they commonly expressed their immense pride at capturing a suspected spy. Within five days of disembarking in France, Private Alfred Thurlow, a bandsman in the Lincolnshire

Regiment, boasted that he had apprehended two German spies in a café before even arriving at the front.[87] Similarly, Lieutenant Arthur Francis Smith, a former Etonian who had commissioned into the Coldstream Guards in 1910, helped catch a spy thought to be concealing carrier pigeons. Smith claimed that the spy was subsequently shot after being interrogated at HQ, thereby affirming the significance of his actions.[88] For some, though, it was more than duty. Private Harding claimed to have witnessed the capture of a spy while serving with the Royal Army Medical Corps:

> At the village a spy was caught up in the church tower signalling by means of the bell we soon had him out and finished him off in the street, no mercy was given, the men barbarous to-wards spys [*sic*].[89]

While Harding's account shows that spies could be suspected anywhere – church bells are hardly a covert form of communication – the fact that the spy was so violently 'finished off' not only indicates that troops were keen to impede German espionage, but he seems almost proud of the incident, implying that catching a spy was like a trophy hunt of sorts.[90]

As a chaplain serving in the 1st Canadian Division, Canon Frederick George Scott thought that 'everyone had a bad attack of spy-fever' in France. After encountering a colonial officer 'who pronounced his "rs" in the back of his throat', Scott suspected the man was a spy and reported his concerns to a nearby sentry. Within a matter of seconds 'eager Canadians with fixed bayonets came out of the building and surrounded the suspicious officer. Canadians were always ready for a bit of sport', clamed Scott. But relevance and meaning could also be found through such excitement. Upon detaining the suspect, Scott described the incident as a 'delightfully weird experience' and wrote that 'it seemed to me that the whole war might depend on our capturing the spy'.[91] Similarly, Lieutenant Kenneth Stuart Hall commented on his disappointment at not catching a spy while out 'hunting' but nevertheless described it as a remarkably exciting affair. He later wrote how spies 'are very good fun and much safer sport than strafing'.[92] Far from a unique analysis, then, Charteris's observation about spy hunting reflects how men in the trenches often comprehended the spy peril. To them, catching spies imitated the trials and tribulations of the most intense and titillating form of sport, and so apprehending one of Germany's secret agents clearly demonstrated one's virility and soldierly bravado.

In a somewhat candid letter George Fear described his engagement with a German spy in single combat. Having been stopped by the 'spy' and dispossessed of his rifle, the assailant then attempted to commandeer his horse:

> He pointed a revolver at me and I was taken unawares so I told him he could take the horse but let me have the rifle. He said he wanted the lot so I said take it. I got off the horse and stepped away from him. He went to get up on the horse so as he did, I had a little friend around my waist, under my overcoat. That was a revolver. So as he got into the saddle I put two rounds into him.[93]

By encountering this 'spy', Fear was able to demonstrate his ingenuity as a warrior. Overcoming this type of enemy required a level of cunning and audacity not necessary against a regular soldier. Defeating a spy not only confirmed his manliness and bravery, but it also proved his identity as a soldier and the strength of his valour:

> I searched him and found a lot of papers on him and it was a lot of plans that he had taken from our guns. I got a lot of praise for that. I was not a bit afraid when he said he would shoot me but of course if I had said no you shan't have my horse, I expect I could have said goodbye … I can account for 16 dead Germans now and hope to account for more yet.[94]

Given that First World War soldiers, the very personification of contemporary notions of masculinity, conveyed ideas of military service and courage through mimicking spy fiction is a testament to the cultural impact of both adventure novels and espionage literature during this period.[95] That men on the Home Front, even more anxious to prove their value and manliness than soldiers in the BEF, also used sensationalized stories of secret agents to demonstrate their manliness is hardly surprising.

In the first outing of John Buchan's Richard Hannay in *The Thirty-Nine Steps* (1915), amateur spy catching was shown to be an effective antidote to the boredom encountered on the Home Front, and many people viewed the outbreak of a spy peril as an opportunity to act out some of their fantasies.[96] Winston Churchill, as First Lord of the Admiralty, gave a vivid description of how he along with Admiral Oliver, the Director of Naval Intelligence, went searching for German spies in September 1914. After arming themselves with pistols Churchill and Oliver stormed a castle in the Scottish Highland thought to be communicating the location of the British Grand Fleet to enemy forces nearby. As they approached the spies' stronghold, Churchill noted how 'suspicion and curiosity went hand in hand, and the excitement of adventure spurred them both'.[97] Indeed, many men on the Home Front revelled in the opportunity to search for spies. Horace Joseph heard one Territorial boasting about killing a spy, supposedly in possession of explosives, while he guarded nearby haystacks – a target of undisputable significance to the German military.[98] Another sentry, this time claiming to be in possession of 'secret documents', supposedly found it necessary to sleep with a loaded revolver just in case the Germans attacked him in the night.[99] Having presumably spent too much time consuming popular fiction, one officer responsible for investigating illicit signalling wrote to the War Office because he feared enemy agents were on to him and had started to follow him.[100] While the latter may have been slightly paranoid, the majority seem to have been motivated more by a desire for entertainment and excitement, because lived experiences of the spy peril distracted people from certain realities and amplified one's sense of importance.[101] Adopting the venerated persona of the amateur spy catcher not only imitated the heroic deeds of popular literature and encapsulated soldierly ideals but, as Charteris's enthusiasm for catching spies indicates, it also demonstrated notions of manliness and ingenuity.[102]

Figure 4.2 Photos of mock captures and executions.
The photo of soldiers in front of a tent shows a sentry post at Redbridge. The soldiers are from E Company, 7th Battalion, the King's Regiment, who were stationed there between 2 September and 8 October 1914. The photo of sailors pretending to execute a spy contains no additional details. Both photos are reproduced here courtesy of Dr Nicholas Hiley who holds the originals in his personal collection.

Although the War Office encouraged much of the interest in espionage among Territorial soldiers, this was exacerbated by the soldiers' readiness to imitate popular fiction. While some were doubtless terrified of facing the enemy, though few would have likely admitted as much, the need to prove one's value through thrilling endeavour spurred them on to engage the German spy menace. Following the outbreak of war, Edward Heron-Allen was involved in establishing the Sussex Volunteers that would defend the south coast in the event of a German invasion and, as a commissioner in the Boy Scouts, had also overseen their efforts to root out German spies.[103] With his first-hand knowledge of those responsible for home defence, Heron-Allen remarked in August 1914 that 'spy-hunting promises to be one of the popular sports this autumn'.[104] Heron-Allen's prophecy proved accurate and the sport of spying soon became a popular activity for soldiers on the Home Front otherwise unable to engage the enemy. While some found the novelty of sentry duty and guarding vulnerable points enough to generate excitement,[105] for people like Richard Orlebar, serving in the Bedfordshire Regiment in Felixstowe in December 1914, the spy peril intensified their sense of exhilaration:

> Last night I was on guard at the 'Naval Oil Tanks', and had a great spy hunt. We drew blank but we have managed to mark down his house and incidentally we fancy we have spotted our man, and he knows nothing at all about it. He is one of these coast signallers and was spotted by H.M.S. *Loyal* signalling while a cruiser was going out of harbour. A landing party came and woke me up and together we went out in search but owing to the awful night we were unable to get anything more than a general direction. We ended up our evening outside a house which we eventually proved to be the house in question … We eventually proved ourselves right because just as day was drawing my sergeant saw signals from the house we surrounded, 10 minutes later the destroyer patrol left the harbour.[106]

By adopting the role of the amateur sleuth, Territorials on sentry duty were able to turn a relatively mundane and often insignificant activity into an exciting pursuit of real importance. Just like soldiers in the BEF, Territorial soldiers responsible for the majority of spy scares in Britain were motivated not by hysteria or manic delusions but by their desire for approval, satisfaction and commendation.

For special constables filling the ranks of the constabularies bereft of officers sent to the front, the excitement offered by spy hunting was equally rousing. As men on the Home Front, special constables likewise sought an emotional connection to the war. To overcome this insecurity one inspector remarked that special constables could think of themselves as soldiers employed in an equally patriotic occupation, but spy catching in particular helped in this regard. In October 1914, for example, Vernon Kell ordered local police to investigate a Danish Butter Syndicate based in south-west London. Matching Kell's own paranoia, two detective inspectors, a divisional detective inspector and a superintendent were on the search alongside a sergeant major and two gunners from Woolwich Arsenal. Their investigation, of course, proved fruitless. But this episode nevertheless highlights the seriousness with which local authorities treated the spy threat. But the involvement of so many officers also suggests that they took a personal interest in espionage for the opportunity and excitement of facing the enemy directly.[107] Indeed, the acting chief constable of Gloucestershire, Maynard Willoughby Colchester-Wemyss, expressed just that. After Colchester-Wemyss had been instructed to follow the movements of Robert Rosenthal in April 1915, he wrote about his disappointment upon learning that Rosenthal was no longer in his jurisdiction because he had become 'quite interested in it'.[108] Given the presumed dangers of spy catching, it could easily be linked with appropriate ideals regarding wartime service, and because the perceived risk was dwarfed only by the assumed rewards of catching a spy, there was much jubilation to be found in such activity. One special constable even joked that his colleagues 'would give their eyes for a German spy'.[109]

That the spy peril was considered a source of excitement can be seen in how communities often responded to spies being captured in their locale. Rumours and reports of German spies, especially early on in the war, mostly centred on success (i.e. the capture of an enemy suspected of heinous crimes) rather than alarm, and the language used to describe such events seldom conveyed fear. Instead, the press regularly depicted spy hunts as thrilling incidents designed to enthuse and engage rather than simply alarm.[110] News of a spy being captured created a buzz within the community, and excited crowds often came out to catch a glimpse of a real secret agent.[111] Incidents like the one reported in Aberdeen in September 1914 became a common spectacle during the initial months of the war:

> Cries of 'German Spy' resounded in Union Street last night shortly after nine o'clock, when a foreign looking man, handcuffed to a stalwart constable of the city police, was escorted along the thoroughfare to the central office in Lodge Walk. The east end in Union Street was crowded at the time, and as the cry spread there was a rush to get a view of the constable and his quarry. Fortunately there was no disorder, and in the absence of accurate information regarding the identity of the apprehended man, there was no hostile demonstration, and the constable experienced no difficulty in taking his captive to the police-office. On inquiry, it was learned that the apprehended man was a foreigner, but was not an enemy agent, and had been apprehended on a minor charge.[112]

Following a similar incident in Exeter the crowd there became noticeably despondent after discovering that the stranger believed to be a German spy turned out to be nothing more than an Irishman on his way to enlist.[113] That people were desperate to catch a glimpse of the infamous German spy suggests that the presence of nefarious agents made communities feel like part of the war by localizing the national effort and bringing a sense of interest with it. Because the capture of a spy resembled military success, there was much cause for a sense of triumph and joy. In many ways they served as a metaphor for Britain's eventual victory against a duplicitous foe.

Although this conception of patriotism closely aligned with existing ideas of masculinity, and despite the majority of early spy scares being conducted by males, British men were not alone in their desire to participate. Following the onset of war females felt similarly compelled to participate in a military capacity and more than 100,000 women served in various paramilitary units across Britain.[114] Members of the Women's Emergency Corps and Women's Voluntary Reserve began donning khaki uniforms and stressed their desire to defend the nation from an invasion. Most joined out of a deep sense of patriotism and, despite the economic costs, it was often seen as an opportunity to provide a sense of adventure as well as demonstrating the efficacy and courage of women.[115] For Beatrice Trefusis, the war offered a 'most thrilling experience', and she wrote in her diary about how glad she was that it was occurring during her lifetime. From March 1915, Trefusis worked in the Censor's Office's under Lieutenant Colonel George Cockerill, Director of Special Intelligence from April 1915. Confiding in her diary, she wrote:

> It is interesting and not a little exciting. All very secret, of course. You are not supposed to tell any but the necessary people that you are even working there – of course no mention of anything of the work that goes on there is allowed outside … Perhaps it would be as well not to write here anything further about it until after the war – perhaps not even then – or mention names of anyone else in it. One certainly derives lots of amusement from the work, and a certain amount of insight into the 'feeling' in various countries. And it's fun to be doing war office work.[116]

Defying the need for secrecy, Trefusis's desire to disclose her wartime activities, whether through her diary or post-war memoirs, reflects an assumption that espionage activity was deemed meaningful and crucial to the war effort. However, she seldom made accusations of illicit espionage. Although Trefusis developed private suspicions about possible German spies, she was incredibly reticent to reveal them publicly.[117] But by expressing a willingness to make sacrifices akin to their male counterparts, women were able to appropriate male versions of patriotism rather than remain passive onlookers. Although many women continued to be employed in traditional female roles, assisting the armed forces in service of their country also helped redefine their identity and establish new gender identities.[118]

***

Spying is about power. Power to dominate your enemies through a contest of deception and intrigue. For this reason the act of spying is commonly portrayed as a matter of life and death between two spies, which often serves as a metaphor for contemporary international struggles and demonstrates how individuals can shape them for the collective good. The assumed significance of covert operations combines with the implicit danger of deception to make spying an endeavour unlike any other. Even today popular representations of spying continue to accentuate the thrill of the 'great game'.

Because historians have previously claimed that spy phobias originated from a widespread paranoia induced by popular espionage fiction, the most common emotion associated with the spy peril has been terror, which also partly explains why 'fever' and 'mania' have been so widely used. But by attributing spy phobias to a desire for inclusion and a commitment to national security, it is possible to identify different feelings that may have resulted from spy fever. First, spy phobias were not simply triggered by people taking the threats contained within invasion and espionage fiction literally. Rather, spy phobias represented an assortment of anxieties and vulnerabilities. Fears of espionage were mostly transitory and relatively insignificant, but the huge cultural impact of the espionage genre shaped the way people thought about their own role and importance during such an unprecedented crisis. Because the figure of the amateur spy catcher had been established as a heroic adventurer able to overcome Britain's foes, the re-enactment of this fantasy in the real world provided a sense of meaning and excitement to individuals otherwise afraid of national decline and personal irrelevance. Spy scares thus helped assuage concerns generated by the reality of conflict and the changes that it had brought about, but it also instilled a belief that non-combatants had a valuable role to play in the nation's war effort.

Nowhere was this more important than on the Home Front. The outbreak of war had quickly challenged the existing status quo for many. The degree of uncertainty, especially in the relationship between the individual and the state, threatened to overthrow existing identities. With the outbreak of war, notions of masculinity were revised according to the rise in popular militarism. As a result, it became important for non-combatants to display feelings and behaviours that had been entwined with national security throughout the preceding decades. By adopting these conventions, civilians could form an emotional connection to the war through a perceived sense of national service. The spy peril thus afforded individuals an opportunity to become involved in the conflict, thereby making them an important facet of the war effort, despite the relative safety of the Home Front. Through this form of participation individuals fashioned a sense of agency among passive onlookers otherwise unable to shape the events around them, which served to alleviate certain fears associated with civilian guilt or masculine insecurity.

Although labels like 'spy fever' and 'spy mania' provided post-war writers a way of distancing themselves from wartime xenophobia and militarism, they do not accurately describe the nature of individuals' feelings generated in response to the First World War. Fears of German secret agents manifested in different ways and arguably reflected broader concerns that were not necessarily linked to espionage or sabotage. While the previous chapter has shown how fear created terror and suspicion, people also found excitement as they sought to rid the country of the enemy within. Expressions of fear were thus often articulated through sporting allegories or likened to adventurous pursuit, which suggests that the espionage peril served to titillate, rather than terrorize. Moreover, although anxiety is often associated with spy fever, this anxiety is invariably attributed to a sense of national peril, when in reality people seemed most anxious about their own role in this new wartime environment. To them, spy catching served to distract people from the boredom or guilt felt on the Home Front. This emotional style, in which excitement was more prominent that either terror or anguish, clearly distinguishes spy fever from a sustained and delirious paranoia. For the individual, at least, spy fever did not resemble a psychological malady.

Part III

COLLECTIVE ANXIETIES, 1914–15

Although the concept of 'spy fever' has often created an impression that individuals' fears of secret agents were akin to psychological disorder, it is much more likely, given that the majority of spy phobias seem rather benign or transient in retrospect, that most people understood 'spy fever' as way of describing a collective response to the enemy within. Public outpouring can appear excitable and frantic, even if individuals were not literally feverish. Whereas few traces of hysteria remain visible in the historical record, it remains possible that 'spy fever' was symptomatic of what modern social scientists refer to as 'mass hysteria' or 'epidemic hysteria', rather than any individual form of psychological illness.[1] Although the idea that groups of people can simultaneously suffer from abnormal illnesses born out of a shared anxiety has only emerged during the latter half of the twentieth century, episodes of mass hysteria have been identified as early as the medieval period.[2]

Much like how spy phobias reflected the unique circumstances of 1914, episodes of mass hysteria build on existing social and cultural concerns and flourish when anticipated threats intertwine with reality. In 1983, amid long-standing Arab-Israeli tensions, various rumours purported that Israel was attacking Palestinians in the West Bank with poisonous gas. No noxious substances were ever used but 947 residents in the West Bank suffered from various psychogenic complaints including fainting, headaches, abdominal pain and dizziness as a direct consequence of the alleged attacks. A similar episode occurred in Georgia in 1989 following political unrest there. Four hundred students reported symptoms of poisoning after rumours suggested that they had been exposed to toxic chemicals used to disperse an opposition rally, when in reality no such countermeasure had been employed. In the wake of the 9/11 terrorist attacks in New York and Washington, DC, anxious Americans produced more than 2,300 anthrax false alarms in the first two weeks of October 2001 alone. In one incident, a man sprayed a mysterious fluid at a Maryland subway station and thirty-five people were treated for nausea, headache and sore throats. The substance was later identified as a relatively harmless window cleaner.[3] In sum, mass hysteria is a social phenomenon in which a perceived danger or threatening scenario provokes an anxiety-induced illness that affects members of a cohesive group. The physical effects caused by this illness are typically exhibited unconsciously and have no organic foundation but can nevertheless transmit widely.[4] Symptoms can range from abdominal pain and headaches to fainting and nausea and even convulsions and pseudoseizures.[5]

According to Francois Sirois, 'diffuse outbreaks' of mass hysteria involve entire communities overwhelmed by the rapid spread of false rumours and beliefs – ostensibly like the anxieties witnessed in August 1914. Notwithstanding the frequent insinuations that popular reactions to the enemy within were hysterical, few if any documented cases describe a somatic defect or physical affliction, and so such behaviour was more likely caused by group anxiety than epidemic hysteria.[6] In cases of spy fever the abnormality was a belief that German spies were present but victims neither regarded themselves as ill nor sought medical attention, thereby distinguishing 'spy fever' from mass hysteria.[7] If we take historical claims of spy fever at face value, therefore, collective spy phobias were probably more in line with what psychiatrists have labelled 'mass delusion' rather than 'epidemic hysteria'.[8]

The question that remains, though, is how widespread was the belief that German spies had infiltrated Britain? Because the study of spy fever has been written as an offshoot of counter-espionage or anti-alienism histories, it is typically based on only fragmentary evidence. The overreliance on right-wing newspapers, which relentlessly spewed vitriolic rhetoric designed to foment popular fears, has led to various distortions in our understanding of the scale and significance of spy phobias. In one of the first histories of secret operations in Britain during the First World War, Sidney Felstead identified a severe and widespread spy fever in Britain. The number of suspicions and complaints involving alleged German spies, he claimed, were 'innumerable'.[9] Cate Haste similarly argued that 'spy mania engulfed the nation', but her assessment was based predominantly on articles published in *The Times* and *Daily Mail*.[10] In his seminal account of British spy fever David French asserts that the frequency with which images of spies appeared in the press serves as evidence that society became receptive to such rhetoric. French's analysis was similarly confined to right-wing publications.[11] While the *Daily Mail* was indeed one of the key publications associated with spy fever, and despite its relative popularity, there remained many millions of Britons who did not buy or even read it.[12]

Cataloguing the extent of spy phobias has been constrained by the difficulties of ascertaining the scale of anti-alienism more generally. Panikos Panayi's early work examining wartime Germanophobia repeatedly emphasizes the magnitude of anti-German sentiment in Britain, which he considers an extension of a widespread spy fever. He claims that the best evidence for quantifying the level of hatred towards Germany was the rate at which British men volunteered for military service.[13] Not only does this statement ignore the majority of British society, including an entire gender, it also overlooks the fact that recruitment was driven by a number of complex political and socio-economic factors and not simply driven by patriotism and idealism alone.[14] It is entirely possible that individuals could passionately support the war effort while also clinging to the liberal values that Britain claimed to represent. In any case, the rate of enlistment was enormously varied and was heavily influenced by each individual's specific circumstances.[15] Although Panayi rightly points out that the right-wing press was most active in forming anti-alienism and Germanophobia, his focus on these publications, as well as political figures from the radical right, obscures any wider perspective. Without contextualizing the extent of ideological support for the ideas espoused by radical elements in British politics, Panayi cannot sufficiently measure the significance of their rhetoric more broadly. There can be no doubt that British anti-alienism grew during the First World War, but there is a difference between passively accepting xenophobic rhetoric and explicitly transforming one's emotional state because of it.[16]

The notion that spy phobias were both prolific and influential during the First World War likely derives from the terminology used to describe the effects of the spy peril. Because spy phobias have often been described as a 'fever' that defied treatment, they are thought of as a sort of 'contagion' that spread violently throughout the population, leading to the assumption that such fears were almost endemic. However, multiple definitions of 'fever' exist. On the one hand, 'fever' relates to a 'disease characterized by an abnormally high body temperature', but it can also denote 'a state of intense nervous excitement or agitation' or 'an intense enthusiasm for or interest in a person, pastime, event, etc., typically widespread but short-lived; and obsession, a craze. Frequently with modifying word indicating the person or object of enthusiasm or interest.'[17] The lack of somatic effects evident in the historical record suggests that people seldom experienced an abnormally high temperature. The latter definition, commonly used alongside a modifying word – like 'spy', for example – seems most appropriate. Although historians have chosen to portray spy fever as a severe psychological ailment that resulted in intense physical symptoms, the limited impact on both the mind and body suggests that these experiences were more akin to a collective obsession or craze.[18]

In the early twentieth century especially, the word fever was frequently used to describe a notable rise in popular passions. 'War fever', for example, was a term given to the excited frenzy that supposedly appeared in the wake of Britain's declaration of war.[19] Under the heading, 'War Fever', the *London Evening Standard* wrote:

> The London crowd has indeed taken every possible opportunity to show its loyalty to the Crown. On Saturday afternoon when the King and Queen drove out, and again in the evening, in front of the palace, the mob gave vent to its feelings in cheering and singing patriotic songs and the 'Marseillaise'. Whitehall seemed to be the vortex of the excitement, and large crowds assembled outside the various government offices, cheering all the celebrities as they came.[20]

This tendency to label collective excitement as feverish raises important questions about 'spy fever'. First, why have historians been so preoccupied with fear and anxiety, when contemporaries were perhaps just as likely to be referring to an excited, rather than terrified, reaction? Second, the scale of war fever – or war enthusiasm, depending on how you want to term it – is not portrayed as a contagion that attacked indiscriminately and has been the subject of much historical revision, so why assume that spy phobias behaved in such a way?[21]

The following three chapters demonstrate that the term 'spy fever' is more appropriate as a concept describing the atmosphere of cultural fascination and collective excitement and anxiety generated by the spy peril. Because the spy peril served different purposes according to the context in which it was depicted, it seems likely that different feelings were felt in response to this enemy within narrative. By highlighting the plurality of emotives conveyed by the spy peril, the following chapters propose that different emotional reactions occurred in different communities, and that all of these experiences should be incorporated into our understanding of 'spy fever'.

To get a better sense of how the spy peril affected society, we must put the scaremongering of the right-wing press into a broader context, because without this perspective, grandiose claims of widespread anxiety remain unsubstantiated. In response to Barbara Rosenwein's notion of 'emotional communities', the following chapters consider the contexts in which spies featured in print to highlight the myriad of feelings that the period of spy fever represented. These findings are significant for they show that the majority of articles in the press referring to spying were not devoted to scaremongering and nor were they symptomatic of a mass hysteria. The first chapter looks specifically at *how* espionage pervaded British discourses to show that while there were undoubtedly shared concerns linked closely to the spy threat, these were not the same as the spy phobias encountered in previous chapters, nor did they reflect a shared delusion or anxiety. In fact, the inclusion of espionage in popular discourse merely provided a fashionable medium to spread old animosities. As such, Chapter 7 associates spy phobias with a particular group – or community – to further refute the historiography's penchant for portraying spy phobias as almost ubiquitous. By ascertaining the community that was most responsible for perpetuating the spy peril we can begin to understand *why* it was so prominent. Moreover, the emotions and attitudes commonly associated with spy phobias can be linked to radical idealists and separated from the mainstream of British politics. The assumed pervasiveness of spy phobias can therefore be called into question. Finally, Chapter 8 places alarm and anxiety into a broader context. It measures the frequency of alarmist rhetoric compared to those that merely reflected a cultural fascination with spying. In doing so, it uncovers *when* and *where* spy phobias were most likely to have been prolific. More importantly, it reveals that society could be captivated by intrigue and engrossed in duplicity without necessarily developing severe fears or anxieties of spies in the real world. Although spy phobias may have been pervasive in one emotional community, this does not indicate that society more broadly subscribed to the same emotional style.

Examining the collective response to the spy peril reveals a plethora of emotives that are indicative of multiple emotional experiences. Anger and hatred became particularly noticeable among radical conservatives, but in other communities with a less chauvinistic orientation, espionage was likely used to create a sense of hope or provide a means to find enjoyment. As a result, our understanding of the term 'spy fever', and how it applied to British society's reaction to the First World War, needs to be extended beyond simply fear and anxiety. 'Spy fever' is better viewed as a period of excited and anxious expectations of what the war might bring. The custom of using images of spies served a number of functions: they allowed society to explore the role of individuals in this grand contest of nations; they placated concerns by distracting audiences from genuine problems; they incited hatred against aliens for their alleged treachery and deceit; but they also encouraged hope and enjoyment through fictional exploits in which Britain consistently prevailed. It would be wrong, therefore, to assume that the spy peril resulted in a single emotional experience. At times, this atmosphere may have doubtless appeared obsessive and frenzied, but there was a mixture of emotions that were all part of society's fascination with espionage. This varied and complex emotional response is what we might term a 'spy fever'.

Chapter 5

CONCERNS ON THE HOME FRONT

During August 1914, the British public were inundated with warnings about perfidious German agents planning an attack from within. Yet beyond August 1914 there was a noticeable change in how the spy peril played out in the press. Public warnings about the dangers of German espionage gradually, and by no means consistently, became more about spreading anti-alienism than mobilizing society against an invasion. Rather than encourage feelings of mistrust against certain individuals thought to be acting suspiciously, alarmist rhetoric began overtly targeting entire demographic groups. As such, immigrants living in Britain became the principal danger facing the nation.[1] Although chauvinism and nationalism were by no means absent from the initial wave of scaremongering in August, during October and November 1914 they were dominant themes. Central to this growing prejudice was the assumption that Germans were naturally malicious and predisposed to treachery and deceit. As such, allegations and reports of espionage proved crucial in convincing society of the urgency and severity of the alien danger more broadly.[2]

Nevertheless, the role of the spy in the growth of anti-alienism during the First World War has been misunderstood. Panikos Panayi considers spy phobias as a precursor to more sinister forms of anti-alienism that culminated with complex theories of a German 'Hidden Hand' that had supposedly controlled Britain since the Middle Ages.[3] He implies that the transformation of spy phobias into more extreme forms of nationalism was a straightforward, linear progression fuelled by an intensifying hatred caused by repeated German atrocities. Describing espionage phobias as 'unsophisticated' or as a primitive form of anti-alienism, however, implies that the spy peril was a separate entity or distinct phase in this phenomenon, which overlooks the complexity of emotional experience. Interpreting the rise of anti-alienism in this way presumes that fear and suspicion were merely replaced by hatred and anger, and that these emotions were either on or off. It is the contention here that rhetoric establishing the espionage threat was not merely a prelude to wartime anti-alienism; the image of the spy was fundamental in sustaining xenophobia and anti-immigrant sentiment beyond the initial period of panic and paranoia. Early attempts to manipulate public opinion and maintain popular hatred towards Germany continually relied upon the existence of an extensive and nefarious system of German espionage, which suggests that the spy peril and Germanophobia were closely intertwined.

The growth of anti-alienism and discrimination witnessed during the First World War was not a straightforward process. This chapter examines how images of espionage expedited growing levels of hostility towards 'outsiders'. It identifies three ways in which spying was used to fan the flames of popular animosity, which together provided a foundation for more extreme prejudices. The chapter starts by examining how spy stories provided a recognizable format to follow and comprehend the war, thereby filling the void created by a lack of war news. Because these narratives depicted spies active in almost every theatre, the figure of the spy became a convenient scapegoat for a variety of blunders and setbacks. By attributing British failings to Germany treachery reports deflected blame and aimed it at 'undesirable outsiders'. In this way espionage rhetoric aligned xenophobia with popular patriotism and made the spy a frequent target of frustration and aggression. Importantly, though, these ways in which spies were used as a vehicle for debate and discussion should not be seen as three distinct phases in a linear development of hostility, as each continued to appear concurrently throughout the autumn and winter of 1914–15. Nevertheless, they do provide a logical escalation and neatly illustrate how the portrayal of the spy helped stimulate a more complex and multifaceted xenophobia.

Whereas suspicion and vigilance were fairly explicit during the early weeks of war, in an effort to mobilize the nation by creating a covert plot against Britain, later iterations of the spy peril appear to have prioritized hatred and anger towards 'outsiders' deemed harmful to the war effort. But as a window into secret diplomacy and international relations, the spy peril also provided glimpses into things that were typically hidden from view but which could likely mean life or death for some. It is entirely possible, therefore, that the spy peril provided comfort by affording individuals a degree of agency during the escalating crisis. To others, vindicating British setbacks by blaming German treachery perhaps also inspired a sense of hope that Britain will eventually prevail because, in fiction at least, the British protagonist always thwarted the advances of German emissaries. By highlighting the varied purposes of the spy peril, and thus the different emotional responses that could be had, this chapter demonstrates that society's obsession with espionage was not purely symptomatic of an uncontrollable anxiety about secret enemies. In doing so, it further shifts our understanding of 'spy fever' away from unsubstantiated claims of hysteria and delusion. Society's fascination with the German spy peril emerged because of an understandable and rational need for information in a time of crisis and the desire to attribute blame during a period of great insecurity. 'Spy fever', it is argued here, provided an outlet for popular frustration and exhilaration created by the changes and challenges brought about by the war and was not simply a product of delusional paranoia.

Keeping up with the war

As an amalgamation of imperial adventure stories and fictional detective work, spy novels have always mirrored international politics and social tensions taking place in the real world.[4] And so, through the depiction of authentic dangers spy novels provide a barometer for measuring the fragility of the political status quo and social order. Rarely are they explorations of intelligence craft or the monotony of surveillance; instead, they aim to portray national vulnerabilities through the representation of the duplicitous or heroic spy.[5] That stories of espionage were fallacious was irrelevant; by envisaging the war through the lens of popular spy fiction, society could celebrate military success as well as mitigate anguish through a shared dialogue and an imagined collective experience. Especially as reliable news was not particularly forthcoming during the early stages of war, rumours of fictional intrigues that closely resembled reality offered a means through which people could figuratively stay abreast of wartime events. Representations of espionage offered a convenient and recognizable interpretation of events unfolding during the war, which could instil a sense of hope by affording people a sense of familiarity and control at a time of crisis, while also reinforcing society's belief in the likelihood of victory.[6]

Rather than take rumour and gossip at face value, and because hearsay invariably embodies ideas or beliefs that are deeply embedded within, historians often view these narratives as a representation of the collective subconscious. As this is otherwise difficult to penetrate, rumours offer a unique way of accessing historical mentalities.[7] Such narratives provide historians with a way of accessing how identities were formed, the dynamics of social interaction and the conventions governing behaviour.[8] Fictional exploits involving spies and counter-spies, therefore, can reveal much about how people adapted to wartime conditions and their efforts to overcome the early challenges brought about by the First World War.

From the BEF's arrival in France until their retreat at Mons, the British public was largely kept in the dark about military activities at the front. Having learnt from his experiences in South Africa, Kitchener deliberately restricted journalists from operating close to the front line, and as a result, society's awareness of the BEF's early engagements was severely limited.[9] To comply with Kitchener's demands the government established a Press Bureau to examine all press releases and instruct editors on what should be downplayed and what should be emphasized. In effect, the bureau could censor, supress or delay any material considered detrimental to the war effort.[10] These restrictions placed great dependence on gossip transmitted via word of mouth, which resulted in a deluge of distorted reports and invented stories.[11] The details that did manage to reach the Home Front were often vague by design and scarcely mentioned the soldiers involved.[12] Philip Gibbs, one of the correspondents on the Western Front from 1915, believed that this only exacerbated anxieties on the Home Front:

Owing to the rigid refusal of the War Office to give any official credentials to correspondents, the British press, as hungry for news as the British public whose little professional army had disappeared behind a deathlike silence, printed any scrap of description, any glimmer of truth, any wild statement, rumour, fairy tale, or deliberate lie, which reached them from France and Belgium.[13]

Owing to her own ignorance about what was going on, Beatrice Trefusis noted how 'everyone has some special bit of rumour, more or less unlikely ... One has so little news from authentic sources, that one seizes any odd rumours with glee – crumbs to live on'.[14] The shortage of wars news inevitably left society in the dark, and not knowing how close Britain was to defeat engendered feelings of insecurity and helplessness. People's reliance on hearsay and rumour was not, therefore, caused entirely by gullibility but desperation. The shortage of credible news meant that society relied on sensationalist stories and rumours of espionage to satisfy their need for information.[15]

It was within this context that rumours and scare stories abounded.[16] Norman Macleod observed how the war had produced 'many rumours of a very definite kind. In first week of war story of a great battle in [North] Sea 6 [British] ships including Iron Duke sunk 19 German – also story that Black Watch cut up in Belgium'. He went on to describe a 'funny story' in which a hairdresser was shot after being found wearing female clothing and concealing secret documents. Macleod surmised that the fact that 'this story had got about shows state of public mind'.[17] Whereas in retrospect many came to disparage 'the way in which we believed every rumour in those early days',[18] it was precisely because many found the initial period of unknowing particularly ominous and greatly feared the receipt of bad news.[19] To compensate, rumours often told of tremendous successes to quell any lingering concerns. Evelyn Diver heard how the Kaiser had shot himself shortly after Britain had declared war, whereas Emily Blathwayt was told that German troops had become severely disheartened after facing the BEF, and more or less everybody seemed to hear about Russian troops landing in Scotland to bolster British and French forces on the Western Front.[20]

This desire for information can be seen in how people meticulously recorded what little news they received and begrudged the scarcity of reliable information about what was happening on the continent.[21] Spy fever seemed to address this concern; the majority of articles containing references to German covert activity were not actually focused on spies operating in Britain but instead sensationalized the activities of suspected spies abroad.[22] As the German army advanced through Belgium, spy stories fixated on Germany's supposed transgressions in the Low Countries.[23] After victory on the Marne had established trench warfare on the Western Front, the principal arena for Germany's spy network became France and Flanders.[24] After the Ottoman Empire entered the conflict in November 1914, and commenced military operations against Russia in the Caucasus, rumours of spies in Turkey quickly appeared in British newspapers.[25] Tales of espionage on the Eastern Front and at Salonika also coincided with major operations there, while escalating tensions between Italy and the Central Powers prompted a spate of spy stories involving the two belligerents.[26] The nature of these reports suggests that the spy peril served as an important metaphor for international diplomacy and military engagements across Europe. Rather than a straightforward enemy-within-complex, therefore, spy stories allowed society to stay apprised of events, figuratively at least, and stay emotionally connected to the conflict. Envisaging the increasingly volatile situation as a trial of wits between two individuals made contemporary events both accessible and engaging, while also concealing some of the more distressing facets of war from the British public.[27]

As well as *informing* society about international goings-on, the spy peril also *involved* local communities in the wider war effort. Of course, many spy stories emphasized nationally significant threats like spies directing U-boat attacks, guiding Zeppelins over Britain or constructing secret gun emplacements, which signalled an impending national disaster.[28] But at the local level, gossip served to enhance a community's connection to the global crisis.[29] At his local choir practice, for instance, Reverend Andrew Clark heard of an apparently tragic incident in which a local sentry had been shot dead by 'a German agent in a motor' while guarding the nearby wireless station. Why the enemy thought it necessary to assassinate the sentry was never questioned, but the resulting blockade ensured that residents of Little Waltham felt a part of the international struggle.[30] Colonel Davidson, stationed at Inverness, wrote to his wife describing the 'exciting times' being had in Scotland upon hearing rumours that nine German spies were captured at Fort William concealing carrier pigeons in their luggage. Presumably Colonel Davidson felt a sense of attachment or significance because of alleged enemy activity in his vicinity.[31] One rumour in St Albans purported that 'a spy [had] been found with plans inside a lemon', and another had been caught tampering with a local well, and so local residents speculated that Germany was seeking to poison their water supply.[32] In doing so, this rumour established St Albans as a strategically vital location, which inflated the significance of the area and the community's importance to the war effort. As a young girl living in the Cotswolds, Peggie Alexander was told:

When a German spy wants to let the German soldiers know what they are to do and what their enemies are doing they draw a cow on a gate, or a fence, or anything they can find, if it is a small cow it means that the road is only weakly defended; a medium cow means that our troops were somewhere near; if it was a large cow it was a warning that there were earthworks or trenches nearby. If the cow's head pointed in the air it meant that the Germans had better send up an aeroplane before advancing.[33]

Although comical, Peggie's story of cows etched onto fences demonstrates how national and local security became synonymous and how communities, even in remote locations, felt part of the wider struggle because all potentially faced the hidden enemy within.[34]

Nevertheless, people could still discern fiction from reality when it was necessary. In recalling an invasion scare, for example, Hilda Davison, a dockworker from Sunderland, wrote that 'we talked about "the invasion", but I don't think we ever dreamt it could really happen'.[35] When Fred Robinson, a machine engineer, heard reports of a great naval battle off the Norfolk coast in August 1914, he similarly doubted its validity.[36] William Campbell, a schoolmaster in Sutherland, sarcastically mocked the story of Russian soldiers arriving in Scotland as nobody could state that they had actually seen it for themselves. People retelling the tale had only ever heard about the arrival of troops from somebody else who had heard it from somebody else.[37] Shortly after the declaration of war, Robert Saunders, a headmaster in Winchester, blamed strict censorship for reducing newspapers to rumour and hearsay and claimed that these were 'far from satisfying' and not credible sources of information.[38] Emily Blathwayt disparaged at the newspapers for being 'so inaccurate that it is difficult to tell how much truth there is in our supposed victories'.[39] Others simply laughed at the inventions in the press or compared them to fairy tales.[40] Even *John Bull* displayed a degree of criticism to such stories. Rather ironically, Horatio Bottomley bemoaned that 'what spoof – and wicked spoof – the Press indulges in when war is on! Nearly everything which appears is pure invention, and, to the initiated, obvious fake.'[41]

While certain individuals may have consumed rumours and spy stories as factual exposés of German espionage and subversion, their existence does not denote a state of mass delusion or hysteria. For some, popular spy fictions provided a useful representation of the international context. By focusing on a clear and identifiable danger rather than an abstract and potentially fatal reality, Britons gained a sense of understanding and agency, which alleviated anxieties linked to a potential defeat. Sensationalist spy stories afforded an interpretation of the crisis that was comforting; they invariably involved German agents being outwitted by the ingenuity of the British protagonist, while Britain's allies abroad were continuously victorious in the face of German treachery. Yet as the reality of war began to reach people on the Home Front, especially after Britain sustained the first civilian casualties of the conflict, the nature of spy rumours began to change. No longer were such stories simply aimed at satisfying a need for information; they also sought to explain Britain's shortcomings.

Spies and scapegoats

Although spy stories provided a recognizable narrative with which people could figuratively stay abreast of wartime events, to fully comprehend and consent to the conflict, society also needed an enemy to focus on and believe that this foe was surmountable. Cate Haste, for instance, argues that the propaganda campaign against spies 'achieved very little in terms of its declared aim – to safeguard the security of the country', but that 'the propagandists were people gripped by war hysteria themselves, who found a convenient scapegoat for the failures of the war in enemy aliens'.[42] Explaining Britain's early setbacks not only became essential to society's understanding of the war but also their acceptance of it. And so, as increasingly ominous news began to reach people in Britain, spies provided a suitable scapegoat that vindicated failure by blaming it on German treachery, rather than allow it to be attributed to British incompetence. Society was already familiar with the methods and objectives of German agents through countless novels and stage productions, and, according to recent reports, spies were already active across all theatres of war. According to this interpretation German spies had the means, motive and opportunity to perpetrate various transgressions against Britain and her allies. It was also impossible to irrefutably deny their involvement since spying is, by its very nature, covert. By deflecting blame and attributing disappointing events to the existence of German spies, these narratives refocused anxieties away from far more troubling concerns over whether Britain could actually overcome Germany's military prowess. The depiction of spies, therefore, often served to maintain confidence and morale as society began to face setback and disappointment.

As various difficulties – both on land and at sea – began to appear in the news, it became increasingly difficult to sustain popular optimism regarding Britain's prospects in the war. After only a few weeks of fighting, Norman Macleod noted how there was a:

> feeling of depression everywhere – public felt loss of Antwerp keenly especially as reports had been so optimistic. Censorship at fault here – loss of Hawke and fear of submarines, German advance on Ostend and Warsaw, darkened London streets had effect as well – marked loss of confidence in Admiralty – this feeling of depression more marked in conversation than in newspapers owing to censorship and no doubt to desire of papers not to injure public confidence.[43]

Fictional exploits of German espionage helped lessen this turmoil, and authors like William Le Queux established the groundwork for blaming spies for anything detrimental to the war effort. In *German Spies in England: An Exposure* (1915), Le Queux claimed that France's military defeat in 1870 was precisely because of German spies that had infiltrated French society so successfully. According to Le Queux, 'the work of a single spy may wreck a campaign and settle the fate of a nation'.[44] Thanks to the secrecy of espionage and ambiguous depictions of secret agents, society was able to blame anything on German spies, ranging from outbreaks of foot and mouth disease to factory explosions, sunken merchantmen, failed assassinations, haystack fires, burst water pipes and, ironically, the spread of 'fake news'.[45] And for some this explanation seemed convincing.[46] A private memorandum produced by MO5g noted how 'popular clamour at the time attributed all sorts of disasters to enemy espionage ... but in no single instance could enquiries at the Admiralty and elsewhere show that these disasters were to anything but other causes. There was no reason whatever to connect them with enemy agency'.[47]

Images of German spies proved very effective as a scapegoat. As the number of troops being killed in France became increasingly difficult to conceal following the army's hasty retreat from Mons, concerns about the BEF's efficacy needed placating.[48] In an attempt to belittle the German army's proficiency, soldiers often wrote home blaming spies for the difficulties faced on the Western Front. Private G. Harding, serving with the Royal Medical Corps in October 1914, wrote that 'shells are bursting in the air like fireworks. The enemy have found our positions by means of spies.'[49] Private Reginald Watts, serving with the 2/28 London Regiment at Bailleul in 1915, made a similar observation:

> On way via Ravelsberg, passed big guns on side of road with dug outs etc. Place had been bombarded day before. Only 1 establishment open, kept by two women. I think they are spies, as every time troops go in they are shelled.[50]

Even by 1916, Lieutenant Kenneth Hall still thought that 'spies are everywhere – they always seem to get wind of our plans'.[51] Similar allegations made their way into the press. The *Aberdeen Evening Express* conveyed one soldier's frustration after his regiment was caught in a 'certain death trap' set by a cunning spy from which few men escaped,[52] and it became common practice to attribute Germany's accurate artillery fire to spies who had infiltrated the British front line.[53]

Perhaps more concerning to many, though, was the fate of the Royal Navy. Ever since Nelson's victory at Trafalgar had assured Britain's supremacy at sea, it had been widely assumed that the Royal Navy was practically invincible. And yet, early encounters with the German Imperial Navy had been less than convincing. Within weeks of declaring war, HMS *Aboukir*, *Cressy* and *Hogue* were all sunk on the same day with around 1,400 British sailors lost. They were torpedoed by *U-9* while patrolling the North Sea to keep the eastern entrance of the English Channel clear of enemy torpedo craft and minelayers. Although the three cruisers were largely obsolete in 1914, there was a public outcry for what it suggested about the Royal Navy's ability to protect Britain and win the war.[54] Admiral Lord Charles Beresford, not one to miss an opportunity to attack the government, publicly condemned the spies who he believed were operating freely on Britain's east coast for their role in sinking the three British cruisers. He claimed to have made inquiries and found undisputed evidence that spies 'had something to do with those cruisers being put down'.[55] When asked by the Director of Public Prosecutions to supply them with this evidence, he declined. Instead, he claimed that 'the danger is increased by a system of enjoining that proof or evidence must be forthcoming that an alien is going to commit some treacherous act before he is arrested or before he is sentenced'.[56]

Whereas the exploits of a single submarine marked a definite shift in naval warfare, the Royal Navy soon fared badly in conventional sea battle as well. After much damage had been inflicted on commercial ships in Southeast Asia by the SMS *Emden*, which was itself supposedly expedited by Germany's vast network of spies,[57] the Royal Navy dispatched a rather outdated fleet under the command of Rear Admiral Christopher Craddock to locate and destroy the remaining German Pacific Fleet. The ensuing Battle of Coronel proved to be ill-fated though, with Admiral Cradock killed, two armoured cruisers sunk and over 1,600 lives lost.[58] With the ascendancy of the Royal Navy in jeopardy after only their first skirmish with the enemy, it was quickly pointed out that Germany maintained 'spies and informants in every port in South America', and that it was they who had surreptitiously conveyed Craddock's position to the German vessels lying in wait.[59]

Beresford's remarks that the east coast was littered with German spies were given further credence after German cruisers bombarded Scarborough, Hartlepool and Whitby in December 1914. Although intelligence reports confirmed that German spies had not been involved,[60] the press bemoaned the lack of security that had allowed a clandestine network of German agents to facilitate such an attack.[61] It was widely reported that the German navy's precision was not coincidental, and one commentator suspected that the German naval gunners had been furnished with accurate intelligence less than a week old.[62] William Le Queux, in his self-appointed role as expert on German intelligence matters, strengthened claims that spies had in fact made the attacks possible.[63] Calls for increased vigilance and more stringent measures against spies gained further momentum as a result.[64] For people like Augustus Alexander the claim that German spies had provided the attackers with information pertaining to the location of the Royal Navy and the composition of British defences, thereby making such an attack possible, was necessary to distract them from far more troubling concerns.[65] Without the spy peril these setbacks were either caused by Germany's naval proficiency and bravery or by Britain's incompetence. Neither was particularly promising. By attributing it to German treachery, the British public could remain hopeful that British skill and ingenuity would eventually prevail once the country had wised up to the enemy's perfidious tactics.

German espionage would later be blamed for such things like the sinking of the *Lusitania* in May 1915,[66] the death of Earl Kitchener in June of the following year[67] and the ongoing struggles against German Zeppelins.[68] Besides framing military events in a familiar context and offering opportunities for celebration, the image of the spy also presented Britain's early difficulties in a way that was both intelligible and palatable to the British public. Whether scapegoating involves a deliberate attempt to divert blame to ensure the survival of the status quo or an unconscious effort to grapple with the tensions caused by known and unknown factors, it is an entirely rational endeavour.[69] The inclusion of the spy here was not necessarily designed to stimulate popular vigilance against strangers or certain activities and was instead focusing more on the need to control foreign or divisive elements within Britain. But according to this narrative, anybody ostensibly opposed to the war effort became likened to a subversive faction that needed ousting.

The alien menace

Although the initial resurgence of the spy peril in August 1914 was closely linked to the threat of invasion and the perceived need to ready society to meet the demands of the war, as the parameters of the conflict became clearer these immediate challenges subsided as people became more accustomed to wartime conditions. From as early as mid-September, though, there was an increasingly virulent narrative that aimed to capitalize on the earlier spy peril. Because foreign espionage had become a primary factor underpinning many of Britain's initial setbacks, society's fear of defeat manifested as anger towards those deemed responsible. As such, it became far easier to ostracize and vilify any person or group considered as an outsider due to concerns that they were secretly plotting against Britain. Constance Peel considered this to an almost inevitable reaction to war:

> Because the state of tense excitement in which we existed upset our judgement and made any event seem possible, and also because if people must go to war and continue to be at war they must be made to hate each other and to go on hating each other, war stories were a feature of our life.[70]

Thus, whereas Shakespeare has been shown to have represented an unmistakable symbol of Englishness vital to the 'cultural self mobilization' of Britain during the conflict, the spy served as the antithesis to British national identity and came to symbolize everything that was opposed to the war effort.[71] Maud Cox recalled how Germans became a 'bogeyman', and that as a result, 'anybody the least bit different was a spy'.[72] Owing to the versatility of the spy peril, it was not simply a precursor to more violent forms of anti-alienism; it was a necessary component that helped sustain popular animosity towards foreign influences in Britain throughout the early stages of the war.

During the winter of 1914 Lord Charles Beresford's divisive and xenophobic campaign rested on the assumption that aliens of all nationalities had been caught spying but then released owing to a lack of evidence. According to Beresford the only way to effectively neutralize the existential threat posed by spies was to legislate against Britain's entire alien population and root out all foreign infiltration.[73] *The Globe* wrote that it is 'infinitely better that a thousand blameless individuals should suffer' than allow a single spy to remain 'free to continue his baneful activities',[74] while Le Queux's exposé on German intelligence methods was little more than a thinly veiled attack against naturalized aliens:

> The 'foreign' spy is not the worst peril; the real danger comes from those who, for years, have made their homes among us, who have married Englishwomen, and have become so familiar to their neighbours that they are in little or no danger of being under the slightest suspicion ... The class of person who is much more dangerous is the so-called 'naturalised' alien. Among these are, no doubt, men who have long ago taken out naturalisation papers for the sole purpose of blinding us, and of being afforded opportunities to pursue their nefarious calling.[75]

The spy peril was frequently used to undermine Britain's immigration policies and the individuals who had benefited from them.[76] According to this narrative, Britain's naturalization laws were nothing more than a subterfuge employed by German agents. Figure 5.1, published in the right-wing pamphlet, *John Bull*, shows an unscrupulous German emblazoned in the Union Jack wielding naturalization

Figure 5.1 'The Spy's Sanctuary'.
Published in *John Bull*, 28 November 1914, p. 15. Illustrated by Frank Holland.

papers as a defence. Despite a superficial loyalty to Britain, a portrait of the Kaiser still adorns the wall behind him, his military uniform is kept in a state of readiness and a plethora of secret documents are scattered across the floor. The caption reads: 'They can't touch me now.'

The first and most obvious target of right-wing vitriol was the German communities in Britain. From the start, it was their apparent proclivity for espionage that incited vicious condemnation.[77] George Makgill, secretary of the Anti-German League, proclaimed that all persons of German blood – regardless of place of birth or national allegiance – constituted a threat because it was known, according to Makgill, that German Secret Service agents settle in hostile countries and become naturalized citizens in order to enact untold damage when needed.[78] The significance of the spy in facilitating wider animosity is clearly evident in the wartime play, *The Female Hun*. The performance depicted the rise of nationalism even at the expense of marital harmony. Following the realization that his German wife was actually a secret agent conspiring against Britain, General Grant, the central protagonist, felt compelled to kill his spouse in order to redeem his national loyalty, since personal bonds had been made subordinate to abstract notions of ethnic solidarity. Nicoletta Gullace argues that *The Female Hun* illustrates that 'notions of fictive kinship, based on an imagined community of blood ties and racial stock, began to undercut the living bonds of neighbourliness, familial affection, and – though far less successfully – marriage'. The premise of the play, she contends, drew upon the prevailing assumption that illicit activity confirmed the belief that Germany was instinctively barbaric, and that as a result, Germans had no place in Britain, even if bound by familial ties.[79] Although reports of German atrocities clearly portrayed the enemy as an uncivilized and ruthless nation, it was only because of the spy peril that the threat of German brutality presented an immediate danger to the British public. Thanks to the inherent secrecy of spying, tangible evidence was seldom required to substantiate such claims, and various undesirables could be associated with illicit activities designed to subvert Britain from within.

While historians have been quick to point out that the German atrocities committed in Belgium were used to expedite a popular Germanophobia, the level of prejudice directed at Belgian refugees demonstrates how the spy sanctioned anti-alienism more broadly.[80] Despite the sympathy that often characterized public sentiment towards Belgians, in practice, ambivalence typically marked both state responses and social relations with the Belgian diaspora.[81] Although the Home Secretary, Reginald McKenna, implored society to treat refugees kindly and directed that no difficulty should be placed in their way, the subsequent growth of anti-alienism during the first months of war led to extensive exclusion zones for aliens, friendly or otherwise.[82] The innate difficulty in classifying immigrants as either 'friendly' or 'unfriendly' meant that aliens in general often became targeted.[83] Despite being welcomed into Britain initially, and notwithstanding the popularity of the Belgian relief cause (there were around 2,000 officially recognized local committees designed to assist Belgians in the UK), refugees began to face hostility because of their alien status, even if they were considered 'friendly' for the most part.[84]

Although the image of 'brave little Belgium' protected refugees at the beginning of the war, a noticeable anti-Belgian sentiment surfaced as the war progressed and frustrations mounted. Given the initial fondness for supporting plucky little Belgium, the spy peril proved essential in framing this discrimination, especially it was all but impossible to easily distinguish between a German and a Belgian.[85] Besides vague accusations that all German waiters and barbers were secret agents, there was very little to identify the appearance or even nationality of potential spies.[86] This then allowed public xenophobes to associate refugees with the threat of espionage. At first, 'two German spies' were 'discovered' in a refugee boat landing at Folkstone, but soon after, reports in the press began to allege that thirty-three spies had been caught attempting to pass as refugees.[87] One reporter claimed to have witnessed first-hand the duplicity of certain 'refugees':

> To show how dangerous the influx of Belgian refugees must be for England, I want to tell you the following: In Folkstone two men came on board who did not look to me like Belgians of Frenchmen, although they spoke very good French and were provided with Belgian passports. I could see this, as they were right in front of me when leaving the train and boarding the steamer. On board the ship I managed to sit next to them, and their conversation was kept up in French. It was nearly all on military matters. All of a sudden, when we were close to the Dutch coast, one of the two broke out with 'Gott se dank wir sind bald da', and from that moment on they talked the purest German imaginable.[88]

Despite the unequivocal welcome given to refugees initially, the Home Office soon bowed to popular clamour and set up prohibited zones that no alien, including Belgian refugees, could enter, and this gave credence to the notion that spies were in fact masquerading as people fleeing from the horrors of war.[89] In reply to the Home Office's scheme, the *Hull Daily Mail* argued that 'it seems cruelly inhospitable to drive away people who have suffered little less than martyrdom, but we are engaged in a very serious game, and we cannot afford to take risks'. They prefaced this by claiming that a further forty German spies had arrived in Britain as refugees, this time at Dover, which implied that drastic measures were in fact necessary:

> There can be no doubt, however, that Britain has been 'spied out', and that spies are still at work ... Sleepy, easy-going Hull must lose its fatal bonhomie, its habit of giving its hand and heart to every glib foreigner of the International gang.[90]

The *Chelmsford Chronicle* likewise suggested that adopting such steps was undoubtedly prudent since 'spies are practically without soul or conscience, and will assume for their purpose, if need be, the garb of angels'.[91] In Bexhill-on-Sea, concerned locals formed a 'Vigilance Committee' to produce a list of refugees because of the 'possibility of danger from spies in the town'.[92] The spy peril was so intertwined with popular patriotism that it offered the radical right a convenient vehicle to convey their xenophobia to a broader audience. This ensured that the spy peril was a notable part of the anti-alien campaign that featured prominently at the start of the First World War.

Because of this versatility, the spy was used to vilify an assortment of perceived threats, which could include anything considered inconsistent with notions of 'Britishness' or 'Englishness'.[93] This was especially true if the object of disdain could be linked at all with Germany. Because of allegations that Roma people originally hailed from Germany, it was declared that they had been spying throughout Europe on Germany's behalf for years.[94] Homosexuality, likewise, was frequently conflated with Prussianism, so much so that sexual decadence became synonymous with German culture and militarism.[95] Any undesirable group thought to be opposing notions of Britishness, either by challenging deep-rooted traditions or through forming separate identities, essentially became a threat to the war effort and thus complicit in subversive and seditious activity. Men caught wearing women's clothing, even if only in jest, were commonly perceived as a threat to orthodox gender identities, themselves crucial in maintaining the provision of men at the Front, and were often suspected of being German spies.[96] Images of spies proved so successful in conveying animosity and fears of 'the other' that it became a generic insult and the cause of several libel suits.[97] Spiteful individuals also used this custom to enact personal vengeance. One such instance saw the dismissal of an unpopular chief engineer of the SS *Santaren* after one of his subordinates denounced him as a German spy while docked at Cardiff.[98] In another case, one man was so enraged by the possibility that his sister would abscond with a German, he reported his future brother-in-law to the authorities as a spy.[99]

Although historians have argued that British anti-Semitism was far less pronounced than in other belligerent nations, the growing significance of anti-immigration discourses meant that many latent resentments were also enabled through anti-German rhetoric.[100] Anti-Semitism, unsurprisingly given the radical right's long-held aversion towards Jewish influences in Britain, was often closely entwined with this type of anti-Germanism.[101] One avid supporter of Leo Maxse pleaded with him to 'keep on hammering at "Britain for the British"' and not for 'cosmopolitan Jews, German spies (of whom England is full yet), and any and every kind of foreigner'.[102] Associating Jews with the alien spy served to fan the flames of popular anti-Semitism, which occasionally resulted in violence, especially when victims were foreign as well Jewish.[103] A Rabbi in Hull, for example, found himself attacked by one angry thug for being, according to his assailant, a secret German spy.[104]

The peril was equally effective in legitimizing class-based hostility. While the middle classes became increasingly suspicious of vagrants and gipsies for polluting the nation, the social and political elite found themselves condemned for harbouring secret agents.[105] Lord Northcliffe wrote to Bonar Law outraged that 'it is beyond question that, for some reason, the Government are protecting spies – and spies in high places'.[106] Hamil Grant, an author who like Le Queux claimed to have an intimate knowledge of German intelligence methods, reasoned that it was almost unavoidable that spies had assumed influential and powerful positions within British society:

The boastful claim of pedigree provides for the writer, at any rate, something of a key to the psychology of the spy. Pride of mythical ancestry is undoubtedly a capital symptom of megalomania, among the conditions of which is the obsession of self-importance, and this would seem to be a widely prevalent disease among the sons of men. The desire to be near important people, to be engaged in no matter how lowly a capacity with men who direct important affairs, to associate in more of less familiar fashion with celebrities, or people highly placed, to count for even and infinitesimal part in the conduct of big events, to have the tips of one's fingers in the particular pie of the moment, to have been 'not altogether out of it', as the cant phrase goes, in any given episode, but all to be known to integral outsiders as having played the role of a fractional insider in any cause – this is an acute mania with a larger part of the human race than is commonly suspected. Megalomania of this kind goes a far way to explain the reason why men fitted for success in the unspectacular and prosaic carers of life will deliberately devote themselves to what must be considered as among the most disreputable of trades.[107]

Rumours that spies occupied or at least had special access to the highest offices of the land attracted much speculation.[108] Henry Morris Upcher, an ornithologist living in Norfolk, became convinced that German spies had infiltrated every level of the British government.[109] Ellen Codringham likewise thought that the 'whole cabinet are either pro German or have so compromised themselves by taking German money in the past that they do nothing for fear of exposure'.[110] Outside of government, affluent members of fashionable London clubs were suspected of concealing German spies who were influencing the British elite.[111] While at the other end of the social spectrum, Frederick Charles Kench, a volunteer coast watcher, witnessed one man 'of the tramping persuasion' suspected of espionage in the nearby town of Wisbech. He claimed that his accuser was so aggressive that he must have 'thought it was Kaiser Bill himself'.[112]

Naturally, the traditional enemies of social order and agents of sedition, trade unionists, socialists and anarchists, were regularly likened to spies.[113] But the war also engendered a new antagonist: the pacifist. Although Cyril Pearce has overturned the consensus that the war was a resoundingly popular cause, and demonstrated that popular opposition was far more prevalent than previously assumed, the pro-war press routinely connected pacifists to German conspiracies in the right-wing press.[114] Men who were failing to match the sacrifices of others, commonly referred to as 'shirkers' or 'skulkers', were singled out and condemned for subverting the war effort through inappropriate behaviour.[115] Whereas the spy peril commonly provided a clear analogy for undesirable elements in society, the association between espionage and pacifism was less direct. Rather than directly claim pacifists were spies, and because those who resisted military service were thought to be the greatest danger to Britain's survival, it was often claimed that they were decidedly *worse* than spies.[116] The *Berwickshire News* thought:

No man is worthy of British citizenship who at this time is eating and drinking and sleeping with great zest and self-satisfaction, and is not caring 'one twopenny damn' for the Nation and the brave fellows who are, like heroes, doing, by day and by night, the awful task which enables these callous, selfish beings to eat, drink and sleep in sanctimonious comfort. Shame on us, if there be any bogus British citizens. Such are worse than the enemy's spies for the latter, after all, are doing something for their country.[117]

Wartime discrimination, whether focused on anti-alienism, homophobia or class-based antagonism, often incorporated the imagery of the foreign spy. By framing particular aversions in this way, the illusion of a 'Kingdom United' was maintained by labelling groups of undesirables as outsiders, while advancing xenophobia by effectively combining discrimination with popular patriotism.

Of course, whether or not these types of incidents reflected widespread and intense spy phobias, or whether spy fever merely provided a vehicle with which to exercise these prejudices, is impossible to discern. But it is clear that, beyond August 1914, the expression of spy phobias in public discourse changed. At the commencement of the war, spy fever reflected a systematic attempt to warn society about illicit activities because such incidents could disrupt mobilization or, worse, facilitate an invasion of the British Isles. By September, though, outsiders in general became a danger because of the possibility that they *could* be spies, and these fears manifested as angry and hate-filled bigotry.

✳✳✳

During the first appearance of 'spy fever' in the British press during the Franco-Prussian War, fears of espionage in France were routinely attributed to two causes. First, the shock of France's mounting defeats needed accounting for, especially as initial reports gave cause for optimism, and so covert forms of treachery provided a convenient scapegoat.[118] Because France's setbacks continued into 1871 it was increasingly believed that duplicitous activity was the only explanation for their mounting defeats.[119] Second, a subsequent lack of detailed information about the war's progress perpetuated the need for fanciful rumours to fill the void.[120] The British ambassador in Paris observed the difficulty in obtaining news about current goings on and noted the prevalence of 'false news' because of France's 'system of secrecy' that ensued after the invasion.[121] This sense of unknowing created a national feeling of impatience and distrust.[122] The *London Daily News* wrote:

The spy fever has begun to rage again with a very vigorous flame. Partly this is due to real discoveries, but partly also to the natural anxieties of a people who are coming to the end of their resources; who find that they can do nothing but wait; and who are troubled – over-troubled – lest the defence of Paris should be endangered by the slightest neglect … as a number of journals here, with the most awful gravity, refuse to state where the shells of the Prussians have fallen on their city, but tell mysteriously of the disasters which have happened to houses in

Street M and Street N; so, more than ever, the people are on their guard against treason, and are disposed to find a spy in every lounger.[123]

Together, the receipt of bad news followed by the absence of any credible information implied a growing sense of disaster. According to the portrayal of France's spy fever in the British press, it was this desperation that exacerbated France's fascination with espionage as these reports rallied the nation against their impending destruction. By establishing an enemy 'other', French society defined itself along patriotic lines that separated individuals in support of the war effort from those who were believed to be undermining it.[124]

These same characteristics can be seen in how British society expressed similar fears during the First World War. Stories that exposed Germany's vast network of secret agents and revealed how their intrigues were being thwarted across the globe filled the void created by a lack of reliable wars news. The continuous ability of Britain and her allies to overcome the nefarious practices of such a corrupt and devious enemy, figuratively at least, created the allusion of national success, which helped maintain confidence in the likelihood of a decisive British victory. Despite some of the harsh realities that Britain faced during the opening stages of the conflict, many of the difficult questions that arose out of these setbacks could be deflected and attributed to a secret and unscrupulous foe. The spy peril's endurance in public discourses, therefore, owed as much to its ability to provide a glimpse into international goings-on. In this sense, spy fever addressed collective anxieties relating to Britain's perceived vulnerability and insecurity. Because it seemingly offered a framework to overcome this trepidation, the spy peril was perhaps just as likely to instil a sense of hope or delight, rather than simply alarm and frustration. Many of the stories and rumours purporting illicit activity actually offered a means of comprehending the war through a familiar cultural framework in which Britain invariably prevailed.

However, because spies had become a convenient scapegoat for a variety of uncomfortable realities, portraying aliens as covert operatives made a growing xenophobia more palatable to the wider public, which, as we shall see, expedited many of the radical right's discriminatory attitudes and policies. The fact that the spy peril was used to inflame popular intolerances shows the level of institutional and cultural interference behind the creation of anti-alien sentiment, particularly during the early stages of the war. This is important for two reasons. First, the fears and intolerances that underpinned this facet of the spy peril were not new and, as such, should not be viewed as a delusional aberration. Words like mania simply reflected the conventional practice of employing psychological conceptions to what some perceived as irregular or disagreeable behaviour.[125] Second, discourses relating to the espionage peril going into the winter of 1914 reveal an emotional style that appears much closer to anger and hatred than the early terror and suspicion of August 1914.

So what does this mean for our understanding of collective spy phobias and the nature of 'spy fever' in Britain during the First World War? Given the various dimensions to the spy peril, society's fascination with espionage presumably resulted from a range of concerns. Analysing the discourses responsible for sustaining spy fever suggests that images of espionage served different purposes depending on the context of the war and so resulted in a range of emotional experiences. It is entirely possible that reports of German intrigues across Europe might have infuriated some but alleviated stress in others. Attributing British setbacks to German spies might have prompted anger against foreign influences and in others sustained hopes that British forces would eventually prevail. And, as the next chapter will show, the expression and dissemination of anti-alien sentiment, clearly designed to whip up hatred and anger, was also likely to prompt tolerance and compassion as people sought to challenge and oppose extremism. Without being able to psychoanalyse people's reactions to the different facets of the spy peril, we cannot know for sure how people may have responded to them. But given the different purposes that the spy peril served, and the range of emotives on display, it would be misguided to assume that spy fever only comprised a single emotional reaction. 'Spy fever' should be thought of as an atmosphere of heightened emotional states that were all in some way influenced by the allusive threat of German secret warfare.

Having separated spy phobias from mass hysteria, the following chapters can begin to assess the scale and significance of espionage phobias, and of spy fever more generally, by associating the fears and anxieties connected to the spy peril with a particular community. By demonstrating how collective anxieties relating to the German spy menace were limited and constrained, despite the prominence of secret warfare across British politics and popular culture, the following chapters make a greater case for incorporating multiple emotional experiences into our understanding of 'spy fever'.

Chapter 6

PUBLIC OPINION AND THE ENEMY WITHIN

The most vicious and explicit form of xenophobia and prejudice that emerged in Britain during the First World War was undoubtedly that of Germanophobia. Because Edwardian Britain had shared many similarities with Germany, wartime Britain needed a way to differentiate itself from the enemy and the spy peril offered an obvious framework to do so. Often, the spy peril was wielded deliberately to have this effect. Hamil Grant's history of secret espionage, for instance, attributed spying and deceit to a particular type of person:

> In the opinion of the great soldier [Napoleon] the best spy is a half-breed who is a natural cosmopolitan and is consequently unaffected by ideas of patriotism ... Modern spies of the professional type, more especially those employed by Germany, fully meet the specifications of Napoleon's idea of the race. The accomplished spy of today is invariably a man of at least quasi-criminal proclivities, a being entirely lacking in a moral sense, a degenerate.[1]

Owing to their alleged proclivity for espionage, the entirety of the German populace, and not just the soldiers committing atrocities, could be construed as intrinsically evil. It was the propensity to spy, therefore, that most clearly distinguished the Germanic race from that of the honourable Briton.[2] William Le Queux, for example, likened Germany's ubiquitous secret service to the barbaric Hun decimating modern civilization.[3] Even the Bible seemingly confirmed the immorality of the German people, given their alleged practices,[4] and as a result, Germans in Britain became the modern equivalent of the anti-Christ:

> The real anti-Christ will be one of the monarchs of his time, a son of Luther, he will invoke God and proclaim himself as his messenger. That prince of lies will swear by the bible. He will represent himself as the instrument of the Most High chastising the corrupt nations. He will not only claim omniscient power, but his innumerable armies will adopt the device 'God with us' and will appear like legions of the devil.
>
> For a long time he will act by deceit and stealth and his spies will overrun all the earth and he will be master of the secrets of the highest.[5]

With links to Lutheranism, absolute monarchy and espionage, the abhorrence and dangers of Germanic culture became explicit. By portraying Germany as having an innate penchant for espionage and intrigue, Germany became more than just a mortal enemy; individual Germans became existential threats to be feared and loathed. It was for this reason that the espionage peril provided a foundation for Germanophobia to flourish.

Nevertheless, just because the spy peril provided grounds for further hostility towards Germans in Britain, the prevalence of espionage in popular culture and politics during the First World War should not necessarily be taken as evidence of a widespread and intense Germanophobia. Despite the prominence of the spy peril, and the inclination of many commentators to use it as a device to incite aggression against Germans living in Britain, much of this rhetoric emanated from radical conservatives, and as such, whether these emotional standards applied to British society as a whole remains to be seen. Much like how Reddy connects emotional regimes to political counterparts, Martha Nussbaum claims that political principles in every society are derived and sustained through cultivating relevant emotions. Even in liberal democracies, politicized emotions are fostered through leadership, education, government policy and culture, without necessarily impinging upon individual autonomy and agency. Opposing political ideologies thus prioritize different emotional styles. By assigning the most extreme anxieties generated by the spy peril to a particular community, it becomes possible to assess the impact and extent of spy phobias because the impact of this emotional style corresponds to the size and influence of the group propagating and consuming such divisive and alarmist rhetoric.

As this chapter will argue, right-wing fanatics were most often responsible for promoting fear and anxiety in response to the German spy threat, while individuals subscribing to a more liberal philosophy subscribed to an alternative emotional standard that prioritized tolerance and acceptance. Although the radical right sought to stimulate certain anxieties, in many cases it appears that they were motivated more by their radical politics than hysteria or delusions akin to a 'spy fever' and so were more interested in removing civil liberties than catching German spies. By subsequently highlighting the limited appeal of the radical right during the opening stages of the First World War, this chapter further questions the ubiquity of spy phobias by associating them with a marginalized ideology. The final section documents the presence of a competing narrative that sought to undermine right-wing assessments of the alien menace. Since emotional standards are shaped by political and ethical ideals, these two competing narratives represent contrasting emotional communities with which society could interact with and use to interpret their own feelings. By focusing on how and why collective anxieties were formed in response to the espionage peril, this chapter aims to shift the historiography away from the assumption that spy phobias became a dominant experience. Despite the prominence of secret warfare in both political discourse and popular culture, the paranoia often associated with the spy peril seems to have resonated mostly with people already susceptible to radical ideals.

Espionage and radical politics

Ever since the unexpected difficulties of fighting the Boers had exposed various weaknesses in the British military-imperial system, society was increasingly conscious of the nation's defences.[6] Edwardian Britain responded with a level of popular militarism that increasingly encroached on the remaining vestiges of Victorian liberalism.[7] As we have already seen, waves of invasions scares helped carry the tide of this militarism, but as war came the spy peril offered an equally useful tool to embolden radical opposition to liberal idealism.[8] In particular, radical figures exaggerated the dangers of espionage specifically to create the impression that the government was failing to respond to the challenges of war, thereby giving them an opportunity to criticize their apparent inertia.[9] Lord Roberts, one the country's foremost military authorities and fervent proponents of radical conservatism, wrote to Leo Maxse, editor of the *National Review*, to encourage him to 'take up the matter of spies in this country' to combat the government's negligence:

> It seems to me we are doing all we can to help the Germans should they, by any possible chance, be able to land a Force on these shores ... What fools we are. People, especially those in authority, are acting as if an invasion of this country could or would never take place.[10]

Maxse had himself been long hoping to 'smash this rotten coalition [led by Asquith's Liberal Unionist Party] into smithereens',[11] and the spy peril provided the perfect opportunity to do so. Outraged at the apparent system of German espionage on the east coast, Lord Leith of Fyvie suggested that the government's bureaucratic confusion and administrative errors were preventing a wholesale restriction on aliens, which exacerbated the threat to the nation's security.[12] Meanwhile, Lord Charles Beresford's efforts to galvanize popular hostility towards enemy aliens were similarly founded on the premise that the government's precautions against spies were hopelessly insufficient.[13] Although the inclusion of the spy may have offered a novelty to radical politics and provided a degree of urgency and necessity to their warnings, attacking liberalism for being too lenient was hardly a new idea. Before the war, liberals demonstrating a commitment to Cobdenite principles were frequently accused of endangering the empire, the security of the nation and the morale of British society.[14] And on the eve of war, Leo Maxse, warned his readers that 'either this country must destroy the Asquith government or the Asquith Government will destroy this country'.[15] To many critics in 1914, liberalism appeared ill-prepared to deal with an international contest of this magnitude. In particular, liberalism seemed to lack the vigour and ruthlessness necessary for victory, and following the declaration of war, ministers failed to produce sufficient legislation to the contrary.[16]

Deliberate attempts to galvanize collective fears by overstating the existence of foreign influences, creating a sense of crisis and urgency and exaggerating various security threats all resemble far-right strategies to legitimize anti-immigration debates.[17] Consequently, the inclusion of a spy peril into conservative discourses merely accentuated a long-standing tradition within British politics. The outbreak of war certainly provided the radical right with a fresh impetus, and so as the initial furore subsided, security discourse shifted from specific localized disturbances involving spies to more centralized policy debates centred on the alien menace, both of which required the existence of a nefarious and comprehensive system of foreign espionage. Beyond the initial spate of spy phobias in August 1914, the resurgence of the spy peril in October 1914 was largely driven by radical conservatives attempting to expedite their cause. Consequently, it would be misguided to uncritically assume that the impact of this divisive rhetoric, and thus the emotional standards maintaining xenophobic and chauvinistic attitudes, extended beyond this community. This section shows why radical conservatives were so invested in the spy peril and how they used depictions of German espionage to grow popular support for their ideology. The degree to which they achieved this objective will be the focus of subsequent sections.

Although both liberals and conservatives questioned the government's policy following the outbreak of war, the most profound criticisms that also employed images of covert plots originated from parliamentarians in both Houses with connections to the radical right. In the Commons, it was William Joynson-Hicks and Lord Charles Beresford who were most instrumental in forming radical opposition to the government's alleged indiscretions.[18] At the beginning of September 1914, Joynson-Hicks pressed McKenna on the necessity of appointing a small non-party committee to advise on the appropriate steps to secure the nation from German spies. He initially seemed content with the Home Secretary's rebuttal that such a committee had been established in 1910 and had fully considered the question of aliens in wartime.[19] Yet only a week later, he suggested the Home Office go so far as to publish the names and addresses of all registered enemy aliens so 'that Englishmen may know with whom they are transacting business'.[20] In November, he reiterated that 'our first duty is to protect ourselves' and claimed he 'would rather that irreparable damage should be done to any individual or individuals rather than our country should be placed in danger even for a moment'. Adamant that rumours of German spies operating in France and Belgium were indicative of threats in Britain, he became outwardly convinced of the government's ineptitude: 'I am quite prepared to say that I believe there are, and that there have been … men who for the interests of the country would have been very much better shot than left where they were. I say that without hesitation.' However, when asked by McKenna whether he could supply the names of these culprits, Beresford came up short.[21] His eagerness to suspend habeas corpus and his ferociousness in advocating a series of ad hoc executions were illustrative of his radical nature, which is itself reflective of the ideological position many notable proponents of the spy peril held.

Beresford gained notoriety for chastising the government in the Commons, but he was also equally influential in extending extremist narratives outside of Parliament. Despite taking an active role in the recruitment campaign during September

1914, during which Beresford actively drew upon conceptions of race to increase volunteering and ironically juxtaposed Prussian militarism and authoritarianism with the more favourable ideals associated with British liberty and democracy, the spy was ostensibly absent from this rhetoric.[22] But by October 1914, Beresford had begun to vehemently target the government's national security strategy. He began holding local meetings to propagate extremist ideology, which sought to emphasize the gravity of the situation and expose the Home Office's failure to recognize the ramifications of the spy peril. As an initial precaution, he recommended that all aliens, naturalized or not, be interned immediately.[23] This local campaigning culminated with a letter released to the press in which he appealed to the country's nationalistic urges to combat the threat of German espionage:

> I appeal to my countrymen to take a strong line of action with regard to the crowd of alien enemies in our midst. They are creating a real danger to the State. Are we to wait for those ordinary commonsense precautions necessary during war until a catastrophe occurs? It is time for plain speaking, for deeds and not words. The plea that there must be some proof or evidence that an alien is going to commit a treacherous act before he can be arrested or sentenced cannot hold water in war time.

After exposing the 'real danger' and the need for an abrupt and profound response, he emphasized the urgency by using the image of 'Poor little Belgium':

> Belgium has suffered countless horrors by the dastardly action of Germans who were naturalised. Immediately [after] war broke out these supposed friends placed all their local knowledge at the disposal of the enemy. Before the war these Germans were considered as friends, and every confidence was placed in their loyalty. A false friend is far more dangerous than a declared enemy.

Unsurprisingly, the prevention of similar circumstances befalling Britain required increased regulations and restrictions placed upon aliens:

> Meetings should be held in every town, and resolutions should be carried protesting against the present state of affairs, and sent to the Premier. We are all one in the country in supporting the Government in all that they do to enable them to fight this war out to a finish, but public men would be traitors if they did not call attention to facts liable to cause disaster. The sooner we recognise the fact that we are at war the better. Numbers of men have been caught red-handed signalling and have been discharged [because there was] 'not sufficient evidence'. German hatred of us is little understood in this country. The doctrine has been forced into the German mind by their Press and in their schools. It blossoms forth in the actions of treacherous spies.[24]

By amplifying the danger confronting the public, Beresford was attempting to highlight what he considered negligence and weakness. More importantly, though, manufacturing a spy peril in this way combined popular xenophobia with national security and military strategy, which added a degree of legitimacy to his pre-existing anti-immigrant agenda.[25] The use of counterfactual comparisons that exaggerated the urgency of the current crisis, the importance of a collective grassroots response and the limitations of existing legislative capabilities, all typify far-right strategies.[26] Beresford's underlying message was therefore consistent with wider attempts to popularize extremist narratives. His rhetoric suggests that he was not overly focused on provoking local vigilance to thwart covert operations and was instead mostly focused on the control and restriction of immigrants more generally, which he had long advocated.

Although William Le Queux declared himself to be apolitical, this was merely a façade to conceal many of the more extreme measures that he endorsed.[27] Like other spy novelists, many of whom were typically sympathetic towards the radical right, Le Queux's stories were seldom more than thinly veiled propaganda.[28] But whereas Beresford aimed his criticisms at liberal ministers, Le Queux claimed that politicians from across the political divide, not just the Liberal Party, had failed to take the German menace seriously:

> Hitherto, the security of our beloved Empire had been disregarded by party politicians, and their attendant sycophants, in their frantic efforts to 'get on' socially, and to pile up dividends. What did 'The City' care in the past for the nation's peril, so long as money was being made?[29]

Le Queux's primary antagonism, then, was the system of governance rather than any one party. Although the Home Office and Reginald McKenna found themselves under repeated attack throughout Le Queux's tirade against the establishment, it was bureaucracy itself that formed the primary villain:

> He [Steinhauer – Chief of German espionage before 1914] made frequent visits to this country: he got to know many German residents here of the better class, whose efforts might be of value to him, and within twelve months – while our red-tape-tangled Government departments closed their eyes and dreamed – he had actively at work a swarm of agents in every dockyard town and garrison where the picking up of information of value would be possible or likely. How he must have smiled![30]

Like Beresford, Le Queux lamented at the need for evidence and legal proceedings:

> As far as can be gathered from Mr McKenna … Nobody is assumed to be a spy unless he is an unnaturalised German. Even if he fulfils this condition, he is then to be caught 'in the act' of spying, or if really strong suspicion be aroused, some evidence against him may be 'looked for'. But until this is 'found', and so long as he complies with the posted up regulation orders, etc., he may continue unmolested. In short, after the steed is stolen, our stable door may be shut.
>   One sighs in despair. Could anything be more hopeless?[31]

In accordance with other radicals, Le Queue's proposed solution was a suspension of habeas corpus:

> We shall never be free from the spy-peril until we recognise with Sherman that during war the military authority is superior to the civil; until we insist with Sir Oliver Lodge that all foreign spies must be shot, and all native ones hanged.[32]

Despite the introduction of draconian legislation in Britain during the First World War, this was not enough to appease radicals hell-bent on eroding civil liberties in the name of security. As a result, the prominence of the spy peril should not be viewed as evidence of a widespread and organic hysteria and can instead be attributed to a deliberate campaign seeking to embolden popular fears and anxieties that would challenge and uproot liberal ideas and policies.

Ultraconservative magazines were thus especially eager to promote the spy as an object of danger and cause for alarm. Despite the oft-repeated remark among radical figures that Britain should fight as one, the *National Review* continued its unrelenting attack on the government's alleged incompetence.[33] It argued that because of 'Haldaneism' and pro-German factions within the Cabinet, Britain had continuously underestimated Germany's belligerence and carelessly brought about a war that the government was unequipped to fight. In a deliberate attempt to incite further opposition, its editor, Leo Maxse, declared:

> It is only by vigilance in the patriotic cause that we shall prevent a continuance of the hideous blunders which were within an ace of ruining our name and our fame ... Politicians do not become capable and trustworthy simply because they have drifted into war. They will require a vigorous 'bingeing up' throughout the war as in the crisis preceding the war.[34]

This appeal for 'vigilance', however, was soon aimed at mobilizing public hostility towards surviving German influences because of the remaining spies who had supposedly 'honey-combed' Britain.[35] While not all aliens were considered dangerous, dutiful citizens were instructed to remain cautious:

> Germany has displayed such genius in the peculiarly dirty business of organising espionage, and employs every stray scoundrel of any nationality who will sell himself for a sufficiently small sum, that we cannot be too careful.[36]

By claiming that the government were acting negligently, and by embellishing the dangers posed by secret agents, the *National Review* manufactured a scenario in which attacking Britain's naturalization laws became a patriotic endeavour.[37] But more importantly, the implicit secrecy of an army of spies helped to validate their conspiratorial fantasies. Central to the *National Review*'s Germanophobia was a belief that a Hanseatic League had been clandestinely subverting British interests since the medieval period.[38] It was only thanks to the prominence of the spy peril that the later myth of a German 'Hidden Hand' found any real resonance.[39]

Images of spying also proved useful in launching one of the most active and vocal radical groups to emerge in Britain during the First World War: the British Empire Union (BEU). Formed in 1915 under its original name, the Anti-German League, it integrated the ideas and objectives from an assortment of pre-war Conservative pressure groups.[40] The creation of the BEU illustrates the close associations between spy phobias and radical politics. The figure of the spy was vehemently capitalized on by the BEU wherever it was beneficial to their interests, but there is little evidence to suggest that the organization took the threat of espionage and covert operations literally.[41] Nonetheless, in response to Britain becoming supposedly 'overrun and swamped' by foreign spies during the years leading up to the outbreak of war, the BEU portrayed themselves as the defenders of British security while advocating ever-restrictive measures:

> We are hunting down agents and spies, but especially we are out to defend British freedom, rights, and privileges ... Those of us who cannot fight in the trenches can assist in expelling the Germans secret societies from our country. Men and women could not do better than enrol themselves in this union, and be your own private detective. Your help will be the greatest value ...
>
> The Anti-German Union has an Intelligence Branch, which investigates reports of suspected espionage, alien enemies at large, and any other information pointing to hidden dangers to our nation. These reports are dealt with accordingly, and are either handed over to the authorities, or are dealt with in some other way which seems appropriate.[42]

Employing images of spying thus served to legitimize discrimination against aliens by conflating it with popular patriotism. Drawing upon the themes of excitement and adventure found in popular culture also made such rhetoric more palatable and appear more mainstream. The practicality and functionality of this imagery meant that depictions of espionage continued to have an enduring role in the construction of popular xenophobia well beyond the autumn of 1914.

That images of spying played a key role in the promotion of radical politics is indisputable, and far-right politicians, newspapers and organizations all had a vested interest in exaggerating the degree and danger of foreign espionage. Since Germany's purported infiltration of Britain had allegedly gone uncontested, it ostensibly necessitated an extreme and swift response: enhanced military powers and legislative capabilities, the mobilization of popular xenophobic hostilities and the removal of complacent politicians. However, attributing these espionage-related anxieties to a specific ideology challenges the suggestion that they were widely experienced. The importance of the spy peril to the expansion of radical conservatism suggests that spy phobias were primarily influential insofar as the radical ideology itself became accepted. Ascertaining the wider impact of the radical right is thus essential in determining how successfully spy phobias gripped the nation.

Outcasts and Xenophobes

The integration of the spy into extremist rhetoric proved useful. When Ada McGuire learnt of the supposed connections between German spies and the sinking of the *Lusitania*, her initial response was to condemn the current system of government. She wrote that 'England is too slow ... Everything must be debated and so valuable time is lost ... In time of war military measures should not be left to a civilian government'. McGuire reckoned that the treasonous activity of spies demanded authoritarian leadership: 'A military staff of experts and naval staff of experts should be able to say "this must be done whether you like it or not". I am sure other countries think we are not half awake.'[43] McGuire's readiness to remove democratic traditions because of setbacks allegedly facilitated by German spies illustrates how radical propaganda became an important framework for interpreting wartime events. Beatrice Trefusis similarly exclaimed:

> There seems no end to the spying and treachery. The papers are all clamouring for more drastic steps to be taken as regards spies – and everyone is furious at the slack and suicidal methods of the Home Office in not interning every enemy alien.[44]

It was not uncommon to believe that 'the spy business [was] a burning question' and that, without more drastic steps, there would be 'popular outbursts against Germans suspected of spying';[45] however, such remarks are not necessarily representative of society as a whole. People's receptiveness towards radical discourse was far more varied than Trefusis's assessment suggested.

The impact of the war on British politics has often been construed in a way that suggests conservative ideology was better prepared to prosecute the war effort.[46] Although all parties had been redefining their relationship with patriotism, it was indeed the Tories who had firmly cemented their image as the most patriotic party during the Edwardian era.[47] Despite their staunchly patriotic stance, however, Conservatives were careful to distinguish their idea of patriotism from both nationalism and jingoism. It would be a mistake, therefore, to assume that the Conservative Party was decidedly anti-German and that it consisted entirely of scaremongers who contributed to the growth of Anglo-German antagonism. There was a sharp divide between the diffidence maintained by the leadership and enthusiastic, but peripheral, elements of the party, many of which emphatically promoted Germanophobia.[48] In fact, radicals often justified their extreme methods on the grounds that Conservative leaders were ineffectual compromisers who needed replacing.[49] By attributing spy phobias to a marginalized form of conservatism distinct from the official party line, we can dissociate widespread fears of espionage and sabotage from central Conservative ideals.

The divide between Conservative leaders and radical elements within the party has frequently been interpreted as a 'crisis of Conservatism', but this argument contains various methodological flaws.[50] Not only does it misinterpret their collective intentions, it also presumes a degree of coherent opposition inside the party, which was almost entirely non-existent.[51] In recent examinations of Edwardian conservatism, Frank McDonough and Rhodri Williams both contend that 'scaremongering' against Germany was limited to 'outcasts' and marginalized 'wild men' who had almost no impact on the direction of the party.[52] Geoffrey Searle describes this 'radical right' as a loose coalition of 'super patriots' who feared imperial decline, constitutional imbalance and increasing class consciousness. They regularly attacked aliens, cosmopolitans, intellectuals, Jews, political parties as well as parliamentary democracy itself, and as a result, radical individuals were largely alienated from all political parties.[53] Consequently, 'the actions of the "radical right" can be interpreted as propaganda exercises designed to weaken the Liberal Party rather than the outward manifestation of deep ideological beliefs'.[54] Starved of the legitimacy afforded by the party's leadership and the political mainstream, any collective alarm that they managed to generate was most likely to have impacted individuals sympathetic to this marginalized ideology.

Although the Edwardian era gave rise to a plethora of radical groups, the most influential was the National Service League that aimed to reduce Britain's aversion to conscription.[55] Despite a superficial rise in popularity, though, the influence of radical groups remained limited. The NSL certainly grew exponentially after its creation in 1902. Fears of Germany's rapid naval expansion had seen the NSL's membership grow from 1,725 in 1904 to 35,000 supporters across fifty branches by 1909. And by 1914, the league's following had expanded even further.[56] Although dissatisfied Conservatives filled its ranks, the leadership sought to obtain support from across the political and social divide.[57] Yet their attempt to inaugurate a cross-party mass movement was an abject failure. The majority of participants continued to derive from long-standing middle-class supporters of the Conservative Party, and so extreme radicals from within the Conservative Party, who had grown deeply concerned about the German threat, provided leadership and direction.[58] In any case, McDonough surmises that 'not many sensible people took these far-fetched stories seriously at the time', and that 'historians who make grandiose claims about the influence of the "radical right" need to appreciate more fully how marginalised and plain "loony" many of its leading figures were'.[59] In a similar vein, Anne Summers portrays them as fundamentally conservative in outlook but completely incapable of securing a mass following.[60] Most of their followers were widely considered to be 'hyper-patriots' or 'ultra-imperialists' who held a simple view of Germany. They were undoubtedly preoccupied with the military and Britain's vulnerability to invasion and derided traditional parties for their negligence and reticence in dealing with the German peril.[61]

Throughout the period, it was also the right-wing press that had been instrumental in exaggerating the German menace and the alien problem in Britain.[62] In August 1914, Horatio Bottomley conceitedly reprinted his profuse warnings that had appeared in *John Bull* prior to the outbreak of war:

> Alone amongst journalists, alone amongst public men, have we been warning the nation, during the past five years, of what was coming; and as will be seen

from the following pages, we have been deadly correct in our information ... We want to impress upon the public mind the fact that we, at any rate, are, and always have been, alive to the true reading of signs and portents which indicate the destiny of our race.[63]

Whereas Bottomley framed the German threat around notions of racial competition, Leo Maxse maintained that he was not anti-German and instead claimed that he was opposed to the 'irresponsible oligarchy called German government'. He thus revered the vibrancy and strength of Germany compared with what he perceived as the more timorous disposition of British politicians intent on maintaining electoral support at the expense of Britain's continued progress and security.[64] Regardless, both thought of themselves an anomaly. Bottomley claimed that he was alone in prophesizing the German menace, while Maxse recognized that he was regarded as a 'disruptive right-wing' Germanophobe by the mainstream. Maxse's self-perception as an outcast on the fringes of conventional political discourse was captured by a typical editorial written in May 1912:

Great Britain herself may be compared to a Titanic obviously plunging at full speed towards certain disaster, because her so-called statesmen refuse to see the obvious or to prepare against the inevitable ... Those are denounced as 'cranks' who call attention to the danger which is apparent to every man with eyes to see.[65]

Despite identifying as a political pariah, Maxse firmly believed in the influence that his tactics could attain,[66] and to a small extent, Maxse was proven right. In 1915, after witnessing the *National Review* finally turn a profit following the outbreak of war,[67] he wrote to Northcliffe proclaiming that 'after having been regarded as a hopeless lunatic for half a generation it is a most curious sensation to be treated as a comparatively sane being, though I do not suppose it will last'.[68]

Notwithstanding his growing popularity, fluctuating memberships of radical groups suggest that the appeal of extremist ideology remained rather limited. The inability of any radical right group to sustain a consistent membership during this period is best explained by separating popular support from a commitment to radical beliefs. Historians have tended to perceive nationalist groups as collectives that entertained relatively homogenous ideas, but in reality, members often held considerably different views from the leadership.[69] Most organizations were typically reliant on material incentives and social activities to encourage participation. Although some individuals undoubtedly joined in support of specific goals, they rarely viewed their involvement as an ideological and political renovation of the British right as the leadership often did. Radical nationalism was thus largely confined to the leadership and was not necessarily shared among its members.[70] Notwithstanding the outbreak of war in 1914 and the opportunities that it offered the radical right, they lacked a unified leadership and a coherent direction. Owing to the deep divides that split radical conservatives, they never amounted to any real alternative to the dominant liberal ethos of the period.[71] And because the

Conservative Party continued to offer refuge for both disgruntled opposition and anxious patriots, it remained a locus for protest against the establishment. Owing to the enduring appeal of the Conservative Party, the majority of British society did not need to resort to radical ideals.[72]

Besides their frequent warnings in press, there is also little evidence that these conservative pressure groups took the espionage threat literally. Beyond the BEU's initial attempt at mass public engagement, the inclusion of spies dwindled as their efforts became far more extremist and conspiratorial.[73] Despite early attempts to conceal their more extreme ambitions using the image of the spy, their primary objectives became increasingly explicit within subsequent propaganda. In a leaflet entitled 'What the British Empire Union Wants', the BEU specifically demanded an immediate closure of all German banks across the British Empire as well as legislation preventing them from reopening after the war. Furthermore, they called for the internment of all enemy aliens, reformed naturalization laws, the suppression of pacifism and pro-Germanism, the prohibition of enemy businesses, a worldwide boycott of Germany and, finally, the regulation of all industrial and commercial enterprises throughout the empire.[74] None of which included or even referred to the spy danger.[75] Increasing employment, rather than combating espionage, became their central objective. They strongly objected to foreign workers undermining the British labour force and candidly called upon society, especially women, to ensure that returning soldiers enjoyed a comfortable and prosperous life by eradicating German commerce from the empire.[76] While the degree of fanaticism is readily apparent, there is little evidence to suggest that espionage and sabotage were predominant concerns. The readiness with which the BEU dispensed with portrayals of the spy menace is perhaps illustrative of a disingenuous concern towards the alleged threat and suggests that their advocacy of it was mainly for publicity purposes. In sum, not only was radicalism a marginal force in British politics, which inevitably constrained the appeal of its ideology, reports of secret agents were often superfluous compared to the more pressing concerns of far-right politics.

The historiography of radical politics during the Edwardian era suggests that support for such groups remained trivial throughout the period, which inevitably limited its influence. More importantly, though, the lack of ideological support even among its associates further constrained the tangible impact that they achieved. People exhibiting spy phobias were the exception, rather than the norm. The *Thanet Advertiser*, for example, recognized that 'spy fever' was 'a disease which is said to afflict a small portion of the community',[77] while Winston Churchill commented that 'there is a well-defined class of people prone to "spy-mania" and whose minds are peculiarly affected by anything in the nature of espionage'.[78] Similarly, Edward Glover, a wartime psychologist examining the relationship between war, fear and morale, found that 'the spy-maniac is usually a "nosey" type of person who is secretly alarmed by the war. He is also a rather aggressive person. Consequently he is unsure of himself, secretly doubtful of the integrity of his own patriotism'.[79] Indeed, spy phobias were regularly associated with reprobates of the lower classes.[80] When referring to an attack of spy fever in Walsall, which caused a surge of anti-alien violence, the *Walsall Advertiser* castigated the 'mob' of 'roughs' and their 'very ugly temper', which gives an indication of how society perceived individuals prone to spy phobias.[81] No individual received greater abuse while in public office during the War than Richard Haldane, but even he believed that this hostility came from only a small section of society.[82]

Despite the popularity of the *Globe* or the *Daily Mail*, radical politics remained subservient to mainstream Conservatism. The *Birmingham Daily Mail* asserted that Northcliffe's *Daily Mail* was playing the German game in portraying Britain as disorganized and weak and was therefore actually 'doing more damage to England than the cleverest German spy who ever set foot in this country'.[83] The continued ability to access a political and emotional community that remained opposed to radical ideals suggests that spy phobias may not have been a dominant social response. Although not every individual who subscribed to the spy rhetoric had to be an avid supporter of radical conservatism, recipients required some form of sympathy towards the objectives of the radical right. While this community expanded somewhat during the First World War, its limited reach suggests that spy phobias did not infect people. These emotions did not resemble a contagion. The spy peril merely liberated pre-existing tendencies, however dormant or animated, within individuals who occupied or interacted with an overly right-wing political and emotional community. But since spy phobias were relatively short-lived even among the community primarily responsible for spreading them, the influence of this particular emotional style should not be overstated.

A tolerant and incredulous public

Although certain Conservatives went to great lengths to impress upon people the dangers of foreign espionage and inculcate fear among the British public, their fabrications and hostility did not go completely unchecked. Rowland Hunt, a noted anti-Semite and Unionist MP for Ludlow,[84] gave a speech in Parliament in September 1914 in which he warned of a completely fictitious enemy:

> Mr Hunt asked the Home Secretary whether, in view of the fact that telegraph wires have been cut and bombs and firearms and carrier pigeons found in possession of alien enemies, he can see his way to pass a short law ordaining that all persons found either attempting to obtain or to communicate information useful to the enemy, or to commit any act of injury or destruction, should be handed over to the military authorities to be dealt with according to military law?

Of course McKenna responded with the simple truth, which was that no malicious acts of this kind had been carried out. He also pointed out that the Defence of the Realm Act already empowered the police and military authorities in such a way as to deal with many subversive threats.[85] But refuting the alleged transgressions of Germany's spy network was not limited to government ministers. The *Arbroath*

Herald likewise disparaged the absurdity of the spy peril and highlighted the dangers that such rhetoric could bring:

> In some cases the hunt for German spies has passed from the ludicrous to the serious. I have heard, and have repeated in this column, some of the funny incidents. But I now call attention to a more grave case where the hunt for German undesirables has been made the occasion of private or political persecution. A decent man of nearly 70 years of age, British born and English by both his father and mother, has been the victim of a galling search and or imprisonment owing to secret information lodged against him. The case turned out to be a mare's nest. It is, however, mentioned that the victim happened to be a keen Liberal who had made himself obnoxious to the local Tory leaders by starting a Liberal Association in a district of notorious Tory darkness and bigotry.[86]

This account makes clear that there was a political incentive behind constructing a secret enemy within. In creating stories about fictitious spies plotting against Britain, radicals sought to instigate anxieties that would bolster support for their ideology. Furthermore, it demonstrates that tolerance and compassion survived despite growing levels of discrimination and persecution. This would have only been possible if an alternative emotional style existed, one that opposed the emotional standards conveyed by radical discourse. This section sheds light on this hitherto neglected response to exaggerated reports of Germany's clandestine exploits in Britain.

Despite the prominence of the spy peril, which has often been used to justify claims of widespread spy phobias, correspondence that exhibit these types of fears also often betrays a lack of awareness or receptiveness to them. One of Maxse's supporters, for example, wrote to him condemning the inertia of the British public:

> The English have for years been far too tolerant of spies planted in their midst and it is really amazing to contemplate the astonishment of the majority of Englishmen when they begin to wake up to the fact that this country is in for a fight to a finish and that the enemy is not altogether outside our own borders. Nothing is more pathetically foolish than the average well to do view of the English country gentleman when he begins to criticise police or military measures taken principally for his own safety.[87]

The contrasting reactions to German espionage can be seen in an account appearing in the *Army and Navy Gazette* in October 1914:

> On the one side there are the benevolent or incredulous public who have not hitherto had the question brought seriously before their notice, who neither realise the danger to the country of individual or organised spies, and that England is so secure that, even if they do exist, they can do no harm; and more mischievous still, the large section of society who, partly from false good nature,

partly from an ill founded sense of superiority, and partly from sheer ignorance and indifference, deliberately close their eyes to the danger which the experience of France and Belgium clearly illustrates is real.

On the other side, we have the almost equally mischievous section that believe the wildest rumours and thoughtlessly advocate measures that cannot possibly be taken.[88]

If, as this account supposes, individual reactions could range between ignorance and apathy to overzealousness and thoughtlessness, any attempt to identify a single collective experience of anxiety will be incredibly difficult. Especially as the second category, the 'large section of society who deliberately close their eyes to the danger', clearly represents a different emotional community complete with a distinct set of emotional standards. Whereas Conservative-Unionist newspapers like the *Daily Mail*, *The Globe* and *John Bull* sympathized with anti-German rioters and occasionally incited further hostility, liberal papers like the *Manchester Guardian* and *Westminster Gazette* routinely deplored chauvinism and xenophobia.[89] It is argued here that attempts to oppose and denounce claims of a German spy peril represented a distinct set of emotions that conflicted with the suspicion, intolerance and animosity that radical xenophobes sought to promote. Individuals' ability to resist certain emotional standards conveyed by the spy peril suggests that the impact of radical discourses was limited, and that extreme anxieties were not as dominant as the prevalence of the spy would suggest.

Despite this rise in conservatism during the First World War, liberalism was not erased following the outbreak of war.[90] Opponents of xenophobia and oppression continued to emphasize the lack of evidence pertaining to German spies and stressed the need for calm and objectivity.[91] Amidst the height of spy fever, the *Nottingham Journal* called on its readers to oppose scaremongering and divisive rhetoric on the grounds that it was targeting already vulnerable people with vitriol:

> Let us again enter the strongest protest against all language calculated to incite suspicion or inflame feeling against the large numbers of innocent foreigners who are obliged to remain in this country in time of war … to raise clamours for the forcible deportation of these unfortunate people is wicked and mischievous.[92]

Espionage phobias were regularly derided as 'ignorant and idiotic' and were condemned by some for being 'more serious even than the operations of the German spy'.[93] To others, the inconsistency and foolishness of the anti-alien and spy rhetoric were noticeably apparent.[94] Having been baited by a local xenophobe, Reverend J. Osbourne attacked the coherency and persuasiveness of his accuser:

> Mr. Ash begins by classifying me with the pro-German element in Bexhill, and he asserts that I am a champion of German Kultur. But these assertions are, of course, considerable untruths … Mr. Ash gives no evidence nor makes any quotation from my letter to prove his point. But what can one expect from a man in a state of ecstacy? [*sic*] In this exalted mood he proclaimed in a former letter that

he knew that every town and village had its spies and secret German agents. Later in the same letter this omniscience was watered down to a 'suspicion', which was a rather tame ending, a sort of drop from the sublime to the ridiculous. The typical line of suggestion (for there is no reasoned argument) is this: If an opponent does not share my ecstatic fury against honourable Anglo-Germans, call him a pro-German ... he is not only dealing in falsehood but utters a farrago of nonsense.[95]

While it was possible to accept espionage and sabotage as legitimate security concerns, the level of hostility shown to foreigners was certainly open to rebuke. Attempts to exaggerate the spy menace to perpetuate an anti-immigrant agenda, therefore, were often exposed for what they were: illogical, inflammatory and inconsistent.

One way of denouncing the hyperbole surrounding the spy threat was to liken the fervent nationalism of the radical right to German authoritarianism and oppression.[96] As such, newspapers frequently juxtaposed Germany's foolish 'spy mania' with Britain's composure and tolerance, to demonstrate Britain's superiority.[97] According to the depiction of events transpiring in Germany, military law had become predominant, state surveillance was dramatically expanded, executions were becoming widespread and the freedom of the press had been all but removed.[98] Such conditions were associated with Prussianism and the 'spy mania and foreigner-baiting' rage led by an excited and overzealous mob.[99] Aliens in Germany, it was asserted, 'are liable to summary arrest, and possibly to mob violence, at the instigation of any fool or busybody who chooses to raise a cry of "spy"'.[100] While these claims were palpably overstated, language such as 'mania', 'crazed' and 'fool' suggested that this type of response was considered abhorrent in Britain. Wilmot Herringham, for example, denounced the 'cowardly people' in Britain attacking innocent people as if they were 'the Berlin mob'.[101] The contemporary association between spy phobias and German despotism implies there was a continued effort to protect freedom and justice by portraying enhanced security restrictions as an affront to civil liberty and public order and thus unbecoming of British politics.

Moreover, as the number of innocent victims of the spy panic grew, their experiences became increasingly difficult to ignore:

> In some cases the hunt for German spies has passed from ludicrous to the serious. I have heard, and have repeated in this column, some of the funny incidents. But I now call attention to a more grave case where the hunt for German undesirables has been made the occasion of private or political persecution. A decent man of nearly 70 years of age, British born and English by both his father and mother, has been the victim of a galling search and imprisonment owing to secret information lodged against him. The case turned out to be a mare's nest.[102]

As a result, correspondence sections in local newspapers regularly displayed society's disapproval of the spy peril. In August 1914, one reader of the *Birmingham Daily Post* deplored the social animosity aimed at suspected individuals:

Sir, – I venture to suggest a note of warning to be considerate in our behaviour to Germans in England... Let the authorities quietly deal with undoubted spies, but do not let us give way to hysterics. It seems to me a great pity that the official notice bears the heading 'Hue and Cry'. This is an absurd and meaningless relic of old times – circulated on to inflame. It should be remembered that many of us have relations and friends stranded on the Continent ... If we are to expect considerate treatment for these, we must show ourselves prepared to extend similar treatment to the stranger within our gates.[103]

But it was not just the impact on the individual victims of spy phobias but the disruption and damage inflicted on the community. Archibald Walker noted how a perceived rise in anti-German feeling created a sense of fear, not of alien subversion but of property damage caused by rioters and troublemakers reacting to the spy peril. Not only were the impacts of spy phobias likened to German repression, they were also decidedly un-British, and for some, violent rioters were far more threatening and concerning than the secret German plots that they were claimed to expose.

Part of the reason why spy phobias appeared so prevalent across British society was because the spread of alarm relied so heavily upon localized threats, like a spy poisoning a county reservoir, blowing up a nearby bridge or signalling to a Zeppelin overhead, as opposed to a more centralized threat against the state. Society's willingness to accept the validity of the spy peril, and subscribe to a particular emotional style, specifically required the existence of an imminent danger to public safety. For this to have been fully realized, secret agents needed to be everywhere and so localized threats were indispensable. As a result, stories of illicit activity appeared across the British Isles, and the breadth of these allegations led to the assumption that spy phobias were ubiquitous. However, because it was reliant on local threats it was also relatively easy to disprove, as the lack of evidence was always quickly apparent.[104] One bewildered resident wrote to the *Belper News*, for example, questioning the claims made about the spy threat:

It is passing strange where all the foolish rumours come from at the present moment with respect to the machinations of German spies in our own district. We hear of bombs being discovered here and there, and detailed plans of roads and railways unearthed in private houses, all in the possession of the police superintendent of Belper. The only detail lacking about these stories is that the superintendent himself knows nothing of the circumstances so glibly related.[105]

A sceptical resident in Arbroath thought it simply implausible that spies would have infiltrated their remote region: 'If German scouters are on the lookout for important places ... they will certainly give our burgh the go-bye.'[106] Similarly, one resident in Bexhill-on-Sea believed his town to be 'the last place where one would find a German, and a spy would not have dared to set foot within the borough'.[107] Equally significant, though, was the enduring sense of community that superseded nationalistic rhetoric:

> Now all of these aliens, especially from Hull, some of who I know quite well, are not in the least guilty. They have lived in England since they were babies, and can neither speak or understand the German language.[108]

In Bradford, the German community had integrated so successfully into the community that many civic figures originated from German families. The town was saturated with German influences ranging from street names to church services, and so a rise in Germanophobia was considered an insult to the town's unity and prosperity.[109] For others, though, this sense of community prevented them from expressing any concerns regarding covert activity for fear of the embarrassment they might face if their accusations were found to be untrue.[110]

As a bastion of radical politics, *The Globe* received explicit opposition to its blatant discrimination. To its credit, some of this was actually published. In August 1914, one reader began questioning the advantages of generating racial hatred, while another condemned those responsible for attacking innocent Germans and looting their property.[111] For others, though, it became a battle to define understandings of patriotism. Whereas radicals maintained that security through discrimination equated to patriotic endeavour, one campaigner sought to re-establish the meaning of 'Englishness' to challenge oppressive narratives:

> I am sorry to think that 'The Globe' could have condescended to such an idle and ill-natured suggestion … It is the duty of every Englishman to remember the traditions of hospitality sacred to Englishmen and do the best to alleviate the distress of those unwittingly stranded in England, to extend help to them in every possible way … The police are quite able to tell us who are possible spies and who it is undesirable to help, but do not let 'The Globe' go mad over spies.[112]

The existence of conflicting opinions, even among a staunchly conservative audience such as readers of the *Globe*, indicates that the readership of a single newspaper was not itself a coherent entity and that even within this demographic, individuals were not obliged to subscribe to a single, consistent emotional style.

A far more subtle way of conveying resistance to the negative emotions promoted by spy peril, though, was through humour.[113] The considerable cultural impact of espionage during the First World War ensured that spies remained an ever-present feature of comedic narratives:

> Sergeant: 'You may have one wish gratified before you die'. Spy: 'May I choose the place in which I shall be shot?' Sgt: 'Certainly!' Spy: 'I wish to be shot in the arm'.[114]

> 'Now, then, what are you doing here at this time of night? Spying, I expect'. 'No. I'm only burgling!' 'I beg you pardon. Sorry I troubled you. Good night'.[115]

Although *Punch*, a leading British satirical magazine, very much intended to 'whip up public hatred of the Boshe' using humorous cartoons, such devices were equally significant in managing one's fear and suffering because comedy was – and is – a place in which problematic issues can be reviewed and discussed.[116] As such, humour provided a space for communication and evaluation that was inherently paradoxical: it could inspire confidence at the same time as causing trepidation and not only unveil hard truths but also distort their reality.[117] Both the proponents of the spy peril and the extremity of spy phobias, therefore, were openly mocked. One of the most popular critiques of the spy peril came in the form of 'Schmidt the Spy'. Created by Alfred Leete in 1914 for the *London Opinion*, Schmidt effectively investigated the hyperbole surrounding the spy peril to highlight the absurdity of many of the accusations. In this way, humour provided an opportunity to openly discuss and internalize dissatisfaction many felt towards what were viewed as negative repercussions of spy fever.[118]

Satirists write not merely out of personal indignation but with a sense of moral vocation and concern for the public interest.[119] As a tool to express discontent, satirical creations offer historians a unique insight into social convention. Given that humour afforded artists and writers the freedom to explore alternatives to contemporary realities, it provided a space to uncover truths omitted elsewhere. Satire also invariably critiques political events and figures and so preserves perceptions of prejudice and oppression.[120] Caricatures of the spy threat were thus a useful way of exposing the baselessness of popular fears as well as ridicule the bigotry conveyed by radical rhetoric:

Mary Jane (at climax of fearful story of German spy): 'And when the police searched the cellars they found enough ambition to blow up the whole of London'.[121]

German spy (seeing a lady with a Belgian hat on): 'Ach! The Englishwomen are forming a Belgian corps. Ah! I have something to report to my beloved Kaiser at last!'[122]

Nurse: 'Goodness me! What 'ave you been doing to your dolls?' Joan: 'Charlie's killed them! He said they were made in Germany, and how were we to know they weren't spies?'[123]

A somewhat bloodthirsty correspondent suggests that those who give information to the enemy should, as of old, be hanged, drawn, and quartered. The quartering seems out of season. Minced spies would be more appropriate.[124]

'If I had my way', writes one correspondent, 'I would shoot every spy on the spot'. 'Yes, but supposing he hasn't got a spot?'[125]

Besides simple jokes, however, political satirists set about highlighting the absurdity of the spy peril:

"*As a precaution against Zeppelins, sentries are posted at night in bomb-proof shelters. They are armed with high-angle guns, and are supplied with special telescopes.*"—SCHMIDT.

Figure 6.1 'The night precautions of the military authorities are investigated'. Alfred Leete, *Schmidt the Spy and His Messages to Berlin* (London, 1916), p. 17.

"*Martial law has been proclaimed, and all picture palaces are under the supervision of field-marshals.*"—SCHMIDT.

Figure 6.2 'The iron hand of discipline is everywhere visible'.
Alfred Leete, *Schmidt the Spy and His Messages to Berlin* (London, 1916), p. 23.

"*There is evidently great discontent in Kitchener's Army, as the squeals of the recruits as they are driven to drill are distinctly heard outside the barracks.*"
—SCHMIDT.

Figure 6.3 'The craven British have to be trained by force'.
Alfred Leete, *Schmidt the Spy and His Messages to Berlin* (London, 1916), p. 45.

Figure 6.4 'The populace in London has risen'.
Alfred Leete, *Schmidt the Spy and His Messages to Berlin* (London, 1916), p. 51.

An officer, who had been warned of a spy, a woman said to have a flaming red head, was worried at lunch by the arrival of three lots of men, each with a red headed woman. Then the regimental sergeant-major saluted and said, in a hoarse whisper, that if I wanted any more there was another in the next farm. This appalling collection of heterogeneous females, all red-headed and all ugly, completely unmanned me, but not for long! I sent the whole boiling off to the Provost-Marshal with a note that I had more arriving later. Result, a motor-orderly to beg me not to send any more, as he had already got a yard full of them, and was at his wits' end to know how to feed or keep them quiet, for they were all fighting![126]

By replacing spies with evilly disposed red-headed women, comics were able to exaggerate spy phobias to foolish proportions and attribute their reactions to an overstated and unjust paranoia. In this way, comics used humour to convey their discontent and criticism of those sustaining the peril to their audiences. Perhaps for this reason, some individuals recorded their amusement, rather than panic, when hearing of rumours exaggerating the German spy menace.[127]

Although the politicized nature of this debate meant that opposition to the spy peril was mostly confined to public discourse, it did occasionally enter the private correspondence of individuals encountering popular spy phobias. James Thomas, Professor of Sculpture at University College London, condemned society for being so easily misled by 'nonsense' theories that were a 'nuisance to dear England' and served only to profit the 'vanity of the Kaiser'.[128] Dr Odlum, while working in internment camps during the war, became incredibly familiar with enemy aliens and stressed that prisoners were 'far, far, far from spies'.[129] Following an incident in which Margaret Constable was suspected as a spy for travelling in a motorcar, she similarly ridiculed the logic (or lack thereof) that prompted the rationale of the mob:

They were only pacified when we told them that it was Colonel Constable's car, one of the women said her husband was a soldier and that she had seen Col. Constable, so they were satisfied (Observe the logic). They later discovered they had been reported to the police, although the police never took it seriously, the officer told them to avoid the side streets because there were many 'excited' people about.[130]

After the capture of a man with a letter, supposedly written using a German cipher, Constable somewhat sarcastically wrote that it was 'conclusive proof' of his unlawful intentions.[131] Constable's willingness to dispute claims of espionage and her inclination to mock the intellectual capacity of individuals perpetuating spy phobias exemplify the endurance of opposing values and emotions that encouraged tolerance rather than hostility.

***

In August 1914, the famed espionage novelist and self-appointed authority on Germany's secret service, William Le Queux, was growing increasingly concerned for his safety. He claimed that because of the many German secrets that he had discovered, he was being sent anonymous letters making threats against his life. Desperate for publicity and attention, he wrote to the Metropolitan Police Commissioner seeking protection to ensure his family's continued safety. He reckoned that his close association with the secret service branch of the War Office, as well as his public persona as a renowned spy catcher, placed him in considerable danger. Despite his pleas, the Metropolitan Police was less than sympathetic. It was stated that Le Queux had undoubtedly 'imagined the receipt of these letters, just as he was imagining that he was in personal danger'. As a result, his requests for protection were repeatedly denied. Scotland Yard attributed his paranoia to narcissistic fantasy:

> Mr Le Queux ... is not a person to be taken seriously and his ways are somewhat tortuous ... In his own eyes he is a person of importance and dangerous to the enemy, who would be glad to get rid of him ... The authorities, who view him in proper perspective, informed him that he would receive such protection as might be deemed necessary and there the matter rests.[132]

It was thus entirely possible to view William Le Queux for what he was – a charlatan and scaremonger, who desired nothing more than to increase his own celebrity.

Despite peddling lies, crackpots like Leo Maxse seem to have genuinely believed that the peril was real. In a private letter to Lord Northcliffe he asked:

> Have you noticed the number of German names in the War Office? The Schlichs, the Bovenschoens, etc. etc. I am told there is also a dangerous man at the Treasury. I have tracked down a son of Krupp's London representative, Major WF Reichwald, who was appointed Assistant Military Secretary and Interpreter to the Commander-in-Chief in India in March 1914, which would give him access to all the plans of the Indian authorities, by whom he was treated with the usual trustfulness. He came to France last autumn as Chief Staff Officer of an Indian Cavalry Division, and appears to have been advised by his British friends, in deference to French susceptibilities, to change his name from Reichwald to Blaker. But unfortunately the Army List was carelessly edited and you will find him put down in the May issue both as Major WF Reichwald in one part, and Major WF Blaker in another. It is not disputed that his father was Krupp's representative in London, but Blaker alias Reichwald is voted 'a good chap' by many British soldiers, who are annoyed with my 'mare's nest'. However the gentleman has had to leave France, but the Authorities are jealously guarding his whereabouts in England preparatory to appointing him to some other confidential post.[133]

Maxse's conspiratorial fantasies are clearly on display, but what is more, Lord Northcliffe appears equally convinced of the threat.[134] In a reply to one of Maxse's latter letters, Northcliffe conveyed his approval of Maxse's hyperbole:

> My dear Leo, what am I to believe? I open one letter and am told that Lord
> Hardinge is Germany's best friend in the country, and I was so impressed by the
> evidence that I sent it on to Robin. I shall begin to believe soon that you are the
> hidden hand.[135]

Aside from merely publicizing the spy peril, presumably to awaken the British
public to the fact that 'we are fighting a battle for our existence as a nation' and
compensate for the lack of genuine war stories needed to instil popular jingoism
and patriotism, Northcliffe also lobbied the opposition to take the matter further.[136]
In November 1914, he wrote to Bonar Law claiming not to be an 'unduly suspicious
or a scarey person' but that:

> it is beyond question that, for some reason, the Government are protecting spies
> in high places ... That our Post Office has German and other spies in many of
> its branches is, I believe, a fact ... The enclosed account of the arrest at Lerwick
> shows that we were right, and we know of other cases.[137]

Far from being a centre of German espionage, the debacle surrounding the Lerwick
Post Office, in which several members of staff were illegally imprisoned, sprung
from allegations – endorsed by Winston Churchill no less – that Shetlanders
were somehow disloyal and favourable to Germany. This then fostered the belief
that spies were active and had established a submarine base somewhere on the
archipelago, but there was of course no truth in this.[138] Notwithstanding the
prominence of spy fever, and the fact that leading proponents of the spy peril
certainly seem to have believed their own fantasises, neither of these indicate that
spy phobias were widely adopted as an emotional response.

   Since emotions are interpreted by social custom, which is shaped by the political
outlook of the individual or group, the expression of collective spy phobias should
be attributed to communities aligned with radical conservatism. The rhetoric
surrounding the spy peril undoubtedly originated from right-wing individuals
and conservative pressure groups to increase popular support for their ideology.
By identifying the origins of scaremongering and highlighting the relative
insignificance of the radical right, this chapter has questioned whether extreme
spy phobias ever became a dominant or protracted collective experience. Despite
the intermittent prominence of radical communities, they remained incoherent,
divided and peripheral to British politics. The failure to generate conformity
among their supporters, as well as the lack of sustained conviction expressed
towards the espionage threat, suggests that this emotional regime seldom enforced
strict emotional discipline. For the majority, spy fever only ever imposed relatively
lenient emotional standards, which may also explain why individual phobias were
often only short-lived experiences.

   Reimagining spy fever as a mixture of emotional standards that all existed
simultaneously across different communities has several implications for
understanding the scale of espionage phobias. Given this diversity, spy fever failed
to dictate stringent emotional values, and individuals were free to ignore or resist

the increasingly prejudicial customs advocated by the radical right. Although Panayi contends that the animosity displayed towards Germans was so intense and widespread that it swept away traditional liberalism, the continued capacity to confront popular discrimination shows that these values had not been entirely abandoned during 1914 and 1915.[139] Owing to the cultural impact of the spy peril and the conspicuousness of espionage phobias, historians have often overstated the significance of such emotions and exaggerated their pervasiveness. But the acceptance of the spy peril as a legitimate concern was limited to a particular community, which was already in possession of latent xenophobic attitudes. Consequently, although the spy peril afforded the radical right greater prominence, liberalism continued to provide an emotional counter-community that could shape wartime experiences.

How far this sort of sentiment pervaded British society is unclear. Less than 3 per cent of all articles surveyed in this study seem to explicitly oppose heightened fears or radical anxieties. However, the fact that different interpretations of the German spy threat existed suggests that a corresponding emotional community also existed. And in the opposing emotional community, spy fever did not simply induce suspicion or alarm, and nor did it inevitably focus frustration and animosity at people considered as 'outsiders'. We should not therefore mistake the prominence of spy fever as indicative of the pervasiveness of literal spy phobias. Now that this chapter has raised the question of pervasiveness, the size and dominant characteristics of spy fever in Britain during the First World War are the subject of the following chapter.

Chapter 7

THE SPY OBSESSION

The political and cultural resistance to popular suspicion and xenophobia suggests that there also existed an emotional refuge from the anxiety and animosity advocated by radical individuals and conservative groups. This leaves us with the question: How extensive were spy phobias? Any attempt to gauge public opinion is obviously fraught with difficulty, and measuring the extent of collective emotion is harder still. Not least because historical sources claiming cognizance of social attitudes or collective emotional states were invariably written for political purposes. Yet this has not prevented historians from using radicals' estimations about popular spy phobias as evidence of the widespread impact of the spy peril. Notwithstanding the value of these sources in unpacking the anxieties that could be associated with secret agents, they reveal little about how receptive society was to them. Lacking objectivity and careful analysis, descriptions of public opinion were crafted as propaganda and should be treated as such. But most importantly, radical figures provide no useful indication of collective anxieties for the simple reason that they make two very distinct and conflicting claims about the magnitude of popular anxieties linked to German spies.

On the one hand there were people like Lord Charles Beresford who, in a speech to Parliament, claimed that 'there is a growing feeling of irritation against those Germans in this country who are suspected of being spies ... there is also a feeling that the measures taken by authorities are far too lenient ... in places like Portsmouth there is a suggestion of making vigilance committees to take the law into their own hands'.[1] Conservatives in both Houses continually harassed the government over the espionage peril and made repeated claims regarding the scale of public anxiety caused by the German spies still at large.[2] For politicians like Beresford, William Joynson-Hicks and the Earl of Crawford, exaggerating the degree of popular condemnation and alarm served to compel the government into adopting the discriminatory measures that they had long been advocating. To gather support for their cause, and for their anti-alien rhetoric to have any impact, people not only needed to believe that German spies were a realistic and imminent danger, but that others were also taking this threat seriously. It was very much in Beresford's interest to exaggerate the social impact of the spy peril and the resulting angst.

Then there are the contrasting allegations, made by people who were similarly jingoistic and xenophobic, that entirely contradict Beresford's assessment. Far from attesting to the prevalence of spy phobias, William Le Queux declared that *German Spies in England: An Exposure* (1915) was purposely written to awaken the British public to the enemy within because, according to Le Queux, people seldom took the threat seriously.[3] He even whinged about the derision that he regularly faced because of his methods:

> I was, at the same time, inundated with letters from persons who openly abused me and called me a liar ... One newspaper wrote, 'There are no spies in England. You are a fool to alarm the public by such a statement. Nobody believes you.'[4]

Leo Maxse, the journalist behind the conservative *National Review*, likewise insinuated that espionage phobias were fairly atypical in his condemnation of those who 'devoted themselves to pooh-poohing the German peril' and who 'discount the German danger as the malignant invention of Teutophobe scaremongers or crazy Jingoes'.[5] In a private letter to Lord Northcliffe, he complained that society remained unmoved by the spy peril and how, even by July 1915, people had still 'not yet begun to realise the extraordinary thoroughness of the German system of espionage established in this country many years before the War'.[6] So whereas politicians exaggerated the scale of a popular spy fever to try and provoke government action, authors and journalist downplayed collective spy phobias to augment their own status and significance. By publicly disparaging the lack of awareness and engagement with the spy peril, Le Queux was seeking to incite frustration and vigilance among his radical supporters by criticizing mainstream responses. Such a narrative had the added benefit of portraying Le Queux as the most important celebrity figure in relation to national security. For him to appear as a visionary, he and his ideas needed to appear exceptional.[7] Claiming that he was 'awakening' society to the German spy peril fulfilled this desire. Using either of these sources to reconstruct the scale of spy fever is therefore problematic. Because espionage phobias could be both widespread and scarce depending on the intentions of the author, they rarely provide useful appraisals of public opinion or sentiment.

So how can historians evaluate the extent of spy phobias or measure something as elusive as popular emotions and attitudes? As mentioned previously, Panikos Panayi reckoned that public opinion could be measured through the politically active and powerful sections of society. This study contends that newspapers, when used systematically, can give us a better idea of the range of opinions being expressed. The language and tone of newspaper coverage can be thought of as both reflective of customary attitudes and emotions and a linguist and cultural resource to interpret circumstances and feelings. Despite not disclosing the impact they had on peoples' emotional states, a comprehensive analysis of newspaper articles containing references to spying is nevertheless symptomatic of the size and characteristics of different emotional communities. Consequently, measuring the frequency of alarmist rhetoric within the overall coverage of the spy peril provides one way of ascertaining the relative significance of the emotional community centred on anxiety and anger and provides further insights into how and why these emotions manifested in response to the spy peril.

To try and accommodate the breadth of emotional experiences on the British Home Front, this analysis has gathered 9,245 articles that mention spying in some way and has categorized them according to their content. The categories are: *spy scares* (reports involving tangible suspects), *alarmist rhetoric* (vague allegations of covert activities with no actual suspects), *popular culture* (fictional or pseudohistorical depictions of spying), *international intrigue* (reports of spies operating oversees) and *opposition* (denunciations of the spy peril).[8] Although cataloguing entries in this way is subjective, and articles can incorporate a range of meanings and agendas, these classifications are designed to distinguish between specific instances of suspicion, the various concerns that developed in association with the peril, the prominence of espionage within popular culture, the role spies played in helping people explain and understand the war as well as the resistance to discriminatory and chauvinistic sentiment. Although this approach is not without limitation, it has produced the first quantitative analysis of spy fever. In doing so, the frequency with which society encountered narratives exaggerating the threat and calling for a heightened emotional state can be contextualized within society's broader interest in spying, and our understanding of 'spy fever' as a description of collective experience can become more nuanced as a result.

Most importantly, the use of local newspapers in this study contrasts with the historiographical focus on national right-wing publications and so incorporates a much wider range of communities and perspectives. Comparing *The Globe* with more mainstream journals clearly highlights the problem with confining the analysis to such sources. Between 4 August 1914 and 31 December 1915, for example, *The Globe* published 925 articles containing references to espionage; ten of the fifteen daily newspapers surveyed published less than half that amount. To put this statistic into context, it equates to over two spy-related articles in every issue of *The Globe*, whereas half of the daily newspapers in this study produced less than one article per issue. *The Globe* was more than twice as likely to feature stories about spies than the majority of newspapers analysed. This is hardly surprising given the radical right's close association with the spy peril (*The Globe* was a fervently right-wing newspaper), but it demonstrates that publications like these were the exception and not the rule. Local newspapers are therefore essential if we are to understand the national implications of the spy peril. No other source can chart the development of spy fever in such a systematic way. So what did the spy peril look like in provincial newspapers?

According to many contemporary reports, outbursts of spy phobias were typically varied and sporadic,[9] and so mapping collective anxiety is practically impossible. Moreover, while there are some geographic trends evident in newspaper coverage, it is just as likely that these disparities were due to the political affiliations of the journal or editor, rather than local concerns or perspectives. With this caveat in mind though, the presence of spy fever in local newspapers does provide some tentative insights into the national ramifications of the spy

Table 7.1 Prevalence of Spying in the Press, 4 August 1914–31 December 1915

	Issues	Spy Articles	Articles per Issue		Issues	Spy Articles	Articles per Issue
The Globe	427	925	2.17	Berwickshire News	74	64	0.86
Faringdon Advertiser	73	121	1.66	Belfast Telegraph	438	368	0.84
Whitby Gazette	74	110	1.49	Thanet Advertiser	73	60	0.82
Fife Free Press	73	98	1.34	Nottingham Journal	436	343	0.79
Dublin Daily Express	441	562	1.27	Hawick Express	74	57	0.77
Diss Express	74	93	1.26	Chelmsford Chronicle	73	54	0.74
Edinburgh Evening News	436	537	1.23	Dorking and Leatherhead Ad.	73	54	0.74
Birmingham Mail	436	537	1.23	Cheshire Observer	72	53	0.74
Penrith Observer	74	89	1.20	Southern Reporter	74	52	0.70
Western Mail	421	505	1.20	Drogheda Independent	73	50	0.68
Cornishman	74	88	1.19	Tamworth Herald	73	49	0.67
Hull Daily Mail	436	513	1.18	Ballymena Observer	74	46	0.62
Shepton Mallet Journal	74	80	1.08	Warwickshire Advertiser	73	43	0.59
Liverpool Echo	436	440	1.01	Arbroath Herald and Ad.	74	43	0.58
Manchester Evening News	439	441	1.00	Glamorgan Gazette	74	37	0.50
Daily Record	448	432	0.96	Brecon County Times	74	37	0.50
Sheffield Independent	445	429	0.96	Caernarvon and Denbigh Herald	73	36	0.49
Aberdeen Evening Express	443	422	0.95	Belper News	74	35	0.47
Bexhill-on-Sea Observer	73	66	0.90	Sligo Champion	72	33	0.46
Leeds Mercury	444	398	0.90	Kilsyth Chronicle	74	32	0.43
Westminster Gazette	438	392	0.89	Nairnshire Telegraph	74	23	0.31
Portsmouth Evening News	437	383	0.88	Kilrush Herald	74	15	0.20

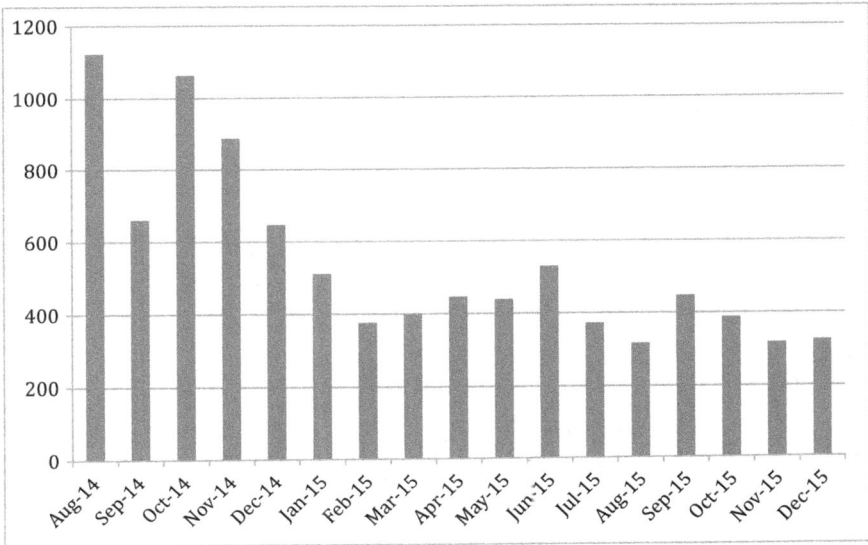

Figure 7.1 Total number of spy-related articles per month.

peril. First, there were small differences in how the spy peril appeared in coastal locations compared with inland regions. Not only were more articles published in coastal areas, but this fixation also contained a higher frequency of alarmist reporting (944 articles compared with 761 inland). Given that espionage anxieties were closely linked to the threat of invasion, especially early in the conflict, 27 per cent of articles appearing in coastal publications were categorized as *alarmist rhetoric*, whereas only 23 per cent of articles published inland featured exaggerated threat assessments or explicit xenophobia. Coastal areas were perhaps more susceptible to this sort of trepidation compared to communities less exposed to a German attack. Second, there were also various discrepancies between urban and rural settings.[10] The latter showed considerably less interest in spying. Table 7.1 indicates that twenty out of the twenty-two newspapers with the lowest proportion of spy-related articles were sold in rural contexts. Given that editors choose subjects based on their appeal to readers, it is perhaps fair to assume that urban communities were more interested in spying as a result. Interestingly, rural newspapers displayed a higher rate of alarm,[11] which suggests that the spy peril was more a source of concern than enjoyment in areas where there were fewer aliens and fewer entertainment venues. Rural areas also suffered more from the lack of up-to-date war news, which possibly exacerbated their anxieties.[12] However, this is all rather speculative. While we cannot say with any certainty that individuals in certain areas suffered more extreme anxieties or frustrations, we can affirm that the emotional standards facilitating those responses were more visible, and therefore more accessible, in coastal and rural contexts. This may have led to spy phobias being more prevalent within these settings.

Table 7.2 Content of Spy-Related Articles by Newspaper. (Number of Articles in Each Category Per Newspaper along with the Percentage of the Total for That Publication)

	Spy Scares	Alarmist Rhetoric	Popular Culture	International Intrigue	Opposition	Total
The Globe	79 (8.5%)	522 (56.4%)	56 (6.1%)	246 (26.6%)	22 (2.4%)	925
Faringdon Ad.	21 (17.4%)	29 (24%)	29 (24%)	38 (31.4%)	4 (3.3%)	121
Whitby Gazette	7 (6.4%)	49 (44.5%)	35 (31.8%)	17 (15.5%)	2 (1.8%)	110
Fife Free Press	17 (17.3%)	35 (35.7%)	14 (14.3%)	30 (30.6%)	2 (2%)	98
Dublin Daily Express	78 (13.9%)	182 (32.4%)	27 (4.8%)	264 (47%)	11 (2%)	562
Diss Express	24 (25.8%)	26 (28%)	14 (15.1%)	25 (26.9%)	4 (4.3%)	93
Edinburgh Evening News	63 (11.7%)	99 (18.4%)	134 (25%)	221 (41.2%)	20 (3.7%)	537
Birmingham Mail	82 (15.3%)	113 (21%)	54 (10.1%)	277 (51.6%)	11 (2%)	537
Penrith Observer	13 (14.6%)	29 (32.6%)	11 (12.4%)	35 (39.3%)	1 (1.1%)	89
Western Mail	76 (15%)	139 (27.5%)	38 (7.5%)	243 (48.1%)	9 (1.8%)	505
Cornishman	22 (25%)	31 (35.2%)	5 (5.7%)	29 (33%)	1 (1.1%)	88
Hull Daily Mail	88 (17.2%)	169 (32.9%)	75 (14.6%)	163 (31.8%)	18 (3.5%)	513
Shepton Mallet Journal	24 (30%)	21 (26.3%)	4 (5%)	31 (38.8%)	0	80
Liverpool Echo	72 (16.4%)	82 (18.6%)	49 (11.1%)	222 (50.5%)	15 (3.4%)	440
Manchester Evening News	63 (14.3%)	77 (17.5%)	35 (7.9%)	260 (59%)	6 (1.4%)	441
Daily Record	44 (10.2%)	85 (19.7%)	94 (21.8%)	199 (46.1%)	10 (2.3%)	432
Sheffield Independent	46 (10.7%)	78 (18.2%)	152 (35.4%)	140 (32.6%)	13 (3%)	429
Aberdeen Evening Express	48 (11.4%)	104 (24.6%)	91 (21.6%)	161 (38.1%)	18 (4.3%)	422
Bexhill-on-Sea Observer	3 (4.5%)	25 (37.9%)	28 (42.4%)	4 (6.1%)	6 (9.1%)	66
Leeds Mercury	69 (17.3%)	110 (27.6%)	86 (21.6%)	120 (30.2%)	13 (3.3%)	398
Westminster Gazette	41 (10.5%)	66 (16.8%)	45 (11.5%)	216 (55.1%)	24 (6.1%)	392
Portsmouth Evening News	82 (21.4%)	85 (22.2%)	64 (16.7%)	146 (38.1%)	6 (1.6%)	383
Berwickshire News	12 (18.8%)	21 (32.8%)	5 (7.8%)	24 (37.5%)	2 (3.1%)	64
Belfast Telegraph	47 (12.8%)	81 (22%)	56 (15.2%)	174 (47.3%)	10 (2.7%)	368
Thanet Ad.	1 (1.7%)	23 (38.3%)	25 (41.7%)	9 (15%)	2 (3.3%)	60
Nottingham Journal	85 (24.8%)	81 (23.6%)	26 (7.6%)	141 (41.4%)	10 (2.9%)	343

	Spy Scares	Alarmist Rhetoric	Popular Culture	International Intrigue	Opposition	Total
Hawick Express	2 (3.5%)	17 (29.8%)	35 (61.4%)	2 (3.5%)	1 (1.8%)	57
Chelmsford Chronicle	12 (22.2%)	20 (37%)	8 (14.8%)	10 (18.5%)	4 (7.4%)	54
Dorking and Leatherhead Ad.	4 (7.4%)	18 (33.3%)	5 (9.3%)	24 (44.4%)	3 (5.6%)	54
Cheshire Observer	9 (17%)	12 (22.6%)	19 (35.8%)	13 (24.5%)	0	53
Southern Reporter	8 (15.4%)	21 (40.4%)	15 (28.8%)	8 (15.4%)	0	52
Drogheda Independent	7 (14%)	20 (40%)	13 (26%)	8 (16%)	2 (4%)	50
Tamworth Herald	9 (18.4%)	14 (28.6%)	15 (30.6%)	11 (22.4%)	0	49
Ballymena Observer	9 (19.6%)	11 (23.9%)	9 (19.6%)	17 (37%)	0	46
Warwickshire Ad.	10 (23.3%)	16 (37.2%)	2 (4.7%)	15 (34.9%)	0	43
Arbroath Herald and Ad.	0	19 (44.2%)	15 (34.9%)	4 (9.3%)	5 (11.6%)	43
Glamorgan Gazette	2 (5.4%)	13 (35.1%)	6 (16.2%)	14 (37.8%)	2 (5.4%)	37
Brecon County Times	2 (5.4%)	16 (43.2%)	12 (32.4%)	7 (18.9%)	0	37
Caernarvon Herald	5 (13.9%)	11 (30.6%)	13 (36.1%)	6 (16.7%)	1 (2.8%)	36
Belper News	4 (11.4%)	4 (11.4%)	5 (14.3%)	20 (57.1%)	2 (5.7%)	35
Sligo Champion	4 (12.1%)	12 (36.4%)	5 (15.2%)	12 (36.4%)	0	33
Kilsyth Chronicle	4 (12.5%)	6 (18.8%)	5 (15.6%)	16 (50%)	1 (3.1%)	32
Nairnshire Telegraph	5 (21.7%)	7 (30.4%)	5 (21.7%)	4 (17.4%)	2 (8.7%)	23
Kilrush Herald	1 (6.7%)	5 (33.3%)	9 (60%)	0	0	15
Total	**1306 (14%)**	**2604 (28%)**	**1448 (16%)**	**3624 (39%)**	**263 (3%)**	**9245**

Table 7.3 Number of Spy-Related Articles Each Month Organized by Content

	Spy Scares	Alarmist Rhetoric	Popular Culture	International Intrigue	Opposition	Total
August 1914	297	311	50	435	30	1123
September 1914	40	190	65	333	33	661
October 1914	111	386	129	393	45	1064
November 1914	111	313	102	315	46	887
December 1914	36	180	109	302	20	647
January 1915	26	153	95	213	24	511
February 1915	8	125	105	127	10	375
March 1915	8	124	128	133	5	398
April 1915	77	102	122	142	3	446
May 1915	136	112	70	110	11	439
June 1915	134	101	83	205	7	530
July 1915	94	86	49	137	6	372
August 1915	20	67	83	137	9	316
September 1915	78	97	87	181	4	447
October 1915	80	99	56	145	7	387
November 1915	18	81	59	158	1	317
December 1915	30	77	56	160	2	325

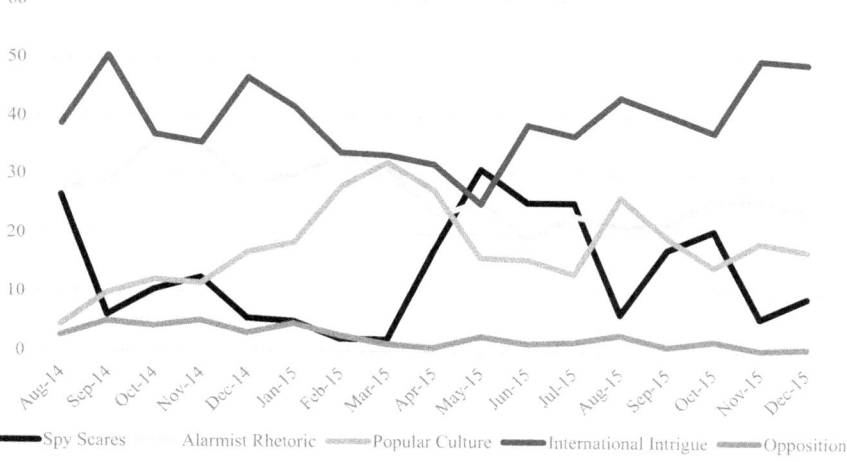

Figure 7.2 Proportional breakdown of spy-related content (as a percentage of the total coverage).

It must also be remembered that people could ostensibly be aware of the peril but remain unaffected by the rhetoric and activities directed towards the danger.[13] John Bamber, for example, noted in his diary that Lancashire was full of 'precaution and preparation for war', but there was never any mention of popular outbursts or reactions towards the spy danger. Notwithstanding the military's efforts to round up German 'devils', any popular anxieties went unnoticed or were deemed unremarkable.[14] Although Peggy Larken recognized the importance of conforming to patriotic narratives, she surmised that few people acted on them. When asked about wartime anti-alienism, she recalled how society was 'taught to hate', and that because of the certain rumours, 'we all thought that these high dignitaries were spies'. But when pressed about her first-hand experiences, Larken insisted that the single German in her village had been 'left alone' by local residents.[15] Larken's insinuation that people remained apathetic to local manifestations of the threat, despite a superficial receptiveness to anti-alien rhetoric, suggests that the popularity of spying in British culture did not reflect a deep commitment to the ideals of the radical right. Consequently, even in areas considered likely targets for German espionage, spy phobias could be noticeably absent. During his time defending the Firth of Forth in 1915, Nowell Turner Smith, a second lieutenant in the Highland Light Infantry, commented on the dearth of public outcry: 'Work is going along quite smoothly. There have been no scares to investigate and no spies to track down.'[16] Of course these are merely snapshots, but the absence of panic challenges the notion that collective anxieties grew to feverish proportions.

This brings us back to the important question: How extensive were spy phobias? Figure 7.1 illustrates that the spy peril was most prominent during the initial five months of the war. After the resurgence of the threat in August 1914, the spy peril peaked again in October but continued to wane thereafter. Several high-profile cases involving genuine German spies in June and September 1915 led to a renewed interest in espionage, but by December 1915 this had lessened considerably. Whereas August 1914 saw the publication of 1,123 articles, which equates to around 2.2 articles per issue, by December 1915 those numbers had dropped to 325 and 0.6, respectively. Meaning that by the end of 1915, spy fever had seriously declined as a cultural and political obsession. Moreover, thirty-four of the newspapers sampled contained at least one mention of spying in every issue during August 1914. Twenty-two publications (i.e. half the entire sample) contained at least two articles for every issue published, with some including as many as four articles per issue during the first month of war. Yet in December the following year, only four newspapers contained one article per issue, nineteen publications produced one article (or less) for every two issues printed and nine newspapers made no mention of spying whatsoever. Thus, despite the efforts of radicals to embellish and promote the threat of German agents, the spy peril was not as conspicuous or as pervasive as some alleged. Any emotional styles that formed in response to the spy peril were thus unlikely to have been dominant emotional standards, at least for much of this period.

We can see this in the way people wrote about their observations and experiences during the war. Even at the height of the spy peril in the press, many individuals appear completely oblivious to the threat. Immediately following the outbreak of war, Bruce Stanbridge recorded his anticipation of the impending conflict but gave no sign that German spies were the cause. As soon as war was declared, he foresaw the unprecedented scale and significance of what was to come and by the end of the month had already recognized that the crisis was 'getting very bad'. While he exhibited some minor concerns regarding the shortage of war news, he never expressed any feelings regarding the spy peril.[17] Although Fannie Fieldsend believed that Britain had 'been drawn into the most stupendous conflict the world has ever known', and her diary diligently recorded significant events, she never once referred to spying.[18] Often peoples' greatest concern was not abstract dangers posed by German espionage but the prospect of food shortages caused by the war itself.[19]

In one remarkable case of indifference, a harbour worker in Aberdeen was duped by a rudimentary ploy. At the height of the spy peril in November 1914, a man claiming to be a Belgian refugee named 'Henry Vander Vin' inquired into the operations of the fishing port there. While Vander Vin cannot be verified as a secret agent, the few German spies operating in Britain were tasked with gathering intelligence about Britain's ports and naval movements, so it seems likely that Vander Vin was a spy or at least somebody posing as one.[20] In any case, the author alleged that following his 'forced exile' from Antwerp, where he had been employed as the Port's chief engineer, he had developed an interest in gathering 'information concerning certain ports of the United Kingdom … to take account of its present position, its dispositions, the conditions under which this industry is carried on both as regards the reception and removal of the fish'. The letter contained an extensive series of questions that, if answered, would betray significant details as to the harbour's vulnerabilities, including the size of Aberdeen's population, the local railway network, the configuration of the harbour and, perhaps most alarmingly, the building materials used to construct the docks there. The author even asked that maps and plans be sent to provide a more complete understanding.[21] Notwithstanding the town clerk's objections, the harbour engineer forwarded the requested information without any due diligence.[22] Despite the potential value of this information to an invading force in need of logistical support, or a naval squadron attempting to attack the harbour, port officials seemed almost entirely unaware, or at least unconcerned, that this person might have been a spy in the employ of a foreign government.[23] Had the harbour staff been seriously affected by spy fever, or had there been an intense atmosphere of panic and anxiety in Aberdeen, such a request would have surely been met with much greater scepticism.

Despite the onset of what would become an unprecedented challenge for Britain militarily, economically and politically, the impacts of war were not necessarily clear to all in 1914.[24] The influx of khaki-clad figures was sometimes the only sign that Britain was at war.[25] While travelling across the south-east of England during Britain's mobilization in August 1914, Horace Joseph saw little disruption and 'no signs of excitement'. On arrival in Tunbridge Wells he maintained that there were 'no signs of anything unusual'.[26] In the same month, Captain Arthur Lloyd-Baker similarly noted how 'contrary to my expectations things where not in a whirl at all'.[27] Even in London, the public often appeared to 'go about their amusements or business as if nothing unusual was happening'.[28] During her visit to a crowded Blackpool beach in April 1915, Edith Usher commented in her diary that you would 'never think there was a war on'.[29] Notwithstanding the enormity of the international crisis, people could seemingly manage their emotions, at least in public, which further challenges the notion that there were frequent outbursts of collective 'mania'. If people struggled to notice signs of a war going on, they must have also been oblivious to the extreme emotions on display because of the spy peril.

So what does this mean for the way we understand the concept of 'spy fever'? Once again a systematic survey of espionage in the press reveals much about the nature of society's fascination with spying. One of the most striking features of this quantitative analysis of spy fever is that scaremongering, jingoism and bigotry were far less prominent than the historiography often implies. Notwithstanding the fact that almost two-thirds of articles printed in *The Globe* can be considered to be in some way alarmist, similar articles only amounted to one quarter of the newspaper coverage across the remainder of the selection. In only fourteen publications did *alarmist rhetoric* feature more frequently throughout the period compared to any other category. Articles containing scaremongering and xenophobia were clearly most prominent numerically and proportionally in October and November 1914 but it waned thereafter. In contrast, the attention given to *international intrigue* remained relatively consistent, aside from a brief drop in May 1915 during the trials of Anton Küferle, Karl Müller and John Hahn, which captivated audiences nationwide for a brief time. Far more space was given to stories of spying abroad: 39 per cent of all articles reported spies active overseas; twenty-two newspapers featured this category most frequently overall; and, in every month of this period, with the exception of May 1915, *international intrigue* was proportionally higher than any other category. In some months, articles in this category accounted for around half of all references to spying. The fact that newspapers most commonly portrayed spying as something taking place in other theatres of war, and not as an imminent threat unfolding in Britain, indicates that the primary emotional response of spy fever would not have been a visceral or literal fear of German secret agents. Only in August 1914 did German spies look like an immediate danger to British society, and even then people seldom expressed or exhibited signs of intense fear.

The most common explanation for the prevalence of spy fever in the historiography has been the rise of anti-German sentiment. But there were undoubtedly other factors involved. The scale of *international intrigue* in newspaper coverage, for instance, suggests that spy stories satisfied a need to stay abreast of wartime developments. While this narrative was undoubtedly sensational, it was also entertaining and distracted from the harsh realities of war. Additionally, 'The Popular Game of Spy' (see Figure 7.3) also suggests that peoples' interest in spying was more than just xenophobia; it was also a form of amusement. Although spy fever is often conflated with radicals' severe Germanophobia, Figure 7.2 shows that the proportion of *alarmist rhetoric* steadily decreased during 1915. That is not to say that radicals became any less chauvinistic or conspicuous in 1915, but this became less apparent as a feature of spy fever.

At the same time as this proportional and numerical decline, the number of articles relating to spies in *popular culture* increased. Most months saw more adverts

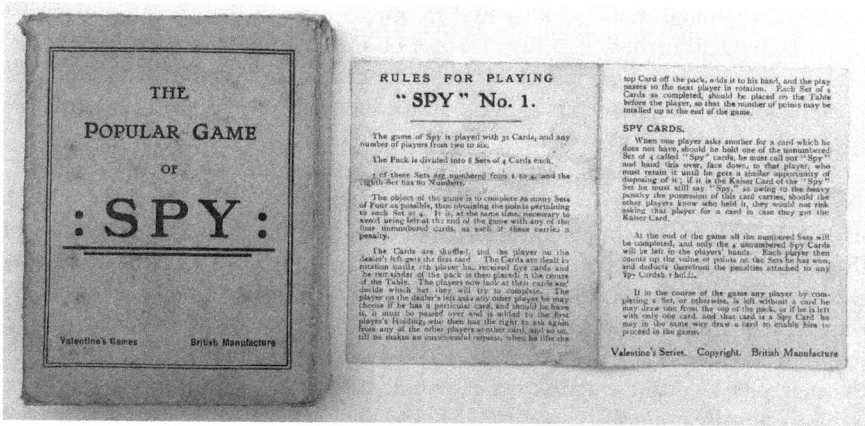

Figure 7.3 'The Popular Game of SPY'.
Game box, instructions and a selection of cards from 'The Popular Game of SPY'. The original item is held by Dr Nicolas Hiley in his personal collections.

and reviews of plays, films and books relating to fictional spies than there were allegations or condemnations of ostensibly real covert activities. This highlights an important yet underappreciated aspect of spy fever. Playhouses and cinema halls became a vital component of wartime culture, in which military successes – or perceived successes – could be celebrated and wartime values reaffirmed. Secret agents were a hugely significant component of this spectacle. The newspapers surveyed report at least fifty-seven plays and sixty-five films were released during the first year and half of war that contained references to spying. Doubtless some of these productions were created as propaganda designed to galvanize popular anxieties relating to the enemy within, but this does not detract from the fact that the spy peril provided a huge source of entertainment during war. This was also partly true for people living in provincial contexts where these art forms were less accessible. This study found sixty-seven spy stories serialized in newspapers; forty-two of these were printed in rural newspapers, and nineteen out of the twenty-eight rural journals all featured stories involving spies. Thus, whereas spy phobias were seemingly most acute in certain geographic contexts, the espionage genre appears to have captivated audiences nationwide.

The fact that different themes were present in newspaper coverage of the spy peril suggests the idea of an enemy within could elicit different feelings depending on how and where it was encountered. The fact that, when taken together, *spy scares* and *alarmist rhetoric* accounted for less than half of all articles concerning spies suggests that fears and anxieties about German espionage were not necessarily the defining features of spy fever. If newspaper coverage was at all reflective of the emotional communities that society interacted with, then spy phobias were most likely not the dominant feelings associated with spy fever. Although they were important, and were certainly prevailing emotions expressed in certain contexts, spy fever embodied a range of experiences and emotions. Owing to the numerous ways in which people could figuratively encounter the enemy within – through military activity, political rhetoric, local gossip, sensationalist journalism or tales of fictional exploits – it would be too simplistic to assume that only a single emotional experience emerged in response.

CONCLUSION

The various chapters of this book have explored the different and sometimes conflicting emotional styles that shaped how feelings were expressed and potentially felt by individuals in response to the spy peril. After taking a closer look at the suspicion and vigilance displayed during August 1914, Parts II and III highlighted the range of emotions that could be felt in response to similar scenarios or anticipated dangers. Whereas Chapter 3 analysed documented cases of fear and panic felt or observed during incidents involving suspected spies, Chapter 4 observed the excitement and joy felt when combating spies. Fear could thus titillate as well as terrorize. The chapters in Part III suggest that anxieties could be both exacerbated and mitigated by the spy peril. Chapter 5 explored how the spy peril may have encouraged calming emotions like hope as well as motivating ones like frustration. Chapter 6 showed that the use of the spy peril could incite hatred and intolerance or inspire compassion and acceptance depending on the community or circumstance in which espionage and intrigue were discussed or encountered. The 'spy fever' witnessed in Britain during the First World War encompassed all of these emotions. Society's fascination – and, at times, obsession – with German's purported spy system, and all the emotions that derived from it, is what we might term a 'spy fever'.

As the prevailing emotional styles associated with the spy peril changed as the context of the war changed, it is impossible to identify a single dominant experience of spy fever. Phobias were only one facet of society's obsession with espionage and were often not the defining experience. Most importantly, there is no clear evidence that any person (not committed to an asylum) developed a serious physiological condition because of, or in relation to, the German spy threat. The inclination to view spy fever as an irrational aberration derives more from retrospective interpretations fashioned during the post-war period, rather than careful analyses of contemporary experiences. People looking back at popular fears and anxieties presumably felt the need to distance themselves from the hyperbole and exaggerated reactions that, with hindsight, were not proportional to the actuality of the threat. Much like how the British sought to chastise the French for fearing the German spy in 1870 by labelling popular fears there as hysterical, writers in the 1920s sought to distance themselves from the xenophobia and militarism that helped instigate and then sustain the conflict. In a 1966 memoir, for example, Ernest Lycette wrote:

Peoples of various nations, led by their leaders as they watched the press and streets during those demented days, fell victim to the hysteria as helplessly as any of the nameless multitudes around them. It seemed as if reason and humanity had ceased. Scares and hysteria of war filled the columns of the press.[1]

The type of language and expression on display here is rather different from how many people recorded their experiences during the conflict. The need to characterize 1914 as a series of 'demented days' and liken popular responses to a form of psychological malady only took hold as society became increasingly disillusioned with the war. Although authors like Basil Thomson portrayed spy phobias as delusions that defied treatment, statements like these do not amount to an objective or carefully conducted assessment of popular opinion, nor do they take into account the complexity of emotional experience. As such, the use of medical terminology to describe popular outbursts of emotion should not force historians to consider spy phobias as a severe physical or psychological condition.

Regardless of how fabricated the threat may have been, the emotions comprising spy fever were hardly irrational. Although sensationalized and distorted from reality, fictional perceptions of espionage acted as a conduit for the expression of various emotions that had been intensified by the outbreak of war. Individuals afflicted were often simply complying with strategies to mobilize society for war, acting out racialist policies emboldened by the crisis, captivated by the thrill of wartime dangers or afraid of the internal and external dangers forged through conflict. Using psychological ailments to describe individuals' emotional states induced by the spy peril is therefore a mistake. Encounters with perceived German spies rarely, if ever, generated hysterical delusions. Terms like 'fever' or 'mania' more accurately depict the fervent collective interest in depictions of German espionage.

Part of the reason why spy fever has been viewed as irrational is the widespread consensus that it formed spontaneously. As an abstract and tenuous threat, though, society needed instructing on when, where and how certain responses became appropriate, and we can see this in how the danger was constructed in popular discourse. The onset of the First World War brought with it demands for greater vigilance and security. While these narratives outlined an elusive threat – treacherous German spies intent on disrupting national mobilization and secretly orchestrating a German invasion – they also encouraged widespread social engagement with the issue. It was widely instructed that strangers be diligently watched and individuals seen loitering near vulnerable locations, even those with little military significance, were to be considered suspect. These warnings were then reinforced by the activities of local authorities. Any 'panic' that did manifest in August 1914 was almost certainly symptomatic of an overzealous search for secret agents by various County Constabularies and Territorial units, which set the tone of popular paranoia. The combination of rhetoric in the press and the willingness of local officials to imitate amateur spy fiction clearly set a precedent and displayed an emotional style with which society could adopt.

However, as the parameters of war became more clearly defined, the emotives contained within the spy peril changed, and so the dominant characteristics of spy fever changed with it. With no precise image of what a German spy might look like, early suspicions assimilated with broader concerns to target anything deemed inappropriate or detrimental to the war effort. Rather than encourage popular vigilance against suspicious-looking individuals, abstract claims of German influence and subversion now promoted antipathy towards the presence of alien communities in accordance with radical conservatism. This divisive rhetoric primarily targeted immigrants, homosexuals, pacifists and socialists and portrayed them as an enemy within by associating them with the German spy threat. This form of hostility was only possible because of the initial aversion and misgivings towards Germans in Britain. Although both reactions (suspicion and then animosity) essentially derived from fears linked with the enemy within, in certain contexts this created a sense of trepidation and in others provoked anger or hatred. Part of the appeal of the spy peril, and thus one of the reasons why spy fever appeared so prevalent, was that it liberated xenophobic and jingoistic sentiments, which some felt necessary to the war effort, not because spy mania was a kind of uncontrollable hysteria.

Whereas some individuals expressed anger or hatred in response to the enemy within, fear also has the potential to provide excitement, depending on the circumstances in which the 'threat' was encountered as well as the disposition of the individuals involved. Although spy fever has been characterized as pessimistic and alarmist, spy novels invariably contain much excitement and provide a valuable distraction from the mundane. Rather than simply construct an existential danger, they also exaggerate the satisfaction and bravado that can be attained through secret service work. This alternative depiction of spying contained a completely distinct set of emotives, which made German spies in the real world a spectacle to behold. Consequently, people were often fascinated to catch glimpses of these infamous secret agents and took tremendous pleasure in pursuing potential suspects.

This brings us back to one of the most common claims made about spy fever: that individuals showing symptoms of spy mania suffered from an inability to distinguish fact from fiction, and that as a result, they became convinced that an army of spies had actually invaded Britain. When we examine the reasons why people felt motivated to hunt for German spies, though, we find a much more nuanced explanation. In reality, spy fever symbolized various concerns that could be conveyed and assuaged thanks to the spy peril. One of the biggest concerns for men on the Home Front, for example, was the guilt or embarrassment they faced for being non-combatants in a distinctly female space. Creating and engaging an enemy at home afforded individuals an allusion of military bravado, which offset the sense of inferiority associated with their civilian status. Fears of inadequacy or irrelevance were therefore just as significant as genuine fears of German spies to the performance of espionage phobias.

With little information reaching the Home Front, fears of defeat could also escalate. Because the spy peril provided a metaphor for the war, in which the scale of conflict became abundantly clear, stories of spies being captured across the globe played a key role in mitigating any residual angst over whether Britain would eventually emerge victorious. By attributing British failures to Germany's dishonest tactics, the image of the spy challenged the belief that military setbacks were caused by incompetence. Reducing the conflict to a trial of wits between two individuals, in which the British protagonist always eventually prevailed, provided reassurance that Britain would emerge victorious against a treacherous and deceitful foe. Without regular news providing coverage of recent events and military operations, people were also vulnerable to concerns about Britain's prospects in the war and the potentially disastrous consequences that could befall them. Fears of the unknown and fears of defeat were thus a key reason as to why stories of spies prevailed so successfully following the onset of war in 1914. Owing to the dearth of 'real' news, people turned to reports of intrigue and subversion as a way to stay abreast of key developments.

Then we have individuals sympathetic to radical conservatism, who greatly feared liberalism and change. Radical conservatives capitalized on the spy peril and used the threat of espionage to promote extreme ideas and advocate stricter, more discriminatory measures. Conservative backbenchers like Lord Charles Beresford and William Joynson-Hicks repeatedly voiced their frustration at the government's perceived negligence in dealing with enemy aliens, which they claimed exacerbated the nation's vulnerability to foreign espionage and subversion. Influential xenophobes and jingoes like Leopold Maxse and Horatio Bottomley used platforms such as *National Review* and *John Bull* to incite hostility towards anything foreign on the grounds that aliens were covertly undermining the ascendancy of Britain and the empire. Utilizing the image of the spy served two long-standing aims of radical conservatives. First, by persistently highlighting the existence of a foreign enemy within Britain, radicals continued their mission to 'expose' the inadequacy of liberalism in matters of security and defence. Second, it challenged the continued effectiveness of Britain's immigration and nationalization policies, a hallmark of Edwardian liberalism, which had been a constant source of indignation among the radical right. How far these individuals and their audiences genuinely believed that spy fiction was imitating reality is obviously impossible to determine, but they were almost certainly also motivated by fears that liberals, immigrants and other groups considered 'outsiders' were weakening British society and damaging the security of the empire.

The spy peril resonated so successfully with British society following the outbreak of war specifically because it embodied a variety of fears that were all intensified because of the crisis and the new and increased challenges that it brought, not because society naively mistook fiction as fact. Spy fever was not an irrational outburst of inexcusable or simple emotions. The spy peril offered a way to interpret new circumstances, grapple with unavoidable realities, discuss the challenges of war and channel emotional responses to its outbreak. Spy phobias represented an assortment of fears: subversion, uncertainty, defeat, inadequacy and change. These emotions were not foolish. The outbreak of war in 1914 threatened to uproot civil society and transform the international political order like nothing before it. Fear was an almost inevitable response. The spy peril gave a voice to those feelings. In doing so, spy fever offered alternative feelings like hope or excitement that could distract from the realities of war. Perhaps this is why spy fever flourished so spectacularly across the globe in 1914.

Anti-German conspiracies, 1915–18

During the early months of the First World War, images of spies and saboteurs saturated political discourse and popular culture in Britain. These caricatures of clandestine operations and intrigues permeated the British psyche in different guises and through a variety of different means. But as the previous chapter has illustrated, the spy peril became far less conspicuous towards the end of 1915. So what became of the enemy within after the relative decline of spy fever?

Just as spy fever was becoming less prominent in British newspapers, a new and more dangerous narrative was beginning to emerge that coalesced and intensified anti-alien hatreds. As the conflict dragged on and war weariness set in, radical politics became increasingly unhinged. Simple stories of spies disrupting and interfering in military and naval operations were no longer sufficient to assuage growing frustrations and distract from the challenges of prolonged warfare. Radical commentators instead turned to conspiratorial fantasies in which sinister forces had taken control of Britain's destiny. Fears of espionage and sabotage essentially mutated into fears of subversion, but this conspiratorial rhetoric was something quite distinct from the broader phenomenon of spy fever. Although radical figures had certainly propagated the spy peril during the early stages of the war, and although fears of subversion share familiar characteristics with spy phobias, the hidden hand conspiracy embodied proto-fascist sentiments that went far beyond anything witnessed during the early months of war. Some of the anxieties present during spy fever were indeed capitalized on by the radical right, who frequently used images of secret warfare to camouflage their ideology using popular vernacular. But while the hidden hand conspiracy built on this facet of the spy peril, it almost certainly represented an entirely distinct emotional experience, one that needs its own methodology to assess.

Whereas spy fever was a reaction to the insecurities and challenges brought about by the outbreak of war, the idea of a hidden hand coalesced frustrations created by the continuation of the war and the perceived inability of the government to find a way to win. Especially as the difficulties of fighting a protracted war were becoming readily apparent to the British public during 1917. The dire military situation that existed by the end of that year – the Bolsheviks had taken power and begun to withdraw Russian forces from the conflict, Italy had suffered a major defeat at Caporetto and British forces had sustained tremendous casualties at Passchendaele – was almost matched by the troubling events at home. The Gotha bombers' intensive bombardment of London and the south-east of England had ramped up the death and destruction inflicted upon civilians,[2] while Germany's unrestricted U-boat campaign drastically worsened the food crisis across the Home Front. Rising food prices had long been a feature of daily life, but this was now compounded by shortages and queues. People were forced to visit multiple establishments trying to find enough to live off and spend an inordinate amount of time waiting in lines doing so. Food shortages were intensely felt from February 1917 but reached a particularly low point in January 1918. Thereafter, the introduction of convoys and more effective food rationing had begun to improve the situation and together they symbolized a hugely important success: the German blockade had failed and the country would not starve. This was a timely victory, for the BEF in France was about to face its most perilous situation yet.[3] In any case, the struggle in 1917 was intimately felt. International setbacks corresponded with severe hardships directly impacting individuals' daily lives and home comforts. People felt angry and frustrated and demanded answers. In response, the radical right put forward a simple, yet conspiratorial, explanation to these troubling questions.

It must be said, however, that concerns about foreign subversion were not entirely borne out of the war weariness that characterized latter stages of the conflict, as we can see traces of them before 1914. But they never reached anywhere near the levels of acceptance that more sophisticated theories achieved during the First World War. The primary individual responsible for concocting this early anti-German conspiracy was none other than Leo Maxse who, in the pages of the *National Review*, claimed that a network of wealthy Germans were secretly manipulating governments across Europe at the behest of their Kaiser. In December 1911, Maxse wrote:

> If the hateful truth be told, there is a large and powerful international syndicate, with ramifications in every capital, including London and Paris, working chiefly through corrupt or cosmopolitan papers, inspired or controlled by that hateful figure the International Jew … These internationalists, alias pro-Germans, demand that, in 'the interests of peace,' Europe shall pass unresistingly under the German yoke.[4]

Maxse warned that German and Jewish immigrants were conspiring together and that 'Hebrew journalists were at the beck and call of German diplomats'. This 'Potsdam Party', as Maxse termed it, had managed to convince soft-headed Englishmen, hypnotized by Hohenzollern flatteries, that Britain was always in the wrong.[5] To Maxse, the German and Jewish 'threats' were synonymous. Indeed, these two immigrant groups could be easily conflated because of the Ashkenazi antecedents of majority of Jewish people living in Britain. But given his extreme anti-Semitism, and owing to Britain's traditional aversion towards conspiratorial rhetoric, these ideas were unappealing to most. While there existed a constant presence of anti-Semitism in Britain, Maxse's claims were far too extreme to penetrate the political mainstream.

Conspiracy theories have seldom gained much traction in Britain during the twentieth century, probably because they have never been tacitly endorsed by government in the way that the red scare was in the United States at the start of the

Cold War or the stab in the back myth in Germany during the 1920s. The 'hidden hand' idea certainly never reached those levels of acceptance or impact, but few conspiracy theories have been as widely circulated in Britain as those concerning obscure influences secretly directing public opinion and government policy during the First World War.[6] Illusions of foreign subjugation were not only able to prosper because of the hardships brought about by the continuation of war, they were partly facilitated by the anti-alien sentiment and legislation that had been enacted because of the conflict. Since naturalized aliens had the same rights as British-born individuals, they were not interned. And because the naturalization process cost money, the majority of naturalized aliens resided among the higher classes of society. Allowing them to remain at liberty led to claims that wealthy and well-connected foreigners had infiltrated military, naval and political networks. This notion of foreign subversion, which built upon the paranoia linked to the spy peril and combined it with the complex conspiratorial fantasies of extremist ideologues, created a formidable narrative that dominated anti-alien discourse between 1915 and 1918.[7]

George Makgill, head of the Anti-German League, penned one of the first major wartime articles dealing with secret German influences in December 1915. In an article in *English Review*, Makgill condemned the freedoms afforded to naturalized Germans and questioned their allegiance:

> Which of us does not know some naturalised German, wealth or well-to-do, who has established himself … he probably gives liberally to the public sports, tips the local police lavishly, and hence is high in the good opinion of the local people … He may subscribe on a princely scale to Party funds. He may even enter Parliament, may perhaps received 'Honours' in return for Party 'services', and be on friendly terms with persons high in office. But when we think of Steiber's injunctions, what guarantee have we that this obliging and useful alien is not a German secret agent?[8]

As well as echoing radicals' disdain for party politics, which he claimed could be taken advantage of by individuals seeking to undermine national interests, he also warned of a coordinated attack on British institutions and government offices. In the same month, Ellis Powell released a series of articles in *Financial News* that elaborated on this 'Unseen Hand'. Here he reported that there was 'a dark element … in the background of the war' and speculated that the German government must have 'a grip on somebody or something, by means of which it is able to defeat our national policy'. Three days later Powell reiterated that 'the Huns have among us some unseen, but indefatigable, coadjutor or coadjutors'. Powell's theories failed to resonate widely until the death of Lord Kitchener aboard HMS *Hampshire* at which point other news outlets began to circulate similar conspiracies. The day after Kitchener's death, the London *Evening News* described 'an Unseen Hand' of Germans controlling unwitting fools within the British establishment, while *John Bull* told of an 'Unseen Hand' that had bribed its way into power and betrayed Britain's revered Minister for War.[9]

In a more detailed account published in February 1917, Powell likened this secret threat to the search for Neptune in 1846. Just as astronomers had observed cosmic anomalies that inspired a search for the object responsible for corrupting gravitational forces, there were, according to Powell, similar signs of manipulation within British politics. The only explanation as to why the government had displayed such lenience towards enemy aliens, he reckoned, was because somebody within government was protecting them.

> The mystery was deepened, as time went on, by the utterly impalpable and inscrutable character of the influence at work. It was omnipotent, but invisible; all-pervasive, but intangible; ubiquitous as the ambient air, but just as impervious to assault or capture; yet it united with these occult characteristics the capacity to strike hard at those who sought to unveil its identify, or to paralyse its treacherous machinations. By linked pressure, long drawn out, and utterly unsuspected by those who were made the instruments of its policy, the Unseen Hand warped a multitude of political, social, economic, and legal forces into consistency with its aim.[10]

While Powell claimed that it was 'superfluous' to name the specific deeds of this 'super-satanic' plot, this did not prevent him from attributing all sorts of setbacks and failures to this malevolent influence and concluding that 'every German interest was protected, and even fostered, in the early days of the war'.[11] In his book, *The Unseen Hand*, Kirton Varley shared many of Powell's conspiratorial delusions but went further. He explicitly called for a new system of governance – essentially a dictatorial regime led by the king along with members of the armed forces – because Parliament had been so corrupted by German power. He contended that propaganda agents dictated public opinion, which in turn shaped policy owing to a party system that was so desperately swayed by popular sentiment. As well as influencing the press, this unseen hand had provoked industrial action, sanctioned the Suffragette movement and incited pacifistic sentiment among the populace to undermine the war effort. Far from being confined to Britain, though, Valey contended that this 'Unseen Hand' had successfully spread its tentacles throughout the world, managing global affairs to suit Germany's interests.[12]

The omnipotence of this diabolical plot was given further credence by Arnold White, who produced one of the most significant contributions to the conspiracy with his book, *The Hidden Hand*, published in September 1917. White claimed to see 'fingerprints' of the hidden hand throughout all departments of state, including Downing Street and the Foreign Office.[13] Owing to the work of this hidden hand Britain's maritime supremacy had been degraded to the point at which its global hegemony was now a mere facade; its agricultural outputs reduced to such a point that it was now wholly reliant and thus subordinate to oversees assistance; and its aerial defences left disorderly and ineffectual thereby exposing its civilians to death and destruction on a daily basis. Moreover, the German financiers who had infiltrated every aspect of finance, industry and commerce had undone Britain's supreme economic might. Armies of German managers and clerks, with the assistance of British politicians and bureaucrats had penetrated businesses up and down the country giving the hidden hand control of Britain's economic policy through bribery and extortion.[14] Only because Fleet Street had been so corrupted by German diplomats, and therefore forced into concealing this almighty intrigue, was society kept in the dark for so long.

While attributing Britain's struggles to this illusive foe made some sense in the context of the war, and was not too dissimilar from the need to use spies as scapegoats for British setbacks, White made some truly bizarre and absurd allegations. Despite the huge amount of support coming to Britain from across the empire, White claimed that the hidden hand had been undermining imperial structures for years. Not only were trade tariffs across the empire apparently set by Germany, he went so far as to claim that Britain had effectively relinquished control of all overseas territories in favour of self-governing regimes that were, according to White, heavily influenced by the Germans residing in those territories.[15] Obviously the king was immune to such influences, being the incorruptible and divine figure that he was, but White reckoned that one of the main objectives of this hidden hand was not just to weaken the monarchy but also to eradicate it completely and destroy the most prestigious and unifying institutions of the British state.[16] The Kaiser's earlier fondness for his grandmother was in fact nothing more than subterfuge designed to create a false sense of affinity between the two nations. White's correspondence suggests that his theories resonated well with his supporters, mostly because the hidden hand acted as a conduit to explain and express an array of discontents, most notably those linked to anti-Semitism.

But the issue of *who* or *what* this hidden hand was rather nebulous. In contrast to Makgill's original suggestion that there was a coordinated attack on government offices by legions of naturalized Germans, Powell reckoned that this 'Arch-Traitor' was just one individual working at the heart of the British establishment:

> We speak idly when we characterize the Unseen Hand as an infirmity, a mere shadowy 'influence', a sentiment, a system, a pro-German susceptibility or suggestibility in high places. The Unseen Hand is undoubtedly an individual person. If the whole of the colossal secrets of German intrigue had been committed to a body of agents, there would long ago have been a leakage ... But if the supreme direction is in the hands of one dominant brain, whose tools are strangers to one another, and in most cases even to the individual whose behest they unconsciously obey, the gigantic secret is safe.[17]

This surreptitious adversary had been preparing for years, had wormed his way into every department of public life and infected the entirety of national policy with 'the virus of Germanism'. While Powell believed that this made the secrecy of the hidden hand more plausible, given that a vast network of agents would be almost impossible to conceal, whether or not a single individual could wield such immense power on Germany's behalf, without also being exposed, also seems rather dubious. Arnold White actually claimed no knowledge of whether a single individual or group of collaborators had organized the systematic domination of Britain, which was strange for somebody who claimed such cognizance of German influences in Britain.[18] Despite his reticent to side with either theory, he undoubtedly considered naturalized enemies as the '47,000' agents of the hidden hand, able to carry out unspeakable acts of evil on its behalf.[19]

For Ian Colvin, who produced one of the more far-fetched theories, the hidden hand was not so much a single entity but more akin to a protracted German economic influence that spanned centuries. In his books, *The Germans in England 1066–1598* (1915) and *The Unseen Hand in English History* (1917), Colvin proposed that Germany, or at least the antecedents of modern Germany, had been attempting to control much of Europe since the Middle Ages. Starting in the medieval period, the Hanseatic League, a group of merchants that Colvin considered innately Prussian, enjoyed tremendous influence over international commerce and dominated European affairs as a result. They could effortlessly enthrone and dethrone monarchs when it suited their interests and shape national policies thanks to their economic supremacy. England was thus at the mercy of the Hanseatic League, which could impose tariffs on imports and exports to render England subservient to its will, block English goods from reaching the continent to cripple local economies, prevent crops from being transported to England to exacerbate food shortages there or simply bribe and extort statesmen and bureaucrats to shape policy decisions.[20] Although Elizabeth I ostensibly ended the direct subjugation of England, partly by banishing German merchants from England, the Hanse's financial influence over European affairs persisted until the Thirty Years' War effectively neutered Germanic power for the following two centuries.

For Colvin, the unseen hand was not simply a treacherous individual or secret organization manipulating foreign governments but any person seeking selfish and irresponsible financial gain. Elizabeth was only able to defeat the Hanse through the actions of the Company of Merchant Adventurers which, unlike most commercial enterprises, worked for the economic interests of the state rather than personal profit. Coordinating and directing commerce in pursuit of national aims was thus imperative. Only through subordinating individual preferences and desires to national endeavour did England become economically independent and liberated from foreign domination.[21] The Merchant Adventurers responsible for freeing England from Hanseatic influence had been thoroughly English in birth and character; neither parent was of foreign birth, he did not marry a foreign woman, nor did he own property abroad. His interests were therefore entirely aligned with England's.[22] Colvin's hidden hand was quite literally an unseen force: selfish profiteering and relentless greed. Such unrestrained ambition made individuals susceptible to corruption which could be exploited. While economic self-sufficiency was imperative, as was an ethnically homogenous workforce, self-serving commercial competition was thought to weaken national prosperity and stability and thereby allow foreign pressures to exert influence over economic policy. As a result, this elusive danger could involve anybody directly supporting a foreign power, along with anybody placing personal interests before those of the nation and inadvertently aiding the enemy in a different way.

There were undoubtedly similarities between the spy peril and the hidden hand conspiracy. While both involved secret enemies undermining Britain from within, the way in which those threats manifested was quite different. Whereas the spy peril warned of secret agents attempting to carry out unspeakable acts designed to weaken the state, later conspiracies sought to identify treasonous activities being conducted from within the establishment itself. But more importantly, later depictions of the enemy within became increasingly anti-Semitic. While Jews were occasionally targeted for being spies early in the war, this hostility was sporadic rather than systematic. The hidden hand conspiracy, on the other hand, was inherently anti-Semitic, even if it was not always explicitly so. Readers would have had little difficulty identifying the 'cosmopolitan financiers' at the heart of the German conspiracy.[23] Unlike spy fever, the hidden hand idea was formed entirely by radicals attempting to exploit society's frustrations and use them to perpetuate their animosities for financial and political gain. Spy fever was more than just xenophobic rhetoric; it embodied a cultural obsession with secret warfare that produced a range of experiences and emotions. The prevalence of spy fever should not therefore be taken as evidence that society was instinctively receptive to more extreme hatreds. The hidden hand theory arose because people needed something to blame for Britain's inability to find a way to end the war, not because fears of espionage and sabotage organically transformed into fears of subversion. But in demonstrating that anti-alien anxieties and animosities were only a relatively small component of spy fever, this book has essentially challenged one of the main assumptions about Germanophobia during the First World War. Historians of anti-alienism typically view spy phobias as a prevailing sentiment in 1914, and therefore because of these ubiquitous fears and anxieties, anti-alienism grew to unprecedented levels. According to this interpretation, the hidden hand theory must have resonated widely because people were already predisposed to paranoia and anti-alien hostility. But if spy phobias were less common than this interpretation originally suggested, what does that mean for subsequent forms of Germanophobia?

Mirroring the methodology employed to assess the impact of spy fever, Panayi primarily uses the prevalence of anti-alien sentiment in right-wing publications and the proliferation of right-wing organizations to show the level of popular support for the hidden hand conspiracy.[24] While there was indeed an increasingly prominent anti-German sentiment displayed in various newspapers, and people almost certainly became more angry and frustrated because of the frequent bombing raids and ongoing food shortages, this does not necessarily mean that the majority of people became rabid xenophobes or fervent proponents of bizarre conspiracies as a result. Adrian Gregory argues that this deepening ideological anti-alienism was mostly driven by middle class anger and was not necessarily universal. We can see this in the relative success of the British Empire Union, for example. The majority of their active branches were located in the south of England and Home Counties. A third of them were all based in London suburbs. Notwithstanding the growing success of radical organizations, this swelling of support did not reflect a nationwide mass movement. In 1917 and 1918 the coalition government also found itself fighting a series of by-elections in London suburbs, and these were themselves fairly revealing about the appeal of radical politics. Candidates from the far-right often did reasonably well but were almost always beaten by the coalition's candidate. This was sometimes only because the radical vote was split between ultra-right-wing candidates. Had the National Party joined forces with the Vigilantes they may have fared slightly better, but overall the electorate remained in favour of the political mainstream, partly because the government was itself enacting many of the policies that the radical right had been advocating, like systematic retaliatory bombing and harsher interment legislation.[25] But if people were not sufficiently swayed to endorse radical politicians, we should not assume that they accepted their rhetoric or conspiracies whole-heartedly.

Ascertaining whether or not individuals actually subscribed to absurd conspiracy theories is obviously rather difficult. But if the hidden hand conspiracy had any major impact on how people thought or felt during the First World War, it was in 1918. At this point it became less about anti-Semitism and more about the middle classes' aversion towards decadence and immorality, which was much more palatable.[26] This sentiment crystallized after Pemberton Billing, MP, publicized a private performance of Oscar Wilde's infamous play, *Salome*. Billing's weekly journal, *Vigilante*, claimed that the sexual and moral debauchery on display in this production was part of an elaborate German plot to undermine Britain's war effort and denounced members of the audience as the hidden hand. Having essentially appropriated White's conspiracy, Billing modified it to suit middle-class concerns about the moral condition of the country. Billing declared that these highly placed traitors – the political and cultural elite – were in fact homosexuals and perverts being blackmailed by the German high command.[27] Not only was homosexuality commonly regarded as a form of subversion, but it had also become effectively synonymous with Germany thanks to the Eulenburg affair that besmirched German politics in the late 1900s. Because sexual perversion was considered inherently un-British, anybody guilty of such offenses must have been corrupted by foreign influences. Ridding the country of sexual deviance was therefore essential. Homosexuals in positions of authority were considered weak-willed and open to exploitation, while purging the country of scandal and decadence was needed to maintain social discipline and prosecute the war effectively.[28]

Spies, sex and corruption proved a powerful concoction in 1918. Especially during Pemberton Billing's trial for criminal libel in May and June, which elevated his conspiracy even further. The star of *Salome*, Maud Allen, felt that the title of Billing's exposé, 'The Cult of the Clitoris', falsely implied that she was a lesbian and so she initialled legal proceedings again him. Billing conducted his own defence and used the courtroom to announce the existence of a book containing 47,000 names, which he claimed revealed the extent of government corruption led by German spies, as much as he did trying to prove Allen's homosexuality.[29] Billing used the platform to question how so many mistakes had been allowed to happen and lamented that so many had died as a result of negligence or ineptitude. He once again condemned the political and cultural elite for their perversion and decadence and reiterated that this was how German spies controlled officials within government, which explained why Britain was failing to win the war. The trial lasted for six days and captivated readers nationwide. Although mainstream newspapers condemned Billing's actions, in dedicating so much attention to the trial they nevertheless broadcast his conspiracies to a much wider audience than the few thousand readers of *Vigilante*. As the trial unfolded at the same time as British forces were hit by powerful German offensives, Billing's trial provided a catalyst for anti-German feeling.[30] And so in July 1918, the threat of German spies was once again at the forefront of British political culture. This proved short-lived, however, as the Allies counter-attacked in August. As the destruction of Germany's forces became increasingly likely, the idea of a German hidden hand quickly faded away.

Throughout Panikos Panayi's seminal work on Germanophobia during the First World War, he repeatedly distinguishes between 'spy fever' and subsequent forms of anti-alien hostility, including the hidden hand conspiracy. And he is right to do so but not because 'spy fever' was 'unsophisticated', as he terms it, compared to more complex hatreds later on. Far from being a simple panic about foreign covert action, spy fever intertwined an assortment of concerns that were all conveyed through fears of espionage and sabotage. Individuals also had contrasting interpretations of the peril that fashioned a myriad of different experiences and emotions. While certain communities undoubtedly used images of spies to encourage anxiety and animosity, others used them to inspire hope or create a sense of excitement. Consequently, although the radical right became fervent proponents of the spy danger, spy fever represented a cultural fascination with secret warfare and was not just a form of anti-alien hostility. The hidden hand conspiracy, on the other hand, was something quite different. The depths of this conspiracy, and the extreme contempt it displayed against Jews, and to a lesser extent homosexuals, liberals and pacifists. places these ideas far outside the mainstream of British politics. The ubiquity of spy fever in 1914 and 1915 in no way supports the notion that individuals developed extreme hatreds towards Germans or any other minority group. There can be no doubt that the search for a hidden hand became a widespread feature of British culture in 1918, but how far this prominence translated into ideological or emotional impact requires a separate study with its own methodology. Whereas this book has used fear and anxiety as focus points for analysis, our understanding of popular anti-alienism during the First World War could surely benefit from additional work looking at the nuances and scale of popular hatred and animosity.

Appendix 1

BREAKDOWN OF HOW ARTICLES WERE CATEGORIZED ACCORDING TO THEIR CONTENT

Spy scares

Articles referring to suspects apprehended or prosecuted
Unidentified suspects pursued and unsuccessfully apprehended

Alarmist rhetoric

Warnings regarding the scale of espionage or the resulting feelings
Vague allegations about what spies are doing or where they are
Discriminating rhetoric or repressive measures against minorities
Articles blaming spies for various mistakes or failures
Criticisms of the government or individual government ministers
Reports of violence against alleged 'spies'

International intrigue

Secret agents interfering with military operations overseas
Spies manipulating international diplomacy
Emissaries undermining internal policies of other states

Popular culture

Reviews and adverts of plays, films or novels
Serialized stories printed in newspapers
Jokes
Pseudohistorical narratives

Opposition

Rhetoric denouncing the validity of the spy peril
Satire exposing the inconsistency or foolishness of the spy peril
Support or tolerance shown to minorities

Not included

Summaries or adverts of news articles appearing elsewhere
Articles that use spy or spied as a synonym for observe or observed
Horse racing updates including horses named 'spy'
Stock market updates including shares named 'spies'

The British Newspaper Archive, which holds digitized copies of the newspapers used in this study, made a quantitative analysis possible. A total of 9,245 articles were collated thanks to the ability to search for keywords used in the text. Search terms included 'spy' (which includes 'spying'), 'spies' and 'espionage'.

Appendix 2

NUMBER OF SPY-RELATED ARTICLES PER MONTH IN
EACH NEWSPAPER SURVEYED

	no. issues	Aug 1914	Sep 1914	Oct 1914	Nov 1914	Dec 1914	Jan 1915	Feb 1915	Mar 1915	Apr 1915	May 1915	Jun 1915	Jul 1915	Aug 1915	Sep 1915	Oct 1915	Nov 1915	Dec 1915	no. spy-related articles	no. of articles per issue
Coastal/Urban																				
Aberdeen Evening Express	443	32	29	54	40	35	26	20	15	10	22	20	17	14	30	16	23	19	422	0.95
Edinburgh Evening News	436	54	36	72	44	42	28	25	29	28	33	23	24	20	22	20	21	16	537	1.23
Hull Daily Mail	436	51	34	58	55	42	41	25	23	29	24	32	12	12	22	24	18	11	513	1.18
Liverpool Echo	436	52	19	45	41	28	19	28	21	21	21	22	24	13	30	22	16	18	440	1.01
Portsmouth Evening News	437	94	24	33	28	22	25	11	13	20	17	26	12	12	16	6	13	11	383	0.88
Western Mail (Cardiff)	421	89	50	77	46	24	21	15	17	12	21	29	16	14	24	14	15	21	505	1.20
Total	2609	372	192	339	254	193	160	124	118	120	138	152	105	85	144	102	106	96	2800	1.07
Coastal/Rural																				
Arbroath Herald and Ad.	74	3	1	8	4	2	4	0	1	1	2	3	2	3	3	3	2	1	43	0.58
Berwickshire News and General Ad.	74	9	8	6	9	5	0	3	3	2	4	3	3	2	3	1	2	1	64	0.86
Bexhil-on-Sea Observer	73	5	7	11	11	3	1	7	4	2	0	2	1	3	3	3	2	1	66	0.90
Caernarvon and Denbigh Herald	73	2	2	3	2	1	4	5	2	5	0	1	2	0	1	0	4	2	36	0.49
Chelmsford Chronicle	73	8	5	10	7	8	3	1	3	0	3	0	2	0	0	1	3	0	54	0.74
Cheshire Observer	72	7	2	6	6	3	6	3	4	3	0	3	5	2	1	0	0	2	53	0.74
Cornishman	74	3	0	10	7	6	5	4	1	5	5	7	6	5	9	6	3	6	88	1.19
Fife Free Press	73	11	4	19	9	7	4	3	5	3	0	10	9	3	2	6	1	2	98	1.34
Glamorgan Gazette	74	3	0	10	2	4	2	1	0	1	3	4	2	1	1	1	1	1	37	0.50
Nairnshire Telegraph	74	1	1	2	2	5	1	1	0	0	1	2	0	3	0	3	1	0	23	0.31
Thanet Ad.	73	4	6	4	10	2	7	1	6	3	4	3	3	3	3	3	0	0	60	0.82
Whitby Gazette	74	13	8	10	12	7	15	7	7	6	7	5	3	1	1	0	4	4	110	1.49
Total	881	69	44	99	81	53	52	36	36	31	29	43	37	26	26	27	23	20	732	3.00

	no. issues	Aug 1914	Sep 1914	Oct 1914	Nov 1914	Dec 1914	Jan 1915	Feb 1915	Mar 1915	Apr 1915	May 1915	Jun 1915	Jul 1915	Aug 1915	Sep 1915	Oct 1915	Nov 1915	Dec 1915	no. spy-related articles	no. of articles per issue
Inland/Urban																				
Birmingham Mail	436	49	37	60	57	41	42	24	20	26	27	30	26	15	28	24	14	17	537	1.23
Daily Record (Glasgow)	448	56	27	53	47	31	21	19	13	39	18	17	20	13	18	15	11	14	432	0.96
Leeds Mercury	444	49	32	41	31	28	19	12	32	30	15	24	14	18	15	20	6	12	398	0.90
Manchester Evening News	439	43	20	39	42	27	24	26	22	26	26	29	16	21	20	12	24	24	441	1.00
Nottingham Journal	436	59	21	22	22	19	25	10	19	14	21	27	14	9	13	14	21	13	343	0.79
Sheffield Independent	445	60	39	41	37	37	19	18	19	19	14	19	16	21	29	15	15	11	429	0.96
Total	2648	316	176	256	236	183	150	109	125	154	121	146	106	97	123	100	91	91	2580	0.97
Inland/Rural																				
Belper News	74	12	5	2	0	1	1	2	3	1	1	1	1	4	1	0	0	0	35	0.47
Brecon County Times	74	0	0	0	1	4	2	2	3	3	1	3	4	7	4	2	1	0	37	0.50
Diss Express	74	9	7	10	7	7	5	1	3	2	5	7	5	4	4	6	2	9	93	1.26
Dorking and Letherhead Ad.	73	5	1	9	4	5	7	2	1	7	0	4	2	1	0	1	4	1	54	0.74
Faringdon Ad.	73	17	8	24	14	11	3	3	4	5	5	7	2	6	4	4	4	0	121	1.66
Hawick Express	74	3	3	6	9	6	6	4	5	6	1	2	2	2	1	0	1	0	57	0.77
Kilsyth Chronicle	74	1	2	2	3	4	1	1	3	3	1	2	2	1	2	1	1	2	32	0.43
Penrith Observer	74	10	10	13	6	6	4	2	7	4	0	4	4	3	3	3	7	3	89	1.20
Shepton Mallet Journal	74	16	11	9	8	4	2	1	0	1	4	7	3	3	3	4	4	1	80	1.08
Southern Reporter (Selkirk)	74	5	1	6	1	5	1	3	2	3	4	5	1	1	4	4	3	3	52	0.70
Tamworth Herald	73	10	3	6	2	1	0	1	2	2	4	1	1	3	4	4	1	4	49	0.67
Warwick and Warwickshire Ad.	73	3	1	1	3	1	1	4	1	2	2	3	5	1	0	11	2	2	43	0.59
Total	884	91	52	88	58	55	33	26	34	39	28	46	32	36	30	39	30	25	742	0.84

	no. issues	Aug 1914	Sep 1914	Oct 1914	Nov 1914	Dec 1914	Jan 1915	Feb 1915	Mar 1915	Apr 1915	May 1915	Jun 1915	Jul 1915	Aug 1915	Sep 1915	Oct 1915	Nov 1915	Dec 1915	no. spy-related articles	no. of articles per issue
London																				
The Globe	427	90	91	105	78	66	45	38	38	55	45	50	32	26	50	52	22	42	925	2.17
Westminster Gazette	438	36	28	43	45	12	27	15	20	17	17	34	20	14	24	14	14	12	392	0.89
Total	865	126	119	148	123	78	72	53	58	72	62	84	52	40	74	66	36	54	1317	1.52
Ireland																				
Belfast Telegraph	438	56	39	47	48	33	10	9	8	8	15	19	10	6	18	15	11	16	368	0.84
Dublin Daily Express	441	74	33	69	72	40	30	14	13	22	30	32	24	18	27	27	17	20	562	1.27
Sligo Champion	72	6	1	2	6	4	0	1	1	0	4	0	1	1	1	4	1	0	33	0.46
Kilrush Herald and Kilkee Gazette	74	0	0	3	2	0	2	1	2	0	2	1	0	1	1	0	0	0	15	0.20
Ballymena Observer	74	7	2	4	2	2	0	1	1	0	5	3	4	1	3	7	2	2	46	0.62
Drogheda Independent	73	6	3	9	5	6	2	1	2	0	5	4	1	5	0	0	0	1	50	0.68
Total	1172	149	78	134	135	85	44	27	27	30	61	59	40	32	50	53	31	39	1074	0.92
TOTAL	9059	1123	661	1064	887	647	511	375	398	446	439	530	372	316	447	387	317	325	9245	1.02

Appendix 3

LIST OF SPY SCARES APPEARING IN PRINT BETWEEN 4 AND 31 AUGUST 1914

Date Appearing in the Press (August 1914)	Location of Incident	Number of Suspects	Identity of Suspect	Instigator of Claim
4	Waltham	1	Herbert Iankewitz	Sentry
4	Hull	2	Unidentified (no gender given)	Sentry
4	Isle of Wight	2	Brothers named Swetz	Police
4	Portsmouth	1	Albert Celso Roderquiz Garcia	War Office
5	Dover	1	Unidentified (no gender given)	Implied sentry
5	Upstreet	1	Unidentified male	Male civilian
5	Edinburgh	2	Unidentified males	Sentry
5	Newcastle	1	Frederick Franz Sukowski	Police
5	Queenstown	1	Frank Townsend Clarke	Undisclosed
5	Barrow	1	Fredrick Apel	War Office
5	Falmouth	1	Johann Engel	War Office
5	Sheerness	1	Franz Heinrich Losel	War Office
5	London	1	Karl Gustav Ernst	War Office
5	Penarth	1	Frederick William Fowler	War Office
5	London	1	Frederick Diederichs	War Office
5	London	1	Adolf Schneider	War Office
5	London	1	August Klunder	War Office
5	Southsea	2	Max Power Heinert	War Office
			Lina Maria Heine	War Office
6	Isle of Wight	1	Unidentified male	Implied sentry
6	Scarborough	1	Unidentified male	Sentry
6	Swansea	1	Frederick James Ireland	Police
6	London	2	Unidentified male	Police
			Unidentified female	
6	London	2	Unidentified males	Undisclosed
6	London	1	Henry Laurens/Max Bernstein Laurens	War Office
7	Bridlington	1	Unidentified male	Civilian
7	Chatham	1	Gerrard Hall	Implied sentry
7	Conway	2	Unidentified males	Male civilian
7	Hull	1	Mr Pinchbeck	Sentry
7	Newcastle	1	Unidentified Male	Sentry

Date Appearing in the Press (August 1914)	Location of Incident	Number of Suspects	Identity of Suspect	Instigator of Claim
7	London	1	William Francis Brown	Police
7	London	3	Unidentified males	Police
7	Holyhead	1	Rev Charles T. Richardson	Undisclosed
7	Maidstone	3	Unidentified (no gender given)	Undisclosed
7	Sunderland	1	Henry Aaron Matteo	Undisclosed
7	Scarborough	3	Unidentified (no gender given)	Undisclosed
7	Mountain Ash	1	Otto Moritz Walter Kruger	War Office
8	Berwick	1	Unidentified male	Civilian
8	Chatham	1	Bernard Ludgate	Implied sentry
8	Belfast	2	Dandt and Mickobeck	Implied police
8	Belfast	1	Paul George Wetzen	Implied police
8	Aberystwyth	1	Gustav E. Lammel	Implied police
8	Brixham	1	Mr Longford	Sentry
8	Liverpool	1	Ambrose Berger	Sentry
8	Sutton-on-Sea	2	Unidentified males	Sentry
8	Sunderland	1	Herman Adolphus Ahless	Sentry
8	Barry	1	Edward John Davies	Sentry
8	London	1	Heinrich Grosse	Police
8	Reading	1	Unidentified male	Police
8	London	1	Reinhard	Undisclosed
8	London	1	Marie Kronauer	War Office
9	Clerkenwell	2	Unidentified males	Undisclosed
9	Rochester	1	John Kaltenbach	Undisclosed
10	Nottingham	1	Max Kuhner	Police
10	Balcombe tunnel	1	Unidentified male	Undisclosed
10	Peterborough	2	Unidentified males	Undisclosed
10	St George's Channel	4	Unidentified males	Undisclosed
10	Spurn	2	Unidentified male Unidentified female	Undisclosed
10	Dunoon	1	Unidentified female	Undisclosed
11	Newcastle	2	Leo and Aloysius Boers	Boy scouts
11	Berwick	1	Unidentified male	Civilian
11	Reading	2	Unidentified males	Implied authorities
11	Aberdeen	2	Unidentified males	Male civilian
11	Belfast	1	John Rockman	Male civilian
11	Birkenhead	1	Unidentified (no gender given)	Sentry
11	London	2	Jacob Mitznian Robert Armstrong	Sentry
11	Dunfermline	1	Unidentified male	Sentry
11	Liverpool	2	Max Dreker John Seyer	Sentry
11	Brighton	1	Unidentified male	Sentry

Date Appearing in the Press (August 1914)	Location of Incident	Number of Suspects	Identity of Suspect	Instigator of Claim
11	Whitburn	1	Unidentified male	Sentry
11	Brentwood	1	Unidentified male	Sentry
11	St Abbs	2	Unidentified males	Sentry
11	Tweedmouth	1	Unidentified male	Sentry
11	Spittal	1	Unidentified male	Sentry
11	Duns	1	Major Sinclair Wemyss	Police
11	Berwick	2	Unidentified males	Police
11	Portsmouth	3	Unidentified (no gender given)	Undisclosed
11	South Shields	1	Pastor Wilhelm Singer	Undisclosed
11	Liverpool	1	Robert Arthur Blackburn	War Office
12	Kilsyth	1	Unidentified male	Undisclosed
13	Paull	1	Unidentified male	Implied authorities
13	Holderness	1	Unidentified male	Implied authorities
13	Howth	1	Unidentified male	Sentry
13	Dover	1	Unidentified male	Sentry
13	Newry	3	B. Beck (male) C. Muller (male) J. Herman (male)	Undisclosed
13	Withernsea	1	Unidentified male	Undisclosed
14	Rochford	2	Unidentified males	Boy scouts
14	Millbrook	2	Unidentified males	Sentry
14	Tollesbury	1	Edgard Austin Colgate	Sentry
14	Dover	1	Charles Hussey	Sentry
14	Milford-on-Sea	1	Vernon Nicholson	Sentry
14	Caernarvon	1	Unidentified male	Undisclosed
14	Wivenhoe	1	Ernest Abberfield	Undisclosed
14	Smithstone	1	Unidentified male	Undisclosed
14	Winchester	2	Unidentified males	Undisclosed
14	Pembrokeshire	1	William Hobday	Undisclosed
15	Kirkcaldy	1	Unidentified female	Civilian
15	Balbriggan	3	Unidentified females	Implied authorities
15	Carrigaline	1	Cecil Walker	Implied sentry
15	Hartlepool	1	Unidentified male	Sentry
15	Undisclosed	3	Unidentified males	Sentry
15	Chester	1	Unidentified male	Police
15	Newcastle	1	Karl Stubenvoll	Police
15	London	2	Keppel Rezriarin Max Bruski	Police
15	Aberdeenshire	1	Unidentified male	Undisclosed
15	Co. Clare	3	Ruby Yanez John Jones Harry Wilson	Undisclosed
15	Newcastle	1	Unidentified male	Undisclosed
17	Brooklands	1	Unidentified male	Sentry

Date Appearing in the Press (August 1914)	Location of Incident	Number of Suspects	Identity of Suspect	Instigator of Claim
17	Winchester	3	William Sidney Joseph Edgar Stringer Richardo Ferrari	Sentry
17	London	1	Oscar Wilhelm Goehling	Police
17	Pembroke	1	David Coher	Undisclosed
18	Edinburgh	1	Unidentified male	Sentry
18	Bembridge	1	Harold Beaumont	Sentry
18	Feltham	2	Max Wilhelm Nagel Charles King	Undisclosed
19	Milngavie	1	Unidentified male	Boy scouts
19	York	1	Isidore Frederick Woolbranch	Sentry
19	Grimsby	1	Richard Clough	Police
19	London	1	Unidentified female	Police
20	Colwyn Bay	1	Lord Kitchener's cousin (female)	Sentry
20	Chatham	1	Unidentified (no gender given)	Sentry
21	Hornsea	1	Unidentified (no gender given)	Implied police
21	Aldershot	1	James Carroll	Sentry
21	Cromer	1	David Winestone	Police
21	Colchester	1	Unidentified male	Undisclosed
22	Kirkcaldy	1	Unidentified male	Civilian
22	Bexhill-on-Sea	1	Dr M. F. Blassneck	Police
22	PenyGraig	1	Unidentified male	Police
24	Paull	4	Unidentified males	Sentry
24	Pembrokeshire	1	Isaac Jacobs (alias Jack Jacobs)	Sentry
25	Berwick	1	Unidentified male	Boy scouts
25	Sprouston	1	Unidentified male	Civilian
25	Torry	1	Unidentified male	Sentry
25	Eyemouth	1	Unidentified male	Sentry
25	Duddinstone	1	Unidentified male	Sentry
25	New Brighton	1	Mr F. W. Green	Sentry
25	Cockburnspath	1	James White	Police
26	Brighton	2	William Eric Guy Clease Carrie Sims	Civilian
26	London	1	Unidentified female	Undisclosed
27	Stenhousemuir	1	Unidentified male	Sentry
27	Harwich	1	William Frederick Whitehead	Sentry
28	Chelmsford	1	Unidentified male	Sentry
29	Undisclosed	1	Unidentified male	Female civilian
29	Eastbourne	1	Unidentified male	Male civilian
31	Killarney	1	Unidentified male	Implied police
31	Dublin	1	Hans Heinsen	Undisclosed

*Each incident is only included once, on the day of its first appearance.

NOTES

Introduction

1 David French, 'Spy Fever in Britain, 1900–1915', *Historical Journal* 21/2 (1978), p. 364.
2 'I-SPY-I', *The Nation* 16/4 (1914), p. 113.
3 Basil Thomson, *Queer People* (London, 2015), p. 37; this definition is repeated in Christopher Andrew, *Secret Service: The Making of the British Intelligence Community* (Sevenoaks, 1986), p. 264; and Catriona Pennell, *A Kingdom United: Popular Responses to the Outbreak of the First World War* (Oxford, 2014), p. 102.
4 Imperial War Museum (IWM) docs. 16020: Memoir of Ernest Lycette, p. 7.
5 IWM docs. 13607: Diary of Norman Macleod, 20 October 1914.
6 Gail Braybon, 'Introduction', in Gail Braybon (ed.), *Evidence, History and the Great War: Historians and the Impact of 1914–18* (Oxford, 2005), pp. 1–2.
7 Adrian Gregory, *The Last Great War: British Society and the First World War* (Cambridge, 2013), p. 26.
8 Janet S. K. Watson, *Fighting Different Wars: Experience, Memory and the First World War in Britain* (Cambridge, 2004), p. 61.
9 Deborah Bauer, 'Villains, Liars, Soldiers, and Patriots: Perceptions of Espionage and the Politics of Emotion in Fin-de-Siècle France', in Simon Ball, Philip Gassert, Andreas Gestrich and Sönke Neitzel (eds), *Cultures of Intelligence in the Era of the World Wars* (Oxford, 2020), pp. 189–98.
10 Catriona Pennell, 'British Society and the First World War', *War in History* 16/4 (2009), p. 506.
11 Claire Langhamer, Lucy Noakes and Claudia Siebrecht (eds), *Total War: An Emotional History* (Oxford, 2020).
12 Pennell, *A Kingdom United*, p. 55.
13 Ute Frevert, 'Emotions in Times of War: Private and Public, Individual and Collective', in Claire Langhamer, Lucy Noakes and Claudia Siebrecht (eds), *Total War: An Emotional History* (Oxford, 2020), p. 22.
14 Claire Langhamer, Lucy Noakes and Claudia Siebrecht, 'Introduction', in Langhamer, Noakes, and Siebrecht, *Total War*, pp. 1–2.
15 Sektion IIIb was established in 1889. Its name was derived from the section with the Third (French) department of the General Staff that had been responsible for intelligence gathering during the Franco-Prussian War: Markus Pöhlmann, 'German Intelligence at War, 1914–1918', *Journal of Intelligence History* 5/2 (2005), p. 27.
16 This lack of funds meant that the German army's intelligence coverage remained limited to France and Russia: Pöhlmann, 'German Intelligence at War', p. 28.
17 Thomas Boghardt, *Spies of the Kaiser: German Covert Operations in Great Britain during the First World War Era* (Basingstoke, 2004), pp. 14–17, 44–6.
18 Steinhauer had initially served in the German navy and trained at the Pinkerton Detective Agency in Chicago, before returning to Berlin and joining the Metropolitan Police. He was a personal friend of the Kaiser and accompanied him on various

foreign trips. From around 1894, he was conducting intelligence missions on behalf of the General Staff and Admiralstab. Gustav Steinhauer, *The Kaiser's Master Spy: The Story as Told by Himself*, edited by S. T. Felstead (London, 1930).

19 Boghardt, *Spies of the Kaiser*, pp. 51–69.

20 French, 'Spy Fever in Britain', pp. 356–7; Nicholas Hiley, 'The Failure of British Counter-Espionage against Germany, 1907–1914', *The Historical Journal* 28/4 (1985), pp. 839–42.

21 Nicholas Hiley, 'Counter-Espionage and Security in Great Britain during the First World War', *English Historical Review* 101/400 (1986), pp. 635–70; Christopher Andrew, *The Defence of the Realm: The Authorized History of MI5* (London, 2010), pp. 15–28.

22 Nicholas Hiley, 'Entering the Lists: MI5's Great Spy Round-Up of August 1914', *Intelligence and National Security* 21/1 (2006), pp. 47–50.

23 Boghardt, *Spies of the Kaiser*, pp. 54–8.

24 Significant effort has gone into establishing and maintaining this version of events: Nicholas Hiley, 'Re-entering the Lists: MI5's Authorized History and the August 1914 Arrests', *Intelligence and National Security* 25/4 (2010), pp. 415–52.

25 Hiley, 'Entering the Lists', pp. 68–9.

26 Boghardt, *Spies of the Kaiser*, p. 80.

27 Ibid., pp. 91–4.

28 Henry Landau, *The Enemy Within: The Inside Story of German Sabotage in America* (New York, 1937); Dan Larsen, 'Intelligence in the First World War: The State of the Field', *Intelligence and National Security* 29/2 (2014), pp. 290–2.

29 For German intrigues in Ireland see: Eunan O'Halpin, 'British Intelligence in Ireland, 1914–1921', in Christopher Andrew and David Dilks (eds), *The Missing Dimension: Governments and Intelligence Communities in the Twentieth Century* (London, 1984), pp. 54–77; Dan Larsen, British Signals Intelligence and the 1916 Easter Rising in Ireland', *Intelligence and National Security* 33/1 (2018), pp. 48–66. For the Middle East see: Yigal Sheffy, 'The Spy Who Never Was: An Intelligence Myth in Palestine, 1914–18', *Intelligence and National Security* 14/3 (1999), pp. 123–42; Polly A. Mohs, *Military Intelligence and the Arab Revolt: The First Modern Intelligence War* (Abingdon, 2008), pp. 39–83. For India: Richard J. Popplewell, *Intelligence and Imperial Defence: British Intelligence and the Defence of the Indian Empire 1904–1924* (London, 1995), pp. 165–99. And finally, for German plots in Morocco see: Harry Richards, 'Room 40 and German Intrigues in Morocco: Re-assessing the Operational Impact of Diplomatic Cryptanalysis during World War I', *Intelligence and National Security* 32/6 (2017), pp. 833–48.

30 Pöhlmann. 'German Intelligence at War', p. 50.

31 Boghardt, *Spies of the Kaiser*, pp. 123–6.

32 Ibid., pp. 129–30.

33 Mark Wheelis, 'Biological Sabotage in World War I', in Erhard Geissler and John Ellis van Courtland Moon (eds), *Biological and Toxin Weapons Research, Development, and Use from the Middle Ages to 1945* (Oxford, 1999), p. 38.

34 Patrick Beesly, *Room 40: British Naval Intelligence, 1914–18* (Oxford, 1984), pp. 200–2.

35 Boghardt, *Spies of the Kaiser*, pp. 126–8.

36 Christopher Andrew, *Secret Service: The Making of the British Intelligence Community* (London, 1986), pp. 264–7. William le Queux was a celebrated spy novelist and dedicated much of his writing to awaking the British public to the invasion and espionage danger that the German menace presented. For more on Le Queux, see

David Stafford, 'Conspiracy and Xenophobia: The Spy Novels of William le Queux, 1893-1914', *Europa* 3 (1982), pp. 489-509.

37 Panikos Panayi, *The Enemy in Our Midst: Germans in Britain during the First World War* (Oxford, 1991), pp. 181-3; James Hampshire, 'Spy Fever in Britain, 1900 to 1914', *The Historian* 72 (2001), p. 24.

38 French, 'Spy Fever in Britain', p. 356. Bernard Porter is a notable exception to this. Porter argues that although popular fears may have appeared trivial or even imaginary, the underlying reasons were understandable and legitimate: *Plots and Paranoia: A History of Political Espionage in Britain 1790-1988* (Abingdon, 2016), p. 120.

39 Marc Bloch, 'Reflections of a Historian on the False News of the War', translated by James P. Holoka, *Michigan War Studies Review* (2013). https://www.miwsr.com/about.aspx.

40 John Horne, 'Public Opinion and Politics', in John Horne (ed.), *A Companion to World War I* (Oxford, 2012), p. 281. Spy phobias also occurred in both World Wars: Panikos Panayi, 'Dominant Societies and Minorities in the Two World Wars', in Panikos Panayi (ed.), *Minorities in Wartime: National and Racial Groupings in Europe, North America and Australia during the Two World Wars* (Oxford, 1993), p. 13.

41 Paul Newman, *A History of Terror: Fear and Dread through the Ages* (Stroud, 2000), pp. 196-7; Corey Robin, *Fear: The History of a Political Idea* (Oxford, 2004), pp. 1-31; Frank Furedi, *Politics of Fear: Beyond Left and Right* (London, 2005), p. 8; Daniel J. Kapust, 'On the Ancient Uses of Political Fear and Its Modern Implications', *Journal of the History of Ideas* 69/3 (2008), pp. 356, 372.

42 Robert S. Robins, *Political Paranoia: The Psychopolitics of Hatred* (New Haven, 1997), pp. 89-94; Newman, *A History of Terror*, pp. 196-7.

43 Daniela L. Caglioti, *War and Citizenship: Enemy Aliens and National Belonging from the French Revolution to the First World War* (Cambridge, 2021), pp. 108, 137-8.

44 Although the Dominions often followed London's precedent, especially in matters of defence, internal ethnic pressures were locally managed, which in some cases fashioned more extreme policies towards ethnic minorities: Kay Saunders, ' "The Stranger in Our Gates": Internment Policies in the United Kingdom and Australia during the Two World Wars, 1914-39', *Immigrants and Minorities* 22/1 (2003), pp. 23-4.

45 Martin Kitchen, 'The German Invasion of Canada in the First World War', *International History Review* 7/2 (1985), pp. 245-60; Gerhard P. Bassler, 'The Enemy Alien Experience in Newfoundland 1914-1918', *Canadian Ethnic Studies* 20/3 (1988), pp. 45-6; Jeffrey A. Keshen, *Propaganda and Censorship during Canada's Great War* (Edmonton, 1996), pp. 5-11.

46 Tilman Dedering, ' "Avenge the Lusitania": The Anti-German Riots in South Africa in 1915', *Immigrants and Minorities* 31/3 (2013), p. 279.

47 R. J. W. Selleck, ' "The Trouble with My Looking Glass": A study of the Attitudes of Australians to Germans during the Great War', *Journal of Australian Studies* 4/6 (1980), pp. 5-6, 21; Gerhard Fischer, 'Fighting the War at Home: The Campaign against Enemy Aliens in Australia during the First World War', in Panayi (ed.), *Minorities in Wartime*, pp. 263-86.

48 Andrew Francis, 'Anti-Alienism in New Zealand during the Great War: The von Zedlitz Affair, 1915', *Immigrants and Minorities* 24/3 (2006), pp. 252-60.

49 Santanu Das, *India, Empire, and First World War Culture: Writings, Images, and Songs* (Cambridge, 2019), pp. 43-4, 72, 93-5, 178.

50 Margaret H. Darrow, *French Women and the First World War: War Stories of the Home Front* (Oxford, 2000), pp. 15, 106, 268–9; Bruno Cabanes, *August 1914: France, the Great War, and a Month That Changed the World Forever* (New Haven, 2016), pp. 133–8.

51 Eric Lohr, *Nationalizing the Russian Empire: The Campaign against Enemy Aliens during World War I* (Cambridge, 2003), pp. 17–20; Peter Gatrell, *Russia's First World War: A Social and Economic History* (Harlow, 2005), pp. 22–9, 178–82; William C. Fuller, *The Foe Within: Fantasies of Treason and the End of Imperial Russia* (Ithaca, 2006), pp. 172–6; Alan Kramer, 'Combatants and Noncombatants: Atrocities, Massacres, and War Crimes', in Horne (ed.), *A Companion to World War I*, p. 193; Christopher Read, *War and Revolution in Russia, 1914–22* (Basingstoke, 2013), pp. 27–8; Joshua Sanborn, *Imperial Apocalypse: The Great War and the Destruction of the Russian Empire* (Oxford, 2014), p. 54; Uğur Ümit Üngör and Eric Lohr: 'Economic Nationalism, Confiscation, and Genocide: A Comparison of the Ottoman and Russian Empires during World War I', *Journal of Modern European History* 12/4 (2014), pp. 508–11; Melissa Kirschke Stockdale, *Mobilising the Russian Nation: Patriotism and Citizenship in the First World War* (Cambridge, 2016), pp. 167–8.

52 Daniela L. Caglioti, 'Why and How Italy Invented an Enemy Aliens Problem in the First World War', *War in History* 21/2 (2014), pp. 144–9; John Gooch, 'Italy before 1915: The Quandary of the Vulnerable', in Ernest R. May (ed.), *Knowing One's Enemies: Intelligence Assessment before the Two World Wars* (Princeton, 2014), pp. 213–15.

53 David Kennedy, *Over Here: The First World War and American Society* (Oxford, 1980), pp. 53–6, 81; Jörg Nagler, 'Victims of the Home Front: Enemy Aliens in the United States during the First World War', in Panayi (ed.), *Minorities in Wartime*, pp. 191–215; Nancy Gentile Ford, *The Great War and America: Civil-Military Relations during World War I* (London, 2008), pp. 57–60; Jennifer D. Keene, *The United States and the First World War* (Abingdon, 2014), pp. 34–6; Michael S. Neiberg, *The Path to War: How the First World War Created Modern America* (Oxford, 2016), pp. 78–82; Zachery Smith, *Age of Fear: Othering and American Identity during World War I* (Baltimore, 2019), pp. 44–6, 52–3; Mark Stout, *World War I and the Foundations of American Intelligence* (Lawrence, 2023), pp. 196–200.

54 Mark Cornwall, 'Austria-Hungary and "Yugoslavia"', in Horne (ed.), *A Companion to World War I*, p. 375; Matthew Stibbe, 'Enemy Aliens, Deportees, Refugees: Internment Practices in the Habsburg Empire, 1914–1918', *Journal of Modern European History* 12/4 (2014), p. 492; Alexander Watson, *Ring of Steel: Germany and Austria-Hungary at War* (London, 2014), pp. 58–9; Holger H. Herwig, *The First World War: Germany and Austria-Hungary 1914–1918* (London, 2014), p. 132; Pieter M. Judson, *The Habsburg Empire: A New History* (Cambridge, 2016), pp. 395–9.

55 Belinda Davis, *Home Fires Burning: Food, Politics, and Everyday Life in World War I Berlin* (Chapel Hill, 2000), p. 40; Huw Strachan, *The First World War, Volume I: To Arms* (Oxford, 2003), p. 106; Jeffrey Verhey, *The Spirit of 1914: Militarism, Myth, and Mobilisation in Germany* (Cambridge, 2004), pp. 75–6; Roger Chickering, *The Great War and Urban Life in Germany* (Cambridge, 2007), pp. 65–9, 312–17; Watson, *Ring of Steel*, pp. 75–8. Probably because of the earlier conflict in 1870 and the use of the Franc-Tireurs against the invading Prussian army, German soldiers in Alsace-Lorraine were particularly conscious of covert activity and armed resistance, leading to a deluge of rumours about spies in their midst. Alan Kramer, '*Wackes* at War: Alsace-Lorraine and the Failure of German National Mobilization, 1914–1918',

in John Horne (ed.), *State, Society and Mobilization in Europe during the First World War* (Cambridge, 1997), p. 108.

56 Eyal Ginion, 'Landscapes of Modernity and Order: War and Propaganda in Ottoman Writing during World War I', in M. Hakan Yavuz and Feroz Ahmad (eds), *War and Collapse: World War I and the Ottoman State* (Utah, 2016), p. 287. At the same time, nations within the empire began to rebel against Ottoman rule: Pamela Dorn Sezgin, 'Greeks, Jews, and Armenians: A Comparative Analysis of Non-Muslim Communities and Nascent Nationalisms in the Late Ottoman Empire through World War I', in Yavuz and Ahmad (eds), *War and Collapse*, p. 323.

57 Donald Bloxham, *The Great Game of Genocide: Imperialism, Nationalism, and the Destruction of the Ottoman Armenians* (Oxford, 2005), pp. 65–8, 71; Taner Akçam, *A Shameful Act: The Armenian Genocide and the Question of Turkish Responsibility* (New York, 2006), pp. 43–6, 97–102.

58 Yiğit Akin, *When the War Came Home: The Ottomans' Great War and the Devastation of an Empire* (Stanford, 2018), p. 53.

59 Y. Doğan Çetinkaya, 'Illustrated Atrocity: The Stigmatisation of Non-Muslims through Images in the Ottoman Empire during the Balkan Wars', *Journal of Modern European History* 12/4 (2014), p. 468; Akin, *When the War Came Home*, p. 73.

60 Çiğdem Oğuz, *Moral Crisis in the Ottoman Empire: Society, Politics, and Gender during WWI* (London, 2021), pp. 65, 90–2.

61 Peter N. Stearns and Carol Z. Stearns, 'Emotionology: Clarifying the History of Emotions and Emotional Standards', *American Historical Review* 90 (1985), pp. 813–36.

62 William M. Reddy, *The Navigation of Feeling: A Framework for the History of Emotions* (Cambridge, 2001), pp. 64, 94–5, 102–4; Jan Plamper, 'The History of Emotions: An Interview with William Reddy, Barbara Rosenwein, and Peter Stearns', *History and Theory* 49 (2010), pp. 239–40.

63 Reddy, *The Navigation of Feeling*, pp. 104–5, 108–9; Monique Scheer employs Reddy's methodology to argue that bodily performance is just as useful as linguist expression to uncover the meaning and experience of emotion: 'Are Emotions a Kind of Practice (and Is That What Makes Them Have a History)? A Bourdieuan Approach to Understanding Emotion', *History and Theory* 51 (2021), pp. 193–220.

64 Katie Barclay, *The History of Emotions: A Student Guide to Methods and Sources* (London, 2020), p. 10.

65 Jan Plamper, *The History of Emotions: An Introduction* (Oxford, 2015), pp. 142–4.

66 Ute Frevert, Christian Bailey, Pascal Eitler, Benno Gammerl, Bettina Hitzer, Margrit Pernau, Monique Scheer, Anne Schmidt, and Nina Verheyen, *Emotional Lexicons: Continuity and Change in the Vocabulary of Feeling 1700–2000* (Oxford, 2014); Barbara H. Rosenwein, *Generations of Feeling: A History of Emotions, 600–1700* (Cambridge, 2016).

67 Martha C. Nussbaum, *Upheavals of Thought: The Intelligence of Emotions* (Cambridge, 2003), p. 4.

68 Rosenwein, *Generations of Feeling*, p. 3.

69 Reddy, *Navigation of Feeling*, p. 32. See also: Martha C. Nussbaum, *Political Emotions: Why Love Matters for Justice* (Cambridge, 2013), pp. 1–5; Martha C. Nussbaum, *Hiding from Humanity: Disgust, Shame, and the Law* (Princeton, 2006), pp. 61–2.

70 Frank Biess, *German Angst: Fear and Democracy in the Federal Republic of Germany* (Oxford, 2020), p. 16.

71 Joanna Bourke, *Fear: A Cultural History* (London, 2006), p. 189.
72 Bourke, *Fear*, pp. 190.
73 Sigmund Freud distinguished phobias from what he termed 'true obsessions', which come with an 'associated emotional state', such as anger, doubt, remorse or anxiety. Phobias, on the other hand, are always accompanied by a state of anxiety. Whereas 'common phobias' reflect exaggerated fears of things that frighten most people, such as death or illness, 'specific phobias' can also include fears of objects or situations not normally considered dangerous or threatening. Sigmund Freud, 'Obsessions and Phobias: Their Psychical Mechanism and Their Aetiology', in *The Standard Edition of the Complete Psychological Works of Sigmund Freud*, iii (London, 1962), pp. 74–81.
74 Bourke, *Fear*, pp. 189.
75 Michael Roper, *The Secret Battle: Emotional Survival in the Great War* (Manchester, 2010), p. 14.
76 This includes six daily newspapers from coastal cities and six from inland cities, twelve weekly newspapers from rural coastal locations and twelve from rural inland locations, two London daily newspapers, and six Irish newspapers (two daily and four weekly).
77 William Reddy conceived of 'emotional regimes' to describe the standards determining how societies think, write and speak about emotions. He describes an emotional regime as 'the set of normative emotions and the official rituals, practices, and emotives that express and inculcate them; a necessary underpinning of any stable political regime'. Of course, this does not mean that there is only ever single emotional standard available to society. 'Emotional refuges', as Reddy terms them, provide safe spaces for the expression of feelings that deviates from the social and political norm. For Reddy, rules about expressing and responding to emotion became integral to political ideals. Reddy, *The Navigation of Feeling*, pp. 124–9; Barbara H. Rosenwein, 'Review of William M. Reddy, *The Navigation of Feeling: A Framework for the History of Emotions*', *American Historical Review* 107/4 (2002), p. 1182; William M. Reddy, 'Sentimentalism and Its Erasure: The Role of Emotions in the Era of the French Revolution', *Journal of Modern History* 72/1 (2000), pp. 109–52.
78 Carol Stearns and Peter Stearns posit that emotional styles act as a set of fashionable trends that shape the rules and methods for emotional expression for a particular group. Emotional styles are not simply cultural attitudes towards a single emotion but an entire cultural framework that organizes the emotional life of a society or subculture within it. An emotional style is unlike an emotional regime, in that it does not demand conformity or exact punishment on those failing to adhere to the dominant standard in its attempt to sustain political ideals. An emotional regime can be thought of as an emotional framework that comprises multiple styles that are all enforced through a central authority. Arguably, then, spy phobias represented an emotional style (or styles, because not all emotional reactions were expressed in the same way) that contributed to and sustained a more encompassing emotional regime enforcing certain attitudes and behaviours. Stearns and Stearns, 'Emotionology', pp. 813–36; Barclay, *History of Emotions*, pp. 35–8; Plamper, 'An Interview with William Reddy, Barbara Rosenwein, and Peter Stearns', p. 243.
79 Each 'Emotional Community', according to Barbara Rosenwein, incorporates its own emotional standards and customs relating to the expression of certain feelings based on the situation in which they are experienced. While there is often a dominant community, which she admits is fairly synonymous with Reddy's Emotional Regime, it always accommodates other 'marginal' spaces and coexists with other competing

groups. As individuals move from one community to another, they are free to adjust their emotional judgements and how they display feelings according to the appropriate convention within that particular community. As a result, an individual can conform to several standards of feeling, each depending on their immediate social environment and circumstance. Barbara H. Rosenwein, 'Worrying about the Emotions in History', *American Historical Review* 107/3 (2002), p. 837; Barbara H. Rosenwein, *Emotional Communities in the Early Middle Ages* (Ithaca, 2006), pp. 1–31; Plamper, 'An Interview with William Reddy, Barbara Rosenwein, and Peter Stearns', pp. 255-61; Rosenwein, *Generations of Feeling*, pp. 3–10.

80 'Mixed emotions' is the idea that categorizing emotions (love, hate, anger, fear) is far too simplistic to account for the complex blend of emotions that people typically experience: Barclay, *History of Emotions*, p. 11.

Part I

1 I. F. Clarke, *The Tale of the Next Great War, 1871–1914: Fictions of Future Warfare and Battles Still-to-Come* (Liverpool, 1995), p. 14.

2 Patrick Longson, 'The Rise of the German Menace: Imperial Anxiety and British Popular Culture, 1896–1903', PhD thesis (University of Birmingham, 2014), p. 10.

3 Patrick Major, 'Britain and Germany: A Love Hate Relationship?', *German History* 26/4 (2008), pp. 457–68; Lothar Reinermann, 'Fleet Street and the Kaiser: British Public Opinion and Wilhelm II', *German History* 26/4 (2008), pp. 469–85.

4 Panikos Panayi, 'German Immigrants in Britain, 1815–1914', in Panikos Panayi (ed.), *Germans in Britain since 1500* (London, 1996), pp. 73–94.

5 Arthur Marwick, *The Deluge: British Society and the First World War* (London, 1965), pp. 89, 171–2.; Colin Holmes, *John Bull's Island: Immigration and British Society* (London, 1992), pp. 86–114; K. D. Ewing and C. A. Gearty, *The Struggle for Civil Liberties: Political Freedom and the Rule of Law in Britain 1914–1945* (Oxford, 2000), p. 43; Gregory, *Last Great War*, pp. 238–41; Gerard De Groot, *Back in Blighty: The British at Home in World War I* (London, 2014), pp. 246–52.

6 Panayi, *Enemy in Our Midst*, p. 184; Nicoletta F. Gullace, 'Friends, Aliens and Enemies: Fictive Communities and the Lusitania Riots of 1915', *Journal of Social History* 39/2 (2005), pp. 345–6; Keir Waddington, '"We Don't Need Any German Sausages Here!" Food, Fear, and the German Nation in Victorian and Edwardian Britain', *Journal of British Studies* 52/4 (2013), pp. 1017–21.

7 Cate Haste, *Keep the Home Fires Burning: Propaganda in the First World War* (London, 1977), p. 108.

8 Panayi, *Enemy in Our Midst*, p. 153.

9 Pennell, *A Kingdom United*, pp. 102–7.

10 Ibid., pp. 105–7.

11 'Appeal to Devonshire. Patriotic Fund Inaugurated. Lord-Lieutenant's Speech. Mayor of Exeter's Strong Comments', *Exeter and Plymouth Gazette*, 8 August 1914, p. 4; 'Spies in Devon', *Western Times*, 11 August 1914, p. 2.

12 Pierre Purseigle shows how local authorities took a particularly important role in mediating between the state and the British public: 'Beyond and Below the Nations: Towards a Comparative History of Local Communities at War', in Jenny Macleod and Pierre Purseigle (eds), *Uncovered Fields: Perspectives in First World War*

Studies, History of Warfare, 20 (Leiden, 2004), pp. 98, 101; and 'Introduction', in Pierre Purseigle (ed.), *Warfare and Belligerence: Perspectives in First World War Studies*, History of Warfare, 30 (Leiden, 2005), p. 26.

13 This was not merely specific to Devon, however. A letter written to Bonar Law about a purported spy explicitly stated that it was a response to a previous debate held in the Commons about espionage: Parliamentary Archives, BL/36/5/13: Papers of Andrew Bonar Law, Letter dated 4 March.

14 IWM docs. 6322: Papers of W. L. B. Tower, Diary entry 1 August 1914.

15 'Alleged Spies', *Daily Mail*, 31 July 1914, p. 3.

16 Joanna Bourke, 'Fear and Anxiety: Writing about Emotion in Modern History', *History Workshop Journal* 55/1 (2003), pp. 119–20.

Chapter 1

1 Liddle DF 148/1/54: Professor A. D. Gardner, Memoir, p. 96.

2 Concerns regarding a channel tunnel had long existed in public debate. Those who opposed the creation of a tunnel did so on the grounds that it could facilitate a French invasion of Britain: Peter Keeling, 'British Liberal Internationalism in Retreat: The Channel Tunnel Controversy and the Naval Defence Act, 1880–1894', PhD thesis (University of Kent, 2018), pp. 160–97.

3 J. A. Hobson, *The Psychology of Jingoism* (London, 1901), p. 7. Antony Taylor has recently argued that William Le Queux's invasion and espionage fictions were themselves reflective of a growing concern for Britain's decaying urban environments which, to Le Queux, were symbolic of national decline: 'At the Mercy of the German Eagle: Images of London in Dissolution in the Novels of William Le Queux', *Critical Survey* 32/1–2 (2020), p. 60.

4 Roy Porter, 'Nervousness, Eighteenth and Nineteenth Century Style: From Luxury to Labour', in Marijke Gijswijt-Hofstra and Roy Porter (eds), *Cultures of Neurasthenia from Beard to the First World War* (New York, 2001), p. 33; Andrew Scull, *Hysteria: The Disturbing History* (Oxford, 2011), pp. 48–9; Tracey Loughran, *Shell-Shock and Medical Culture in First World War Britain* (Cambridge, 2020), pp. 74–5.

5 Smith, *Age of Fear*, p. 20; Mathew Thompson, 'Neurasthenia in Britain: An Overview', in Gijswijt-Hofstra and Porter, *Cultures of Neurasthenia*, pp. 77, 80.

6 Raymond F. Betts, 'The Allusion to Rome in British Imperialist Thought of the Late Nineteenth and Early Twentieth Centuries', *Victorian Studies* 15/2 (1971), pp. 149–59; Linda Dowling, 'Roman Decadence and Victorian Historiography', *Victorian Studies* 28/4 (1985), pp. 579–607; Norman Vance, 'Anxieties of Empire and the Moral Tradition: Rome and Britain', *International Journal of the Classical Tradition* 18/2 (2011), pp. 246–61. Britain's leaders, however, refused to acknowledge any erosion in their national position and remained confident that measures could be devised to meet the emerging challenges: Aaron Friedberg, *The Weary Titan: Britain and the Experience of Relative Decline, 1895–1905* (Princeton, 1988), pp. 292–3.

7 Thompson, 'Neurasthenia in Britain', p. 88.

8 Norman Longmate, *Defending the Island: From Caesar to the Armada* (London, 1990); and Norman Longmate, *Island Fortress: The Defence of Great Britain 1603–1945* (London, 1991).

9   John Gooch, *The Prospect of War: Studies in British Defence Policy, 1847–1942* (Abingdon, 1981), p. 1; David Morgan-Owen, *The Fear of Invasion: Strategy, Politics, and British War Planning, 1880–1914* (Oxford, 2017), p. 1.

10 'Why Are We at War?', *Derbyshire Courier*, 15 August 1914, p. 4.

11 See, for example, Caroline Playne, *The Pre-War Mind in Britain: An Historical Review* (London, 1928).

12 'Panic' was often used to denigrate people holding different views to those of the author: David Morgan-Owen, 'Scares, Panics, and Strategy: The Politics of Security and British Invasion Scares before 1914', *Diplomacy and Statecraft* 33/3 (2022), pp. 449–50.

13 It was by no means a dominant emotional regime. It has been clearly demonstrated that a widespread affinity for invasion fiction did not correspond to widespread fears of foreign attack: Christian K. Melby, 'Empire and Nation in British Future-War and Invasion-Scare Fiction, 1871–1914', *Historical Journal* 63/2 (2020), pp. 389–410.

14 Morgan-Owen, *Fear of Invasion*, pp. 15–17.

15 There was little in the way of centrally directed strategy during this period, and British strategy here can best be understood as an 'aggregate of quasi-independent naval and military efforts' that were increasingly subject to political oversight and influence: Morgan-Owen, *Fear of Invasion*, pp. 11–12.

16 War with France had not been fully discounted, despite the signing of the Entente Cordiale in 1904, since the Russo-Japanese War (1904–5) threatened to precipitate an Anglo-French conflict. Russia's advances into Asia also endangered Britain's rule in India, and the Kaiser's bellicosity and desire for empire placed Germany firmly in competition with Britain, especially as Wilhelm's support for the Boers had soured relations between the two nations.

17 Morgan-Owen, *Fear of Invasion*, pp. 117–19.

18 Matthew Seligmann, 'Switching Horses: The Admiralty's Recognition of the Threat from Germany, 1900–1905', *International History Review* 30/2 (2008), pp. 239–58; and 'Britain's Great Security Mirage: The Royal Navy and the Franco-Russian Naval Threat, 1898–1906', *Journal of Strategic Studies* 35/6 (2012), pp. 861–86; John Gooch, *The Plans of War: The General Staff and British Military Strategy c. 1900–1916* (London, 1974), pp. 278–85; Hew Strachan, 'The British Army, Its General Staff and the Continental Commitment 1904–14', in David French and Brian Holden Reid (eds), *The British General Staff: Reform and Innovation, 1890–1939* (London, 2005), pp. 63–4.

19 Morgan-Owen, *Fear of Invasion*, pp. 134–5.

20 Matthew Seligmann, *Spies in Uniform: British Military and Naval Intelligence on the Eve of the First World War* (Oxford, 2006), pp. 185–6.

21 Seligmann, *Spies in Uniform*, pp. 161–5; Morgan-Owen, *Fear of Invasion*, pp. 136–7.

22 Strachan, 'The British Army', p. 76; Morgan-Owen, *Fear of Invasion*, pp. 165–6.

23 Ian Beckett, Timothy Bowman, and Mark Connelly, *The British Army and the First World War* (Cambridge, 2017), p. 94.

24 A. J. A. Morris, *The Scaremongers: The Advocacy of War and Rearmament, 1896–1914* (Abingdon, 2014) p. 3.

25 Ibid., pp. 4–6; Keith Robbins, *Politicians, Diplomacy and War in Modern British History* (London, 1994), p. 135.

26 Howard Moon, 'The Invasion of the United Kingdom: Public Controversy and Official Planning, 1888–1918', PhD thesis (University of London, 1968), p. 20; See also I. F.

Clarke, 'Forecasts of Warfare in Fiction 1803–1914', *Comparative Studies in Society and History* 10/1 (1967), pp. 11–24.

27   Moon, 'Invasion of the United Kingdom', pp. 19–24.

28   *Hansard*, House of Lords, 11 May 1888, cols 6–7; C. H. Nugent, 'Thoughts upon Invasion and upon the Means Available, or Which May Be Made Available at a Few Weeks Notice, for Securing Our Coast Line Generally against Sudden Attack', *Royal United Services Institution Journal* 32/143 (1888), p. 165.

29   Quoted in Moon, 'Invasion of the United Kingdom', pp. 27–9.

30   'Our Real National Peril. The Opened Door for a French Raid on London', *Review of Reviews*, 22 December 1899, p. 148.

31   TNA PRO 30/40/3: Papers of Major General Sir John Charles Ardagh, letter dated 22 December 1899.

32   Even the Queen wrote to Salisbury in January 1900 to express her concerns regarding the efficacy of the nation's defences in light of naval expansion occurring abroad.

33   Moon, 'Invasion of the United Kingdom', pp. 129–31, 140–4.

34   TNA CAB 17/17: Universal Military Training 1905, Correspondence between Roberts and Balfour.

35   Morris, *Scaremongers*, pp. 5–7; J. Lee Thompson, *Politicians, the Press, and Propaganda: Lord Northcliffe and the Great War, 1914–1919* (London, 1999), p. 13; J. Lee Thompson, *Northcliffe: Press Baron in Politics, 1865–1922* (London, 2000), p. 206.

36   H. M. Hyndman, a leading left-wing figure and founder of Britain's Socialist Party in 1881, espoused invasion fears akin to those of Leopold Maxse, probably the most deluded and vociferous critic of Germany in Edwardian Britain.

37   A. M. Matin, 'Securing Britain: Figures of Invasion in Late-Victorian and Edwardian Fiction', PhD thesis (Columbia University, 1997) p. v. See also Rhodri Williams, *Defending the Empire: The Conservative Party and British Defence Policy 1899–1915* (New Haven, 1991).

38   Arthur Marwick, *The Deluge: British Society and the First World War* (London, 1965). For early revisionist accounts see Trevor Wilson, *The Myriad Faces of War: Britain and the Great War, 1914–1918* (Cambridge, 1986); Gerard De Groot, *Blighty: British Society in the Era of the Great War* (London, 1996). Neither Wilson nor De Groot significantly altered our understanding of anti-German sentiment.

39   Marwick, *The Deluge*, p. 90.

40   Wilson, *Myriad Faces of War*, p. 161; De Groot, *British Society in the Era of the Great War*, p. 157.

41   Panayi, *Enemy in Our Midst*, p. 41.

42   Adrian Gregory, for instance, observes a gradual increase in anti-German sentiment that culminated with the sinking of the *Lusitania* in May 1915: *Last Great War*, p. 62.

43   Marwick argued that the popular press merely followed contemporary attitudes rather than led them, while the government played almost no part in early propaganda efforts. Marwick, *The Deluge*, p. 91; Gary S. Messinger, *British Propaganda and the State in the First World War* (Manchester, 1992), p. 2.

44   Holmes, *John Bull's Island*, p. 57.

45   Ibid., pp. 57–61; Donald M. MacRaild, *Irish Migrants in Modern Britain, 1750–1922* (Basingstoke, 1999), pp. 155–74; Panikos Panayi, *An Immigration History of Britain: Multicultural Racism since 1800* (London, 2014), p. 223.

46   Holmes, *John Bull's Island*, pp. 65–70. See also William Rubinstein, *A History of the Jews in the English Speaking World: Great Britain* (Basingstoke, 1996).

47   Holmes, *John Bull's Island*, pp. 64.

48 Panayi, *An Immigration History*, p. 229.

49 Ibid., pp. 74–81.

50 But, at the same time, there was little indication of an extensive hostility towards immigrants: Holmes, *John Bull's Island*, p. 84. See also: Colin Holmes, *A Tolerant Country? Immigrants, Refugees and Minorities in Britain* (London, 1991), p. 14; Panikos Panayi, *Immigration, Ethnicity and Racism, in Britain, 1815–1945* (Manchester, 1994), pp. 102–3, 114–24.

51 See also David Cannadine, *Victorious Century: The United Kingdom, 1800–1906* (Milton Keynes, 2018), pp. 364–5.

52 David Cesarani, 'An Alien Concept? The Continuity of Anti-Alienism in British Society before 1940', *Immigrants and Minorities* 11/3 (1992), pp. 26–34.

53 Holmes, *John Bull's Island*, p. 62; Paul Kennedy, *The Rise of the Anglo-German Antagonism 1860–1914* (London, 1980).

54 Paul Kennedy, 'Idealists and Realists: British Views of Germany, 1864–1939', *Transactions of the Royal Historical Society* 25 (1975), pp. 139–40; Major, 'Britain and Germany', p. 461; Dominic Geppert and Robert Gerwarth, 'Introduction', in Dominic Geppert and Robert Gerwarth (eds), *Wilhelmine Germany and Edwardian Britain: Essays on Cultural Affinity* (Oxford, 2008), pp. 6–7.

55 John Mander, *Our German Cousins: Anglo-German Relations in the 19th and 20th Centuries* (London, 1974), p. 196; Jörn Leonhard, 'Construction and Perception of National Images: Germany and Britain, 1870–1914', *The Linacre Journal* 4 (2000), pp. 48, 52–3; Major, 'A Love Hate Relationship', p. 462. This political antipathy did not remove the entrenched cultural affinity, however: Richard Scully, *British Images of Germany: Admiration, Antagonism and Ambivalence, 1860–1914* (Basingstoke, 2012), pp. 60–2, 184–5. Conversely, the Boer War also marked a divisive point in the development of German attitudes towards Britain: Martin Kröger, 'Imperial Germany and the Boer War', in Keith Wilson (ed.), *The International Impact of the Boer War* (Abingdon, 2014), pp. 25–39.

56 Kennedy, 'Idealists and Realists', p. 141.

57 Kennedy, 'Idealists and Realists', pp. 137–46; Scully, *British Images of Germany*, pp. 69–70, 86, 93.

58 Kennedy, 'Idealists and Realists', pp. 137–46.

59 Jan Rüger, 'Revisiting the Anglo-German Antagonism', *Journal of Modern History* 83/3 (2011), p. 587. See also Leonhard, 'Construction and Perception of National Images', p. 49.

60 Major, 'A Love Hate Relationship', p. 458; Thomas Weber, *Our Friend the Enemy: Elite Education in Britain and Germany before the First World War* (Stanford, 2008), p. 93. Likewise in Germany, it was quite possible to be culturally Anglophile at the same time as being politically Anglophobic: Leonhard, 'Construction and Perception of National Images', pp. 45, 56; Major 'A Love Hate Relationship', p. 458.

61 Between 1900 and 1914, in particular, popular discourse repeatedly agonized over what Germany should and could mean for British fortunes: Scully, *Images of Germany*, p. 319.

62 Kennedy, 'Idealists and Realists', p. 142.

63 Kennedy, 'Idealists and Realists', pp. 142–6; Leonhard, 'Construction and Perception of National Images', p. 50; Scully, *Images of Germany*, pp. 113–7.

64 Rüger, 'Revisiting the Anglo-German Antagonism', pp. 583, 588, 601–2.

65 Jews were often blamed for the perceived decline: Panayi, *Immigration, Ethnicity and Racism*, p. 117.

66 Major, 'A Love Hate Relationship', p. 462.

67 Scully, *Images of Germany*, pp. 112, 125.

68 The year 1896 marked a definite shift in both political and cultural perceptions of Germany thanks to the Kaiser's interference in the Transvaal: see Matthew Seligmann, *Rivalry in Southern Africa, 1893–99: The Transformation of German Colonial Policy* (Basingstoke, 1998); and Patrick Longson, 'The Rise of the German Menace: Imperial Anxiety and British Popular Culture, 1896–1903', PhD thesis (University of Birmingham, 2014).

69 Reinermann, 'Fleet Street and the Kaiser', pp. 472–6; Scully, *Images of Germany*, pp. 228–60. The Kaiser's own perception of Britain was equally inconsistent: John C. G. Röhl, ' "The Worst of Enemies": Kaiser Wilhelm II and His Uncle Edward VII', in Geppert and Gerwarth, *Wilhelmine Germany and Edwardian Britain*, pp. 48–65.

70 Panayi, 'German Immigrants in Britain, 1815–1914', pp. 88–9.

71 Ibid., p. 90.

72 Leonhard, 'Construction and Perception of National Images', p. 47. Homes contends that popular antipathy results from a multitude of factors, including stereotypes, numbers of immigrants, wartime phobias, economic conditions and the perception of a group as unassailable or as competition: Holmes, *John Bull's Island*, pp. 299–301.

73 Waddington, 'Food, Fear, and the German Nation', pp. 18–20.

74 Stella Yarrow, for example, suggested that wartime Germanophobia was evidence of a much wider and deep-rooted xenophobia that was exacerbated following reports of German atrocities: 'The Impact of Hostility on Germans in Britain, 1914–1918', *Immigrants and Minorities* 8/1–2 (1989), pp. 98, 109; Gullace, 'Friends, Aliens and Enemies', p. 347.

75 Harry Richards, 'The Nationalisation of War, the Rise of Psychology, and the Creation of "Spy Fever" in the British Press', *War and Society*, published online 20 February 2025.

76 'The Police and the Spy System', *John Bull*, 4 September 1854, p. 9.

77 Richards, 'Creation of "Spy Fever" in the British Press', published online 20 February 2025.

78 'Reviews', *Lincolnshire Chronicle*, 5 May 1871, p. 3.

79 Richards, 'Creation of "Spy Fever" in the British Press', published online 20 February 2025.
    Although spy phobias were seldom on display in Britain until after the turn of the century, allegations of clandestine German activity in France continued to appear in the British press long after 1870 and mostly involved suspicious-looking Germans sketching vulnerable targets, loitering near military installations or their involvement in the French railway network – all of which would become familiar tropes used during the First World War: 'From Our Paris Correspondent', *Manchester Courier and Lancashire General Advertiser*, 28 July 1883, p. 5; 'General News', *The Globe*, 24 December 1883, p. 2; 'Arrest of a Supposed German Spy', *Cardiff Times*, 12 January 1884, p. 5; 'Arrest of a German Spy', *Northern Whig*, 4 September 1884, p. 5; 'Another German Spy Story', *Shields Daily Gazette*, 14 September 1885, p. 4; 'Another German Spy in France', *Evening Herald*, 18 October 1895, p. 2.

80 David A. T. Stafford, 'Spies and Gentlemen: The Birth of the British Spy Novel, 1893–1914', *Victorian Studies* 24/4 (1981), p. 492; Roger T. Stearn, 'The Mysterious Mr

Le Queux: War Novelist, Defence Publicist and Counterspy', *Critical Survey* 32/1–2 (2020), pp. 37–8.

81 William Le Queux, *The German Spy System from Within* (London, 1914), p. 41.

82 French stories told of an army of German spies commanded by Bismarck's chief of police, Wilhelm Stieber: Bauer, 'Villains, Liars, Soldiers, and Patriots', p. 193.

83 This was precisely the point being made by Hamil Grant in publishing a detailed account of Prussian espionage during the Franco-Prussian War in 1915: *Spies and Secret Service: The Story of Espionage, Its Main Systems and Chief Exponents* (London, 1915), pp. 190–4.

84 I. F. Clarke, *Voices Prophesising War, 1763–1984* (Oxford, 1966), p. 72; Joseph S. Meisel, 'The Germans Are Coming! British Fiction of a German Invasion 1871–1913', *War, Literature and the Arts* 2/2 (1990), p. 43; Scully, *Images of Germany*, p. 94.

85 Scully, *Images of Germany*, pp. 110–11.

86 Erskine Childers, *The Riddle of the Sands*, edited by David Trotter (Oxford, 2008), p. 68.

87 Ibid., p. 75.

88 Joseph Conrad, *The Secret Agent: A Simple Tale* (Oxford, 2007), pp. 17–20.

89 Ibid., p. 110.

90 Ibid., pp. 23–4.

91 Stearn, 'The Mysterious Mr Le Queux', p. 24.

92 David Trotter, 'The Politics of Adventure in the Early British Spy Novel', in Wesley K. Wark (ed.), *Spy Fiction, Spy Films and Real Intelligence* (London, 1991), p. 39.

93 William Le Queux, *The Man from Downing Street* (London, 1904), p. 5.

94 Le Queux's earlier work also reflected this paradigm. *The Great War in England in 1897*, for example, only features Count von Beilstein as the main antagonist as opposed to armies of hidden saboteurs.

95 William le Queux, *The Invasion of 1910 with a Full Account of the Siege of London* (Toronto, 1906), pp. 16–7, 28–9.

96 William le Queux, *Spies of the Kaiser: Plotting the Downfall of England* (London, 1908), p. 66.

97 Trotter, 'The Politics of Adventure', p. 42.

98 E. Phillips Oppenheim, *Mysterious Mr. Sabin* (New York, 1905).

99 E. Phillips Oppenheim, *The Great Secret* (Boston, MA, 1908), pp. 56–9, 229–30, 286.

100 Leo Maxse, one the most prominent radicals and exponents of the spy peril, was commended for launching attacks against innocent waiters and hairdressers, for intriguers were still at large but there was no tangible threat to pin it on. West Sussex Record Office, Maxse Mss 3/2/1/370: Papers of Leo Maxse, Letter from David Lindsay, 7 January 1915. TNA HO 45/10727/254753: WAR. Activities of Enemy Agents.

101 French, 'Spy Fever in Britain', p. 356.

102 Hampshire, 'Spy Fever in Britain, 1900 to 1914', p. 24.

103 Danny Laurie-Fletcher, *British Invasion and Spy Literature, 1871–1918* (Cham, 2019), p. 83.

104 See also Andrew, *Secret Service*, p. 267; Childers, *The Riddle of the Sands*, p. viii.

105 Jonathan Rose, 'Rereading the English Common Reader: A Preface to a History of Audiences', *Journal of the History of Ideas* 53/1 (1992), p. 48.

106 Harry Wood, 'External Threats Mask Internal Fears: Edwardian Invasion Literature 1899–1914', PhD thesis (University of Liverpool, 2014), p. 9.

107 Between 1871 and 1914, there were only two years without a novel alluding to future conflict published in Britain, and between 1880 and 1900, there were three English stories to every French one, while Germany produced half of the number that appeared in France. Clarke, 'Forecasts of Warfare in Fiction 1803–1914', pp. 1–25.

108 'Diplomats and a Spy', *Daily Mail*, 6 April 1911, p. 7; 'German Espionage Mystery', *Daily Mail*, 12 February 1913, p. 6; 'Gold Beater as Spy', *Daily Mail*, 20 October 1911, p. 5; 'Spy Mania Interventions', *Daily Mail*, 20 December 1911, p. 5; 'Spies in England', *Daily Mail*, 18 May 1908, p. 8; 'German Spies', *Daily Mail*, 5 October 1909, p. 7; 'The Russian Spy', *Daily Mail*, 4 February 1909; 'Police Spies and Bombs', *Daily Mail*, 10 October 1911, p. 7; 'German Espionage', *Daily Mail*, 1 April 1909, p. 4; 'Spies and the Law', *Daily Mail*, 8 September 1910, p. 4.

109 'Spies in England', *Daily Mail*, 18 May 1908, p. 8; 'Single Spies', *Daily Mail*, 27 July 1909, p. 6; 'A Spy Drama', *Daily Mail*, 3 February 1909, p. 5.

110 The *Quarterly Review* claimed that 'Germany already possesses in this country such an intelligence system as no other nation has ever maintained upon the territory of another … There are in this country some 50,000 German waiters … The blow will fall when and where we least expect it'. Quoted in Morris, *The Scaremongers*, pp. 157–8.

111 'King of Spies Lynched', *Daily Mail*, 6 August 1908, p. 5; 'The Russian Spy', *Daily Mail*, 4 February 1909, p. 5; 'Spy Shot in the Street', *Daily Mail*, 9 August 1910, p. 6; 'Spies at Potsdam', *Daily Mail*, 10 August 1910, p. 7; 'Diplomats and a Spy', *Daily Mail*, 6 April 1911, p. 7; 'Woman Spy', *Daily Mail*, 17 July 1911, p. 7; 'Escaped Spy Home Again', *Daily Mail*, 1 January 1912, p. 9; 'Russo-German Espionage', 29 June 1912, p. 6; 'Wireless Espionage', *Daily Mail*, 11 April 1913, p. 6; 'Espionage Arrests', *Daily Mail*, 12 April 1913, p. 5.

112 'Substitute for Spies', *Daily Mail*, 15 May 1909, p. 5; 'Spies within the Camp', *Daily Mail*, 30 September 1910, p. 4.

113 'Spy Mania Inventions', *Daily Mail*, 20 December 1911, p. 5; 'German Spy Mania', *Daily Mail*, 28 May 1914, p. 5.

114 'German Spy Mania', *Daily Mail*, 26 August 1910, p. 5. For information on Brandon and Trench see Seligmann, *Spies in Uniform*, p. 9; Keith Jeffrey, *MI6: The History of the Secret Intelligence Service 1909–1949* (London, 2011), p. 25.

115 'Spy Mania', *Daily Mail*, 24 May 1909, p. 7.

116 'German Spy Mania', *Daily Mail*, 12 September 1910, p. 5; 'German Spy Mania', *Daily Mail*, 13 September 1910, p. 5.

117 'German Spy Mania', *Daily Mail*, 27 September 1910, p. 7; 'German Spy Mania', *Daily Mail*, 16 September 1910, p. 5.

118 'Spy Trial in Germany', *Daily Mail*, 9 December 1911, p. 5; 'German Spy Sentences', *Daily Mail*, 15 December 1911, p. 8.

119 Quoted in 'A Host of Spies', *Daily Mail*, 11 December 1911, p. 10.

120 'The Law and Spies', *Daily Mail*, 10 September 1910, p. 5.

121 The *Daily Mail* was notoriously Germanophobic: Gregory, *Last Great War*, p. 47.

122 Nicoletta Gullace has made a similar argument elsewhere: *The Blood of Our Sons: Men, Women and the Renegotiation of British Citizenship during the Great War* (Basingstoke, 2002), p. 10. Such narratives also served to reassure society that preparations for war, as well as the war itself, could be governed by a system of rules and codes making it less chaotic and more familiar: Thomas Hitchner, 'Edwardian Spy Literature and the Ethos of Sportsmanship: The Sport of Spying', *English Literature in Transition* 53/4 (2010), p. 427.

Chapter 2

1 TNA WO 32/13745: Legal Authority for Military and Police Guarding Railways to Challenge and Fire on People, Report of Inquest: Testimonies of Private Wagner, Bugler Hardy, and Private Calfe.

2 Hiley, 'Re-Entering the Lists', pp. 415–52.

3 'German Spies in London', *Aberdeen Evening Express*, 7 August 1914, p. 2; 'Sensational Raid. Rifles and Ammunition Seized in London', *Manchester Evening News*, 7 August 1914, p. 2.

4 'Arrested as a Spy', *Western Mail*, 3 August 1914, p. 3; 'The Onslaught at Liege', *Hull Daily Mail*, 6 August 1914, p. 1; 'The Spy Cry', *Daily Record*, 8 August 1914, p. 1; 'Arrest of Spies in France', *Manchester Evening News*, 10 August 1914, p. 2.

5 'Wholesale Espionage. 100 Germans Shot', *Portsmouth Evening News*, 11 August 1914, p. 6; 'Network of Spies in Belgium. Hundreds Arrested: Rifles, Bombs, and Wireless Found', *Birmingham Mail*, 11 August 1914, p. 3; '2,000 Spies Arrested in Belgium', *Hull Daily Mail*, 12 August 1914, p. 5; '100 Spies Shot in Belgium', *Aberdeen Journal*, 12 August 1914, p. 6.

6 'Catching Spies in Belgium. Remarkable Incidents', *Western Daily Press*, 15 August 1914, p. 8.

7 'War Notes', *Derby Daily Telegraph*, 12 August 1914, p. 2; '"I Spy." How They Played It on Wee Wullie', *Motherwell Times*, 21 August 1914, p. 5.

8 'Emissaries of Destruction', *Birmingham Mail*, 8 August 1914, p. 3.

9 Radical politicians attempting to stimulate anti-alien sentiment equally relied upon presumed events transpiring elsewhere: Joynson-Hicks, *Hansard*, 12 November 1914.

10 'Points for Patriots', *John Bull*, vol. XVII, no. 429, 22 August 1914, p. 10.

11 'Precautions', *Buckingham Advertiser and Free Press*, 15 August 1914, p. 8; 'Martial Law. Protection against Spies', *Portsmouth Evening News*, 14 August 1914, p. 5; 'Important Notice and Warning', *Nairnshire Telegraph and General Advertiser*, 25 August 1914, p. 3.

12 'Our London Letter. The Spy Danger', *Derby Daily Telegraph*, 12 August 1914, p. 4.

13 Aberdeenshire and Aberdeen City Archives, POL/E/2/1: Elginshire Constabulary, General Order Book, Order no. 52, 22 August 1914. This was not a unique occurrence; see Bodleian Library Special Collections, MS. Eng. Hist. e. 89, Papers of Andrew Clark, Diary entry 14 September 1914, p. 53.

14 Norfolk Record Office C/PO 1/11: Books of Memorandum Issued by Chief Constable, 10–31 August 1914, pp. 71, 85. A similar order was apparently given in Lincolnshire: Lincolnshire Archives, 9-FANE/1/1/4/5: Papers of Helen Beatrice Fane, Diary entry 22 August 1914.

15 TNA KV 1/10: Kell's diary, 9 December 1910, p. 48.

16 East Sussex Record Office, SPA 5/6/8: Records of the Sussex Police Authority, Hastings Constabulary, Extracts from the Watch Committee Minutes, dated 8 August 1914, p. 29.

17 West Sussex Record Office, GOODWOOD MSS 1274: Letters and instructions to the West Sussex Volunteer Civil Guard and Special Constables 1914–18, 'West Sussex Civil Guard', dated 17 August 1914.

18 West Sussex Record Office, GOODWOOD MSS 1274: Letter from Chief Constable to the Duke of Richmond, dated 25 August 1914.

19 Surrey History Centre, CC98/7/2: Review of Surrey in WWI by the Chief Constable.

20 Pennell, *A Kingdom United*, pp. 55–6.

21 Pierre Purseigle, 'Beyond and Below', in Macleod and Purseigle (eds), *Uncovered Fields*, p. 98; and 'Introduction', in Puseigle (ed.), *Warfare and Belligerence*, pp. 25–6.

22 IWM docs. 10943: Papers of Major General Sir Vernon Kell, reel no. 1, 'The Control of Civil Populations in War' (1930), p. 17.

23 TNA KV 1/2: Espionage in Time of Peace, DMO to CGS, 31 December 1908, p. 10.

24 Aberdeenshire and Aberdeen City Archives, POL/B/4/5: Banffshire Constabulary, Ballindalloch, General Order Book, 3 November 1914.

25 Leicestershire Record Office, DE 3831-37: Leicestershire Constabulary Records, General Order Book, 7–10 August 1914.

26 Leicestershire Record Office, DE 5491-104-1: Leicestershire Constabulary Records, Superintendents Meetings Minutes, 6 August 1914, p. 1.

27 Derbyshire Record Office, D3376/Box 6/1: General Order Book, no. 284/313, 5 August 1914.

28 Derbyshire Record Office, D3376/Box 1/3: County Copy Correspondence Book, 1914–20.

29 Gwent Archives, D709/47: Newport Constabulary Records, Police Order Book, 21 August 1914.

30 Gwent Archives, D2113/23: Griffithstown Police Records, General Order Book, 15 August 1914.

31 Gwent Archives, D2113/19: Griffithstown Police Records, Information Book, May 1914–December 1916. This is supported by instructions given to constables and the activities recorded in Sergeant's journals: Gwent Archives, D2113/130: Griffithstown Police Records: Constable's Information Book, June 1914–July 1915; and D2113/136: Constable's Information Book, July 1914–September 1921; and D2113/57: Sergeant's Journals: Charles Nurdern, January 1914–March 1915.

32 For example, see 'The Spy Scare', *Bedfordshire Times and Independent*, 28 August 1914, p. 5.

33 'Taken for a Spy', *Leicestershire Chronicle*, 29 August 1914, p. 7.

34 'A Survey at Home', *Bedfordshire Times and Independent*, 21 August 1914, p. 8; 'Spies and Spies', *Bucks Herald*, 15 August 1914, p. 6.

35 'Lying Tales', *Northampton Mercury*, 21 August 1914, p. 4.

36 This is explored further in Chapter 6.

37 French, 'Spy Fever in Britain', p. 365; Panayi, *Enemy in Our Midst*, pp. 154–5; Pennell, *A Kingdom United*, p. 106.

38 McKenna, *Hansard*, 9 September 1914.

39 TNA HO 45/10729/255193: Internment and Treatment of Enemy Subjects, letter written to Edward Henry dated 25 August 1914 and the subsequent report written by Edward Troup, 27 August 1914.

40 Ibid.: Arrest of German and Austrian Reservists in the Provinces, 2 September 1914.

41 Frederick Apel, Johann Engel, Gustave Ernest, August Kludner, Adolf Schneider, Lina Heine, Celso Rodriquez, Otto Kruger, Friedrich Diedrichs, and Frederick Fowler featured on Kell's SWL list and were be rounded up following the declaration of war. Heinrich Grosse had been imprisoned after an investigation by MO5(g) in 1912 and would be recommitted for the same offence in 1914. The husband of Lina Heine, Max Power Heinert, was not on Kell's arrest list, but as arresting officers arrived on the scene, they thought it best to take no chances and arrested him along with her. Kell had also monitored Marie Kronauer and Frederick James Ireland since they were the husband and nephew, respectively, of known German agents. Other suspects

in this selection would end up being retrospectively added to Kell's register, despite never featuring in MO5(g)'s potential suspects list, simply to embolden the great spy round up of August 1914 myth and add to Kell's reputation. Hiley, 'Entering the Lists', pp. 46–76.

42 Although these arrests did not necessarily represent popular fears, they did arguably go on to shape the public's perception of espionage given that these suspects featured in almost a fifth of all articles referring to spy scares during this period.

43 Liddle GS 1027: Jock Dunning Macleod, Diary entry 10 August 1914; Tammy Proctor, *Civilians in a World at War, 1914–1918* (London, 2010), pp. 14–15.

44 Peter Dennis, *The Territorial Army 1906–1940* (Royal Historical Society: Studies in History 51, Woodbridge, 1987), pp. 16–29; Ian Beckett, 'The Territorial Force', in Ian Beckett and Keith Simpson (eds), *A Nation in Arms: The British Army in the First World War* (Barnsley, 2004), p. 130.

45 Timothy Bowman and Mark Connelly, *The Edwardian Army: Recruiting, Training, and Deploying the British Army 1902–1914* (Oxford, 2012), p. 146.

46 Henry Wilson Papers, 2/75/2: Callwell to Wilson, 1 September 1914.

47 K. W. Mitchinson, *Defending Albion: Britain's Home Army, 1908–1919* (Basingstoke, 2005), p. 54. This order made its way to the Territorial units, which most likely increased their alertness and anxiety: Surrey History Centre, QWRS/30/SLADEN/2/1: Papers of St Barbe Russell Sladen, Diary entry 5 August 1914.

48 Mitchinson, *Defending Albion*, pp. 59–60.

49 Spy scares were not just the product of nervous apprehension. Territorials also planned to go out on patrol with the deliberate intention of finding and catching a 'spy': Liddle DF 087: Roderick Macleod, Diary entry 12 August 1914.

50 Mitchinson, *Defending Albion*, p. 60.

51 Ibid., p. 60.

52 'Mistaken for a Spy', *Dover Express*, 14 August 1914, p. 5.

53 'Coroner as a Spy', *Western Mail*, 25 August 1914, p. 6.

54 Surrey History Centre, QRWS/30/MERR/1/p24/1: 'Reminiscences of LW Smith', pp. 34, 50.

55 Gloucestershire Archives, D3549/33/1/19: Papers of Arthur Barwick Lloyd-Baker, Diary entry 11 August 1914.

56 Brian W Harvey and Carol Fitzgerald (eds), *Edward Heron-Allen's Journal of the Great War: From Sussex Shore to Flanders Fields* (Chichester, 2002) p. 12.

57 'Midnight 'Spy' Incident. Excitement Caused at Dunfermline', *Edinburgh Evening News*, 11 August 1914, p. 2.

58 'Cyclist Wounded by Sentry', *Liverpool Echo*, 11 August 1914, p. 4.

59 'A Newcastle Chase', *Portsmouth Evening News*, 8 August 1914, p. 7.

60 'Capture of Supposed Spy on the Humber. Defending Soldier Wounded', *Hull Daily Mail*, 3 August 1914, p. 6.

61 'Soldier Shot by Supposed Spy', *Hull Daily Mail*, 17 August 1914, p. 1.

62 Caithness Archives, C/NC/1/13: Caithness Constabulary Records, Occurrence Book, 15 August 1914.

63 On 5 August, a twenty-year-old Morrice enlisted at Sefton Park barracks and was serving as a gunner with 1st Lancashire Brigade RGA on Bidston Hill garrison duty. Stephen McGreal, *Liverpool in the Great War* (Barnsley, 2014), p. 32.

64 'War Items', *Exeter and Plymouth Gazette*, 12 August 1914, p 3; 'Sentry Shot Dead. Sensational Affair Near Birkenhead', *Manchester Evening News*, 11 August 1914, p. 2.

65 'Sentry Death at Chatham', *Birmingham Daily Post*, 21 August 1914, p. 7. Smith had enlisted at Mill Hill in Middlesex in July 1913 and was serving in 6th Battalion, Duke of Cambridge's Own (Middlesex) Regiment. Stephen Wynn, *Chatham in the Great War* (Barnsley, 2017), p. 14.

66 'War and Sport in the North of England', *Edinburgh Evening News*, 19 September 1914, p. 9. For a similar observation, see 'Bon-Accord Gossip', *Aberdeen Evening Express*, 12 September 1914, p. 2.

67 Defence planners had long realized that public opinion impacted strategy, and how destabilizing popular panic could be, so strategists were focused on impeding popular agitation and anxiety, not exacerbating them: David Morgan-Owen, 'Strategy, Rationality, and the Idea of Public Opinion in Britain, 1870–1914', *Historical Research* 94/264 (2021), pp. 397–418.

68 TNA CAB 3/2/62: Attack on the British Isles from Oversea, 15 April 1914; TNA CAB 3/2/72: Attack of the British Isles from Oversea, 9 May 1914; TNA CAB 3/2/73: Attack of the British Isles from Oversea, 14 September 1914.

69 TNA CAB 3/2/62: Attack on the British Isles from Oversea, 15 April 1914, pp. 5–7.

70 Major C. B. Brackenbury, 'The Intelligence Duties of the Staff Abroad and at Home', *RUSI Journal* 19 (1876), p. 244.

71 Ibid., p. 250.

72 TNA PRO 30/40/2: Papers of Sir Charles Ardagh, Letter from Brackenbury, 7 April 1896; Andrew, *Secret Service*, pp. 44–8. Henry Brackenbury served in intelligence posts in Sedan and Ireland, where he was affectionately known as Britain's 'spy master general'. He was later appointed as director of the Intelligence Branch (IB) in 1886, and then in 1887, he became the first Director of Military Intelligence (DMI).

73 As Director of Military Operations (DMO) both Ewart (DMO, 1906–10) and Wilson (DMO, 1910–14) had influential positions relating to the War Office's planning and defence schemes. Both men shared Brackenbury's opinion that Germany's secret service was a threat to British security and should be resolutely defeated. Henry Wilson Papers, 3/3/7: Lecture: 'Intelligence in Peace and War', 13 November 1907; TNA KV 1/2: Espionage in Time of Peace: War Office Memorandum, letter from Ewart dated 2 December 1908, p. 7; TNA KV 4/313: Military Administration of Occupied Territory in Time of War, 22 April 1922.

74 This was not exceptional; in a lecture delivered at the Staff College in Quetta, a former intelligence officer in the Indian army, Captain Claud H. G. Black, similarly drew upon recent experiences of the Franco-Prussian War. TNA WO 106/6148: 'Secret Service', undated Lecture by Captain C. H. G. Black, p. 8. When Edmonds provided the CID with evidence of Germany's covert intrigues in Britain, he began by pointing to the tradition of espionage within the German army that had supposedly led to France's downfall in 1870. TNA CAB 16/8: The Question of Foreign Espionage, 30 March 1909, p. 3.

75 LHMA, Papers of James Edmonds, 4/1/1-40: Intelligence in European Warfare, January 1908, pp. 3–5.

76 'Intelligence in European Warfare', p. 8.

77 IWM docs. 22580: Papers of George Eric Row Gedye, GER3/71, 'Value of Intelligence. No. 2'.

78 TNA KV 1/2: Letter from Ewart to C. G. S. dated 2 December 1908, p. 7.

79 TNA WO 33/694: Home Defence. Central Force Scheme, p. 9.

80 TNA WO 17/90: Notes on the Work and Methods of Foreign Secret Service Agents, October 1912, pp. 179–81. This familiar trope seems to have resonated with soldiers: St Barbe Russell Sladen Papers, Diary entry 6 August 1914.

81 TNA WO 33/688: A War Book for the War Office, August 1914, p. 16.

82 LHMA, Papers of James Edmonds, V/5/13: 4th Division Standing Orders, 1 May 1914; TNA WO 33/651: Principal Questions Connected with Home Defence, p. 18. When a sentry defending the Humber from ill-disposed persons shot a civilian for failing to halt after three challenges, the commanding officer displayed no alarm or remorse. His indifference towards the action of the sentry suggested that it was routine and expected and not abnormal in anyway. TNA WO 95/5453: Commander Royal Artillery (Humber Defences) War Diary, 16 August 1914.

83 TNA WO 33/694: Home Defence. Central Force Scheme, pp. 8–9, 12–13.

84 TNA CAB 38/15/13: Home Ports Defence Committee, 'It's Constitution, Functions, and Procedure', 1 July 1909. This included assigning responsibility for the security of such locations and outlining the measures to be adopted in peacetime, before the outbreak of war and during future conflict: TNA CAB 17/28: Safeguarding of Vulnerable Points, 1909–1911. 'Home Ports Defence Committee. Note by the Secretary'. Vulnerable points included 'magazines, dockyards, large oil-stores, cable landing stations, wireless stations, private shipbuilding yards, railway bridges, tunnels, and other vulnerable points', p. 2.

85 TNA CAB 17/28: 'Home Ports Defence Committee, Notes for 2nd Meeting. Protection of Vulnerable Points', p. 55.

86 TNA CAB 17/107: Memorandum on the Principles Concerning the Defence of the United Kingdom, November 1910, p. 19; TNA CAB 17/29: Arming of the Police, 1910.

87 TNA CAB 17/28: 'The Protection of Magazines', p. 122.

88 TNA KV 1/35: F Branch Report on the Prevention of Espionage (1921), p. 39.

89 TNA KV 1/10: Kell's diary, 15–17 June 1910, p. 6. This is consistent with the apathy of the Aberdeenshire constabulary noted earlier.

90 Ibid. Kell's diary, 20 March and 20 April 1911, pp. 61–6.

91 TNA WO 32/9098: Duties of the Police in the Event of War, September 1911, pp. 2–3.

92 TNA KV 1/39: G Branch Report on the Investigation of Espionage (1921), pp. 30–2.

93 TNA CAB 17/90: Notes on the Work of Counter-Espionage, October 1913, pp. 182–4.

94 TNA WO 33/688: A War Book for the War Office, pp. 16–9.

95 TNA HO 144/10128: The Duties of the Police in the Event of War (1914), 'Strengthening the Police Force', p. 1.

96 TNA CAB 38/15/16: Report of a Sub-Committee Appointed to Consider the Question of Foreign Espionage in the UK (1909), p. 6; Basil Thomson, *Queer People* (London, 2015), p. 35.

97 TNA HO 144/10128: Section 5, 'Protection of Vulnerable Points', pp. 2–3.

98 TNA KV 1/35: F Branch Report on the Prevention of Espionage, pp. 21–2; TNA KV 1/37: Prevention of Espionage (1914–21), Appendix B, p. 8.

99 TNA HO 158/16: Home Office Circulars dated 30 July and 3 August 1914.

100 The Marquess of Londonderry condemned the negligence displayed by the Home Secretary in which 'he placed the responsibility on every single department except his own'. In response to McKenna delegating the entire responsibility of counter-espionage to chief constables, Londonderry highlighted the ambiguity and vagueness of the Home Office's policing strategy. *Hansard*, 18 November 1914.

101 Moreover, protecting vulnerable points from sabotage was one of several additional duties assigned to the police in August 1914: Clive Emsley, *The English Police: A Social and Cultural History* (Harlow, 1996), p. 124.

102 The Home Secretary's primary influence over provincial policing was in the appointment of chief constables. Constabularies had a large degree of autonomy and could resist requests that were considered inappropriate for police. Clive Emsley, *The Great British Bobby: A History of British Policing from the 18th Century to the Present* (London, 2010), p. 87; Mary Fraser, *Policing the Home Front 1914–1918: The Control of the British Population at War* (Abingdon, 2020), p. 26.

103 TNA WO 32/9098: Duties of the Police in the Event of War, Letter dated 22 February 1913.

104 Emsley, *The English Police*, p. 125.

105 In MI5's post-war 'official history' written in 1921, it was declared that in peacetime, there was no apparatus for separating friendly and innocent aliens from potential suspects, and so every alien needed monitoring. TNA KV 1/35: F Branch Report on the Prevention of Espionage (1921), p. 47.

106 Ibid. Section 2, Lt. McAnally to Treasury Solicitor, Letter dated 21 August 1914.

107 Ibid. Section 3, 'Inquest on Civilian Named Carroll at Aldershot'.

108 Ibid. Report of Inquest: 'Notice'.

109 Ibid. Section 5, Letter dated 25 August 1914.

110 Diary of St Barbe Russell Sladen, 6 August 1914.

111 TNA WO 32/13745: Section 3, 'Inquest on Civilian Named Carroll at Aldershot'.

112 Ibid. Section 7, Letter dated 29 August 1914.

113 Library and Archives Canada, RG9 III A1, vol. 29, file 8-1-29: Captain McInnes to Colonel F. A. Reid, Letter dated 12 April 1916.

114 Library and Archives Canada, MG30-E61, MITCHELL, Charles Hamilton, vol. 16: II Corps to North Midland Division, 3 April 1915.

Part II

1 Loughran, *Shell-Shock and Medical Culture*, pp. 52–5.

2 Mark S. Micale, *Approaching Hysteria: Disease and Its Interpretations* (Princeton, 1995), p. 25; Elaine Showalter, *Hystories: Hysterical Epidemics and Modern Culture* (New York, 1998), pp. 14–16; Scull, *Hysteria*, pp. 31–4, 42.

3 Loughran, *Shell-Shock and Medical Culture*, pp. 68–9.

4 M. Paciaronei and J. Bogousslavsky, 'The Borderland with Neurasthenia', in J. Bogousslavsky (ed.), *Hysteria: The Rise of an Enigma* (New York, 2014), p. 149; Loughran, *Shell-Shock and Medical* Culture, pp. 55–9.

5 Scull, *Hysteria*, p. 42.

6 Loughran, *Shell-Shock and Medical Culture*, p. 71.

7 Harry Richards, 'The Nationalisation of War, the Rise of Psychology, and the Creation of "Spy Fever" in the British Press', *War and Society*, published online 20 February 2025. In October 1914, Edward Heron-Allen even referred to a sudden outbreak of knitting as a 'disease': *Heron-Allen's Journal*, p. 22.

8 French, 'Spy Fever in Britain', p. 365; Pennell, *A Kingdom United*, p. 102. For other examples, see Hampshire, 'Spy Fever in Britain', p. 24.

9 Richards, 'The Creation of "Spy Fever" in the British Press'.

10 West Yorkshire Archives Service Wakefield, Menston Asylum Records, C488/7/2/80: Female Case Book vol 41 (1915), Patient 10672, p. 177.

11 Menston Asylum Records, C488/7/2/82: Female Case Book vol. 41 (1916), Patient 11378, p. 528.

12 Menston Asylum Records, C488/7/Box 5: Loose Leaf Case Notes, Patient 12658.

13 Menston Asylum Records, C488/7/Box 4: Loose Leaf Case Notes, Patient 11987.

14 Menston Asylum Records, C488/7/2/81: Female Case Book vol. 42 (1915–16), Patient 10967, p. 281.

15 Alexander Morison, *Outlines of Mental Diseases* (Edinburgh, 1826). Quoted in Kenneth S. Kendler, 'The Origin of Our Modern Concept of Mania in Texts from 1780 to 1900', *Molecular Psychiatry* 25 (2020), p. 1978.

16 Kendler, 'Origin of Our Modern Concept of Mania', pp. 1975–80; Claire Hilton, *Civilian Lunatic Asylums during the First World War: A Study of Austerity on London's Fringe* (Cham, 2021), p. 75.

17 Likewise, 'fever' has been used to refer to numerous diseases of unknown origin and so was also easily applied to popular spy phobias: Gian Franco Gensini and Andrea A. Conti, 'The Evolution of the Concept of "Fever" in the History of Medicine', *Journal of Infection* 49/2 (2004), pp. 85–7.

18 Stearns and Stearns, 'Emotionology', p. 830.

19 The applicability of 'mania' and 'fever' to describe cases of mass hysteria, a twentieth-century concept relating to the collective psyche, will form the basis of Part III.

Chapter 3

1 These fears and anxieties, however, were never referred to as a spy fever until after the Franco-Prussian War had given rise to the term: Richards, 'Creation of Spy Fever in the British Press' (Forthcoming).

2 Marianne Elliot, 'French Subversion in Britain in the French Revolution', in Colin Jones (ed.), *Britain and Revolutionary France: Conflict, Subversion and Propaganda* (Exeter, 1983), p. 40; Clive Emsley, 'The Impact of the French Revolution on British Politics and Society', in Ceri Crossley and Ian Small (eds), *The French Revolution and British Culture* (Oxford, 1989), p. 42.

3 David Eastwood, 'Patriotism and the English State in the 1790s', in Mark Philp (ed.), *The French Revolution and British Popular Politics* (Cambridge, 1991), p. 150.

4 Clive Emsley, 'Revolution, War and the Nation State: The British and the French Experiences, 1789–1801', in Philp (ed.), *The French Revolution*, pp. 100–3; Eastwood, 'Patriotism and the English State', p. 159.

5 Jenny Uglow, *In These Times: Living in Britain through Napoleon's Wars, 1793–1815* (London, 2014), p. 366.

6 Although this story has most likely been the subject of much embellishment, this in of itself reflects the climate of paranoia that existed: Paul Chrystal and Simon Crossley, *Hartlepool through Time* (Stroud, 2011), p. 25.

7 F. H. Hinsley and C. A. G. Simkins, *British Intelligence in the Second World War, Vol. Four: Security and Counter-Intelligence* (London, 1990), pp. 47–62; Richard Thurlow, 'The Evolution of the Mythical British Fifth Column, 1939–46', *Twentieth Century British History* 10/4 (1999), pp. 477–98; Brian Simpson, *In the Highest Degree Odious: Detention in Wartime Britain* (Oxford, 1992), pp. 147–71; Glyn Prysor, 'The

"Fifth Column", and the British Experience of Retreat, 1940', *War in History* 12/4 (2005), pp. 418–47.

8 IWM docs.12152: Ernest Read Cooper Papers, 'Nineteen Hundred and War Time', p. 2.

9 Helen Beatrice Fane Papers, Diary entry 8–9 August 1914.

10 Liddle DF 129: Beatrice Morwenna Trefusis, Diary entry 26 October 1914.

11 Liddle DF 114: Florence Schuster, Diary entry 12 September 1914.

12 Rosenwein, *Generations of Feeling*, pp. 5–6.

13 George Aston, *Secret Service* (London, 1930), p. 82.

14 Photography, motor vehicles and flashing lights had clearly been identified as a cause for concern: Le Queux, *German Spies in England*, pp. 129–30; Blumenfeld, *RBD's Diary*, p. 223.

15 'Spy Peril', *Shepton Mallet Journal*, 25 September 1914, p. 5; 'German with a Cut-down Name', *Portsmouth Evening News*, 8 May 1915, p. 3; 'A Friendly German', *Thanet Advertiser*, 19 June 1915, p. 7; 'No Register but Anxious to Catch Spies', *Warwick and Warwickshire Advertiser*, 16 October 1915, p. 3. WLB Tower Papers, Diary entry 20 August 1914; Diary of Andrew Clark, vol. III, 26 October 1914, p. 143.

16 Bodleian Library Special Collections, MS. Eng. Hist. e. 91, Diary of Andrew Clark, vol. IV, 15 November 1914, p. 214; TNA AIR 1/550/16/15/27: MT1(b) Intelligence Summary, 10 March 1915, Appendix D: Letter from Chief Constable, Lewes, 18 March 1915.

17 Unfortunately for Bfaff, he was later interned as a law-abiding citizen anyway. Lincolnshire Archives, REGI/5/798: Records of the Lincolnshire Regiment, 19 December 1914.

18 TNA AIR 1/550/16/15/27: MT1(b) Intelligence Summary, 25 March 1915, paragraph 57. Especially dachshunds, given their symbolic representation of Germany: Liddle DF 043: Barbara Duguid, 'The Unforgivable Years 1914–1918' (1984), p. 10.

19 TNA AIR 1/550/16/15/27: MT1(b) Intelligence Summary, 24 November 1914, Appendix A: Illicit signalling report. Previous rumours had claimed that Germans spies were dressing as nuns in Belgium to hide their wireless equipment: 'Spies Dressed as Nuns', *Manchester Evening News*, 13 August 1914, p. 4; 'Spies in Guise of Nuns', *Liverpool Echo*, 15 August 1914, p. 3; 'Germans Disguised as Nuns and Priest', *Leeds Mercury*, 15 August 1914, p. 5.

20 TNA ADM 131/120: Plymouth Station Correspondence, 'Suspected Enemy Agents', pp. 4–8.

21 IWM docs. 7142: Papers of Gabrielle Mary West, Diary entry 30 December 1914.

22 Highland Archive Centre, D758/1: Lars J. Skarpnes, Memoir of Scandinavians at Loch Morlich during the First World War (1973), p. 3.

23 Kell, of course, took the matter very seriously, but the investigation was eventually dropped after Unmack proved he was born in Australia and was therefore of British nationality. Surrey History Centre, CC98/14/8: Records of the Surrey Constabulary, Enquiry regarding alleged German origin of pro-German rector Edward Unmack.

24 Tim Lynch, *Yorkshire's War: Voices of the First World War* (Stroud, 2014), p. 35. See also, 'The Man Who Loitered', *Portsmouth Evening News*, 14 August 1914, p. 7; 'Amusing Spy Hunting Incident', *Edinburgh Evening News*, 18 August 1914, p. 3; 'Coroner as a "Spy"', *Western Mail*, 25 August 1914, p. 6; 'Dutchman to be Deported', *Chelmsford Chronicle*, 7 May 1915, p. 3.

25 Bodleian Library Special Collections, MS. Eng. Hist. e. 90, Diary of Andrew Clark vol. III, 24 and 26 October 1914, pp. 125, 143.

26 The warnings and threat assessments given to soldiers in the BEF will be discussed in the following chapter.

27 Leicestershire Record Office 2913/3/5/3: Papers of Donald L. Weir, Letter to his mother, 19 November 1914.

28 The use of homing pigeons was equally as ominous to some. NMM WHI/185: Arnold White Papers, an exposition of foreign espionage in Britain entitled 'German Spies'. Dated 26 August 1914. See also 'The Risks We Run', *Globe*, 2 October 1914, p. 6; 'Spy Peril', *Birmingham Mail*, 9 October 1914, p. 5; 'Pigeon with German Message', *Manchester Evening News*, 26 October 1914, p. 2; 'Homing Pigeons in War', *The Scotsman*, 27 October 1914, p. 9.

29 TNA ADM 131/119: Plymouth Station Correspondence, Spies and Anti-Espionage Measures, 1914–18, pp. 180–416. The local military authorities became so convinced that German spies were signalling to vessels offshore that they refused to believe the truth when cases of signalling were proven to be false. Instead, they assumed that it was the lack of local organization that prevented cases from being properly investigated. TNA AIR 1/550/16/15/27: MT1(b) Intelligence Summary, 1 November 1914, paragraph 8. They later concluded that 'no such system as was foreshadowed by MO5 exists', but they nevertheless continue investigating cases of alleged signalling. TNA AIR 1/550/16/15/27: MT1(b) Intelligence Summaries, 11 December 1914, paragraph 3, and 20 January, paragraph 3.

30 Parliamentary Archives, LG/D/20/2/55: Papers of David Lloyd George, Letter dated 1 November 1915.

31 Fife Archives, A/ABG/1/11: Monteith Family Papers, Rev. W. N. Monteith to his wife, Letter dated 4 December 1914, pp. 6–10. See also IWM docs. 12089: Papers of Charles Cuthbert Aston, Letter dated 9 July 1915.

32 IWM sound. 9417: John Raymond Mallalieu (1986) reel 1.

33 TNA ADM 131/120: Plymouth Station Correspondence, 'Suspected Enemy Agents – Aliens Regulations Censorship', pp. 115–32.

34 TNA KV 1/37: Prevention of Espionage 1914–21, Appendix B, p. 8. Newspapers also frequently equated sketching with spying: 'Suspected Spy Arrested', *Dumfries and Galloway Standard*, 8 August 1914, p. 5; 'Sketching the Fort', *Western Mail*, 8 August 1914, p. 3; 'Spy's Unfinished Love Letter', *Liverpool Echo*, 15 August 1914, p. 2; 'A Military Sketch', *Portsmouth Evening News*, 17 October 1914, p. 5; 'Spy Scare at Kirkcaldy', *Edinburgh Evening News*', 19 October 1914, p. 3; 'Amusing Incident at Newlyn', *Cornishman*, 14 January 1915, p. 4. Photography became equally indicative of spying; see 'Funny Us', *John Bull*, vol. XVII, no. 435, 3 October 1914, p. 2; NMM WHI/185: Arnold White Papers, Letter dated 5 October 1914; IWM docs. 6996: Papers of M. Coules, Journal, June 1914–November 1915, p. 22.

35 Aberdeenshire and Aberdeen City Archives, B82: Records of Banffshire Constabulary, Daily Occurrence Book of the Junior Constable, 1914–17, 7 August 1914.

36 Gloucestershire Archives, D2659/27/21: Papers of Mary Blathwayt, Diary entry 8 October 1914.

37 Essex Record Office, D/DU 418/15: Papers of George H. Rose, Diary entry 6 August 1914.

38 Caithness Archives, C/NC/1/13: Caithness Constabulary Records, Occurrence Book, 5 August 1914.

39   TNA AIR 1/550/16/15/27: MT1(b) Intelligence Summary, 10 March 1915, paragraph 27.

40   TNA HO 45/10727/254753: Activities of Enemy Agents, Aliens in Motor Cars, Circular to Police, 5 August 1914; 'Mistaken for Spies', *Birmingham Mail*, 7 October 1914, p. 3; Liddle DF ZEP 45: A. E. Bumpuss, Letter dated 19 October 1915.

41   Sean O'Connell, *The Car and British Society: Class, Gender and Motoring, 1896–1939* (Manchester, 1998), pp. 150–70.

42   Helen Long, *The Edwardian House: The Middle-Class Home in Britain 1880–1914* (Manchester, 1993), p. 5.

43   Bodleian Library Special Collections, MS. Eng. Hist. e. 92, Diary of Andrew Clark vol. V, 21 November 1914, p. 81; Bonar Law Papers, BL/36/4/63: Letter dated 23 February 1915; Norfolk Record Office, MC 1631/4, 847X7: Papers of Walter Rye, Letter to his sister, 19 April 1915.

44   IWM docs. 15227: Papers of Arthur Reginald Read, 'The Great War – 1914'.

45   Liddle DF GA ZEP 21: William Foster, Letter dated 19 April 1915.

46   East Ridings Record Office, Papers of Margaret Elizabeth Strickland-Constable, Diary entry 11 June 1915. Spies in vehicles directing Zeppelins to their target became a widespread rumour. One man wrote to Arnold White, an extremely right-wing xenophobe, claiming to have seen a man and a woman travelling at great speed on a motorcycle many times. The suspects allegedly carried a flashing light that faced upwards, which was supposedly conclusive proof of their illicit activity: NMM WHI/186: Arnold White Papers, Letter dated 7 June 1915.

47   Tami Davis Biddle, *Rhetoric and Reality in Air Warfare: The Evolution of British and American Ideas about Strategic Bombing, 1914–1945* (Oxford, 2002), pp. 13–15.

48   Margaret Elizabeth Strickland-Constable Papers, Diary entry 10 June 1915.

49   It was not uncommon for an entire family to come under suspicion: Liddle GS 0569: Lord Forester, Diary entry 28 August 1914; *Punch*, 26 August 1914, p. 179.

50   TNA AIR 1/550/16/15/27: MT1(b) Intelligence Summary, 11 December 1914, Appendix B: suspicious motor car.

51   Mary Anderson, *A Few More Memories* (London, 1936), pp. 145–6.

52   Henry de Halsalle, *Who Goes There? Being an Account of the Secret Service Adventures of 'Ex-Intelligence' during the Great War of 1914–1918* (London, 1927), p. 189.

53   'Germans in Britain', *Daily Herald*, 10 August 1914, p. 1; 'Germans in England. Reassuring the Public', *Birmingham Mail*, 10 August 1914, p. 3.

54   'War Notes', *Derby Daily Telegraph*, 29 August 1914, p. 2.

55   IWM docs.10729: Anonymous Home Front Diary, 8 August 1914; Lincolnshire Archives, 9-FANE/1/1/4/6: Papers of Helen Beatrice Fane, Diary entry 9 October 1914.

56   TNA AIR 1/550/16/15/27: MT1(b) Intelligence Summary, 1 November 1914, paragraph 2.

57   Arnold White received numerous letters from readers thankful that the authorities were finally awake to the peril: NMM WHI/186: Arnold White Papers, Letters dated 11 and 21 October 1914. See also 'The German Spy', *Aberdeen Evening Express*, 10 October 1914, p. 2; 'The Spy Danger', *Dumfries and Galloway Standard*, 10 October 1914, p. 2; 'Two Traitors Within Our Gates', *John Bull*, vol. XVII, no. 437, 17 October 1914, p. 4.

58   *Daily Herald*, 24 October 1914, p. 1.

59   'Lord Chief Justice's View', *Edinburgh Evening News*, 20 May 1915, p. 5.

60 Although Thomson described it as a malady that 'defied treatment', he mentions one public official who relentlessly reported the sightings of suspicious people from across the country. All of them were German spies, but the authorities remained idle in the face of such a threat. In response, Thomson invented the character of 'von Burstorph', who was responsible for all of the alleged sightings. Claiming that the authorities were vigorously attempting to apprehend von Burstorph, this one official went 'away quite happy since he knew that the authorities were doing something', *Queer People*, p. 45.

61 Hiley, 'Counter-Espionage and Security', pp. 638–9; Hiley, 'Entering the Lists', p. 48.

62 Apart from Lincoln, all were apprehended by MO5: Thomas Boghardt, *Spies of the Kaiser: German Covert Operations in Great Britain during the First World War Era* (Basingstoke, 2004).

63 Although people occasionally recorded the details of important spy trials, there is little evidence that they experienced an intense emotional reaction to them: Lincolnshire Archives, 9-FANE/1/1/4/12: Papers of Helen Beatrice Fane, Diary entry 5 June 1915.

64 The first bombs dropped on Britain fell from a seaplane during a raid over Dover. Susan R. Grayzel, *At Home and under Fire: Air Raids and Culture in Britain from the Great War to the Blitz* (Cambridge, 2013), p. 24.

65 Captain Joseph Morris, *The German Air Raids on Great Britain 1914–1918* (London, 1969), pp. 30–53; Jerry White, *Zeppelin Nights: London in the First World War* (London, 2014), pp. 124–30.

66 Jeremy Black, *Air Power: A Global History* (London, 2016) p. 24.

67 The moral effect of dropping explosives from the air had been anticipated for over a century: Davis Biddle, *Rhetoric and Reality in Air Warfare*, p. 12; Grayzel, *At Home and under Fire*, pp. 7–14.

68 Liddle DF 043: Barbara Duguid, 'The Unforgivable Years 1914–18' (1984), p. 10; Liddle RNMN 025: G. H. Bickmore, Manuscript recollections (1984), p. 5.

69 Liddle RNMN REC 060: T. H. Kirk, Typescript Recollections (1980), p. 1.

70 IWM docs.276/3728: Letters Describing Zeppelin Raids; Liddle DF GA ZEP 31: M. Burton, 'A Coward Goes to War'; Liddle DF GA ZEP 37: Recollections of J. Southall.

71 Edward Glover, *The Psychology of Fear and Courage* (Harmondsworth, 1940), p. 26; Liddle DF GA ZEP 41: R. Herring, Letter dated 5 September 1979; Liddle DF 16: Dorothy Bowes, 'Looking Back to 1914–18' (1991), p. 3.

72 Liddle DF GA HAB 4: A. S. Hare, '1st World War' (undated).

73 Frank Meeres, *Norfolk's War* (Stroud, 2016), p. 53.

74 Liddle DF 018: Elizabeth Bracher, 'Memories of War I' (undated).

75 In contrast to her intimate fears of Zeppelins outlined below, Hilda Davison observed that people talked about 'the invasion' but claimed that few thought that it could ever happen: Liddle DF 40: Hilda W. Davison, 'Memories of the Great War' (1981), p. 10. Whereas Louisa Harris noted how the authorities warned about the grave peril of invasion, she seems to have felt most anxious for her friend living in London on account of the air raids targeting the capital: Liddle DF 062: Louisa Charlotte Harris, Diary entries 21 July and 26 September 1915.

76 Hilda W. Davison Papers, 'Memories of the Great War' (1981), p. 5.

77 Liddle DF 032: Elizabeth Cockayne, 'Recollections of the First World' (undated).

78 Liddle DF 020: Norah S. Bristow, Manuscript recollections (1981).

79 IWM docs. 16155: Memoir of J. W. Barrett, p. 5.

80 IWM docs. 15021: Diary of Mrs Purbrook, p. 10; Grayzel, *At Home and under Fire*, p. 32.

81 Liddle DF GA ZEP 33: M Moseley-Williams, 'Experiences at Cuffley'; Liddle DF GA ZEP 42: G. H. Elliot, Letter dated 19 May 1981.

82 Diary of Helen Beatrice Fane, 7 June 1915. Although the theory of the knock-out blow remained primitive prior to the First World, the possibility of airships being used to destroy key arsenals and dockyards, and thereby disrupt Britain's mobilisation, was widely expected: Brett Holman, *The Next War in the Air: Britain's Fear of the Bomber, 1908–1941* (Farnham, 2014) pp. 191–2.

83 Liddle DF 036: Dame Margery Irene Corbett-Ashby, Letters to her mother dated 2 April and 29 November 1916; West Yorkshire Archives Service Bradford, WYB335/4: Papers of Edith Usher, Diary entries 14 April and 15 June 1915; Surrey History Centre, 6782/25: Papers of Lucy Broadwood, Diary entry 10 May 1915; IWM docs.8594: Papers of George Howard Williams, Diary entries 7 and 9 September 1915.

84 While in London to see his son before he left for France, James Hissey asked a taxi driver to show him around the damage caused by Zeppelins: IWM docs. 14225: Hissey Family Letters, Letter from James John Hissey dated 17 September 1915. Second Lieutenant Eric Whitehead (RFC) similarly examined the damage caused by a Zeppelin and advised his mother to use the basement for protection: Liddle DF GA ZEP 26: Eric Whitehead, Letter dated 22 September 1915.

85 James John Hissey clearly believed espionage was a potential threat but was not hysterical because of it. His desire to witness the damage caused by air raids in an intimate way suggests a much greater fascination with Zeppelins, compared to spies, for instance, that was presumably driven by their destructive and overtly threatening capabilities. For James's spy phobias see Hissey Family Letters, Letters from James John Hissey dated 30 March and 17 July 1915.

86 Gloucestershire Archives, D2659/24/14: Papers of Emily Blathwayt, Diary entry 8 October 1914.

87 IWM docs. 5593/H: Papers of Ada McGuire, Letter dated 31 May 1915.

88 Grayzel, *At Home and under Fire*, pp. 20–4.

89 Dame Margery Irene Corbett-Ashby Papers, Letter from Capt. Ashby, dated 3 September 1916.

90 Liddle DF 004: Olive Armstrong, Diary entry 2 November 1915.

91 IWM docs.13471: Papers of John Lawton, Letters to his parents dated 19 March 1916 and another sent sometime in the spring of 1916.

92 Liddle DF GA ZEP 24: L. B. Stanley, Letter dated 10 September 1915.

93 Lucy Broadwood Papers, Diary entries 25 January and 18 May 1915.

94 Liddle DF 060: Nell Hague, Letter to her husband, 7 June 1915 (written at 1 am).

95 Nell Hague, Letter to her husband, 7 June 1915 (written later in the day).

96 This was particularly acute in East Anglia, given that it was directly under the flight path. Zeppelins would often unleash their bombardment there because they mistook it for their actual target, or they released the remaining explosives before making the return journey. See Liddle DF GA ZEP 20: 'Zeppelins over East Anglia'; Liddle DF GA ZEP 29: East Anglican Magistrate's Diary.

97 IWM docs. 12358: Papers of H. Miller, Diary of Jeanne Berman, 8 June 1915.

98 Liddle DF GA ZEP 40: Recollections of W. Pritchett (Undated). For a similar experience see Dame Margery Irene Corbett-Ashby Papers, Letter to her mother, 29 November 1916.

99 Ernest Read Cooper Papers, 'Nineteen Hundred and War Time', p. 4.

100 The inaccuracy of Zeppelin bombers was clearly not known or anticipated here. Dame Margery Irene Corbett-Ashby, Letter to her mother, 29 December 1915; Liddle DF GA ZEP 27: Harry Innes, Letter dated 24 June 1916.

101 Nell Hague Papers, Letter to her husband, 9 June 1915.

102 Emily Blaythwayt Papers, Diary entry 16 December 1914; Harvey and Fitzgerald, *Edward Heron-Allen's Journal of the Great War* p. 57; Grayzel, *At Home and under Fire*, pp. 46–62.

103 John Lawton Papers, Letter to his parents dated 4 February 1916.

104 IWM docs. 2589: Papers of Lydia Peile, Diary entries 1 and 19 March 1916.

105 Florence Schuster Papers, Diary entry 31 October 1914.

106 Hissey Family Letters, Letter from James John Hissey dated 1 December 1914.

107 IWM docs. 5744: Papers of F. T. Lockwood, Diary entry 14 April 1915.

108 Grayzel, *At Home and under Fire*, p. 70.

109 Liddle DF 164: Memoirs of Margaret Ulph Currie (1984). This was far from an isolated incident. Performers regularly continued through air raid warnings, much to the delight of cheering audiences. Liddle DF 082: M. B. Maclean, 'War Memories of a Women's Legion Motor Driver', p. 17.

110 IWM docs. 11174: Papers of J. H. Merivale, Letter from Maggie Turner to Hattie Turner dated 10 September 1915.

111 He noted how he was forced to board a train because his taxi driver refused to take him on account of being 'terrified of the Zeps'.

112 Liddle DF GA ZEP 28: Andrew Clark, collection of undated letters (b).

113 Liddle DF GA ZEP 30: Flora Jane Evans, Letter to her Mother, 28 November 1916.

114 Nell Hague Papers, letters to her husband dated 7 June 1915.

115 Liddle CO 066: Albert Murray, Letter from 'Winifred', 7 July 1917; Papers of William Foster, Letter dated 20 July 1917.

116 Liddle Collection, DF 081: Alison MacIntyre, Diary entry 20 January 1915.

117 Westminster Archives, 1257/1: Papers of Archibald Walker, Diary entry 6 September 1915.

118 'Zeppelins and Psychology', *The Times*, 10 September 1915. Quoted in Grayzel, *At Home and under Fire*, p. 39.

119 Grayzel, *At Home and under Fire*, pp. 39–41, 61–2.

120 Nell Hague Papers, Letter to her husband, 7 June 1915; Liddle DF/Zeppelins/42: Papers of G. H. Elliot, Letter dated 15 May 1981.

Chapter 4

1 The role spy stories played in helping people understand international events is explored in detail in the following chapter.

2 Nicholas Hiley, 'Decoding German Spies: British Spy Fiction 1908–18' *Intelligence and National Security* 5/4 (1990), pp. 56, 76.

3 It was only for this reason that people like Armgaard Karl Graves, briefly employed by German Naval Intelligence, and Ignatius Timothy Trebitsch-Lincoln, a Hungarian con artist, were able to profit from fabricated stories that exaggerated the risks and rewards of spying as well as the significance and heroism that could be obtained through clandestine intrigue and espionage. Armgaard Karl Graves, *The Secrets of*

the German War Office (New York, 1914), pp. 17–37; Ignatius Timothy Trebitsch-Lincoln, *Revelations of an International Spy* (New York, 1916).

4 Hitchner, 'The Sport of Spying', p. 415.

5 Although Le Queux's stories also frequently featured amateur heroics that defined the enemy's plots, the difference was in their scale of intrigue and subversion that separated Le Queux's novels from earlier stories such as *Kim* or *Riddle of the Sands*. *Kim* was also still political in that it reaffirmed racial stereotypes and prejudices that maintained the British Empire, but it did little to explicitly incite xenophobia or animosity in the same way that Le Queux would later come to epitomize.

6 Watson, *Fighting Different Wars*, p. 41.

7 Fifteen suspects did not have their personal details included.

8 In his popular work on the 'reality' of German espionage, Lionel James, a pseudonym used by William Le Queux, wrote that women were very rarely officially employed as spies. According to James/Le Queux, women could not be trusted with state secrets because they could easily become infatuated with men seeking to betray them: *The German Spy System from Within*, pp. 71, 106. See also Grant, *Spies and Secret Service*, pp. 23–4; Constance Kell, *A Secret Well Kept: The Untold Story of Sir Vernon Kell, Founder of MI5*, edited by Chris Northcott (London, 2017), p. 118; papers of Arnold White, WHI/186, Undated letter, p. 2. Although White recognized the potential danger of female spies, he argued that few in Britain took the threat of enemy women seriously.

9 However, as the war went continued, women were increasingly portrayed as a threat. Since female citizenship was defined by her husband's nationality, and because this ambiguity was exacerbated by 'sexual anger' directed at women occupying new roles, women were increasingly targets of the enemy within rhetoric: Tammy Proctor, *Female Intelligence: Women and Espionage in the First World War* (New York, 2003), pp. 29–51.

10 George Mosse, *The Image of Man: The Creation of Modern Masculinity* (Oxford, 1996), p. 52; Jessica Meyer, *Men of War: Masculinity and the First World War in Britain* (Basingstoke, 2011), pp. 5–10.

11 John Tosh, *Manliness and Masculinities in Nineteenth Century Britain* (Edinburgh, 2005), p. 192.

12 Meyer, *Men of War*, p. 6. This was juxtaposed with continental rivals who were regularly portrayed as inherently feminine: Robert McGregor, 'The Popular Press and the Creation of Military Masculinities in Georgian Britain', in Paul Higate (ed.), *Military Masculinities: Identity and the State* (London, 2003), pp. 143–4.

13 Graham Dawson, *Soldier Heroes: British Adventure, Empire and the Imagining of Masculinities* (London, 1994); Michael Paris, *Warrior Nation: Images of War in British Popular Culture, 1850–2000* (London, 2000). Wartime propaganda also strongly reiterated these themes and the idea of sacrifice depicted by the National War Aims Committee commonly portrayed male actions on images of the 'ultimate sacrifice' achieved through martial death: David Monger, *Patriotism and Propaganda in First World War Britain: The National War Aims Committee and Civilian Morale* (Liverpool, 2012), p. 107.

14 Robert Baden-Powell, *My Adventures as a Spy* (Stroud, 2014), p. 33.

15 Stafford, 'Spies and Gentlemen', p. 503; David Trotter, 'The Politics of Adventure in the Early British Spy Novel', *Intelligence and National Security* 5/4 (1990), p. 31.

16 Clive Bloom, *Spy Thrillers, from Buchan to le Carré* (Basingstoke, 1990), p. 3.

17 Stafford, 'Spies and Gentlemen', p. 491; Bloom, *Spy Thrillers, from Buchan to le Carré*, p. 1.

18 Le Queux, *Spies of the Kaiser*, pp. 12–16.
19 Lionel James, *The German Spy System from Within* (London, 1914), p. 7.
20 Oliver S. Buckton, *Espionage in British Fiction and Film since 1900: The Changing Enemy* (London, 2015), pp. 31–3.
21 Scully, *Images of Germany*, p. 115.
22 Escott Lynn, *In Khaki for the King* (London, 1915), p. 70.
23 George Robb, *British Culture and the First World War* (Basingstoke, 2002), pp. 182, 196.
24 Lechmere Worrall and J. E. Harold Terry, *The Man Who Stayed at Home* (London, 1916), p. 143. See also 'Why We Wrote It. Chat with Authors of the "Spy" Play', *The Globe*, 11 December 1914, p. 1.
25 Mary Luckhurst, 'A Wounded Stage: Drama and World War I', in Mary Luckhurst (ed.), *A Companion to Modern British and Irish Drama 1880–2005* (Oxford, 2006), pp. 302–3.
26 Worrall and Terry, *The Man Who Stayed at Home*, p. 143.
27 Joanna Bourke, *Dismembering the Male: Men's Bodies, Britain and the Great War* (London, 1996), pp. 13–14; Laura Ugolini, *Civvies: Middle-Class Men on the English Home Front, 1914–18* (Manchester, 2017), pp. 4–7. But this crisis in masculinity had been developing since at least 1870. The advocacy of women's rights, the influence of new mass media, frequent periods of labour unrest and the advent of new technologies all threatened to question the most important presuppositions on which society was based. See Mosse, *The Image of Man*, pp. 78–9. Notwithstanding the importance of soldiering to masculine identity, most men of military age chose not to volunteer and faced widespread disapproval as a result: Gregory, *Last Great War*, pp. 89–90.
28 Miriam Cooke and Angela Woollacott, 'Introduction', in Miriam Cooke and Angela Woollacott (eds), *Gendering War Talk* (Princeton, 1993), p. IX; Gullace, *The Blood of Our Sons*, pp. 2–3; Meyer, *Men of War*, p. 9; Ugolini, *Middle-Class Men on the English Home Front*, p. 6.
29 Gullace, *Blood of Our Sons*, p. 42. Michael Roper also contends that since masculinity is conceived of as an idea created by social convention, this approach leaves unanswered questions about how codes of masculinity related to the behaviour and disposition of individual actors. Without analysing experience, masculinity can only be perceived as a set of abstract codes. By examining the connections between masculine ideals and physical manifestations of suspicion, this chapter can offer new insights into how the war generated new forms of self-expression. Michael Roper, 'Between Manliness and Masculinity: The "War Generation" and the Psychology of Fear in Britain, 1914–1950', *Journal of British Studies* 44/2 (2005), p. 345.
30 'The Dawn of Britain's Greatest Glory', *John Bull*, vol. XVII, no. 428, 15 August 1914, p. 4.
31 Ugolini, *Middle-Class Men on the English Home Front*, p. 4. This was compounded by a popular belief that the struggle represented an opportunity to assert one's manliness by defending women from the horrors of war: Bourke, *Dismembering the Male*, pp. 76–123; Robb, *British Culture and the First World War*, pp. 58–60; Alexander Wilkinson, *The Church of England and the First World War* (Cambridge, 2014), pp. 94–6.
32 British manhood was juxtaposed with German brutality There were three characters: Germany – the brutal militarist, Britain – the chivalric rescuer and Belgian – the suffering women who had been metaphorically raped. Conversely,

national danger was associated with failed manliness. Gullace, *Blood of Our Sons*, pp. 33–46.

33 Alexander Watson, *Enduring the Great War: Combat, Morale and Collapse in the German and British Armies, 1914–1918* (Cambridge, 2009), p. 53.

34 Quoted in Lynch, *Yorkshire's War*, p. 30.

35 Cambridgeshire Archives, 531/F/1: Papers of Reverend Canon Percy G. Ward, Diary entries 1 January and 26 May 1915.

36 Thomson, *Queer People*, p. 37.

37 Ugolini, *Middle-Class Men on the English Home Front*, pp. 7, 51. Tammy Proctor similarly argues that the distinction between soldier and civilian is an anachronistic construct. The divide between the home and fighting front was never entirely clear. Although propaganda regularly augmented this gendered division, such dichotomies fail to capture the multiple identities and experiences of war. As a consequence, the imaginary boundary separating the civilian from the conflict was not necessarily apparent. Proctor, *Civilians in a World at War*, pp. 3–15.

38 Proctor, *World at War*, pp. 15, 37, 80, 110.

39 Later renamed the British Empire Union.

40 *Nantwich Guardian*, 24 September 1915, p. 7.

41 'Local Committees', *The Globe*, 21 October 1914, p. 3.

42 'The Spy Danger', *The Globe*, 24 November 1914, p. 3.

43 Le Queux, *German Spies in England*, p. 115.

44 Andrew Clark thought that individuals mistrustful of strangers believed it to be an obligation or duty during wartime. Diary of Andrew Clark, vol. II, 28 September 1914, p. 131.

45 'The Spy Danger', *The Globe*, 17 October 1914, p. 10. The same notice was reprinted at least twenty-six times between October 1914 and April 1915.

46 'Things "The Globe" Does Not Regret', *The Globe*, 22 November 1915, p. 4.

47 However, the apparent 'spy' was nothing more than an elderly lady with a German accent. Diary of Andrew Clark, vol. II, 26 September 1914, p. 124.

48 'War Items', *Shepton Mallet Journal*, 21 August 1914, p. 3.

49 'Soldier Runs Amok', *The Globe*, 15 March 1915, p. 7.

50 'Our Boys', *Westminster Gazette*, 18 December 1914, p. 7.

51 Liddle DF 001: Augustus Gordon Stewart, Diary entry 20 September 1914.

52 Augustus Gordon Stewart Papers, Transcript of Interview (1976), Diary entry 5 October 1914; Liddle DF 002: Arthur Hoyer Alexander, Scrapbook diary, 1914–15.

53 It was not uncommon for children to react in this way: Following the east coast raid in December 1914, one schoolboy grew equally determined to prove his value and offered his services to defend 'a bridge or something'. If not allowed, it was professed, he 'will go to fight in France [anyway] and pity the poor spy they get hold of'. *Manchester Evening News*, 19 December 1914, p. 2; *The Cornishman*, 31 December 1914, p. 8. Like all civilians, children had been explicitly called upon to participate and indoctrinated on the importance of sacrifice. Lancashire Record Office, PR 2908/9/5: 'What You Can Do for Your country: An Appeal to the Boys and Girls of the Empire' (1915).

54 'Armed German Spy', *Dover Express*, 2 October 1914, p. 5; 'The Alleged Spy Story', *Dover Express*, 9 October 1914, p. 5.

55 William Freeland Waddell, *The Patriot and the Spies* (London, 1915), pp. 12–15.

56 Ibid., p. 16.

57 Ibid., pp. 22–3.

58 Ibid., pp. 60–9.

59 Ibid., pp. 80–101.

60 Ibid., pp. 9, 50.

61 Ibid., pp. 9–10.

62 Ibid., pp. 132–4.

63 'Hunting Out the Spies', *Daily Herald*, 24 October 1914, p. 7.

64 'The Patriots', *Nantwich Guardian*, 30 October 1914, p. 5.

65 Contemporary psychologists and historians alike have both observed that fear was most prominent among those who felt helpless: Watson, *Enduring the Great War*, p. 29.

66 Winston Spencer Churchill, *Thoughts and Adventures: Churchill Reflects on Spies, Cartoons, Flying, and the Future*, edited by James W. Muller (Delaware, 2009), p. 90.

67 TNA WO 106/6151: Lecture on Intelligence Duties in the Field by Count Gleichen, March 1908.

68 Kell, *A Secret Well Kept*, pp. 108–13; Andrew, *Secret Service*, p. 124.

69 Robert Baden-Powell, *My Adventures as a Spy* (Stroud, 2014), p. 52. Similarly, Richard Hannay likened spying to a sporting contest between two huntsmen in which only the victor survives: John Buchan, *Greenmantle* (London, 1916), p. 52. David Trotter has argued that early spy novels were designed to instil a belief that excitement and adventure were key if Britain was to avoid further degeneracy and national decline: 'The Politics of Adventure', p. 42.

70 Glenn R. Wilkinson, *Depictions and Images of War in Edwardian Newspapers, 1899–1914* (Basingstoke, 2003), pp. 71–88.

71 Liddle GS 0872: C. G. W. Joss, Letter dated 20 May 1915.

72 TNA WO 123/199: BEF Routine Orders, 18 August 1914.

73 TNA WO 95/1440: Third Army Memorandum, 28 July 1915.

74 Surrey History Centre, QRWS/30/MER/1/p139/3: Papers of Col. L. W. Merrow-Smith, Scrapbook.

75 TNA WO 123/200: BEF Routine Orders, 3 March 1916.

76 Pöhlmann, 'German Intelligence at War', p. 34.

77 IWM docs. 6731: Papers of Geoffrey Archibald Loyd, Diary entry 15 August 1914; IWM docs. 8061: Papers of Percival Charles Cobb, Diary entries 18 and 19 September 1914; IWM docs. 12911: Papers of Albert Edward Gumm, Diary entries 21 September and 1 November 1914; IWM docs. 18918: Papers of G. Harding, Diary entry 6 November 1914; IWM docs. 11822: Papers of G. O. Chambers, Diary entry 15 January 1915; IWM docs. 12588: Papers of Kenneth Stuart Hall, Letter dated 5 January 1916.

78 Chris Kempshall, *British, French and American Relations on the Western Front, 1914–1918* (Cham, 2018), p. 97.

79 Percival Charles Cobb Papers, Diary entries 29 August, 2 September, 3 December 1914; IWM docs. 11573: Papers of W. V. Hindle, Diary entry 7 June 1915; Leicestershire Record Office, DE 3695/116: Papers of Arthur Percival Marsh, Letter to his fiancé dated 27 June 1915.

80 IWM docs. 5094: Papers of R. A. Watts, Diary entry 8 May 1915; Biographical details came from TNA WO 372/21/47466: Medal Card of Raymond A. Watts.

81 Leicestershire Record Office, 22D63/190/1: Diary of Lt. Col. Herbert Stoney Smith, 31 December 1914. Boasting of being employed as a spy was not uncommon either: R. A. Watts Papers, Diary entry 7 June 1915.

82 P. C. Cobb Papers, Diary entry 1 September 1914.

83 In her study of masculinity during the First World War, Jessica Meyer argues that the difficulty in comprehending and explaining experiences of combat forced soldiers to rely on abstractions that had been central to pre-war concepts of manliness. Meyer, *Men of War*, pp. 9, 45–6.

84 John Charteris, *At GHQ* (London, 1931), p. 43.

85 For examples see Rudyard Kipling, *Kim*, p. 257; Childers, *Riddle of the Sands*, p. 188; E. Phillips Oppenheim, *Mysterious Mr. Sabin*, p. 19. Le Queux also wrote spy novels, as well as counter-spy novels, such as *Secrets of the Foreign Office* (1903) and *The Man from Downing Street* (1904), which similarly focused on the gentleman spy.

86 IWM docs. 17100: Papers of J. G. Coulson, Diary entry 18 June 1916.

87 Lincoln Museum, LINRM, 2000/16: Papers of Alfred Thurlow, Diary entry 10 March 1915.

88 IWM docs. 11782: Papers of Arthur Francis Smith, Diary entry 6 November 1914.

89 IWM docs. 18918: Papers of G. Harding, Diary entry 22 October 1914.

90 Patrols boasting about capturing daring spies seem to have been fairly prevalent: Arthur Francis Smith Papers, Diary entry 21 August 1914; Albert Edward Gumm Papers, Diary entry 29 September 1914.

91 Canon Frederick George Scott, *The Great War as I Saw It* (Toronto, 1922), pp. 83–4. Much like soldiers in the BEF, Canadian troops were similarly warned about the dangers of German espionage and instructed to remain vigilant: Library and Archives Canada RG9 III C-3, vol. 4039, folder 11, file 7: 3rd Canadian Infantry Battalion, 1st Canadian Infantry Brigade, Notes on the Prevention of Espionage and Leakage of Information (May 1916).

92 IWM docs. 12582: Papers of Kenneth Stuart Hall, Letters dated 9 January and 17 January 1916.

93 IWM docs. 16328: Papers of George Fear, Letter dated 29 November 1914.

94 Ibid.

95 Stories involving soldiers, usually local residents, catching spies on the Western Front were a frequent source of pride and admiration in newspapers. 'Cheshires Capture Spy', *Cheshire Observer*, 27 March 1915, p. 10; 'Another Kilsyth Soldier's Experiences', *Kilsyth Chronicle*, 23 April 1915, p. 1. While British civilians abroad equally found excitement and pride in disclosing their own efforts to thwart a German spy: Thomas A. Baggs, *Back from the Front: An Eyewitness's Narrative of the Beginnings of the Great War of 1914* (London, 1914), pp. 46–8.

96 John Buchan, *The Thirty-Nine Steps* (New York, 1915), pp. 11, 38, 64. For some at least, spy catching did provide a welcome respite to the boredom experienced on the Home Front: IWM docs. 13271: Anonymous Royal Naval Division Memoir, First World War (undated).

97 Churchill, *Thoughts and Adventures*, pp. 92–5.

98 Horace W. B. Joseph Papers, Diary entry 4 October 1914, p. 102.

99 Gloucestershire Archives, D3549/33/1/19: Papers of Arthur Barwick Lloyd-Baker, Diary entry 9 August 1914.

100 TNA AIR 1/550/16/15/27: Home Defence Intelligence Summaries, MT1(b) Intelligence Summary, 8–24 November 1914.

101 Horace W. B. Joseph Papers, Diary entry 30 May 1915, p. 164.

102 The excitement of clandestine operations was frequently likened to military activity. During a ruse to escape Germany, Stewart, a surgeon and not a spy, began 'tingling all over with a sudden sense of danger – tingling as a soldier tingles as he awaits the

command to charge'. Burton E. Stevenson, *Little Comrade: A Tale of the Great War* (New York, 1915). p. 93.

103 Given his fondness for spy hunting, Heron-Allen allegedly spent several hours each night ensuring that the Scouts were diligently watching for German spies: Harvey and Fitzgerald, *Heron-Allen's Journal*, pp. 7, 12, 17.

104 Harvey and Fitzgerald, *Heron-Allen's Journal*, p. 13.

105 Surrey History Centre, QRWS/30/MERR/1/p24/1: Personal Reminiscences of L. W. Smith, p. 31; Leicestershire Record Office, 22D63/409: Memories of a Trench Rat by Jack Horner, p. 16.

106 Liddle GS 1205: Richard Astry Bourne Orlebar, Letter dated 1 December 1914.

107 TNA AIR 1/550/16/15/27: Home Defence Intelligence Summaries, Confidential Report from O. C. Woolwich Garrison to Eastern Command HQ, 19 October 1914.

108 Gloucestershire Archives, D37/1/50: Correspondence of Maynard Willoughby Colchester-Wemyss, Letter to the King of Siam, dated 16 April 1915.

109 'Xmas Night with the Special Constables', *Westminster Gazette*, 29 December 1914, p. 4.

110 'Supposed Spy Shot. A Newcastle Chase', *Portsmouth Evening News*, 8 August 1914, p. 7; 'Midnight Spy Incident. Excitement at Dunfermline', *Edinburgh Evening News*, 11 August 1914, p. 2; 'Exciting Incident in Wigan', *Wigan Observer and District Advertiser*, 15 August 1914, p. 6; 'Spy Scare at Shepton Mallet. Veterinary Surgeon Bitten with the Mania. Territorial Officer's Exciting Adventure', *Taunton Courier and Western Advertiser*, 19 August 1914, p. 8; 'Supposed Spy Chase at Torry. A Daring Escapade', *Aberdeen Evening Express*, 25 August 1914, p. 3; 'Shadowing a "Spy". Exciting Incident at Cardiff', *Western Mail*, 8 September 1914, p. 6; 'Spy Hunt Comedy. Exciting Incident at Scarborough', *Birmingham Mail*, 18 December 1914, p. 4.

111 'Tring', *Bucks Herald*, 12 December 1914, p. 10.

112 '"Spy" Scare in Aberdeen', *Aberdeen Evening Express*, 9 September 1914, p. 2.

113 'Amusing Spy Story at Exeter', *Western Times*, 14 August 1914, p. 5.

114 Angela Woollacott, 'Sisters and Brothers in Arms: Family, Class, and Gendering in World War I Britain', in Cooke and Woollacott (eds), *Gendering War Talk*, p. 143; Susan R. Grayzel, *Women and the First World War* (Harlow, 2002) p. 43.

115 Krisztina Robert, 'Gender, Class, and Patriotism: Women's Paramilitary Units in First World War Britain', *International History Review* 19/1 (1997), pp. 52–4.

116 Beatrice M. Trefusis Papers, Diary entry for March 1915.

117 Beatrice M. Trefusis Papers, Diary entry 26 October 1914.

118 Robert, 'Gender, Class, and Patriotism', p. 65.

Part III

1 Which are also known as 'mass psychogenic illness' or 'mass sociogenic illness'.

2 Leslie P. Boss, 'Epidemic Hysteria: A Review of the Published Literature', *Epidemiologic Reviews* 19/2 (1997), p. 233.

3 Robert E. Bartholomew and Simon Wessely, 'Protean Nature of Mass Sociogenic Illness: From Possessed Nuns to Chemical and Biological Terrorism Fears', *British Journal of Psychiatry* 180 (2002), pp. 302–3.

4 Ibid., p. 300.

5 Boss, 'Epidemic Hysteria', p. 233.

6 'Group anxiety' can be defined as the rapid spread of a seemingly irrational belief, in which no illness symptoms are reported: Robert E. Bartholomew, 'Epidemic Hysteria: A Review of the Published Literature', *American Journal of Epidemiology* 151/2 (2000), p. 206.

7 Simon Wessely, 'Mass Hysteria: Two Syndromes?', *Psychological Medicine* 17 (1987), p. 110.

8 In this context, 'delusion' refers not to a persistent pathological belief associated with psychosis but to the perpetuation of falsehood and rumour surrounding a particular threat or event: Bartholomew, 'Epidemic Hysteria', p. 206.

9 Sidney Theodore Falstead, *German Spies at Bay: Being an Actual Record of the German Espionage in Great Britain during the Years 1914–1918* (New York, 1920), pp. 41–4.

10 Haste, *Keep the Home Fires Burning*, p. 110.

11 French, 'Spy Fever in Britain', p. 356.

12 Robbins, *Politicians, Diplomacy and War*, p. 90.

13 Panayi, *Enemy in Our Midst*, p. 4.

14 Gregory, *Last Great War*, pp. 73–81; Pennell, *A Kingdom United*, pp. 156–62.

15 For example, men employed in commercial or distribution trades volunteered in far greater numbers than industrial workers, transport operatives or agricultural labourers. Textile workers were the most reluctant to enlist, given the increased prosperity in the clothing trade caused by the war. The superior wages received by dockworkers, railwaymen and miners all discouraged enlistment, while unemployment in the building trade resulted in a higher than average rate of enlistment: Ian Beckett, 'The Nation in Arms, 1914–1918', in Beckett and Simpson (eds), *A Nation in Arms*, pp. 7–11.

16 The issue with Panayi's assessment of Germanophobia stems from what he regards as 'public opinion'. Panayi rightly differentiates between what can be objectively assessed and the thoughts and feelings of every member of British society. However, his analysis of 'public opinion' only includes the 'politically active and powerful sections of the population'. This overly top-down approach means that the ambiguity and variety of collective emotions becomes lost. Panayi, *Enemy in Our Midst*, p. 3.

17 *Oxford English Dictionary*, 3rd edn (2019), accessed online June 2023.

18 Or Beatlemania, for example.

19 Gregory, *Last Great War*, p. 27.

20 'The War Fever', *London Evening Standard*, 10 August 1914, p. 9. See also, 'The War Fever', *Daily Citizen*, 4 August 1914, p. 5.

21 Pennell, *A Kingdom United*, pp. 35–56.

Chapter 5

1 F. Harrison, *The German Peril: Forecasts 1864–1914, Realities 1915, Hopes 191-* (London, 1915), pp. 233–5. Anthony D. Smith notes that total war provoked contradictory trends. A desire to enhance national solidarity was juxtaposed by simultaneous efforts to solidify individual group homogeneity through reinforcing, even exacerbating, class structure and ethnic division: 'War and Ethnicity: The Role

of Warfare in the Formation, Self-Images and Cohesion of Ethnic Communities',
Ethnic and Racial Studies 4/4 (1981), p. 387.

2   'War News', *Berwickshire News and General Advertiser*, 15 September 1914, p. 3;
'When Victory Is Won', *Portsmouth Evening News*, 22 October 1914, p. 3; 'The
Venomous Reptiles', *Edinburgh Evening Express*, 22 January 1915, p. 3; Harrison, *The
German Peril*, p. 17.

3   Panayi, *Enemy in Our Midst*, pp. 153–83.

4   Bloom, *Spy Thrillers*, p. 1.

5   Stafford, *The Silent Game*, p. 3.

6   Catriona Pennell similarly argues that rumours of Russian soldiers landing in
Scotland not only provided language to express fear but that it also acted as a unifying
force and that this shared belief inspired hope at a time of crisis: 'Believing the
Unbelievable: The Myth of the Russians 'with Snow on Their Boots' in the United
Kingdom, 1914', *Cultural and Social History* 11/1 (2014), p. 73.

7   David Coast and Jo Fox. 'Rumour and Politics', *History Compass* 13/5 (2015),
pp. 224–6.

8   Hans-Joachim Neubauer, *The Rumour: A Cultural History* (London,1999), p. 24.

9   For some, the government's strict control of war news was designed to prevent
information reaching the spies who were already in Britain: Horace W. B. Joseph
Papers, Diary entry 9 August 1914, p. 11. For further entries regarding the lack of war
news see 13–26 August 1914, pp. 13–36.

10 Robb, *British Culture and the First World War*, p. 134.

11 Diary of Andrew Clark, vol. III, 30 October 1914, p. 150.

12 Martin Farrar, *News from the Front: War Correspondents on the Western Front* (Stroud,
1998), pp. x–xv, 41.

13 Philip Gibbs, *Adventures in Journalism* (London, 1923), p. 217. Only from May 1915
did the War Office accept their responsibility to provide the British public with
officially accredited reports of the fighting.

14 Beatrice Morwenna Trefusis papers, Diary entries 6 and 21 August 1914.

15 Tamotsu Shibutini argues that the circulation of rumour is a process in which society
construct its own self-serving explanations for ambiguous or ineffable situations.
Improvised News: A Sociological Study of Rumor (New York, 1966), p. 199.

16 Liddle DF 003: Katrine Margaret Alexander, Diary entry 24 November 1914; John
Terraine, *The Smoke and the Fire: Myths and Anti-Myths of War, 1861–1945* (London,
1992); John Horne and Alan Kramer, *German Atrocities, 1914: A History of Denial*
(New Haven, 2001); David Clarke, *The Angel of Mons* (Chichester, 2004); James
Hayward, *Myths and Legends of the First World War* (Stroud, 2002); Pennell, 'Believing
the Unbelievable'.

17 IWM docs. 13607: Papers of Norman Macleod, Diary entries 25 August, 3 September
and 17 October 1914.

18 Miss M. Coules Papers, p. 8. See also Dorothy Bowes, 'Looking Back to 1914–18'
(1991), p. 3.

19 Gloucestershire Archives, D3981/45: Papers of William Thomas Swift, Diary entries
2–30 August 1914; Cambridgeshire Archives, 531/F/1: Papers of Reverend Canon
P. G. Ward, Diary entry 5 August 1914; Gloucestershire Archives D3355/8: Papers
of Canon Rowan Ernest Grice-Hutchinson, Diary entry 21 September 1914. Even
in 1915, people were still lamenting the lack of reliable war news: IWM docs.
14225: Hissey Family letters, Letter dated 16 August 1915.

20 Cambridgeshire Archives, R109/064/4: Papers of Evelyn Diver, Diary entry 15 August 1914; Emily Blathwayt Papers, Diary entry 17 August 1914; William Thomas Swift Papers, Diary entry 31 August 1914.

21 Canon Rowan Ernest Grice-Hutchinson Papers, Diary entry 12 August 1914.

22 As Chapter 8 will show, 39 per cent of the 9,245 articles surveyed depicted activities of spies abroad. Spy stories related to Germany's clandestine activity across the globe; America, Angola, Australia, Bosnia, Bulgaria, Denmark, Canada, China, Egypt, Finland, Gibraltar, Greece, Hong Kong, India, Mexico, Morocco, the Pacific Islands, South Africa, Spain and Sweden all featured in espionage tales.

23 In August 1914, 48 per cent of articles involving German spies abroad referred to incidents in Belgium.

24 Between September and November 1914, 47 per cent of articles containing reports of spies abroad related to activity in France.

25 Although the Bergmann Offensive opened the fighting in the Caucasus, it was principally a Russian initiative. The flurry of reports pertaining to espionage in Turkey therefore coincided with the first major engagement between Russian and Ottoman forces during the Battle of Sarikamish (22 December 1914–17 January 1915). 'Condemned as a Spy', *Birmingham Mail*, 17 December 1914, p. 3; 'A Greek Subject's Sentence', *Western Mail*, 26 December 1914, p. 4; 'In Constantinople', *Globe*, 30 December 1914, p. 3; 'Greece and Turkey', *Aberdeen Evening Express*, 9 January 1915, p. 3; 'Foreigners in Stambul', *Daily Record*, 11 January 1915, p. 3.

26 The majority of spy stories relating to the Eastern Front emerged during the exact period following the Silesian Offensive (11 November – 6 December 1914) and the Russian offensive in the Carpathians (2 January – 12 April 1915). 'Czar and the Peasant', *Edinburgh Evening News*, 5 December 1914, p. 5; 'Germans Outwitted', *Leeds Mercury*, 12 December 1914, p. 5; 'The Fight for Warsaw', *Birmingham Daily Mail*, 26 December 1914, p. 3; 'River Dammed with Corpses', *Aberdeen Evening Express*, 26 December 1914, p. 3; 'Grim Struggle for Warsaw', *Liverpool Echo*, 26 December 1914, p. 3; 'Batoum to Archangel', *Edinburgh Evening News*, 5 January 1915, p. 2; 'Germans Driven to Death', *Aberdeen Evening Express*, 6 January 1915, p. 2.
Twenty-seven reports of spies in Salonika were published between 20 October and 31 December 1915, which followed the Battle of Krivolak (18 October – 4 November 1915), the first engagement on the Salonika Front. Only one article had previously mentioned spies in Salonika in March 1915. 'Salonika', *Hull Daily Mail*, 20 October 1915, p. 5; 'Spies and the Salonika Landing', *Western Mail*, 25 October 1915, p. 5; 'A Bishop as a Spy', *Daily Record*, 11 November 1915, p. 5; 'Spies at Salonika', *Birmingham Daily Mail*, 20 November 1915, p. 6; 'Swarms of Spies in Salonika', *Aberdeen Evening Express*, 26 November 1915, p. 4; 'The Spies of Salonika', *Liverpool Echo*, 26 November 1915, p. 5.
Almost half of reports relating to Italy between August 1914 and December 1915 appeared in the British press just as Italy declared war and as the First Battle of the Isonzo began (23 June – 7 July 1915). 'Austria and Italy. Signs of Imminent Rupture', *Daily Record*, 22 March 1915, p. 5; 'Germans in Italy', *Liverpool Echo*, 22 March 1915, p. 5; 'Keep an Eye on Germans!', *Manchester Evening News*, 23 March 1915, p. 7; 'Kaiser's Double Arrested in Italy', *Edinburgh Evening News*, 5 April 1915, p. 5; 'Italians Clearing the Country of Spies', *Globe*, 19 April 1915, p. 1; 'Diplomat-Thief-Spy. Wanted at Rome', *Globe*, 28 April 1915, p. 4; 'Germans and Austrians Arrested in Italy', *Birmingham Daily Mail*, 12 May 1915, p. 3; Rioting in Milan. An Anti-German Outburst', *Portsmouth Evening News*, 28 May 1915, p. 6; 'Spy Peril', *Birmingham Mail*,

31 May 1915, p. 2; 'Italian Campaign', *Nottingnam Journal*, 29 June 1915, p. 3; 'Spies Sentenced', *Birmingham Mail*, 8 July 1915, p. 4; 'Official Reports. Italy', *Edinburgh Evening News*, 10 July 1915, p. 5.

27 Rather than admit military failure, for instance, newspapers commonly attributed such distressing rumours to the activities of German spies. It was recommended, therefore, that people take little notice of the difficulties experienced at the front: 'Story of the War', *Leeds Mercury*, 19 August 1914, p. 2; 'Our London Letter', *Diss Express*, 28 August 1914, p. 6; 'London Letter', *Whitstable Times and Herne Bay Herald*, 29 August 1914, p. 4; 'More False News', *Dumfries and Galloway Standard*, 9 January 1915, p. 2.

28 G. M. West Papers, Diary entry 1 February 1915, p. 6; Ada McGuire Papers, Letter dated 31 May 1915; Surrey History Centre, 2572/1/71: Papers of Thomas Cecil Farrer, Letter from Evangeline Farrer, dated 7 August 1916; Holman, 'Constructing the Enemy Within', pp. 22–42.

29 For the difference between rumour and gossip see Coast and Fox, 'Rumour and Politics', p. 223.

30 Diary of Andrew Clark, vol. IV, 5 November 1914, p. 96.

31 Caithness Archives, C/P/566/76/13: Papers of Margret 'Grettie' Davidson correspondence, letter from Colonel Davidson (1914).

32 Surrey History Centre, 6782/25: Papers of Lucy Broadwood, Diary entry 7–8 September 1914.

33 Katrine Margaret Alexander, Transcript of Interview (1976), p. 1.

34 Proctor, *Civilians in a World at War*, p. 20.

35 Hilda W. Davison, 'Memories of the Great War', p. 10.

36 IWM docs. 11335a: Papers of Frederick Arthur Robinson, Diary entry 6 August 1914.

37 Highland Archive Centre, D432/1/8: Papers of William Campbell, 1914 Diary (most entries do not include dates, but this was probably written sometime in September 1914).

38 IWM docs. 6570: Papers of Robert Saunders, Diary entry 8 August 1914.

39 Emily Blathwayt Papers, Diary entry 8 October 1914.

40 William Thomas Swift Papers, Diary entry 28 September 1914; Hissey family letters, 28 December 1914.

41 'War "News"!', *John Bull*, vol. XVII, no. 428, 15 August 1914, p. 1. See also Adrian Gregory, 'A Clash of Cultures: The British Press and the Opening of the Great War', in Troy R. E. Paddock (ed.), *A Call to Arms: Propaganda, Public Opinion, and Newspapers in the Great War* (London, 2004), p. 16.

42 Haste, *Keep the Home Fires Burning*, p. 138.

43 Norman Macleod Papers, Diary entries 14–16 October 1914.

44 Le Queux, *German Spies in England*, pp. 96, 118–19.

45 'Milngavie Flooded', *Daily Record*, 14 August 1914, p. 4; 'Story of the War', *Leeds Mercury*, 19 August 1914, p. 2; 'Our London Letter', *Diss Express*, 28 August 1914, p. 6; 'Epidemic of Falsehood', *Whitstable Times and Herne Bay Herald*, 29 August 1914, p. 4; 'Agricultural Notes', *Southern Reporter*, 3 September 1914, p. 3; 'Bumbles Letter from Beeford', *Hull Daily Mail*, 31 October 1914, p. 3; 'Attempt on King Albert and French President', *Aberdeen Evening Express*, 3 November 1914, p. 3; '800 French Horses Killed', *Portsmouth Evening News*, 11 November 1914, p. 6; 'The Alien Peril', *Nottingham Journal*, 13 November 1914, p. 3; 'More False News', *Dumfries and Galloway Standard*, 9 January 1915, p. 2; 'Two Vessels Sunk in the Irish Sea', *Fife Free Press and Kirkcaldy Guardian*, 27 February 1915, p. 2; 'Who Caused the Lerwick

Explosion?', *Aberdeen Evening Express*, 22 April 1915, p. 5; 'Foot and Mouth Disease in Wiltshire', *Warwick and Warwickshire Advertiser*, 20 November 1915, p. 7.

46 Lucy Broadwood Papers, Diary entry 14 April 1915.

47 TNA KV 1/46: G Branch Report, Appendix C, Memorandum by Major R. J. Drake (1916).

48 Farrar, *News from the Front*, pp. 2–65, esp. 18.

49 IWM docs. 18918: Papers of G. Harding, Diary entry 20 October 1914.

50 IWM docs. 5094: Papers of Reginald A. Watts, Diary entry 19 June 1915.

51 IWM docs. 12582: Papers of Kenneth Stuart Hall, Letter to his mother dated 5 January 1916.

52 After the 'ambush', the battalion were left with around 2 to 300 survivors after an initial strength of 1,150 men, according to Corporal Smith, B Company, Gordon Highlanders: 'Scottish Regiments' Heavy Losses', *Aberdeen Evening Express*, 11 September 1914, p. 3.

53 'The Military Position', *Westminster Gazette*, 17 October 1914, p. 1; 'A Soldier's Thought of Warfare', *Liverpool Echo*, 12 January 1915, p. 5; 'Spy in the British Lines', *Edinburgh Evening News*, 4 March 1915, p. 3; 'Hull Man's Account', *Hull Daily Mail*, 21 May 1915, p. 2.

54 Sir Julian S. Corbett, *Naval Operations Vol. I: To the Battle of the Falklands December 1914* (London, 1920), pp. 175–7.

55 Lord Charles Beresford, *Hansard*, 12 November 1914.

56 TNA HO 45/10756/267450: The 'Spy Peril' and the Question of Interning all Enemy Aliens. Lord Charles Beresford – Guy Stephenson, 9 October 1914.

57 'The Price of Dreadnoughts', *Cheshire Observer*, 24 October 1914, p. 5; 'What the Military Experts Say', *Aberdeen Evening Express*, 11 November 1914, p. 2; 'Alien Enemy Sentenced', *Hull Daily Mail*, 26 November 1914, p. 6.

58 Corbett, *Naval Operations Vol. I*, pp. 347–57.

59 The Earl of Crawford, *Hansard*, 25 November 1914; 'Today's Naval News', *Hull Daily Mail*, 5 November 1914, p. 4; 'Fear for the Good Hope', *Liverpool Echo*, 5 November 1914, p. 6; 'The Good Hope', *Portsmouth Evening News*, 5 November 1911, p. 3; 'The Good Hope', *Western Mail*, 6 November 1911, p. 5.

60 TNA CAB 45/263: Raids on the Coast of Great Britain: British Intelligence Reports, nos 1–2 dated 3 November and 16 December 1914, respectively.

61 For the response to the East Coast Raid: 'Territorials' Baptism of Fire', *Aberdeen Evening Express*, 17 December 1914, p. 2; 'Stories of the Raid', *Liverpool Echo*, 17 December 1914, p. 8; 'Spies on the East Coast', *Portsmouth Evening News*, 17 December 1914, p. 6; 'The Search for Spies', *Edinburgh Evening News*, 18 December 1914, p. 6; 'Spying at Scarborough', *Portsmouth Evening News*, 19 December 1914, p. 5; 'Spy Work at Scarbro', *Liverpool Echo*, 21 December 1914, p. 4; 'Spies on the East Coast', *Western Mail*, 21 December 1914, p. 10.

62 'East Coast Spies. How the German Fire Was Directed', *Exeter and Plymouth Gazette*, 22 December 1914, p. 9.

63 Le Queux, *German Spies in England*, p. 70.

64 'The Bombardment and Its Lessons', *Whitby Gazette*, 24 December 1914, p. 6.

65 Augustus Gordon Stewart Alexander Papers, Diary entry 16 December 1914.

66 'Lusitania. Resumption of the Official Enquiry', *Birmingham Mail*, 16 June 1915, p. 4; 'Lusitania's Speed Explained', *Liverpool Echo*, 16 June 1915, p. 5; 'The Lusitania Inquiry. Were Germans on Board?', *Daily Record*, 17 June 1915; 'The Spy Danger', *Western Mail*, 17 June 1915, p. 4.

67 'German Spies', *Daily Record*, 7 June 1916, p. 2; 'The Spy Theory', *Liverpool Echo*, 7 June 1916, p. 7; 'Menace of the Hun Spy. Kitchener Tragedy', *Aberdeen Evening Express*, 8 June 1916, p. 2; 'Lord Kitchener and His Staff Drowned at Sea. Possible Work of a Spy', *Taunton Courier and Western Advertiser*, 14 June 1916, p. 6.

68 For local disturbances thought to aid Zeppelin raids: 'Agricultural Notes', *Southern Reporter*, 3 September 1914, p. 3; 'Bumbles Letter from Beeford', *Hull Daily Mail*, 31 October 1914, p. 3; 'Airship Raid on Norfolk Coast', *Hull Daily Mail*, 20 January 1915, p. 5; 'News of Air Raids', *Hull Daily Mail*, 20 August 1915, p. 3. See also Papers of L. B. Stanley, Letter dated 10 September 1915.

69 Tom Douglas, *Scapegoats: Transferring Blame* (London, 2003), p. 108.

70 C. S. Peel, *How We Lived Then, 1914–1918: A Sketch of Social and Domestic Life in England during the War* (London, 1929), p. 43.

71 Matthew C. Hendley, 'Cultural Mobilization and British Responses to Cultural Transfer in Total War: The Shakespeare Tercentenary of 1916', *First World War Studies* 3/1 (2012), pp. 25–49.

72 Van Emden and Humphries, *All Quiet on the Home Front*, p. 67. See also, De Groot, *British Society in the Era of the Great War*, p. 159.

73 *Hull Daily Mail*, 13 October 1914, p. 1; Tony Kushner and Katherine Know, *Refugees in an Age of Genocide: Global, National and Local Perspectives during the Twentieth Century* (London, 2001), p. 46.

74 'For the Public Safety', *The Globe*, 16 November 1914, p. 4.

75 Le Queux, *German Spies in England*, pp. 65, 81, 136, 172.

76 Peel, *How We Lived Then*, p. 42. *John Bull* commenced a particularly vociferous campaign against naturalized Germans in Britain: 'Spies, Bombs and Butchery', *John Bull*, vol. XVII, no. 439, 31 October 1914, p. 4; 'Kent Police, Note', *John Bull*, vol. XVII, no. 440, 7 November 1914, p. 3; 'The Rich Enemy within Our Gates', *John Bull*, vol. XVII, no. 440, 7 November 1914, p. 10; 'The Spy Peril', *John Bull*, vol. XVII, no. 441, 14 November 1914, p. 1; 'Spot Those Spies', *John Bull*, vol. XVII, no. 442, p. 7; 'Those Spies', *John Bull*, vol. XVII, no. 443, 28 November 1914, p. 1.

77 While radicals seemed to believe that Germans were somehow predisposed to spying and treachery, even moderates thought it logical that Germans would naturally want to assist the fatherland somehow: Harvey and Fitzgerald, *Heron-Allen's Journal of the Great War*, p. 13.

78 Sir George Makgill, 'The War of Liberation: The German Invasion', *The English Review*, December 1915, pp. 479–80.

79 Gullace, 'Friends, Aliens, and Enemies', pp. 345–6.

80 For historians connecting anti-alienism with alleged German atrocities see John Stevenson, *British Society 1914–45* (Harmondsworth, 1984), pp. 55–6; Holmes, *John Bull's Island*, pp. 97–8; Horne and Kramer, *German Atrocities*, pp. 212–25.

81 Peter Cahalan, *Belgian Refugee Relief in England during the Great War* (New York, 1982), p. 259; Holmes, *John Bull's Island*, pp. 100–2; Kushner and Knox, *Refugees in an Age of Genocide*, p. 52. IWM docs. 77/156/1: Papers of G. M. West, Diary entries 20–30 November 1914, 1 February 1915.

82 Cahalan, *Belgian Refugee Relief*, pp. 11, 58–9; David Saunders, 'Aliens in Britain and the Empire during the First World War', *Immigrants and Minorities* 4/1 (1985), p. 9; Tony Kushner, 'Local Heroes: Belgian Refugees in Britain during the First World War', *Immigrants and Minorities* 18/1 (2010), p. 11.

83 Saunders, 'Aliens in Britain and the Empire', pp. 10–11. Similarly, while serving in France, Geoffrey Lloyd noted how soldiers even 'experienced the greatest difficulty

in distinguishing between English and German uniforms': Geoffrey Archibald Lloyd Papers, Diary entry 11 September 1914.

84 Kushner and Knox, *Refugees in an Age of Genocide*, p. 61.

85 'German or Belgian', *The Globe*, 26 October 1914, p. 6; 'Spy Precautions', *Cornishman*, 29 October 1914, p. 6; 'Swiss or German?', *The Globe*, 28 December 1914, p. 3; Kushner, 'Local Heroes', pp. 3–7.

86 'Waiter, etc., as Spies', *Aberdeen Evening Express*, 14 September 1914, p. 4; 'Knights of the Napkin', *John Bull*, vol. XVII, no. 434, 26 September 1914, p. 3; Papers of Frederick Arthur Robinson, Diary entry 22 October 1914; 'Identifying Germans', *The Globe*, 24 October 1914, p. 4; 'The Work Not Ended', *John Bull*, vol. XVII, no. 441, 14 November 1914, p. 2; Felstead (ed.), *Steinhauer*, p. 51.

87 'Supposed Spies Arrested', *Portsmouth Evening News*, 14 October 1914, p. 8; 'Refugee Spies', *Faringdon Advertiser and Vale of the White Horse Gazette*, 17 October 1914, p. 6.

88 Which translates to 'thank god we will be there soon'. 'German Spy Peril', *Western Mail*, 27 October 1914, p. 5.

89 'Belgian Refugees to Leave Hull', *Hull Daily Mail*, 19 October 1914, p. 6; 'East Coast Closed to Refugees', *Faringdon Advertiser and Vale of the White Horse Gazette*, 24 October 1914, p. 7; 'Belgian Refugees and the Protection against Spies', *Thanet Advertiser*, 24 October 1914, p. 3.

90 'A Hard Necessity: The Refugees', *Hull Daily Mail*, 20 October 1914, p. 4.

91 'A Wise Precaution', *Chelmsford Chronicle*, 23 October 1914, p. 4.

92 'No Additional Refugees Should Be Received', *Bexhill-on-Sea Observer*, 31 October 1914, p. 5.

93 Cesarani, 'An Alien Concept?', p. 36.

94 'Liberating the Gipsies', *Hull Daily Mail*, 30 April 1915, p. 6.

95 Homosexuals from across Europe, especially those in positions of influence, were regularly seen as weak-willed men vulnerable to blackmail, which encouraged notions of conspiracy: Philip Hoare, *Wilde's Last Stand: Decadence, Conspiracy and the First World War* (London, 1997), pp. 25, 43.

96 ' "Spies" on Brighton Pier', *Portsmouth Evening News*, 26 August 1914, p. 5; 'In Female Garb', *Liverpool Echo*, 12 December 1914, p. 3; 'Spy Alarm at Leith', *Edinburgh Evening News*, 7 September 1915, p. 4. See also Diary of Andrew Clark, vol. II, 28 September 1914, p. 131; Diary of Albert Edward Gumm, 2 November 1914.

97 'Battle at Lambhill Tongues Used as Missiles', *Kilsyth Chronicle*, 16 October 1914, p. 6; 'Col. George Cornwallis West', *Cheshire Observer*, 16 January 1915, p. 3; 'Police Courts', *Warwick and Warwickshire Advertiser*, 21 August 1915, p. 3; 'Sandbach Petty Sessions', *Nantwich Guardian*, 10 September 1915, p. 3; 'Woman's Allegation', *Thanet Advertiser*, 18 September 1915, p. 5; 'Plausible Young Man', *Western Mail*, 24 September 1915, p. 7; 'Temper of an Audience', *Shepton Mallet Journal*, 5 November 1915, p. 6; 'Unfounded Espionage Charge', *Edinburgh Evening News*, 13 January 1915, p. 2; 'Libel Based on Mistake', *Hull Daily Mail*, 13 January 1915, p. 2; 'The German Spy Allegations', *Edinburgh Evening News*, 31 March 1915, p. 6; 'Libel Reflecting on His Good Name', *Liverpool Echo*, 30 July 1915, p. 5. See also Le Queux, *German Spies in England*, p. 116.

98 Liddle RNMN 316: Albert Robert Williamson, Diary entry 14 November 1914.

99 'A Prussian Spy's Pernicious Schemes', *John Bull*, vol. XVII, no. 442, 21 November 1914, p. 18.

100 Colin Holmes, *Anti-Semitism in British Society, 1876–1939* (Abingdon, 1979), pp. 137–40; Shmuel Almog, 'Antisemitism as a Dynamic Phenomenon: "The Jewish Question" in England at the End of the First World War', *Patterns of Prejudice* 21/4 (1987), pp. 3–18; David Cesarani, 'An Embattled Minority: The Jews in Britain during the First World War', *Immigrants and Minorities* 8/1 (1989), pp. 61–76.

101 BL Add MSS 62225: Northcliffe Papers, vol. LXXIII, Letter from Leo Maxse, 29 October 1915.

102 West Sussex Record Office, Maxse Mss 3/2/1/370: Papers of Leo Maxse, Letter from Gordon Reid, 9 May 1915.

103 NMM WHI/185: Papers of Arnold White, Letter dated 6 October 1914; NMM WHI/186: Papers of Arnold White, Letter dated 16 October 1914. Cesarani, 'Anti-Alienism in England after the First World War', p. 7; Cesarani. 'An Embattled Minority', pp. 64–5; Pennell, *A Kingdom United*, p. 98.

104 'Hull Minister's Ordeal', *Hull Daily Mail*, 5 November 1915, p. 5.

105 'Spies in High Places', *Birmingham Mail*, 2 September 1914, p. 3; 'The Great Spy Peril. Pro-German Sympathy in High Places', *John Bull*, vol. XVII, no. 438, 24 October 1914, p. 4; Liddle GS 0861: Papers of Major General Dudley Graham Johnson, Letter dated 27 October 1914. See also the claims of Armgaard Karl Graves in his popular book, *The Secrets of the German War Office*, p. 32. For tramps and vagabonds suspected of espionage, see 'Derby Vagrant's Amazing Hallucination', *Nottingham Journal*, 23 March 1915, p. 4; 'Spies in Cornwall?', *Cornishman*, 25 March 1915, p. 3.

106 Bonar Law Papers, BL/35/2/10: Letter dated 6 November 1914.

107 Grant, *Spies and Secret Service*, p. 26.

108 'Highly Placed Germans', *The Globe*, 31 October 1914, p. 10; Caithness Archives C/P/125/14: Letter from Sir E. L. Lucas to Miss Cargill, 9 August 1915.

109 Norfolk Record Office, OLL 3330/1-9, 759X7: Letter from H. M. Upcher regarding fears of German spies at Cromer, 8 February 1915. See also Maxse papers, Mss 3/2/1/370: Letter from Gordon Reid, 18 May 1915.

110 West Sussex Record Office, Maxse Mss 3/2/1/370: Papers of Leo Maxse, Letter from Ellen Codringham, 24 May 1915.

111 'Danger at Clubs', *The Globe*, 31 August 1914, p. 7; TNA HO 45/10756/267450: Metropolitan Police Special Branch report, 17 July 1916.

112 Northamptonshire Record Office, N23/1: Papers of Frederick C Kench, Diary entry 13 March 1915.

113 'By the Way', *Globe*, 25 August 1914, p. 4; 'Two Traitors within Our Gates', *John Bull*, vol. XVII, no. 437, 17 October 1914, p. 5; 'London Socialists and German Spies', *Edinburgh Evening News*, 16 November 1914, p. 4; 'Strong Speaking by Members', *Fire Free Press and Kirkcaldy Guardian*, 13 March 1915, p. 3; 'Workers' Defence', *Birmingham Mail*, 15 June 1915, p. 6; 'Men and Matters', *Globe*, 26 June 1915, p. 9. This was a view shared by MO5(g) as early as 1909: TNA KV 1/2: Edmonds lecture entitled 'Espionage in Time of Peace' (January 1909).

114 Cyril Pearce, *Comrades in Conscience: The Story of an English Community's Opposition to the Great War* (London, 2001); Richard Thurlow, *The Secret State: British Internal Security in the Twentieth Century* (Oxford, 1995), p. 60. Paul Laity similarly shows that the British peace movement was the strongest and most active in Europe. More importantly, it resolutely opposed every British war and military intervention right up until 1914: *The British Peace Movement 1870–1914* (Oxford, 2001), p. 214.

115 Pennell, *A Kingdom United*, p. 78.

116 TNA HO 45/10741/263275: Letter from Rev. Pollock-Hill to Reginald McKenna, 27 August 1914.
117 'Workers and Shirkers', *Berwickshire News and General Advertiser*, 13 October 1914, p. 3.
118 'Paris Transformed', *London Daily News*, 9 September 1870, p. 5; 'The Story of the Spy Nicholas Schull', *Banbury Advertiser*, 24 November 1870, p. 2; Alistair Horne, *The Fall of Paris: The Siege and the Commune 1870–1* (London, 1965), p. 46; Michael Howard, *The Franco-Prussian War: The German Invasion of France, 1870–1871* (London, 2003), p. 121.
119 'Affairs in Paris', *Yorkshire Post and Intelligencer*, 18 January 1871, p. 4; 'The Capitulation', *Dublin Daily Express*, 30 January 1871, p. 2.
120 Robert Henrey (ed.), *Letters from Paris 1870–1875* (London, 1942), p. 110; Howard, *Franco-Prussian War*, p. 224.
121 TNA FO 146/1476: Lyons to Granville, 20 July 1870.
122 TNA FO 156/1476: Lyons to Granville, 25 and 29 July 1870.
123 'War Letters. News from Paris', *London Daily News*, 17 January 1871, p. 5.
124 *Bradford Observer*, 8 March 1871, p. 2; *Whitehaven News*, 9 March 1871, p. 4.
125 William Thomas Swift Papers, Diary entry 4 August 1914.

Chapter 6

1 Grant, *Spies and Secret* Service, p. 20.
2 Ibid., p.22. See also 'Notes on the War', *Chelmsford Chronicle*, 13 November 1914, p. 2; 'Spies in Business', *Whitby Gazette*, 27 November 1914, p. 10.
3 Le Queux, *German Spies in England*, p. 45.
4 Grant, *Spies and Secret Service*, p. 18; 'Baptist Pastor as a Pelican in the Wilderness', *Chelmsford Chronicle*, 6 November 1914, p. 2; 'The Society Papers', *Faringdon Advertiser and Vale of the White Horse Gazette*, 7 November 1914, p. 2. See also David Cesarani, 'Anti-Alienism in England after the First World War', *Immigrants and Minorities* 6/1 (1987), p. 5; Yarrow, 'The Impact of Hostility on Germans in Britain', p. 98.
5 'Monk's Startling Prophecy', *Belper News*, 23 October 1914, p. 2; 'The Anti-Christ', *Shepton Mallet Journal*, 30 October 1914, p. 3; 'A Prophecy of the War', *Dumfries and Galloway Standard*, 25 November 1914, p. 7.
6 Gooch, *The Prospect of War*, p. 9; John Gooch, 'Britain and the Boer War', in George J. Andreopoulos and Harold E. Selesky (eds), *The Aftermath of Defeat: Societies, Armed Forces, and the Challenge of Recovery* (Yale, 1994), pp. 40–3; Glenn R. Wilkinson, ' "The Blessings of War': The Depiction of Military Force in Edwardian Newspapers', *Journal of Contemporary History* 33/1 (1998), pp. 98, 115.
7 Summers, 'Militarism in Britain before the Great War', pp. 104–23; John Gooch, 'Attitudes to War in Late Victorian and Edwardian England', in Brian Bond and Ian Roy (eds), *War and Society: A Yearbook of Military History Volume 1* (London, 1977), pp. 88–102; Matthew Johnson, 'The Liberal Party and the Navy League in Britain before the Great War', *Twentieth Century British History*, 22/2 (2011), p. 163.
8 'Civilian Volunteers', *Birmingham Mail*, 15 August 1914, p. 3; 'German Spies Handicapping our Navy on the East Coast', *Western Times*, 15 September 1914, p. 5; 'Thoughts on the War', *Chelmsford Chronicle*, 16 October 1914, p. 7.

9   Rowland Hunt, *Hansard*, 27 August 1914; Earl Stanhope, *Hansard*, 10 September 1914; Joynson-Hicks, *Hansard*, 12 November 1914; Marquess of Londonderry, *Hansard*, 18 November 1914; Lord Leith of Fyvie, *Hansard*, 25 November 1914; Wilson, *The Myriad Faces of War*, pp. 198–9.

10 West Sussex Record Office, Maxse Mss 3/2/1/469: Leopold Maxse Papers, Letter from Lord Roberts, 20 October 1914.

11 BL Add MS 62225: Lord Northcliffe Papers, vol. LXXIII, Letter from Leopold Maxse, 16 November 1910.

12 TNA HO 45/10756/267450: ALIENS The 'Spy Peril' and the question of interning all enemy aliens. Lord Leith of Fyvie to the House of Lords, 25 November 1914.

13 'Alien Spy Peril', *Portsmouth Evening News*, 18 November 1914, p. 6; 'The Espionage Danger', *Western Mail*, 19 November 1914, p. 4. Horatio Bottomley made similar accusations: 'Foes at Home', *John Bull*, vol. XVII, no. 432, 12 September 1914, p. 11.

14 Stephen E. Koss, *Lord Haldane: Scapegoat for Liberalism* (London, 1969), p. 152; Geoffrey Searle, 'The "Revolt from the Right" in Edwardian Britain', in Paul Kennedy and Anthony James Nicholls (eds), *Nationalist and Racialist Movements in Britain and Germany before 1914* (London, 1981), p. 25; Frans Coetzee and Marilyn Shevin Coetzee, 'Rethinking the Radical Right in Germany and Britain before 1914', *Journal of Contemporary History* 21/4 (1986), p. 517; Nigel Keohane, *The Party of Patriotism: The Conservative Party and the First World War* (Farnham, 2010), p. 105.

15 Morris, *The Scaremongers*, p. 383; John Hutchinson, *Leopold Maxse and the National Review, 1893–1914: Right-Wing Politics and Journalism in the Edwardian Era* (London, 1989), p. 461.

16 Koss, *Haldane: Scapegoat for Liberalism*, pp. 152–5; TNA HO 45/10756/267450: 'The "Spy Peril" and the Question of Interning All Enemy Aliens', House of Lords, 25 November 1914.

17 Richard Thurlow, *Fascism in Britain: From Oswald Mosley's Blackshirts to the National Front* (London, 2006), pp. 3–4; Roger Eatwell, *Fascism: A History* (London, 2003), pp. 222–7; Stanley G. Payne, *A History of Fascism 1914–45* (Madison, 1995), pp. 35–41.

18 'Spies', *Evening Dispatch*, 28 August 1914, p. 1; 'Home Secretary and the Spy Question', *Coventry Evening Telegraph*, 28 August 1914, p. 3; 'The Spy Peril. Lord C. Beresford and the Home Office', *Dublin Daily Express*, 3 October 1914, p. 5; 'Lord C. Beresford and Alien Spies', *Exeter and Plymouth Gazette*, 3 October 1914, p. 3; 'Lord C. Beresford and the Spy Question', *Western Gazette*, 16 October 1914, p. 10.

19 Joynson-Hicks, *Hansard*, 9 September 1914.

20 Ibid., 16 September 1914.

21 Joynson-Hicks – McKenna, *Hansard*, 12 November 1914.

22 'Lord C. Beresford's Call', *Portsmouth Evening News*, 1 September 1914, p. 2; 'Lord Charles' Beresford's Appeal', *Yorkshire Post and Leeds Intelligencer*, 4 September 1914, p. 3; 'Lord Charles' Beresford's Appeal', *Birmingham Daily Post*, 7 September 1914, p. 8; 'Call to Arms at Halifax', *Yorkshire Post and Leeds Intelligencer*, 15 September 1914, p. 3; 'Lord Charles Beresford's Recruiting Campaign', *Leeds Mercury*, 17 September 1914, p. 4. The spy, however, was not absent from recruitment campaigns for long: 'Romford's Call for Men', *Chelmsford Chronicle*, 18 September 1914, p. 2; 'Great Recruitment Meeting at Kirkcaldy', *Fife Free Press and Kirkcaldy Guardian*, 24 October 1914, p. 3; Recruitment Meeting at Lockerbie', *Dumfries and Galloway Standard*, 25 November 1914, p. 6.

23 'Lord Charles Beresford and Alien Spies. An Infamous System', *Aberdeen Evening Express*, 3 October 1914, p. 4. Haste, *Keep the Home Fires Burning*, p. 114; Pennell, *A Kingdom United*, p. 112.
24 'Alien Enemies. Our Danger from Within', *Daily Record*, 13 October 1914, p. 2; 'Alien Enemies in Our Midst. Lord Chas. Beresford's Appeal', *Western Daily Press*, 13 October 1914, p. 5; 'False Friends in Our Midst. Lord C. Beresford and the Spy Danger', *Leeds Mercury*, 13 October 1914, p. 2; 'Enemies in England', *Cornishman*, 22 October 1914, p. 7.
25 Frans Coetzee, *For Party or Country? Nationalism and the Dilemmas of Popular Conservatism in Edwardian England* (Oxford, 1990), p. 96. For specific examples see L. J. Maxse, *Germany on the Brain or, the Obsession of a 'Crank': Gleanings from the National Review, 1899–1914* (London, 1915).
26 Peter Davies and Derek Lynch, *The Routledge Companion to Fascism and the Far Right* (London, 2002), p. 168.
27 In *German Spies in England*, Le Queux claimed that he was no party politician: 'My worst enemy could never call me that. I have never voted for a candidate in my life, for my motto has ever been "Britain for the British"' (p. 13). His public lectures were also styled as 'non-political': Surrey History Centre, ELIAA/1/p144/1: Lt-Col Elias Morgan Scrapbook.
28 In *The Riddle of the Sands*, for example, Erskine Childers explicitly called out ministers for failing to take national security seriously, while endorsing the creation of a naval reserve to shore up British defences (pp. 3, 89). See also Stafford, *The Silent Game*, pp. 6, 11; David Trotter, 'The Politics of Adventure', pp. 31–2.
29 Le Queux, *German Spies in England*, pp. 41–2.
30 Ibid., pp. 71, 103.
31 Ibid., p. 82.
32 Ibid., p. 104.
33 Maxse specifically wrote that 'at this crisis of our fate the British Empire is at the mercy of a cabal of short-sighted at self-seeking partisans, who will be tempted to subordinate permanent national interests to passing party exigencies'. 'Partisans and Patriotism', *National Review*, no. 381, November 1914.
34 'Episodes of the Month', *National Review*, no. 379, September 1914.
35 'What Every Cabinet Minister Knew', *National Review*, no. 381, November 1914.
36 'Undesirable Aliens', *National Review*, no. 382, December 1914.
37 *John Bull* similarly lambasted Britain's traditional hospitality to foreigners in this way: 'Points for Patriots', *John Bull*, vol. XVII, no. 429, p. 10.
38 Ian D. Colvin, *The Germans in England 1066–1598* (London, 1915), pp. xi–xxxi.
39 Panayi, 'The Hidden Hand', p. 257.
40 First, Beresford, Joynson-Hicks and the Lord Leith of Fyvie were all prominent members of the BEU, which provided a degree of unity and continuity with earlier associations. Second, their ideology was far from unique. They replicated Ian Colvin's conspiracy theories regarding the German 'Hidden Hand' and appropriated the Tariff Reformers' advocacy of imperial unity. Panayi, 'The British Empire Union', p. 125.
41 IWM docs. K52496-4: BEU no. 8, 'Britain in the Web of the German Spider'; K52496-5: BEU no. 9, 'What the British Empire Union Wants'; K52496-9: BEU no. 13, 'Germans in London the 'Mysterious Hand' of Influence at Work'; K52496-17: BEU no. 23, 'What the British Empire Union Advocates'.
42 'Anti-German Union Being Formed in Hull', *Hull Daily Mail*, 21 September 1915, p. 2; similar depictions were made elsewhere: 'The Enemy Alien Danger', *Western*

Mail, 6 November 1915, p. 8; 'Anti-German Demonstration in London', *Manchester Evening News*, 28 May 1915, p. 5; 'Spies in England', *Portsmouth Evening News*, 18 June 1915, p. 4.

43 Ada McGuire Papers, Letter dated 31 May 1915.

44 Beatrice Trefusis Papers, Diary entry 15 November 1914.

45 IWM docs. 6570: Papers of R. Saunders, Letter dated 1 November 1914.

46 Robert Blake, *The Conservative Party from Peel to Thatcher* (London, 1985), pp. 195–6; Trevor Wilson, *The Downfall of the Liberal Party 1914–35* (London, 1966), p. 55; Keohane, *The Party of Patriotism*, pp. 2–11.

47 Paul Readman, 'The Liberal Party and Patriotism in Early Twentieth Century Britain', *Twentieth Century British History* xii (2001), pp. 269–302.

48 Searle, 'The "Revolt from the Right"', p. 25; Frank McDonough, *The Conservative Party and Anglo-German Relations, 1905–1914* (Basingstoke, 2007), p. 9; Keohane, *The Party of Patriotism*, pp. 103, 209–11.

49 Gregory D. Phillips, 'Lord Willoughby de Broke: Radicalism and Conservatism', in J. A. Thompson and Arthur Mejia (eds), *Edwardian Conservatism: Five Studies in Adaption* (London, 1988), p. 78.

50 Eric Hobsbawm, *Industry and Empire: From 1750 to the Present Day* (London, 1968), p. 163; Paul Kennedy, 'The Pre War Right', in Kennedy and Nicholls, *Nationalist and Racialist Movements in Britain and Germany*, p. 1; Martin Blinkhorn, *Fascists and Conservatives: The Radical Right and the Establishment in Twentieth Century Europe* (London 1990), p. 2.

51 This idea was first conceived by Geoffrey Searle in 'The Revolt from the Right' but was initially challenged by Alan Sykes. Sykes argued that the radical right was 'all but swamped in a sea of traditional Conservatives defending traditional causes' to suggest that the 'Crisis of Conservatism' was over, but he mistakes the decline of tariff reform for the demise of a 'radical' alternative and confuses tactical disagreements with arguments over political principals. In fact, the radical right was at least as active and influential during the First World War as they had been beforehand. Searle, 'The "Revolt from the Right" in Edwardian Britain'.

52 Williams, *Defending the Empire*, p. 2; McDonough, *The Conservative Party and Anglo-German Relations*, p. 138.

53 G. C. Webber, 'Intolerance and Discretion: Conservatives and British Fascism, 1918–1926', in Tony Kushner and Kenneth Lunn (eds), *Traditions of Intolerance: Historical Perspectives on Fascism in Britain* (Manchester, 1989), p. 155. Panikos Panayi arrives at similar conclusions: 'Review Article: National and Racial Minorities in Total War', *Immigrants and Minorities* 9/2 (1990), p. 193.

54 Keohane, *The Party of Patriotism*, pp. 8, 14.

55 Coetzee and Coetzee, 'Rethinking the Radical Right', p. 516; Stuart Ball, *The Conservative Party and British Politics, 1902–1951* (London, 1995), p. 54; McDonough, *The Conservative Party and Anglo-German Relations*, p. 108.

56 McDonough, *The Conservative Party and Anglo-German Relations*, p. 108.

57 Coetzee, *For Party or Country*, p. 41.

58 McDonough, *The Conservative Party and Anglo-German Relations*, pp. 108–9.

59 Ibid., p. 113. Along with the Navy League, the National Service League shared the label of 'scaremonger': Coetzee, *For Party or Country*, p. 41.

60 Anne Summers, 'The Character of Edwardian Nationalism: Three Popular Leagues', in Kennedy and Nicholls (eds), *Nationalist and Racialist Movements*, pp. 68–87.

61 McDonough, *The Conservative Party and Anglo-German Relations*, p. 110.

62 Adrian Bingham and Martin Conboy, *Tabloid Century: The Popular Press in Britain, 1896 to the Present* (Oxford, 2015), pp. 28, 203–5. Horatio Bottomley referred to the 'great debt of gratitude' the nation owed to the *Daily Mail* and the *Evening News*, for example. 'Spies, Bombs and Butchery', *John Bull*, vol. XVII, no. 439, 31 October 1914, p. 4.

63 'The Voice in the Wilderness That Was Heard at Last', *John Bull*, vol. XVII, 428, 15 August 1914, p. 6.

64 'A "Tame" Reichstag', *National Review*, October 1908, in Maxse, *Germany on the Brain*, pp. 257–8.

65 'The Titanic', *National Review*, May 1912, in Maxse, *Germany on the Brain*, p. 320. Maxse first realized that the majority of the Conservative Party no longer believed as he did following the issues over tariff reform in 1912. After the failure of this cause that he had supported so vigorously, Maxse became so engrossed in his own efforts to discredit the Liberal Party that he was no longer averse to encouraging internal dissent among Conservatives. Hutchinson, *Leopold Maxse and the National Review*, pp. 405–6.

66 BL Add MS 62225: Lord Northcliffe papers LXXIII, Letter from Leo Maxse, 16 November 1910, f.21; Henry Wilson Papers, 2/73/59: Letter from Leo Maxse, 26 September 1914.

67 West Sussex Record Office, Maxse Mss 3/2/1/445: 'The National Review's Computations of Profit'.

68 Lord Northcliffe papers LXXIII, Letter from Leo Maxse, 8 July 1915, f.64. Maxse was also told by the Earl of Crawford that half the Cabinet were increasingly in favour of a more vigorous approach, long advocated by Maxse, suggesting that his ideals were becoming more palatable to society. West Sussex Record Office, Maxse Mss 3/2/1/370: Papers of Leo Maxse, Letter from David Lindsay, 7 January 1915.

69 Jan Rüger convincingly argues that interest in militaristic pageantry and entertainment should not be mistaken as a popular militarism that complimented or affirmed government strategies, and that not every participant identified themselves as part of a 'warrior nation': *The Great Naval Game: Britain and Germany in the Age of Empire* (Cambridge, 2009), pp. 124–5.

70 Coetzee and Coetzee, 'Rethinking the Radical Right', pp. 521–9.

71 Thurlow, *Fascism in Britain*, pp. 2–3.

72 Geoffrey Crossick, 'The Emergence of the Lower Middle Class in Britain', in Geoffrey Crossick (ed.), *The Lower Middle Class in Britain 1870–1914* (London, 1977), pp. 40–4; Searle, 'The "Revolt from the Right" in Edwardian Britain', p. 35; Summers, 'Character of Edwardian Nationalism', p. 84.

73 IWM docs. K52496-4: BEU no. 8, 'Britain in the Web of the German Spider'; and K52496-9: BEU no. 13, 'Germans in London the 'Mysterious Hand' of Influence at Work'.

74 IWM docs. K52496-5: BEU no. 9, 'What the British Empire Union Wants'.

75 IWM docs. K52496-20: BEU no. 9, 'Aims and Objects'; BEU no. 23, 'What the British Empire Union Advocates'.

76 IWM docs. K52496-2: BEU no. 3, 'British Wages for British Pockets'; K52496-7: BEU no. 11, 'What Our Men Will Want'; K52496-21: BEU no. 12, 'Women of the Empire This Is Your War!'

77 *Thanet Advertiser*, 2 January 1915, p. 4.

78 Churchill, *Thoughts and Adventures*, p. 89. However, this did not stop Churchill from ingratiating himself with this group of people. In September 1914, he delivered

a speech as First Lord of the Admiralty during which he professed to receive daily evidence of German espionage in Britain: 'Naval Lord's Speech', *Chelmsford Chronicle*, 25 September 1914, p. 2.

79   Glover, *Psychology of Fear and Courage*, p. 54.

80   'The Enemy in Our Midst', *Manchester Courier and Lancashire General Advertiser*, 21 October 1914, p. 4.

81   'Spy Mania', *Walsall Advertiser*, 15 August 1914, p. 5. Lucy Broadwood similarly described how attacks on aliens were being carried out by 'rough people': Papers of Lucy Broadwood, Diary entry 13 May 1915.

82   Richard Haldane, *Richard Burdon Haldane: An Autobiography* (London, 1929), p. 284.

83   'Playing the German Game', *Hull Daily Mail*, 24 May 1915, p. 6.

84   Hunt later joined the far-right National Party in 1917.

85   TNA HO 45/10727/254753: Alien Enemies Possession of Firearms, Carrier Pigeons etc., 12 September 1914.

86   'Victim of the Spy Crusade', *Arbroath Herald*, 6 November 1914, p. 2.

87   Maxse Papers, Mss 3/2/1/469: Letter from Shelley Scarlett, 1 September 1914.

88   'The Spy Question', *Army and Navy Gazette*, 17 October 1914, p. 5.

89   Panayi, 'Anti-German Riots', p. 188; Robb, *Culture and the First World War*, p. 9.

90   Stuart Hall and Bill Schwarz, 'State and Society, 1380–1930', in Mary Langan and Bill Schwarz (eds), *Crisis in the British State, 1880–1930* (London, 1985), pp. 7–32; Matthew Johnson, 'The Liberal War Committee and the Liberal Advocacy of Conscription in Britain, 1914–1916', *The Historical Journal* 51/2 (2008), pp. 399–420; Keohane, *The Party of Patriotism*, p. 6.

91   'Registration of Aliens', *Bexhill-on-Sea Observer*, 22 August 1914, p. 5; 'Spy Allegations', *Aberdeen Evening Express*, 28 August 1914, p. 3; 'Enemies in Our Midst', *Diss Express*, 18 September 1914, p. 3; 'Comments on Current Topics', *Edinburgh Evening News*, 12 October 1914, p. 4; 'Is the Spy Question Killed?', *Edinburgh Evening News*, 19 October 1914, p. 4; 'The Treatment of Alien Enemies', *Hull Daily Mail*, 23 October 1914, p. 4; 'Amusing Kirkcaldy "Scare" Story', *Edinburgh Evening News*, 26 October 1914, p. 2; 'Spy Gossip', *Fifeshire Advertiser*, 5 January 1915, p. 3; 'Police Work in Wartime', *Dorking and Leatherhead Advertiser*, 9 January 1915, p. 8; 'The Lords and Invasion', *Whitby Gazette*, 15 January 1915, p. 6.

92   'Spy Hunting Mania', *Nottingham Journal*, 8 August 1914, p. 4.

93   'The Spy Scare', *Aberdeen Evening Express*, 8 August 1914, p. 4; 'Chelsea Gossip', *Chelsea News and General Advertiser*, 6 November 1914, p. 5; 'The German Spy', *Arbroath Herald*, 23 October 1914, p. 4.

94   Cambridgeshire Archives, 531/F/1: Papers of Rev. Canon P. G. Ward, Diary entry 25 October 1915.

95   'The Rev. J. Osborne and the War', *Bexhill-on-Sea Observer*, 21 November 1914, p. 2.

96   'The Aliens' Portion', *Dublin Daily Express*, 17 August 1914, p. 4; 'Spies in England', *Liverpool Echo*, 15 October 1914, p. 5; 'Chaplain's Life in Germany', *Warwick and Warwickshire Advertiser*, 17 July 1915, p. 4.

97   'British Aeroplane Raid Spreads Terror', *Western Mail*, 2 October 1914, p. 6; 'Berwickshire Lady's Experiences in Germany', *Berwickshire News and General Advertiser*, 6 October 1914, p. 6; 'Germans Enfiladed', *Aberdeen Evening Express*, 6 November 1914, p. 3; 'Irish Nun's Story of the Germans', *Dorking and Leatherhead Advertiser*, 17 July 1915, p. 8.

 98 'Short shrift for Spies', *Portsmouth Evening News*, 7 August 1914, p. 6; 'Germany
     from the Inside', *Bexhill-on-Sea Observer*, 5 September 1914, p. 2; 'Through German
     Goggles', *Aberdeen Evening Express*, 23 November 1915, p. 2.
 99 'Berlin News', *Portsmouth Evening News*, 20 August 1914, p. 3; 'A Song of Blood',
     Whitby Gazette, 21 August 1914, p. 4.
100 'Danger of Mob Violence', *Western Mail*, 8 August 1914, p. 5.
101 'Plea for Fair Play', *Stroud Journal*, 14 August 1914.
102 'Victim of the Spy Crusade', *Arbroath Herald*, 6 November1914, p. 2. This incident
     also demonstrates the widening ideological divide taking place within society.
     The 'suspect' was targeted because of connections to a Liberal Association in a
     notoriously right-wing district, which made him an adversary of the local Tory
     leadership and, consequently, a target of mob vigilance under the portents that he
     was a spy.
103 'Germans in England', *Birmingham Daily Post*, 11 August 1914, p. 2.
104 Although Pamala Horn's study of English rural life during the First World War
     includes a number of frivolous spy stories, she concedes that they were usually
     caused by the government's defensive measures and were not necessary characteristic
     of rural attitudes: Pamala Horn, *Rural Life in England in the First World War* (Dublin,
     1984), pp. 36–8.
105 *Belper News*, 11 September 1914, p. 2.
106 'Walking in Darkness', *Arbroath Herald and Advertiser for the Montrose Burghs*, 25
     September 1914, p. 4.
107 'Town Talk', *Bexhill-on-Sea Observer*, 13 March 1914, p. 4.
108 'Aliens on the Coast', *Hull Daily Mail*, 5 February 1915, p. 6.
109 Lynch, *Yorkshire's War*, p. 36. Lynch, however, does also highlight anti-German
     activity across Yorkshire more generally, pp. 36–41.
110 John St Loe Strachey Papers, STR/10/3/5: Letter dated 19 October 1914.
111 'Germans in England', *The Globe*, 25 August 1914, p. 6; 'Fairplay to Germans', *The
     Globe*, 28 October 1914, p. 4.
112 'Germans in England', *The Globe*, 21 August 1914, p. 8.
113 Parodying the invasion and spy genres had been well established by comics such as
     A. A. Milne and P. G. Wodehouse during the previous decade: Charles Lowe, 'About
     German Spies', *Contemporary Review* 97 (January 1910), pp. 42–56; A. A. Milne,
     'The Secret of the Army Aeroplabe', *Punch* (26 May 1909), p. 366; P. G. Woodhouse,
     'The Swoop! Or How Clarence Saved England: A Tale of the Great Invasion', in P.
     G. Woodhouse, *The Swoop! And Other Stories* (New York, 1979), pp. 2–25. Nicholas
     Hiley, 'The Play, the Parody, the Censor and the Film', *Intelligence and National
     Security* 6/1 (1991), p. 222; Harry Wood, 'Sharpening the Mind: The German Menace
     and Edwardian National Identity', in Naomi Carle, Samuel Shaw and Sarah Shaw
     (eds), *Edwardian Culture: Beyond the Garden Party* (Abingdon, 2018), pp. 115–32.
114 *Monmouthshire Beacon*, 17 September 1915, p. 8.
115 *Portsmouth Evening News*, 11 August 1915, p. 6.
116 Barbara Duguid Papers, 'The Unforgivable Years, 1914–1918' (1984),
     p. 9; Proctor, *Female Intelligence*, p. 37; Linda D. Henman, 'Humor as a Coping
     Mechanism: Lessons from POWs', *Humor* 14/1 (2001), pp. 83–94; Andreas C.
     Samson and James J. Gross, 'Humour as Emotion Regulation: The Differential
     Consequences of Negative versus Positive Humour', *Cognition and Emotion* 26/2
     (2012), pp. 375–84.

117 Clémentine Tholas-Disset and Karen A. Ritzenhoff, 'Introduction', in Clémentine Tholas-Disset and Karen A. Ritzenhoff (eds), *Humor, Entertainment, and Popular Culture during World War 1* (Basingstoke, 2015), p. 1.
118 Koenraad Du Pont, 'Nature and Functions of Humor in Trench Newspapers (1914–1918)', in Tholas-Disset and Ritzenhoff (eds), *Humor, Entertainment, and Popular Culture during World War 1*, p. 112; Edward Madigan, ' "Sticking to a Hateful Task": Resilience, Humour, and British Understandings of Combatant Courage, 1914–1918', *War in History* 20/1 (2013), p. 93.
119 Ruben Quintero, 'Introduction: Understanding Satire', in Ruben Quintero (ed.), *A Companion to Satire: Ancient and Modern* (Oxford, 2011), p. 1.
120 Jill E. Twark, 'Approaching History as Cultural Memory through Humour, Satire, Comics and Graphic Novels', *Contemporary European History* 26/1 (2017), p. 176.
121 *Reading Mercury*, 31 October 1914, p. 8.
122 *Faringdon Advertiser and Vale of the White Horse Gazette*, 19 December 1914, p. 2.
123 *Reading Mercury*, 24 October 1914, p. 8.
124 *Faringdon Advertiser*, 2 January 1915, p. 6.
125 *Bucks Herald*, 27 February 1915, p. 3.
126 *Portsmouth Evening News*, 13 February 1915, p. 2.
127 Norman Macleod Papers, Diary entry 16 September 1914; Thomas Swift Papers, Diary entry 28 September 1914.
128 Norfolk Record Office, MC 2235/1/32/107, 943XB: Papers of Peter Henry Emerson, Letter dated 19 October 1914.
129 Liddle TR 05 58: Tape recording of Dr Odlum (1981).
130 East Ridings Record Office, DDST/1/8/2/1: Papers of Margaret Elizabeth-Constable, Diary entry 10 June 1915.
131 East Ridings Record Office, DDST/1/8/2/2: Papers of Margaret Elizabeth-Constable, Diary entry for December 1915.
132 TNA MEPO 3/243: William Le Queux Request for Personal Protection (1914–15).
133 BL Add MS 62225: Papers of Lord Northcliffe, vol. LXXIII, Letter from Leo Maxse, 8 July 1915, f.65.
134 BL Add MS 62159: Papers of Lord Northcliffe, vol. VII, Letter to Admiral Fisher, 29 December 1914, f.20.
135 Papers of Lord Northcliffe LXXIII, Letter to Leo Maxse, 20 December 1916, f.80. It is unclear which Lord Hardinge Maxse was originally referring to. An article in *Truth*, however, had similarly criticized Lord Charles Hardinge, Viceroy of India, of taking a soft approach to Germans: 'Germans in India', *Truth*, 13 October 1915.
136 BL Add MS 62327: Papers of Lord Northcliffe CLXXV, Letter to Herbert Asquith, 3 November 1914, f.59.
137 BL Add MS 62158: Lord Northcliffe Papers, vol. VI, Letter to Bonar Law, f.26.
138 Margaret Flaws, *Spy Fever: The Post Office Affair* (Lerwick, 2009).
139 Panayi, *Enemy in Our Midst*, p. 153.

Chapter 7

1 Lord Charles Beresford, *Hansard*, 28 August 1914.
2 'Danger of Aliens', *Western Mail*, 11 November 1914, p. 11; The Earl of Crawford, *Hansard*, 25 November 1914.

3   Le Queux, *German Spies in England*, p. 8.

4   Ibid., pp. 14–19.

5   'Undesirable Aliens', *National Review*, no. 382, December 1914.

6   BL Add MS 62225, vol. LXXIII, Northcliffe Papers, Letter from Leo Maxse, 8 July 1915.

7   So impressed by his own work was he that he claimed the War Office, comparatively at least, knew nothing about German espionage: 'War Office and Britain's Deadly Peril', *Liverpool Echo*, 14 April 1915, p. 7.

8   The first category, 'Spy Scares', refers to all instances in which individuals were suspected of conducting illicit activities, whether that be through official investigations and prosecutions or ad hoc spy hunts. 'Alarmist Rhetoric' includes intangible reports of covert activities that exaggerate the threat, make claims about the scale of popular agitation, contain references to anti-alien sentiment or behaviour or criticize the government. 'Popular Culture' includes all adverts and reviews of books, plays, and films that make references to spies as well as historical narratives that involve cases of espionage, sabotage or intrigue. The final category, 'Opposition', includes rhetoric in favour of showing tolerance to aliens and opposes popular prejudices as well as satirical caricatures of the spy peril designed to highlight the idiocy of such attitudes and feelings.

9   'Spy Mania', *Walsall Advertiser*, 22 August 1914, p. 4.

10 The number of issues printed in urban publications means that they essentially formed the average. To have a fair comparison between urban and rural newspapers, the same number of issues from each group would have to be analysed, which is made difficult by the fact that rural papers were printed weekly, rather than daily.

11 Thirty-three per cent compared with 26 per cent in urban papers.

12 Pennell, *Kingdom United*, p. 44.

13 Surrey History Centre, The Lennards of Clare Lodge, 10181/1: Diary entry 7 August 1914; Diary of Emily Marion Blathwayt, 30 October 1914.

14 Lancashire Archives and Record Office DDX 1841/1/40: Bamber Family Records, John Bamber Diary, 8–10 August 1914.

15 IWM Sound. 13386: Eileen Margaret 'Peggy' Larken (1993) reels 1 and 2. Even if untrue or a slightly distorted memory, any hostility aimed at von Herkimer went seemingly unnoticed by Larken suggesting that it was insignificant in her local context.

16 Liddle GS/1640: Papers of N. A. Turner-Smith, Diary entry 23 August 1915, p. 36.

17 Bedfordshire Record Office, X978/5: Papers of Bruce J. Stanbridge, Diary entry for August 1914.

18 The diary attentively recorded the diplomatic context, which nations were entering the war, where fighting was taking place, how events were affecting the continent, the fighting capabilities of British troops and comments by prominent figures. Lincolnshire Archives, MISC DEP 265/32: Papers of Fannie Rainey Fieldsend, Diary entry 5 August 1914.

19 IWM docs. 74/135/1: Papers of Reverend J. Mackay, Diary entry 4 August 1914; Papers of M. Coules, Journal, June 1914–November 1915, p. 5; Harry Miller Papers, Diary of Jeanne Berman, 6 August 1914; Norman Macleod Papers, Diary entry 18 August 1914.

20 Boghardt, *Spies of the Kaiser*, p. 91.

21 Aberdeen City Archives, Aberdeen Harbour Records, CA/14/4/31: Harbour Commissioner's Incoming Letter Book 1914–16, 1 November 1914, p. 78b.

22 Ibid., 4 December 1914, p. 78c.

23 This type of request was more than enough to warrant suspicion. The editor of *The Spectator*, for example, wrote to the Foreign Secretary, Edward Grey, after receiving two mysterious letters purportedly from foreign attaches. He requested that the police investigate simply because of their anonymity. John St Loe Strachey Papers, STR/7/8/26: Letter dated 18 February 1915.

24 Diary of Andrew Clark, vol. II, 25 September 1914, p. 110; Northcliffe Papers, vol. CLXXV, Letter from Northcliffe to General Wilson, dated 17 November 1914.

25 Plymouth and West Devon Record Office, 511/1: Papers of Charles Calmady-Hamlyn, Letter from W. Eares, 8 August 1914; Helen Beatrice Fane Papers, Diary entry 1 October 1914.

26 Bodleian Library Special Collections, MSS. Top. Oxon. e. 288, Diary of Horace William Brindley Joseph, 14 August 1914, pp. 17–18.

27 Arthur Barwick Lloyd-Baker Papers, Diary entry 5 August 1914.

28 Frederick Arthur Robinson Papers, Diary entry 13 August 1914.

29 West Yorkshire Archives Service, Bradford, WYB335/4: Papers of Edith Usher, Diary entry 4 April 1915.

Conclusion

1   IWM docs. 16020: 'An account by Ernest Lycette of his life as a young man and soldier in the years between 1911 and 1921' (1966).

2   On 25 May 1917, an attack by twenty-three Gotha bombers killed 95 people and injured a further 192 in a single raid. For context, Zeppelins killed 556 people throughout the entirety of the war.

3   Gregory, *Last Great War*, pp. 213–16, 234.

4   'Episodes of the Month', *National Review*, no. 346 (December 1911), p. 499.

5   'Episodes of the Month', *National Review*, no. 350 (April 1912), p. 189.

6   Panayi, 'Hidden Hand', pp. 254–5.

7   Ibid., p. 257.

8   George Makgill, 'The German Invasion', *English Review* XXI (December 1915), pp. 487–8.

9   Panayi, 'Hidden Hand', pp. 260–1.

10 Ellis Powell, 'The Unseen Hand: The Case for a Judicial Investigation', *National Review* 408 (February 1917), p. 751.

11 Powell, 'The Unseen Hand', p. 752.

12 Panayi, 'Hidden Hand', pp. 262–3.

13 Arnold White, *The Hidden Hand* (London, 1917), p. 16.

14 Ibid., pp. 235–7.

15 Ibid., pp. 38–41.

16 Ibid., p. 48.

17 Powell, 'The Unseen Hand', p. 754.

18 White, *Hidden Hand*, p. 17.

19 Ibid., p. 195.

20 Ian D. Colvin, *The Unseen Hand in English History* (London, 1917), p. 7.
21 Ibid., pp. 15–16, 133.
22 Ibid., pp. 6–7.
23 Gregory, *Last Great War*, pp. 238–41.
24 Panayi, 'Hidden Hand', pp. 267–70.
25 Gregory, *Last Great War*, pp. 234–5.
26 Although it was alleged that Jews had been sexually corrupting Britain by maintaining an army of prostitutes spreading venereal disease and causing more harm than any weapon conceivable: Panayi, 'Hidden Hand', p. 265.
27 Hoare, *Wilde's Last Stand*, pp. 91–8; Angus McLaren, *Twentieth-Century Sexuality: A History* (Oxford, 1999), pp. 9–10.
28 Hoare, *Wilde's Last Stand*, pp. 1, 25–39.
29 Panayi, 'Hidden Hand', pp. 266–7.
30 The trial coincided with the Third Battle of the Aisne, in which the German army advanced 34 miles in less than a week.

BIBLIOGRAPHY

Archival sources

Aberdeenshire and Aberdeen City Archives
    Aberdeen Harbour Records
    Banffshire Constabulary Records
    Elginshire County Constabulary Records
Bedfordshire Record Office
    Bruce J. Stanbridge Papers
Bodleian Library Special Collections
    Andrew Clark Diary
    Horace William Brindley Joseph Diary
British Library
    Alfred Harmsworth, Viscount Northcliffe, Papers
Caithness Archives
    Caithness County Constabulary Records
    Margaret Davidson Correspondence
    Collection of Letters from or to people in Caithness
Cambridgeshire Archives
    Evelyn Diver Diary
    Reverend Canon P. G. Ward Diary
Centre for Buckinghamshire Studies
    Buckinghamshire Constabulary Records
Derbyshire Record Office
    Derbyshire Constabulary and Borough Constabularies Records
    John Hunter of Belper Papers
East Ridings Record Office
    Margaret Elizabeth Strickland-Constable Papers
East Sussex Record Office
    Sussex Police Authority Records
Essex Record Office
    George H. Rose Papers
    Essex County Constabulary Records
    'Syd's Memoires'
Fife Archives
    Monteith Family Papers
Gloucestershire Archives

Maynard W. Colchester-Wemyss Correspondence
Stroud Journal Extracts
Emily Marion Blathwayt Diary
Mary Blathwayt Diary
Canon Rowan Ernest Grice-Hutchinson Diary
William Thomas Swift Diary
Arthur Barwick Lloyd-Baker Diary
Gwent Archives
Griffithstown Police Station Records
Newport Constabulary Records
Hull History Centre
Hull City Police Records
Robert Redhead Papers
Imperial War Museum
Anonymous Home Front Diary
Anonymous Royal Naval Division Memoir
Leaflets Produced by the British Empire Union
Letters Describing Zeppelin Raids
Ada McGuire Papers
Arthur Reginald Read Papers
E. R. Cooper Papers
F. T. Lockwood Papers
G. M. West Papers
George Fear Papers
H. Miller Papers
Major General Sir Vernon Kell Papers
Miss M. Coules Papers
Olive Armstrong Papers
Reverend J. Mackay Papers
Robert Saunders Papers
W. L. B. Tower MBE Papers
W. V. Hindle Papers
Sound Recording of Eileen Margaret Larken
Sound Recording of John Raymond Mallalieu
Sound Recordings of James Davidson Pratt
Mrs Purbrook Papers
Albert Edward Gumm Papers
Augustus Gordon Stewart Papers
Charles Cuthbert Aston Papers
Ernest Lycette Papers
Geoffrey Archibald Loyd Papers
G .O. Chambers Papers
Arthur Francis Smith Papers
J. G. Coulson Papers
Norman Macleod Papers

Field Marshal Henry Wilson Papers
Percival Charles Cobb Papers
Kenneth Stuart Hall Papers
J. W. Barrett Memoir Papers
G. Harding Papers
R. A. Watts Papers
Hissey Family Papers
John Lawton Papers
Inverness Archive
J. Skarpnes Papers
William Campbell Diary
Lancashire Archives and Record Office
Bamber Family Records
Leicestershire Record Office
Leicestershire Constabulary Records
Leicestershire Regiment Records
Lord Lieutenant's Papers
Arthur Percival Marsh Papers
Donald L. Weir Papers
Lieutenant Colonel Herbert Stoney Smith Diary
Memories of a Trench Rat by Jack Horner
Library and Archives of Canada
RG9 Canadian Expeditionary Force
Liddle Collection, Brotherton Library, University of Leeds
Extracts from an East Anglican Magistrate's Diary
G. H. Bickmore Papers
Jock Dunning Macleod Papers
A. E. Bumpuss Papers
A. S. Hare Papers
Albert Murray Papers
Albert Robert Williamson Papers
Arthur Hoyer Alexander Papers
Barbara Duguid Papers
Barbara Dunn Papers
Beatrice Morwenna Trefusis Papers
C. G. W. Joss Papers
Dame Elizabeth Cockayne Papers
Dame Margery Irene Corbett-Ashby Papers
Dorothy Bowes Papers
Elizabeth Bracher Papers
Florence Schuster Papers
Frederick Arthur Robinson Papers
Frederick H. Hunt Papers
G. H. Elliot Papers
Harry Innes Papers

Hilda W. Davison Papers
J. Southall Papers
K. M. Alexander Papers
L. B. Stanley Papers
Lord Cecil Forester Papers
M. Burton Papers
Major General Dudley Graham Johnson Papers
Margaret Ulph Currie Papers
N. A. Turner-Smith Papers
Nell Hague Papers
Norah S. Bristow Papers
Professor A. D. Gardiner Papers
R. Herring Papers
Reverend Wolstan Dixie Churchill Papers
Richard Astry Bourne Orlebar Papers
T. H. Kirk Papers
W. Pritchett Papers
William Foster Papers
Sound Recording of Dr Odlum
I. Vivienne Duchenne Papers
Louisa Charlotte Harris Papers
Alison MacIntyre Papers
Roderick Henry MacLeod Papers
Augustus Gordon Stewart Papers
Liddle Hart Centre for Military Archives, King's College London
James Edmonds Papers
Lincoln Museum
Alfred Thurlow Diary
Lincolnshire Archives
Fane of Fulbeck Papers
Fannie Rainey Fieldsend Papers
Lincolnshire Regiment Records
National Maritime Museum
Arnold White Papers
Norfolk Record Office
Norfolk County Constabulary Records
Oliver Locker-Lampson MP Collection
Peter Henry Emerson Papers
Walter Rye Papers
Northamptonshire Record Office
Frederick Charles Kench Papers
Parliamentary Archives
Bonar Law Papers

John St Loe Strachey Papers
Lloyd George Papers
Ralph David Blumenfeld Papers
Plymouth and West Devon Record Office
    Charles Calmady-Hamlyn Papers
Stoke City Archives
    Stoke on Trent City Police Records
Surrey History Centre
    Edith Mary Ware Diary
    Ethel Lousia Hutchinson Duperier Diary
    Lieutenant Colonel St Barbe Russell Sladen Diary
    Beatrice Ethel Maclagan Diary
    Richard Onslow Papers
    L. W. Smith Personal Reminiscences
    Lucy Broadwood Diary
    Lieutenant Colonel Elias Morgan Scrapbook
    Colonel L W. Merrow-Smith Scrapbook
    Susan Lushington Papers
    Surrey Constabulary Records
    The Lennards of Clare Lodge Family Diary
The National Archives
    Admiralty
    Air
    Cabinet Office
    Domestic Records of the Public Record Office
    Home Office
    Metropolitan Police
    Security Service (MI5)
    War Office
Westminster Archives
    Archibald Walker Diary
West Sussex Record Office
    The Goodwood Estate Archives
    West Sussex Constabulary Records
    Leopold Maxse Papers
West Yorkshire Archives Service: Bradford
    Edith Usher Diary
West Yorkshire Archives Service: Wakefield
    Menston Asylum Records

Newspapers and periodicals

Aberdeen Evening Express
Aberdeen Journal

Arbroath Herald and Advertiser
Army and Navy Gazette
Ballymena Observer
Banbury Advertiser
Bedfordshire Times and Independent
Belfast Telegraph
Belper News
Berwickshire News
Bexhill-on-Sea Observer
Birmingham Daily Post
Birmingham Mail
Bradford Observer
Brecon County Times
Buckingham Advertiser and Free Press
Bucks Herald
Caernarvon Herald
Cardiff Times
Chelmsford Chronicle
Chelsea News and General Advertiser
Cheshire Observer
Contemporary Review
Cornishman
Daily Citizen
Daily Record
Derby Daily Telegraph
Derbyshire Courier
Diss Express
Dorking and Leatherhead Advertiser
Dover Express
Drogheda Independent
Dublin Daily Express
Dumfries and Galloway Standard
Edinburgh Evening News
English Review
Evening Herald
Exeter and Plymouth Gazette
Faringdon Advertiser and Vale of the White Horse Gazette
Fife Free Press
Glamorgan Gazette
Hawick Express
Hull Daily Mail
John Bull
Kilrush Herald

Kilsyth Chronicle
Leeds Mercury
Leicestershire Chronicle
Liverpool Echo
London Evening Standard
Manchester Courier and Lancashire General Advertiser
Manchester Evening News
Monmouthshire Beacon
Motherwell Times
Nairnshire Telegraph
Nantwich Guardian
National Review
Northampton Mercury
Northern Whig
Nottingham Journal
Penrith Observer
Portsmouth Evening News
Punch
Reading Mercury
Review of Reviews
Royal United Services Institution Journal
Sheffield Independent
Shepton Mallet Journal
Shields Daily Gazette
Shipley Times
Sligo Champion
Southern Reporter
Stroud Journal
Tamworth Herald
Thanet Advertiser
The Globe
The Nation
Truth
Vigilante
Walsall Advertiser
Warwick and Warwickshire Advertiser
Western Daily Press
Western Mail
Western Times
Westminster Gazette
Whitby Gazette
Whitehaven News
Whitstable Times
Yorkshire Post and Intelligencer

Published primary sources

Asquith, Margot. *The Autobiography of Margot Asquith*. 2 vols. Vol. 2. London: Thornton Butterworth, 2022.

Aston, George. *Secret Service*. London: Faber and Faber, 1930.

Baden-Powell, Robert. *My Adventures as a Spy*. Stroud: Amberley, 2014.

Baggs, Thomas A. *Back from the Front: An Eyewitness's Narrative of the Beginnings of the Great War of 1914*. London: F&C Palmer, 1914.

Blumenfeld, R. D. *RDB's Diary, 1887–1914*. London: William Heinemann, 1930.

Buchan, John. *The Thirty-Nine Steps*. New York: George H Doran, 1915.

Charteris, John. *At GHQ*. London: Cassell, 1931.

Childers, Erskine, and David Trotter (eds). *The Riddle of the Sands*. Oxford: Oxford University Press, 2008.

Churchill, Winston Spencer, and James W. Muller (eds). *Thoughts and Adventures: Churchill Reflects on Spies, Cartoons, Flying, and the Future*. Wilmington, NC: ISI, 2009.

Colvin, Ian D. *The Germans in England, 1066–1598*. London: National Review, 1915.

Colvin, Ian D. *The Unseen Hand in English History*. London: National Review, 1917.

Conrad, Joseph. *The Secret Agent: A Simple Tale*. London: Penguin, 2007.

Corbett, Julian S. *Naval Operations Vol. I: To the Battle of the Falklands December 1914*. London: Longmans, Green, 1920.

Emden, Richard Van, and Steve Humphries (eds), *All Quiet on the Home Front: An Oral History of Life in Britain during the First World War*. London: Headline, 2003.

Falstead, Sidney Theodore. *German Spies at Bay: Being an Actual Record of the German Espionage in Great Britain during the Years 1914–1918*. New York: Brentano's, 1920.

Gibbs, Philip. *Adventures in Journalism*. London: Harper, 1923.

Grant, Hamil. *Spies and Secret Service: The Story of Espionage, Its Main Systems and Chief Exponents*. London: Grant Richards, 1915.

Graves, Armgaard Karl. *The Secrets of the German War Office*. New York: AL Burt, 1914.

Haldane, Richard. *Richard Burdon Haldane: An Autobiography*. London: Hodder and Stoughton, 1929.

Halsalle, Henry De. *Who Goes There? Being an Account of the Secret Service Adventures of 'Ex-Intelligence' during the Great War of 1914–1918*. London: Hutchinson, 1927.

Harrison, F. *The German Peril: Forecasts 1864–1914, Realities 1915, Hopes 191-*. London: T Fisher Unwin, 1915.

Harvey, Brian W., and Carol Fitzgerald (eds), *Edward Heron-Allen's Journal of the Great War: From Sussex Shore to Flanders Fields*. Chichester: Phillimore, 2002.

Hobson, J. A. *The Psychology of Jingoism*. London: Grant Richards, 1901.

James, Lionel. *The German Spy System from Within*. London: Hodder & Stoughton, 1914.

Kell, Constance, and Chris Northcott (eds). *A Secret Well Kept: The Untold Story of Sir Vernon Kell Founder of MI5*. London: Bloomsbury, 2017.

Kipling, Rudyard, and Susan Cooper (eds). *Kim*. London: Penguin, 2011.

Landau, Henry. *The Enemy Within: The Inside Story of German Sabotage in America*. New York: G. P. Putnam's, 1937.

Le Queux, William. *German Spies in England: An Exposure*. Toronto: Thomas Langton, 1915.

Le Queux, William. *The German Spy System from Within*. London: Hodder and Stoughton, 1914.

Le Queux, William. *The Invasion of 1910 with a Full Account of the Siege of London*. Toronto: Macmillan, 1906.

Le Queux, William. *The Man from Downing Street* London: Hurst & Blackett, 1904.

Le Queux, William. *Spies of the Kaiser: Plotting the Downfall of England*. London: Hurst & Blackett, 1908.

Leete, Alfred. *Schmidt the Spy and His Messages to Berlin*. London: Duckworth, 1916.

Lynn, Escott. *In Khaki for the King*. London: W & R Chambers, 1915.

Mary Anderson, Mary. *A Few More Memories*. London: Hutchinson, 1936.

Maxse, L. J. *Germany on the Brain or, the Obsession of a 'Crank': Gleanings from the National Review, 1899–1914*. London: National Review, 1915.

Oppenheim, Phillips, E. *The Great Secret*. Boston, MA: Colonial Press, 1908.

Oppenheim, Phillips, E. *Mysterious Mr. Sabin*. New York: McKinley, Stone & Mackenzie, 1905.

Peel, C. S. *How We Lived Then, 1914–1918: A Sketch of Social and Domestic Life in England during the War*. London: Bodley Head, 1929.

Scott, Canon Frederick George. *The Great War as I Saw It*. Toronto: F. D. Goodchild, 1922.

Steinhauer, Gaustav, and Sidney Felstead (eds). *The Kaiser's Master Spy: The Story as Told by Himself*. London: John Lane, 1930.

Stevenson, Burton E. *Little Comrade: A Tale of the Great War*. New York: Henry Holt, 1915.

The Earl of Oxford and Asquith, *Memories and Reflections: 1852–1927, Vol.2*. London: Cassell, 1928.

Thomson, Basil. *Queer People*. London: Forgotten, 2015.

Trebitsch-Lincoln, Ignatius Timothy. *Revelations of an International Spy*. New York: Robert M. McBride, 1916.

Waddell, William Freeland. *The Patriot and the Spies*. Paisley: Alexander Gardner, 1915.

White, Arnold. *The Hidden Hand*. London: Grant Richards, 1917.

Wodehouse, P. G. *The Swoop! And Other Stories*. New York: Seabury, 1979.

Worral, Lechmere, and J. E. Harold Terry. *The Man Who Stayed at Home*. London: Samuel French, 1916.

Secondary literature

Books

Akçam, Taner. *A Shameful Act: The Armenian Genocide and the Question of Turkish Responsibility*. New York: Metropolitan, 2006.

Akin, Yiğit. *When the War Came Home: The Ottomans' Great War and the Devastation of an Empire*. Stanford, CA: Stanford University Press, 2018.

Andrew, Christopher. *The Defence of the Realm: The Authorized History of MI5*. London: Penguin, 2010.

Andrew, Christopher. *Secret Service: The Making of the British Intelligence Community*. Sevenoaks: Sceptre, 1986.

Ball, Stuart. *The Conservative Party and British Politics, 1902–1951*. London: Longman, 1995.

Barclay, Katie. *The History of Emotions: A Student Guide to Methods and Sources*. London: Bloomsbury, 2020.

Beckett, Ian, Timothy Bowman, and Mark Connelly. *The British Army and the First World War*. Cambridge: Cambridge University Press, 2017.

Beesly, Patrick. *Room 40: British Naval Intelligence, 1914–18*. Oxford: Oxford University Press, 1984.

Biddle, Tami Davis. *Rhetoric and Reality in Air Warfare: The Evolution of British and American Ideas about Strategic Bombing, 1914–1945*. Princeton, NJ: Princeton University Press, 2002.

Biess, Frank. *German Angst: Fear and Democracy in the Federal Republic of Germany*. Oxford: Oxford University Press, 2020.

Bingham, Adrian, and Martin Conboy. *Tabloid Century: The Popular Press in Britain, 1896 to the Present*. Oxford: Peter Lang, 2015.

Black, Jeremy. *Air Power: A Global History*. London: Rowman & Littlefield, 2016.

Blake, Robert. *The Conservative Party from Peel to Thatcher*. London: Methuen, 1985.

Bloom, Clive. *Spy Thrillers, from Buchan to le Carré*. Basingstoke: Palgrave Macmillan, 1990.

Bloxham, Donald. *The Great Game of Genocide: Imperialism, Nationalism, and the Destruction of the Ottoman Armenians*. Oxford: Oxford University Press, 2005.

Boghardt, Thomas. *Spies of the Kaiser: German Covert Operations in Great Britain during the First World War Era*. Basingstoke: Palgrave Macmillan, 2004.

Bourke, Joanna. *Dismembering the Male: Men's Bodies, Britain and the Great War*. London: Reaktion Books, 1996.

Bourke, Joanna. *Fear: A Cultural History*. London: Virago, 2006.

Bowman, Timothy, and Mark Connelly. *The Edwardian Army: Recruiting, Training, and Deploying the British Army 1902–1914*. Oxford: Oxford University Press, 2012.

Buckton, Oliver S. *Espionage in British Fiction and Film since 1900: The Changing Enemy*. London: Lexington, 2015.

Cabanes, Bruno. *August 1914: France, the Great War, and a Month That Changed the World Forever*. New Haven, CT: Yale University Press, 2016.

Caglioti, Daniela L. *War and Citizenship: Enemy Aliens and National Belonging from the French Revolution to the First World War*. Cambridge: Cambridge University Press, 2021.

Cahalan, Peter. *Belgian Refugee Relief in England during the Great War*. New York: Garland, 1982.

Cannadine, David. *Victorious Century: The United Kingdom, 1800–1906*. London: Penguin, 2018.

Chickering, Roger. *The Great War and Urban Life in Germany*. Cambridge: Cambridge University Press, 2007.

Chrystal, Paul, and Simon Crossley. *Hartlepool through Time*. Stroud: Amberley, 2011.

Clarke, David. *The Angel of Mons*. Chichester: Wiley, 2004.

Clarke, I. F. *The Tale of the Next Great War, 1871–1914: Fictions of Future Warfare and Battles Still-to-Come*. Liverpool: Liverpool University Press, 1995.

Clarke, I. F. *Voices Prophesising War, 1763–1984*. Oxford: Oxford University Press, 1966.

Coetzee, Frans. *For Party or Country? Nationalism and the Dilemmas of Popular Conservatism in Edwardian England*. Oxford: Oxford University Press, 1990.

Darrow, Margaret H. *French Women and the First World War: War Stories of the Home Front*. Oxford: Berg, 2000.

Das, Santanu., *India, Empire, and First World War Culture: Writings, Images, and Songs*. Cambridge: Cambridge University Press, 2019.

Davies, Peter, and Derek Lynch. *The Routledge Companion to Fascism and the Far Right*. London: Routledge, 2002.

Davis, Belinda. *Home Fires Burning: Food, Politics, and Everyday Life in World War I Berlin*. Chapel Hill: University of North Carolina Press, 2000.

Dawson, Graham. *Soldier Heroes: British Adventure, Empire and the Imagining of Masculinities*. London: Routledge, 1994.

De Groot, Gerald. *Back in Blighty: The British at Home in World War I*. London: Random House, 2014.

De Groot, Gerald. *Blighty: British Society in the Era of the Great War*. London: Longman, 1996.

Dennis, Peter. *The Territorial Army 1906–1940*. Royal Historical Society: Studies in History 51, 1987.

Douglas, Tom. *Scapegoats: Transferring Blame*. London: Routledge, 2003.

Eatwell, Roger. *Fascism: A History*. London: Pimlico, 2003.

Ewing, K. D., and C. A. Gearty. *The Struggle for Civil Liberties: Political Freedom and the Rule of Law in Britain 1914–1945*. Oxford: Oxford University Press, 2000.

Farrar, Martin. *News from the Front: War Correspondents on the Western Front*. Stroud: Sutton, 1998.

Flaws, Margaret. *Spy Fever: The Post Office Affair*. Lerwick: Shetland Times, 2009.

Ford, Nancy Gentile. *The Great War and America: Civil-Military Relations during World War I*. London: Bloomsbury, 2008.

Frevert, Ute et al. *Emotional Lexicons: Continuity and Change in the Vocabulary of Feeling 1700–2000*. Oxford: Oxford University Press, 2014.

Friedberg, Aaron. *The Weary Titan: Britain and the Experience of Relative Decline, 1895–1905*. Princeton, NJ: Princeton University Press, 1988.

Fuller, William C. *The Foe Within: Fantasies of Treason and the End of Imperial Russia*. Ithaca, NY: Cornell University Press, 2006.

Furedi, Frank. *Politics of Fear: Beyond Left and Right*. London: Continuum, 2005.

Galston, William A. *Liberal Purposes: Goods, Virtues, and Diversity in the Liberal State*. Cambridge: Cambridge University Press, 1991.

Gatrell, Peter. *Russia's First World War: A Social and Economic History*. Harlow: Pearson Longman, 2005.

Glover, Edward. *The Psychology of Fear and Courage*. Harmondsworth: Penguin, 1940.

Gooch, John. *The Plans of War: The General Staff and British Military Strategy c. 1900–1916*. London: Routledge, 1974.

Gooch, John. *The Prospect of War: Studies in British Defence Policy, 1847–1942*. Abingdon: Routledge, 1981.

Grayzel, Susan R. *At Home and under Fire: Air Raids and Culture in Britain from the Great War to the Blitz*. Cambridge: Cambridge University Press, 2013.

Grayzel, Susan R. *Women and the First World War*. Harlow: Pearson, 2002.

Gregory, Adrian. *The Last Great War: British Society and the First World War*. Cambridge: Cambridge University Press, 2013.

Gullace, Nicoletta. *The Blood of Our Sons: Men, Women and the Renegotiation of British Citizenship during the Great War*. Basingstoke: Palgrave, 2002.

Haste, Cate. *Keep the Home Fires Burning: Propaganda in the First World War*. London: Allen Lane, 1977.

Hayward, James. *Myths and Legends of the First World War*. Stroud: Sutton, 2002.

Henry, Robert (ed.). *Letters from Paris 1870–1875*. London: Dent, 1942.

Herwig, Holger H. *The First World War: Germany and Austria-Hungary 1914–1918*. London: Bloomsbury, 2014.

Hilton, Claire. *Civilian Lunatic Asylums during the First World War: A Study of Austerity on London's Fringe*. Cham: Springer International, 2021.

Hinsley, F. H., and C. A. G. Simkins. *British Intelligence in the Second World War, Vol. Four: Security and Counter-Intelligence*. London: HMSO, 1990.

Hoare, Philip. *Wilde's Last Stand: Decadence, Conspiracy and the First World War*. London: Duckworth, 1997.

Hobsbawm, Eric. *Industry and Empire: From 1750 to the Present Day*. Harmondsworth: Penguin, 1968.

Holman, Brett. *The Next War in the Air: Britain's Fear of the Bomber, 1908–1941*. Abingdon: Routledge, 2014.

Holmes, Colin. *Anti-Semitism in British Society, 1876–1939*. Abingdon: Routledge, 1979.

Holmes, Colin. *John Bull's Island: Immigration and British Society*. Basingstoke: Macmillan, 1992.

Holmes, Colin. *A Tolerant Country? Immigrants, Refugees and Minorities in Britain*. London: Faber and Faber, 1991.

Horn, Pamela. *Rural Life in England in the First World War*. Dublin: Gill & Macmillan, 1984.

Horne, Alistair. *The Fall of Paris: The Siege and the Commune 1870–71*. London: Macmillan, 1965.

Horne, John, and Alan Kramer. *German Atrocities, 1914: A History of Denial*. New Haven, CT: Yale University Press, 2001.

Howard, Michael. *The Franco-Prussian War: The German Invasion of France, 1870–1871*. London: Routledge, 2003.

Howard, Michael. *War in European History*. Oxford: Oxford University Press, 2009.

Hutchinson, John. *Leopold Maxse and the National Review, 1893–1914: Right-Wing Politics and Journalism in the Edwardian Era*. London: Garland, 1989.

Judson, Pieter M. *The Habsburg Empire: A New History*. Cambridge: Harvard University Press, 2016.

Keegan, John. *A History of Warfare*. London: Pimlico, 2004.

Keene, Jennifer D. *The United States and the First World War*. Abingdon: Routledge, 2014.

Kempshall, Chris. *British, French and American Relations on the Western Front, 1914–1918*. Cham: Springer International, 2018.

Kennedy, David. *Over Here: The First World War and American Society*. Oxford: Oxford University Press, 1980.

Kennedy, Paul. *The Rise of the Anglo-German Antagonism 1860–1914*. London: Allen and Unwin, 1980.

Keohane, Nigel. *The Party of Patriotism: The Conservative Party and the First World War*. Farnham: Ashgate, 2010.

Keshen, Jeffrey A. *Propaganda and Censorship during Canada's Great War*. Edmonton: University of Alberta Press, 1996.

Koss, Stephen E. *Lord Haldane: Scapegoat for Liberalism*. New York: Columbia University Press, 1969.

Kushner, Tony, and Katherine Know. *Refugees in an Age of Genocide: Global, National and Local Perspectives during the Twentieth Century*. London: Frank Cass, 2001.

Laity, Paul. *The British Peace Movement 1870–1914*. Oxford: Clarendon Press, 2001.

Laurie-Fletcher, Danny. *British Invasion and Spy Literature, 1871–1918*. Cham: Springer International, 2019.

Lohr, Eric. *Nationalizing the Russian Empire: The Campaign against Enemy Aliens during World War I*. Cambridge: Harvard University Press, 2003.

Long, Helen. *The Edwardian House: The Middle-Class Home in Britain 1880–1914*. Manchester: Manchester University Press, 1993.

Longmate, Norman. *Defending the Island: From Caesar to the Armada*. London: Grafton, 1990.

Longmate, Norman. *Island Fortress: The Defence of Great Britain 1603–1945*. London: Hutchinson, 1991.

Loughran, Tracey. *Shell-Shock and Medical Culture in First World War Britain*. Cambridge: Cambridge University Press, 2020.

Lynch, Tim. *Yorkshire's War: Voices of the First World War*. Stroud: Amberley, 2014.

Macedo, Stephen. *Diversity and Distrust: Civic Education in a Multicultural Democracy*. Cambridge: Harvard University Press, 2000.

Macedo, Stephen. *Liberal Virtues: Citizenship, Virtue, and Community in Liberal Constitutionalism*. Oxford: Clarendon, 1990.

MacRaild, Donald M. *Irish Migrants in Modern Britain, 1750–1922*. Basingstoke: Macmillan, 1999.

Mander, John. *Our German Cousins: Anglo-German Relations in the 19th and 20th Centuries*. London: J. Murray, 1974.

Marwick, Arthur. *The Deluge: British Society and the First World War*. London: Bodley Head, 1965.

McDonough, Frank. *The Conservative Party and Anglo-German Relations, 1905–1914*. Basingstoke: Palgrave Macmillan, 2007.

McGreal, Stephen. *Liverpool in the Great War*. Barnsley: Pen & Sword Military, 2014.

McLaren, Angus. *Twentieth-Century Sexuality: A History*. Oxford: Blackwell, 1999.

Meeres, Frank. *Norfolk's War*. Stroud: Amberley, 2016.

Messinger, Gary S. *British Propaganda and the State in the First World War*. Manchester: Manchester University Press, 1992.

Meyer, Jessica. *Men of War: Masculinity and the First World War in Britain*. Basingstoke: Palgrave Macmillan, 2011.

Micale, Mark S. *Approaching Hysteria: Disease and Its Interpretations*. Princeton, NJ: Princeton University Press, 1995.

Mitchinson, K. W. *Defending Albion: Britain's Home Army, 1908–1919*. Basingstoke: Palgrave Macmillan, 2005.

Mohs, Polly A. *Military Intelligence and the Arab Revolt: The First Modern Intelligence War*. Abingdon: Routledge, 2008.

Monger, David. *Patriotism and Propaganda in First World War Britain: The National War Aims Committee and Civilian Morale*. Liverpool: Liverpool University Press, 2012.

Morgan-Owen, David. *The Fear of Invasion: Strategy, Politics, and British War Planning, 1880–1914*. Oxford: Oxford University Press, 2017.

Morris, A. J. A. *The Scaremongers: The Advocacy of War and Rearmament, 1896–1914*. Abingdon: Routledge, 2014.

Morris, Joseph. *The German Air Raids on Great Britain 1914–1918*. London: Pordes, 1969.

Mosse, George. *The Image of Man: The Creation of Modern Masculinity*. Oxford: Oxford University Press, 1996.

Neiberg, Michael S. *The Path to War: How the First World War Created Modern America*. Oxford: Oxford University Press, 2016.

Neubauer, Hans-Joachim. *The Rumour: A Cultural History*. London: Free Association Books, 1999.

Newman, Paul. *A History of Terror: Fear and Dread through the Ages*. Stroud: Sutton, 2000.

Nussbaum, Martha C. *Hiding from Humanity: Disgust, Shame, and the Law*. Princeton, NJ: Princeton University Press, 2006.

Nussbaum, Martha C. *Political Emotions: Why Love Matters for Justice*. Cambridge: Harvard University Press, 2013.

Nussbaum, Martha C. *Upheavals of Thought: The Intelligence of Emotions*. Cambridge: Cambridge University Press, 2003.

O'Connell, Sean. *The Car and British Society: Class, Gender and Motoring, 1896–1939*. Manchester: Manchester University Press, 1998.

Oğuz, Çiğdem. *Moral Crisis in the Ottoman Empire: Society, Politics, and Gender during WWI*. London: Bloomsbury, 2021.

Panayi, Panikos. *The Enemy in our Midst: Germans in Britain during the First World War*. Oxford: Berg, 1991.

Panayi, Panikos. *Immigration, Ethnicity and Racism, in Britain, 1815–1945*. Manchester: Manchester University Press, 1994.

Panayi, Panikos. *An Immigration History of Britain: Multicultural Racism since 1800*. London: Routledge, 2014.

Paris, Michael. *Warrior Nation: Images of War in British Popular Culture, 1850–2000*. London: Reaktion, 2000.

Payne, Stanley G. *A History of Fascism 1914–1945*. Madison: University of Wisconsin Press, 1995.

Pearce, Cyril. *Comrades in Conscience: The Story of an English Community's Opposition to the Great War*. London: Francis Boutle, 2001.

Pennell, Catriona. *A Kingdom United: Popular Responses to the Outbreak of the First World War*. Oxford: Oxford University Press, 2014.

Plamper, Jan. *The History of Emotions: An Introduction*. Oxford: Oxford University Press, 2015.

Popplewell, Richard J. *Intelligence and Imperial Defence: British Intelligence and the Defence of the Indian Empire 1904–1924*. London: Cass, 1995.

Porter, Bernard. *Plots and Paranoia: A History of Political Espionage in Britain 1790–1988*. Abingdon: Routledge, 2016.

Proctor, Tammy. *Civilians in a World at War, 1914–1918*. New York: New York University Press, 2010.

Proctor, Tammy. *Female Intelligence: Women and Espionage in the First World War*. New York: New York University Press, 2003.

Read, Christopher. *War and Revolution in Russia, 1914–22*. Basingstoke: Palgrave Macmillan, 2013.

Reddy, William M. *The Navigation of Feeling: A Framework for the History of Emotions*. Cambridge: Cambridge University Press, 2001.

Robb, George. *British Culture and the First World War*. Basingstoke: Palgrave Macmillan, 2002.

Robbins, Keith. *Politicians, Diplomacy and War in Modern British History*. London: Hambledon Press, 1994.

Robin, Corey. *Fear: The History of a Political Idea*. Oxford: Oxford University Press, 2004.

Robins, Robert S. *Political Paranoia: The Psychopolitics of Hatred*. New Haven, CT: Yale University Press, 1997.

Roper, Michael. *The Secret Battle: Emotional Survival in the Great War*. Manchester: Manchester University Press, 2010.

Rosenwein, Barbara H. *Emotional Communities in the Early Middle Ages.* Ithaca, NY: Cornell University Press, 2006.

Rosenwein, Barbara H. *Generations of Feeling: A History of Emotions, 600–1700.* Cambridge: Cambridge University Press, 2016.

Rüger, Jan. *The Great Naval Game: Britain and Germany in the Age of Empire.* Cambridge: Cambridge University Press, 2009.

Sanborn, Joshua. *Imperial Apocalypse: The Great War and the Destruction of the Russian Empire.* Oxford: Oxford University Press, 2014.

Scull, Andrew. *Hysteria: The Disturbing History.* Oxford: Oxford University Press, 2011.

Scully, Richard. *British Images of Germany: Admiration, Antagonism and Ambivalence, 1860–1914.* Basingstoke: Palgrave Macmillan, 2012.

Seligmann, Matthew. *Rivalry in Southern Africa, 1893–99: The Transformation of German Colonial Policy.* Basingstoke: Palgrave Macmillan, 1998.

Seligmann, Matthew. *Spies in Uniform: British Military and Naval Intelligence on the Eve of the First World War.* Oxford: Oxford University Press, 2006.

Shibutini, Tamotsu. *Improvised News: A Sociological Study of Rumor.* Santa Barbara, CA: Bobbs-Merrill, 1966.

Showalter, Elaine. *Hystories: Hysterical Epidemics and Modern Culture.* New York: Columbia University Press, 1998.

Simpson, Brian. *In the Highest Degree Odious: Detention in Wartime Britain.* Oxford: Oxford University Press, 1992.

Smith, Zachery. *Age of Fear: Othering and American Identity during World War I.* Baltimore, MD: John Hopkins University Press, 2019.

Stevenson, John. *British Society 1914–45.* Harmondsworth: Allen Lane, 1984.

Stockdale, Melissa Kirschke. *Mobilising the Russian Nation: Patriotism and Citizenship in the First World War.* Cambridge: Cambridge University Press, 2016.

Stout, Mark. *World War I and the Foundations of American Intelligence.* Lawrence: University Press of Kansas, 2023.

Strachan, Huw. *The First World War, Volume I: To Arms.* Oxford: Oxford University Press, 2003.

Terraine, John. *The Smoke and the Fire: Myths and Anti-Myths of War, 1861–1945.* London: Leo Cooper, 1992.

Thompson, J. Lee. *Northcliffe: Press Baron in Politics, 1865–1922.* London: John Murrey, 2000.

Thompson, J. Lee. *Politicians, the Press, and Propaganda: Lord Northcliffe and the Great War, 1914–1919.* London: Kent State University, 1999.

Thurlow, Richard. *Fascism in Britain: From Oswald Mosley's Blackshirts to the National Front.* London: I.B. Tauris, 2006.

Thurlow, Richard. *The Secret State: British Internal Security in the Twentieth Century.* Oxford: Blackwell, 1995.

Tosh, John. *Manliness and Masculinities in Nineteenth Century Britain.* Edinburgh: Pearson Longman, 2005.

Uglow, Jenny. *In These Times: Living in Britain through Napoleon's Wars, 1793–1815.* London: Faber and Faber, 2014.

Ugolini, Laura. *Civvies: Middle-Class Men on the English Home Front, 1914–18.* Manchester: Manchester University Press, 2017.

Verhey, Jeffrey. *The Spirit of 1914: Militarism, Myth, and Mobilisation in Germany.* Cambridge: Cambridge University Press, 2004.

Watson, Alexander. *Enduring the Great War: Combat, Morale and Collapse in the German and British Armies, 1914–1918*. Cambridge: Cambridge University Press, 2009.

Watson, Alexander. *Ring of Steel: Germany and Austria-Hungary at War*. London: Penguin, 2014.

Watson, Janet S. K. *Fighting Different Wars: Experience, Memory and the First World War in Britain*. Cambridge: Cambridge University Press, 2004.

Weber, Thomas. *Our Friend the Enemy: Elite Education in Britain and Germany before the First World War*. Stanford, CA: Stanford University Press, 2008.

White, Jerry. *Zeppelin Nights: London in the First World War*. London: Random House, 2014.

Wilkinson, Alexander. *The Church of England and the First World War*. Cambridge: Lutterworth Press, 2014.

Wilkinson, Glenn R. *Depictions and Images of War in Edwardian Newspapers, 1899–1914*. Basingstoke: Palgrave Macmillan, 2003.

Williams, Rhodri. *Defending the Empire: The Conservative Party and British Defence Policy 1899–1915*. New Haven, CT: Yale University Press, 1991.

Wilson, Trevor. *The Downfall of the Liberal Party, 1914–35*. London: Collins, 1966.

Wilson, Trevor. *The Myriad Faces of War: Britain and the Great War, 1914–1918*. Cambridge: Polity, 1986.

Wynn, Stephen. *Chatham in the Great War*. Barnsley: Pen & Sword Military, 2017.

Journal articles

Almog, Shmuel. 'Antisemitism as a Dynamic Phenomenon: "The Jewish Question" in England at the End of the First World War', *Patterns of Prejudice* 21/4 (1987): 3–18.

Bartholomew, Robert E. 'Epidemic Hysteria: A Review of the Published Literature', *American Journal of Epidemiology* 151/2 (2000): 206–7.

Bartholomew, Robert E., and Simon Wessely. 'Protean Nature of Mass Sociogenic Illness: From Possessed Nuns to Chemical and Biological Terrorism Fears', *British Journal of Psychiatry* 180 (2002): 300–6.

Bassler, Gerhard P. 'The Enemy Alien Experience in Newfoundland 1914–1918', *Canadian Ethnic Studies* 20/3 (1988): 42–62.

Betts, Raymond F. 'The Allusion to Rome in British Imperialist Thought of the Late Nineteenth and Early Twentieth Centuries', *Victorian Studies* 15/2 (1971): 149–59.

Bloch, Marc. 'Reflections of a Historian on the False News of the War', trans. James P. Holoka, *Michigan War Studies Review* (2013).

Boss, Leslie P. 'Epidemic Hysteria: A Review of the Published Literature', *Epidemiologic Reviews* 19/2 (1997): 233–43.

Bourke, Joanna. 'Fear and Anxiety: Writing about Emotion in Modern History', *History Workshop Journal* 55/1 (2003): 111–33.

Caglioti, Daniela L. 'Why and How Italy Invented an Enemy Aliens Problem in the First World War', *War in History* 21/2 (2014): 142–69.

Cesarani, David. 'An Alien Concept? The Continuity of Anti-Alienism in British Society before 1940', *Immigrants and Minorities* 11/3 (1992): 24–52.

Cesarani, David. 'Anti-Alienism in England after the First World War', *Immigrants and Minorities* 6/1 (1987): 5–29.

Cesarani, David. 'An Embattled Minority: The Jews in Britain during the First World War', *Immigrants and Minorities* 8/1 (1989): 60–81.

Çetinkaya, Y. Doğan. 'Illustrated Atrocity: The Stigmatisation of Non-Muslims through Images in the Ottoman Empire during the Balkan Wars', *Journal of Modern European History* 12/4 (2014): 460–78.

Clarke, F. 'Forecasts of Warfare in Fiction 1803–1914', *Comparative Studies in Society and History* 10/1 (1967): 1–25.

Coast, David, and Jo Fox. 'Rumour and Politics', *History Compass* 13/5 (2015): 222–34.

Coetzee, Frans, and Marilyn Shevin Coetzee. 'Rethinking the Radical Right in Germany and Britain before 1914', *Journal of Contemporary History* 21/4 (1986): 515–37.

Dedering, Tilman. ' "Avenge the Lusitania": The Anti-German Riots in South Africa in 1915', *Immigrants and Minorities* 31/3 (2013): 256–88.

Dowling, Linda. 'Roman Decadence and Victorian Historiography', *Victorian Studies* 28/4 (1985): 579–607.

Francis, Andrew. 'Anti-Alienism in New Zealand during the Great War: The von Zedlitz Affair, 1915', *Immigrants and Minorities* 24/3 (2006): 251–76.

French, David. 'Spy Fever in Britain, 1900–1915', *Historical Journal* 21/2 (1978): 355–70.

Gensini, Gian Franco, and Andrea A. Conti. 'The Evolution of the Concept of "Fever" in the History of Medicine', *Journal of Infection* 49/2 (2004): 85–7.

Gullace, Nicoletta F. 'Friends, Aliens and Enemies: Fictive Communities and the Lusitania Riots of 1915', *Journal of Social History* 39/2 (2005): 345–67.

Hampshire, James. 'Spy Fever in Britain, 1900 to 1914', *The Historian* 72 (2001).

Hendley, Matthew C. 'Cultural Mobilization and British Responses to Cultural Transfer in Total War: The Shakespeare Tercentenary of 1916', *First World War Studies* 3/1 (2012): 25–49.

Henman, Linda D. 'Humor as a Coping Mechanism: Lessons from POWs', International Journal of *Humor Research* 14/1 (2001): 83–94.

Hiley, Nicholas. 'Counter-Espionage and Security in Great Britain during the First World War', *English Historical Review* 101/400 (1986): 635–70.

Hiley, Nicholas. 'Decoding German Spies: British Spy Fiction 1908–18', *Intelligence and National Security* 5/4 (1990): 55–79.

Hiley, Nicholas. 'Entering the Lists: MI5's Great Spy Round-Up of August 1914', *Intelligence and National Security* 21/1 (2006): 46–76.

Hiley, Nicholas. 'The Failure of British Counter-Espionage against Germany, 1907–1914', *The Historical Journal* 28/4 (1985): 835–62.

Hiley, Nicholas. 'The Play, the Parody, the Censor and the Film', *Intelligence and National Security* 6/1 (1991): 218–28.

Hiley, Nicholas. 'Re-entering the Lists: MI5's Authorized History and the August 1914 Arrests', *Intelligence and National Security* 25/4 (2010): 415–52.

Hitchner, Thomas. 'Edwardian Spy Literature and the Ethos of Sportsmanship: the Sport of Spying', *English Literature in Transition* 53/4 (2010): 413–30.

Johnson, Matthew. 'The Liberal Party and the Navy League in Britain before the Great War', *Twentieth Century British History*, 22/2 (2011): 137–63.

Johnson, Matthew. 'The Liberal War Committee and the Liberal Advocacy of Conscription in Britain, 1914–1916', *The Historical Journal* 51/2 (2008): 399–420.

Kapust, Daniel J. 'On the Ancient Uses of Political Fear and Its Modern Implications', *Journal of the History of Ideas* 69/3 (2008): 353–73.

Kendler, Kenneth S. 'The Origin of Our Modern Concept of Mania in Texts from 1780 to 1900', *Molecular Psychiatry* 25 (2020): 1–11.

Kennedy, Paul. 'Idealists and Realists: British Views of Germany, 1864–1939', *Transactions of the Royal Historical Society* 25 (1975): 137–56.

Kitchen, Martin. 'The German Invasion of Canada in the First World War', *International History Review* 7/2 (1985): 245–60.

Kushner, Tony. 'Local Heroes: Belgian Refugees in Britain during the First World War', *Immigrants and Minorities* 18/1 (2010): 1–28.

Larsen, Dan. 'Intelligence in the First World War: The State of the Field', *Intelligence and National Security* 29/2 (2014): 282–302.

Larsen, Dan. British Signals Intelligence and the 1916 Easter Rising in Ireland', *Intelligence and National Security* 33/1 (2018): 1–19.

Leonhard, Jörn. 'Construction and Perception of National Images: Germany and Britain, 1870–1914', *The Linacre Journal* 4 (2000): 45–67.

Madigan, Edward. ' "Sticking to a Hateful Task": Resilience, Humour, and British Understandings of Combatant courage, 1914–1918', *War in History* 20/1 (2013): 76–98.

Major, Patrick. 'Britain and Germany: A Love Hate Relationship?', *German History* 26/4 (2008): 457–68.

Meisel, Joseph S. 'The Germans Are Coming! British Fiction of a German Invasion 1871–1913', *War, Literature and the Arts* 2/2 (1990): 41–77.

Melby, Christian K. 'Empire and Nation in British Future-War and Invasion-Scare Fiction, 1871–1914', *Historical Journal* 63/2 (2020): 389–410.

Morgan-Owen, David. 'Scares, Panics, and Strategy: The Politics of Security and British Invasion Scares before 1914', *Diplomacy and Statecraft* 33/3 (2022): 442–73.

Neiburg, Michael. 'Review of John Keegan, A History of Warfare', *Journal of Social History* 29/2 (1995): 466–7.

Nye, Robert A. 'Review of William M. Reddy's *The Navigation of Feeling: A Framework for the History of Emotions*', *Journal of Modern History* 75/4 (2003): 920–3.

Panayi, Panikos. 'Review Article: National and Racial Minorities in Total War', *Immigrants and Minorities* 9/2 (1990): 178–94.

Pennell, Catriona. 'Believing the Unbelievable: The Myth of the Russians with "Snow on Their Boots" in the United Kingdom, 1914', *Cultural and Social History* 11/1 (2014): 69–87.

Pennell, Catriona. 'British Society and the First World War', *War in History* 16/4 (2009): 506–18.

Plamper, Jan. 'The History of Emotions: An Interview with William Reddy, Barbara Rosenwein, and Peter Stearns', *History and Theory* 49 (2010): 237–65.

Pöhlmann, Markus. 'German Intelligence at War, 1914–1918', *Journal of Intelligence History* 5/2 (2005): 25–54.

Prysor, Glyn. 'The "Fifth Column", and the British Experience of Retreat, 1940', *War in History* 12/4 (2005): 418–47.

Readman, Paul. 'The Liberal Party and Patriotism in Early Twentieth Century Britain', *Twentieth Century British History* 12/3 (2001): 269–302.

Reddy, William M. 'Sentimentalism and Its Erasure: The Role of Emotions in the Era of the French Revolution', *Journal of Modern History* 72/1 (2000): 109–52.

Reinermann, Lothar. 'Fleet Street and the Kaiser: British Public Opinion and Wilhelm II', *German History* 26/4 (2008): 469–85.

Richards, Harry. 'Room 40 and German Intrigues in Morocco: Re-assessing the Operational Impact of Diplomatic Cryptanalysis during World War I', *Intelligence and National Security* 32/6 (2017): 833–48.

Robert, Krisztina. 'Gender, Class, and Patriotism: Women's Paramilitary Units in First World War Britain', *International History Review* 19/1 (1997): 52–65.

Roper, Michael. 'Between Manliness and Masculinity: The "War Generation" and the Psychology of Fear in Britain, 1914–1950', *Journal of British Studies* 44/2 (2005): 343–62.

Rose, Jonathan. 'Rereading the English Common Reader: A Preface to a History of Audiences', *Journal of the History of Ideas* 53/1 (1992): 47–70.

Rosenwein, Barbara H. 'Review of William M. Reddy's *The Navigation of Feeling: A Framework for the History of Emotions*', *American Historical Review* 107/4 (2002): 1181–2.

Rosenwein, Barbara H. 'Worrying about the Emotions in History', *American Historical Review* 107/3 (2002): 821–45.

Rüger, Jan. 'Revisiting the Anglo-German Antagonism', *Journal of Modern History* 83/3 (2011): 579–617.

Samson, Andreas C., and James J. Gross. 'Humour as Emotion Regulation: The Differential Consequences of Negative versus Positive Humour', *Cognition and Emotion* 26/2 (2012): 375–84.

Saunders, David. 'Aliens in Britain and the Empire during the First World War', *Immigrants and Minorities* 4/1 (1985): 5–27.

Saunders, Kay. '"The Stranger in Our Gates": Internment Policies in the United Kingdom and Australia during the Two World Wars, 1914–39', *Immigrants and Minorities* 22/1 (2003): 22–43.

Scheer, Monique. 'Are Emotions a Kind of Practice (and Is That What Makes Them Have a History)? A Bourdieuian Approach to Understanding Emotion', *History and Theory* 51 (2021): 193–220.

Seligmann, Matthew. 'Britain's Great Security Mirage: The Royal Navy and the Franco-Russian Naval Threat, 1898–1906', *Journal of Strategic Studies* 35/6 (2012): 861–86.

Seligmann, Matthew. 'A Prelude to the Reforms of Admiral Sir John Fisher: The Creation of the Home Fleet, 1902–3', *Historical Research* 83/221 (2010): 506–19.

Seligmann, Matthew. 'Switching Horses: The Admiralty's Recognition of the Threat from Germany, 1900–1905', *International History Review* 30/2 (2008): 239–58.

Selleck, R. J. W. '"The Trouble with My Looking Glass": A Study of the Attitudes of Australians to Germans during the Great War', *Journal of Australian Studies* 4/6 (1980): 2–25.

Sheffy, Yigal 'The Spy Who Never Was: An Intelligence Myth in Palestine, 1914–18', *Intelligence and National Security* 14/3 (1999): 123–42.

Smith, Anthony D. 'War and Ethnicity: The Role of Warfare in the Formation, Self-images and Cohesion of Ethnic Communities', *Ethnic and Racial Studies* 4/4 (1981): 375–97.

Stafford, David. 'Conspiracy and Xenophobia: The Spy Novels of William le Queux, 1893–1914', *Europa* 3 (1982): 163–86.

Stafford, David A. T. 'Spies and Gentlemen: The Birth of the British Spy Novel, 1893–1914', *Victorian Studies* 24/4 (1981): 489–509.

Stearn, Roger T. 'The Mysterious Mr Le Queux: War Novelist, Defence Publicist and Counterspy', *Critical Survey* 32/1–2 (2020): 17–58.

Stearns, Peter N., and Carol Z. Stearns. 'Emotionology: Clarifying the History of Emotions and Emotional Standards', *American Historical Review* 90 (1985): 813–36.

Stibbe, Matthew. 'Enemy Aliens, Deportees, Refugees: Internment Practices in the Habsburg Empire, 1914–1918', *Journal of Modern European History* 12/4 (2014): 479–99.

Summers, Anne. 'Militarism in Britain before the Great War', *History Workshop Journal* 2/1 (1976): 104–23.

Taylor, Antony. 'At the Mercy of the German Eagle: Images of London in Dissolution in the Novels of William Le Queux', *Critical Survey* 32/1–2 (2020): 59–78.

Thurlow, Richard. 'The Evolution of the Mythical British Fifth Column, 1939–46', *Twentieth Century British History* 10/4 (1999): 477–98.

Trotter, David. 'The Politics of Adventure in the Early British Spy Novel', *Intelligence and National Security* 5/4 (1990): 30–54.

Twark, Jill E. 'Approaching History as Cultural Memory through Humour, Satire, Comics and Graphic Novels', *Contemporary European History* 26/1 (2017): 175–87.

Üngör, Uğur Ümit, and Eric Lohr: 'Economic Nationalism, Confiscation, and Genocide: A Comparison of the Ottoman and Russian Empires during World War I', *Journal of Modern European History* 12/4 (2014): 500–22.

Vance, Norman. 'Anxieties of Empire and the Moral Tradition: Rome and Britain', *International Journal of the Classical Tradition* 18/2 (2011): 246–61.

Waddington, Keir. ' "We Don't Need any German Sausages Here!" Food, Fear, and the German Nation in Victorian and Edwardian Britain', *Journal of British Studies* 52/4 (2013): 1017–42.

Wessely, Simon. 'Mass Hysteria: Two Syndromes?' *Psychological Medicine* 17 (1987): 109–20.

Wilkinson, Glenn R. ' "The Blessings of War": The Depiction of Military Force in Edwardian Newspapers', *Journal of Contemporary History* 33/1 (1998): 97–115.

Yarrow, Stella. 'The Impact of Hostility on Germans in Britain, 1914–1918', *Immigrants and Minorities* 8/1–2 (1989): 97–112.

Chapters in edited volumes

Armon-Jones, Claire. 'The Thesis of Constructionism', in Rom Harré, *The Social Construction of Emotions*. Oxford: Blackwell, 1986.

Bauer, Deborah. 'Villains, Liars, Soldiers, and Patriots: Perceptions of Espionage and the Politics of Emotion in Fin-de-Siècle France', in Simon Ball, Philip Gassert, Andreas Gestrich and Sönke Neitzel, *Cultures of Intelligence in the Era of the World Wars*. Oxford: Oxford University Press, 2020.

Beckett, Ian. 'The Nation in Arms, 1914–1918', in Ian F. W. Beckett and Keith Simpson, *A Nation in Arms: A Social Study of the British Army in the First World War*. Barnsley: Pen and Sword, 2004.

Beckett, Ian. 'The Territorial Force', in Ian Beckett and Keith Simpson, *A Nation in Arms: The British Army in the First World War*. Barnsley: Pen and Sword, 2004.

Braybon, Gail. 'Introduction', in Gail Braybon, *Evidence, History and the Great War: Historians and the Impact of 1914–18*. Oxford: Berghahn Books, 2005.

Cooke, Miriam, and Angela Woollacott. 'Introduction', in Miriam Cooke and Angela Woollacott, *Gendering War Talk*. Princeton, NJ: Princeton University Press, 1993.

Cornwall, Mark. 'Austria-Hungary and 'Yugoslavia', in John Horne, *A Companion to World War I*. Oxford: Blackwell, 2012.

Crossick, Geoffrey. 'The Emergence of the Lower Middle Class in Britain', in Geoffrey Crossick, *The Lower Middle Class in Britain 1870–1914*. London: Croom-Helm, 1977.

Du Pont, Koenraad. 'Nature and Functions of Humor in Trench Newspapers (1914–1918)', in Clémentine Tholas-Disset and Karen A. Ritzenhoff, *Humor, Entertainment, and Popular Culture during World War 1*. Basingstoke: Palgrave Macmillan, 2015.

Eastwood, David. 'Patriotism and the English State in the 1790s', in Mark Philp, *The French Revolution and British Popular Politics*. Cambridge: Cambridge University Press, 1991.

Elliot, Marianne. 'French Subversion in Britain in the French Revolution', in Colin Jones, *Britain and Revolutionary France: Conflict, Subversion and Propaganda*. Exeter: Exeter University Press, 1983.

Emsley, Clive. 'The Impact of the French Revolution on British Politics and Society', in Ceri Crossley and Ian Small, *The French Revolution and British Culture*. Oxford: Oxford University Press, 1989.

Emsley, Clive. 'Revolution, War and the Nation State: The British and the French Experiences, 1789–1801', in Mark Philp, *The French Revolution and British Popular Politics*. Cambridge: Cambridge University Press, 1991.

Fischer, Gerhard. 'Fighting the War at Home: The Campaign against Enemy Aliens in Australia during the First World War', in Panikos Panayi, *Minorities in Wartime: National and Racial Groupings in Europe, North America and Australia during the Two World Wars*. Oxford: Berg, 1993.

Freud, Sigmund. 'Obsessions and Phobias: Their Psychical Mechanism and Their Aetiology', in *The Standard Edition of the Complete Psychological Works of Sigmund Freud*, iii. London: Hogarth Press, 1962.

Frevert, Ute. 'Emotions in Times of War: Private and Public, Individual and Collective', in Claire Langhamer, Lucy Noakes and Claudia Siebrecht, *Total War: An Emotional History*. Oxford: Oxford University Press, 2020.

Geppert, Dominic, and Robert Gerwarth. 'Introduction', in Dominic Geppert and Robert Gerwarth, *Wilhelmine Germany and Edwardian Britain: Essays on Cultural Affinity*. Oxford: Oxford University Press, 2008.

Ginion, Eyal. 'Landscapes of Modernity and Order: War and Propaganda in Ottoman Writing during World War I', in M. Hakan Yavuz and Feroz Ahmad, *War and Collapse: World War I and the Ottoman State*. Salt Lake City: University of Utah Press, 2016.

Gooch, John. 'Attitudes to War in Late Victorian and Edwardian England', in Brian Bond and Ian Roy, *War and Society: A Yearbook of Military History Volume 1*. London: Croom Helm, 1977.

Gooch, John. 'Britain and the Boer War', in George J. Andreopoulos and Harold E. Selesky, *The Aftermath of Defeat: Societies, Armed Forces, and the Challenge of Recovery*. New Haven, CT: Yale University Press, 1994.

Gooch, John. 'Italy before 1915: The Quandary of the Vulnerable', in Ernest R. May, *Knowing One's Enemies: Intelligence Assessment before the Two World Wars*. Princeton, NJ: Princeton University Press, 2014.

Gregory, Adrian. 'A Clash of Cultures: The British Press and the Opening of the Great War', in Troy R. E. Paddock, *A Call to Arms: Propaganda, Public Opinion, and Newspapers in the Great War*. London: Bloomsbury, 2004.

Hall, Stuart, and Bill Schwarz. 'State and Society, 1880–1930' in Mary Langan and Bill Schwarz, *Crisis in the British State, 1880–1930*. London: Hutchinson, 1985.

Harré, Rom. 'An Outline of the Social Constructionist Viewpoint', in Rom Harré, *The Social Construction of Emotions*. Oxford: Blackwell, 1986.

Horne, John. 'Public Opinion and Politics', in John Horne, *A Companion to World War I*. Oxford: Blackwell, 2012.

Kennedy, Paul. 'The Pre War Right', in Paul Kennedy and Anthony James Nicholls, *Nationalist and Racialist Movements in Britain and Germany before 1914.* Basingstoke: Palgrave Macmillan, 1981.

Kramer, Alan. 'Combatants and Noncombatants: Atrocities, Massacres, and War Crimes', in John Horne, *A Companion to World War I.* Oxford: Blackwell, 2012.

Kramer, Alan. '*Wackes* at War: Alsace-Lorraine and the Failure of German National Mobilization, 1914–1918', in John Horne, *State, Society and Mobilization in Europe during the First World War.* Cambridge: Cambridge University Press, 1997.

Kröger, Martin. 'Imperial Germany and the Boer War', in Keith Wilson, *The International Impact of the Boer War.* Abingdon: Routledge, 2014.

Luckhurst, Mary. 'A Wounded Stage: Drama and World War I', in Mary Luckhurst, *A Companion to Modern British and Irish Drama 1880–2005.* Oxford: Blackwell, 2006.

McGregor, Robert. 'The Popular Press and the Creation of Military Masculinities in Georgian Britain', in Paul Higate, *Military Masculinities: Identity and the State.* London: Praeger, 2003.

Nagler, Jörg. 'Victims of the Home Front: Enemy Aliens in the United States during the First World War', in Panikos Panayi, *Minorities in Wartime: National and Racial Groupings in Europe, North America and Australia during the Two World Wars.* Oxford: Berg, 1993.

O'Halpin, Eunan. 'British Intelligence in Ireland, 1914–1921', in Christopher Andrew and David Dilks, *The Missing Dimension: Governments and Intelligence Communities in the Twentieth Century.* London: Macmillan, 1984.

Paciaronei, M., and J. Bogousslavsky. 'The Borderland with Neurasthenia', in J. Bogousslavsky, *Hysteria: The Rise of an Enigma.* New York: Karger, 2014.

Panayi, Panikos. 'Dominant Societies and Minorities in the Two World Wars', in Panikos Panayi, *Minorities in Wartime: National and Racial Groupings in Europe, North America and Australia during the Two World Wars.* Oxford: Berg, 1993.

Panayi, Panikos. 'German Immigrants in Britain, 1815–1914', in Panikos Panayi, *Germans in Britain since 1500.* London: Hambledon Press, 1996.

Phillips, Gregory D. 'Lord Willoughby de Broke: Radicalism and Conservatism', in J. A. Thompson and Arthur Mejia, *Edwardian Conservatism: Five Studies in Adaption.* London: Croom Helm, 1988.

Porter, Roy. 'Nervousness, Eighteenth and Nineteenth Century Style: From Luxury to Labour', in Marijke Gijswijt-Hofstra and Roy Porter, *Cultures of Neurasthenia from Beard to the First World War.* New York: Rodopi, 2001.

Purseigle, Pierre. 'Beyond and Below the Nations: Towards a Comparative History of Local Communities at War', in Jenny Macleod and Pierre Purseigle, *Uncovered Fields: Perspectives in First World War Studies.* Leiden: Brill, 2004.

Purseigle, Pierre. 'Introduction', in Pierre Puseigle, *Warfare and Belligerence: Perspectives in First World War Studies.* Leiden: Brill, 2004.

Quintero, Ruben. 'Introduction: Understanding Satire', in Ruben Quintero, *A Companion to Satire: Ancient and Modern.* Oxford: Blackwell, 2011.

Röhl, John C. G. '"The Worst of Enemies": Kaiser Wilhelm II and His Uncle Edward VII', in Dominic Geppert and Robert Gerwarth (eds), *Wilhelmine Germany and Edwardian Britain: Essays on Cultural Affinity.* Oxford: Oxford University Press, 2008.

Searle, Geoffrey. 'The "Revolt from the Right" in Edwardian Britain', in Paul Kennedy and Anthony James Nicholls, *Nationalist and Racialist Movements in Britain and Germany before 1914.* Basingstoke: Palgrave Macmillan, 1981.

Sezgin, Pamela Dorn. 'Greeks, Jews, and Armenians: A Comparative Analysis of Non-Muslim Communities and Nascent Nationalisms in the Late Ottoman Empire through World War I', in M. Hakan Yavuz and Feroz Ahmad, *War and Collapse: World War I and the Ottoman State*. Salt Lake City: Utah University Press, 2016.

Strachan, Hew. 'The British Army, Its General Staff and the Continental Commitment 1904–14', in David French and Brian Holden Reid, *The British General Staff: Reform and Innovation, 1890–1939*. Abingdon: Routledge, 2005.

Summers, Anne. 'The Character of Edwardian Nationalism: Three Popular Leagues', in Paul Kennedy and Anthony Nicholls, *Nationalist and Racialist Movements in Britain and Germany before 1914*. Basingstoke: Palgrave Macmillan, 1981.

Tholas-Disset, Clémentine, and Karen A. Ritzenhoff. 'Introduction', in Clémentine Tholas-Disset and Karen A. Ritzenhoff, *Humor, Entertainment, and Popular Culture during World War 1*. Basingstoke: Palgrave Macmillan, 2015.

Thompson, Mathew. 'Neurasthenia in Britain: An Overview', in Marijke Gijswijt-Hofstra and Roy Porter, *Cultures of Neurasthenia from Beard to the First World War*. New York: Rodopi, 2001.

Trotter, David. 'The Politics of Adventure in the Early British Spy Novel', in Wesley K. Wark, *Spy Fiction, Spy Films and Real Intelligence*. Abingdon: Routledge, 1991.

Webber, G. C. 'Intolerance and Discretion: Conservatives and British Fascism, 1918–1926', in Tony Kushner and Kenneth Lunn, *Traditions of Intolerance: Historical Perspectives on Fascism in Britain*. Manchester: Manchester University Press, 1989.

Wheelis, Mark. 'Biological Sabotage in World War I', in Erhard Geissler and John Ellis van Courtland Moon, *Biological and Toxin Weapons Research, Development, and Use from the Middle Ages to 1945*. Oxford: Oxford University Press, 1999.

Wood, Harry. 'Sharpening the Mind: The German Menace and Edwardian National Identity', in Naomi Carle, Samuel Shaw and Sarah Shaw, *Edwardian Culture: Beyond the Garden Party*. Abingdon: Routledge, 2018.

Woollacott, Angela. 'Sisters and Brothers in Arms: Family, Class, and Gendering in World War I Britain', in Miriam Cooke and Angela Woollacott, *Gendering War Talk*. Princeton, NJ: Princeton University Press, 1993.

PhD dissertations

Keeling, Peter. 'British Liberal Internationalism in Retreat: The Channel Tunnel Controversy and the Naval Defence Act, 1880–1894', PhD thesis (University of Kent, 2018).

Longson, Patrick. 'The Rise of the German Menace: Imperial Anxiety and British Popular Culture, 1896–1903', PhD thesis (University of Birmingham, 2014).

Matin, A. M. 'Securing Britain: Figures of Invasion in Late-Victorian and Edwardian Fiction', PhD thesis (Columbia University, 1997).

Moon, Howard. 'The Invasion of the United Kingdom Public Controversy and Official Planning, 1888–1918', PhD thesis (University of London, 1968).

Wood, Harry. 'External Threats Mask Internal Fears: Edwardian Invasion Literature 1899–1914', PhD thesis (University of Liverpool, 2014).

INDEX